Macro-Micro Linkages in Sociology

AMERICAN SOCIOLOGICAL ASSOCIATION PRESIDENTIAL SERIES

Volumes in this series are edited by successive presidents of the American Sociological Association and are based upon sessions at the Annual Meeting of the organization. Volumes in this series are listed below.

JAMES F. SHORT, Jr.
The Social Fabric: Dimensions and Issues (1986)

MATILDA WHITE RILEY
in association with
BETTINA J. HUBER and BETH B. HESS
**Social Structures and Human Lives:
Social Change and the Life Course, Volume 1** (1988)

MATILDA WHITE RILEY
Sociological Lives: Social Change and the Life Course, Volume 2 (1989)

MELVIN L. KOHN
Cross-National Research in Sociology (1989)

HERBERT J. GANS
Sociology in America (1990)

JOAN HUBER
Macro-Micro Linkages in Sociology (1991)

JOAN HUBER and BETH E. SCHNEIDER
The Social Context of AIDS (1991)

The above volumes are available from Sage Publications.

PETER M. BLAU
Approaches to the Study of Social Structure (1975, out of print)

LEWIS A. COSER and OTTO N. LARSEN
The Uses of Controversy in Sociology (1976, out of print)

J. MILTON YINGER
Major Social Issues: A Multidisciplinary View (1978, out of print)

AMOS H. HAWLEY
Societal Growth: Processes and Implications (1979, out of print)

HUBERT M. BLALOCK
Sociological Theory and Research: A Critical Approach (1980, out of print)

ALICE S. ROSSI
Gender and the Life Course (1985, Aldine Publishing Co.)

KAI ERIKSON and STEVEN PETER VALLAS
The Nature of Work: Sociological Perspectives (1990, Yale University Press)

Joan Huber
editor

Macro-Micro Linkages in Sociology

American Sociological Association Presidential Series

AMERSON COLLEGE LIBRARY

 SAGE PUBLICATIONS
The International Professional Publishers
Newbury Park   London   New Delhi

HM
24
.M1755
1991

For information address:

SAGE Publications, Inc.
2455 Teller Road
Newbury Park, California 91320

SAGE Publications Ltd.
6 Bonhill Street
London EC2A 4PU
United Kingdom

SAGE Publications India Pvt. Ltd.
M-32 Market
Greater Kailash I
New Delhi 110 048 India

Printed in the United States of America

Library of Congress Cataloging-in-Publication Data

Main entry under title:

Macro-micro linkages in sociology / editor, Joan Huber.
    p. cm. — (American Sociological Association presidential series)
    Includes bibliographical references and index.
    ISBN 0-8039-4103-X.   ISBN 0-8039-4104-8 (pbk.)
    1. Macrosociology.   2. Microsociology.   3. Sociology—United States.   I. Huber, Joan, 1925-   .   II. Series.
    HM24.M1755   1991
    301—dc20   90-24238
                                                                 CIP

FIRST PRINTING, 1991

Sage Production Editor: Diane S. Foster

Contents

About the Authors

RAE LESSER BLUMBERG has research interests focused on theories of gender stratification and gender and development. Her publications include *Stratification: Socioeconomic and Sexual Inequality, Making the Case for the Gender Variable: Women and the Wealth and Well-Being of Nations,* and "A General Theory of Gender Stratification" in *Sociological Theory 1984.* She is Associate Professor of Sociology at the University of California, San Diego, and has done field research on gender and development in over a dozen countries around the world, most recently in Ecuador, Nigeria, Guatemala, and the Dominican Republic.

CRAIG CALHOUN is Professor of Sociology and Chair of the International Studies Curriculum at the University of North Carolina at Chapel Hill. He works mainly in historical and political sociology and social theory. His most recent publications include "Classical Sociology and the Revolutions of 1848" and "Populist Politics and Large Scale Social Integration," both in *Sociological Theory,* and *Habermas and the Public Sphere* (MIT Press, forthcoming). He was teaching and doing research in Beijing at the time of the 1989 prodemocracy protests. His book on that movement will be published in 1991 by the University of California Press.

RANDALL COLLINS is Professor of Sociology at the University of California, Riverside. His books include *Weberian Sociological Theory* (1986), *Theoretical Sociology* (1988), and *Sociology of Marriage and Family: Gender, Love and Property* (third edition, coauthored with Scott Coltrane, 1990).

KAREN S. COOK is Professor of Sociology and Director of the Center for Studies in Social Psychology of the University of Washington. She also chairs the Social Psychology Section of the American Sociological Association and edits *Social Psychology Quarterly.* Her recent publications include *Social Exchange Theory* (1987) and *The Future of Sociology* (1988, edited with Edgar Borgatta). Her research interests focus on social exchange theory, power, networks, distributive justice, and organizational behavior. In 1990-1991, she was President of the Pacific Sociological Association.

PAUL DiMAGGIO is Associate Professor in the Sociology Department at Yale University. He has written widely on organizational analysis and sociology of culture and edited *Nonprofit Enterprise in the Arts, Structures of Capital: The Social Organization of Economic Life* (with Sharon Zukin), and *The New Institutionalism in Organizational Analysis* (with Walter Powell). Formerly Executive Director of Yale's Program on Non-Profit Organizations and a Fellow of the Center for Advanced Study in the Behavioral Sciences (1984-1985) and the John Simon Guggenheim Memorial Foundation (1990), he is completing a book on the social organization of the high-culture arts in the United States.

BARBARA ENTWISLE, Associate Professor of Sociology at the University of North Carolina at Chapel Hill, has published articles in the *American Sociological Review, American Journal of Sociology,* and *Demography* on macro-micro linkage in social demography. She is currently working on two volumes that extend her earliest work, one that uses WFS data from 36 developing countries to examine reproductive behavior within national contexts and the other on local contexts and their implications in rural Egypt. In addition, she is studying contraceptive choice in an environment of rapid social and economic change in rural Thailand.

MICHAEL HECHTER is currently a Fellow at the Center for Advanced Study in the Behavioral Sciences (1990-1991) and Professor of Sociology at the University of Arizona. In addition to many articles in professional journals, his books include *Principles of Group Solidarity, Internal Colonialism, The Microfoundations of Macrosociology* (editor), *Social Institutions: Their Emergence, Maintenance and Effects* (coeditor), and *Towards a Scientific Understanding of Values* (coeditor).

JOAN HUBER taught at Notre Dame and at the University of Illinois, Urbana-Champaign. She is currently Dean of the College of Social and Behavioral Sciences at Ohio State University. She was President of the American Sociological Association in 1989 and is Chair of the Committee on Women's Employment and Related Issues for the National Research Council. Her research interests are in gender stratification.

ALAN C. KERCKHOFF is Professor of Sociology at Duke University. His recent research has been concerned with social mobility processes in Great Britain and the United States. He is the author of *Getting Started: Transition to Adulthood in Great Britain.* A follow-up volume, *Diverging Pathways: Social Structure and the Life Course,* is in preparation.

KAREN OPPENHEIM MASON joined the East-West Population Institute, East-West Center, Honolulu, Hawaii, in July 1990 after 17 years on the faculty of the University of Michigan. Her research focuses on family, gender, and demographic change in Asia and the United States, with special emphasis on the status of women and its relationship to population aging, fertility decline, and the health/mortality transition. Recent projects have explored the impact of child care costs on women's employment and fertility decisions in the United States and the effects of women's status on fertility decline in five Asian countries. In 1990, she served as Second Vice-President of the Population Association of America; she currently cochairs the IUSSP's Scientific Committee on Gender and Population.

WILLIAM M. MASON is Professor of Sociology and Social Statistics at the University of California, Los Angeles. At the time the chapter in this collection was written, he was Professor of Sociology and Director of the Population Studies Center at the University of Michigan. His recent interests have included the methodology of multilevel analysis, the comparative analysis of fertility, and political alienation. He is currently studying infant and child mortality in China.

SARA S. McLANAHAN is Professor of Sociology and Public Affairs at Princeton University. Her primary interests are the family and family policy, poverty and inequality, and gender stratification. She is currently involved in several research projects dealing with the effects of marital disruption on children's economic and social well-being. She is also working on an evaluation design for child support provisions of the Family Support Act (1988). She has published numerous articles in books and scholarly journals and is coauthor of *Single Mothers and Their Children: A New American Dilemma*.

SAMUEL H. PRESTON is Frederick J. Warren Professor of Demography and Chair of the Sociology Department at the University of Pennsylvania. He is a member and former Director of the Population Studies Center. His most recent research (with Michael Haines) will appear in *Fatal Years: Child Mortality in Late Nineteenth Century America* (Princeton University Press for the National Bureau of Economic Research, 1991). He has also written on issues of marriage and divorce, aging populations, and technical demography.

BARBARA F. RESKIN is Professor of Sociology at the University of Illinois, Urbana-Champaign. She has been selected Sociologists for Women in Society/Cheryl Allyn Miller Lecturer on Women and Social Change and elected Vice President of the American Sociological Association. Her research on sex segregation appears in *Sex Segregation in the Workplace: Trends, Explanations, Remedies; Women's Work, Men's Work: Sex Segregation on the Job* (with Heidi Hartmann); and *Job Queues, Gender Queues: Explaining Women's Inroads into Male Occupations* (with Patricia Roos) and in several articles and chapters. She continues to study sex segregation, sex differentiation, and other mechanisms that maintain women's subordination.

TIMOTHY M. SMEEDING is Professor of Economic and Public Administration at Syracuse University. He is also overall Project Director of the Luxembourg Income Study Project as well as Research Associate in the Metropolitian Studies Program at Syracuse. He has published extensively in the areas of poverty, income measurement, income distribution, generational equity, and social policy toward children and their families in such journals as *Science, American Economic Review,* and *Journal of Policy Analysis and Management.* He has served as a consultant to several National Academy of Science committees, including the Committee on Child Development Research and Public Policy.

MARTA TIENDA is Professor of Sociology and Public Policy at the University of Chicago and Associate Director of the Population Research Center of NORC and the University of Chicago. She coauthored *The Hispanic Population of the United States* (Russell Sage, 1987) and coedited *Divided Opportunities: Poverty, Minorities and Social Policy* (Plenum, 1988) and *Hispanics in the U.S. Economy* (Academic Press, 1985). Her research interests and writings focus on race and gender inequality and various aspects of the sociology of economic life, including persistent poverty and welfare participation, labor market processes, and the economic consequences of immigration.

SUSAN COTTS WATKINS is Associate Professor in the Department of Sociology and a member of the Population Studies Center at the University of Pennsylvania. Her work is at the intersection of demography, comparative and historical sociology, and social history. She recently finished a book, *From Provinces into Nations* (Princeton University Press, 1990), that describes the decline in demographic diversity within the countries of Western Europe between 1870 and 1960. She is currently editing a volume of papers on the demography of immigrants based on the 1910 U.S. Census.

WILLIAM JULIUS WILSON is the Lucy Flower University Professor of Sociology and Public Policy and former Chair of the Sociology Department at the University of Chicago. He has written *Power, Racism and Privilege,*

The Declining Significance of Race, The Truly Disadvantaged, and *Social Isolation* (forthcoming). He coedited *Through Different Eyes* and edited *The Ghetto Underclass.* He was President of the American Sociological Association (1989-90), a MacArthur Prize Fellow, a Fellow of the American Academy of Arts and Sciences, a Fellow of the American Association for the Advancement of Science, and a member of the American Philosophical Society.

MORRIS ZELDITCH, Jr., is Professor and Chair of the Department of Sociology, Stanford University. He coedited the recently published *Sociological Theories in Progress: New Formulations* (Sage, 1989), the introduction to which addresses the micro-macro problem, and the forthcoming *Theoretical Research Programs: Studies in Theory Growth.*

Introduction

The 1989 annual meeting of the American Sociological Association in San Francisco had, perhaps for the first time, two themes. One was the AIDS crisis, a health care nightmare now becoming a topic of sociological research. The other theme, and the theme of this volume, concerns the interrelations of macro and micro theory and research. It is a broad theme, almost as broad as the discipline itself. There is good reason for such breadth.

The privilege of choosing a theme for the annual meeting increases the tendency for presidents to take themselves very seriously. As Erving Goffman observed in the presidential address he was too sick to deliver in San Francisco in 1982, presidents of scholarly associations find a podium attached to the office. They are encouraged to feel that what they represent is just what their intellectual community wants represented. Presenting their addresses, presidents come to feel like temporary guardians of the discipline. "However large or oddly shaped the hall, their self swells out to fill it" (Goffman 1983, p. 1). Sobering—thus the macro-micro theme, which is broad enough to encompass almost everybody's favorite obsession.

The interrelationships of macro- and micro-level theories, variables, and concepts are confronted by most social and behavioral scientists daily in teaching and research. Most of us deal with these interrelationships as best we can, often by simplifying complex situations to make sense of a small subset of reality. Implicitly, the causal arrows neatly point in one direction although common sense and research make all of us aware that everything interacts with everything else.

The problem is how to untangle the snarl of causal arrows. Under what conditions do individuals affect the societies in which they live? Under what conditions do societies affect individual destinies? An old joke says that economists explain why people make certain choices; sociologists explain why they don't have any to make. The comparison is funny. The reality is sobering. Neither discipline has solved the problem of conceptualizing and analyzing the simultaneous interaction between individuals and societies.

In the last few decades, however, interest in what is usually called the micro-macro problem has been growing. But agreement is widespread that the problem remains unsolved. I hope that the chapters in this volume will carry us a little closer to a solution.

The volume begins with my 1989 presidential address, which puts the issue into historical context. Few scholars debated macro and micro relations until the 1960s when George Homans tried to reduce sociology to individual behavior in his 1963 presidential address, "Bringing Men Back In." Except for the catchy title—sociologists have been bringing things back in ever since—Homans's attack on macrosociology elicited little response from structuralists, most of whom carried on with little concern for social psychology. Instead, Homans's attack provided a convenient rubric for symbolic interactionists and ethnomethodologists to show how their own work contributed to knowledge of social structure. Thus much work on the micro-macro problem focused only on a subset of issues: the effects of "qualitative" micro variables (observed with little regard for replicability) on loosely defined macro variables.

In the past few years, however, scholars like Coleman and Blau have been joined by an increasing number of theorists, social psychologists, and structural sociologists who probe the macro-micro issue and who, like Homans, see social and behavioral science research as requiring a theory that generates hypotheses that can be tested by replicable methods. Consequently, the chapters in this volume demonstrate how the analysis of micro-macro interrelations has broadened and deepened.

All of the chapters in this volume were presented in plenary or thematic sessions at the 1989 annual meeting. They are grouped in ways that highlight certain approaches to the problem.

The first group deals primarily with metatheoretical issues. The authors discuss ways of thinking about the problem that can help to bring substantive problems into better focus. Karen Cook ("The Micro Foundations of Social Structure: An Exchange Perspective") discusses exchange theory, which she sees as one theoretical approach to social structure that is microsociological. Michael Hechter's response ("From Exchange to Structure") points out that what ultimately determines actors' interests is subjective; this fundamental insight must be given its due. Craig Calhoun ("The Problem of Identity in Collective Action") uses events in China in spring 1989 to show that accounting for high-risk actions need not rely on ideas of psychological debility or mystically substitute class interests for individual ones. Rather, action that is risky and apparently self-sacrificing can be seen as rational and self-saving. Paul DiMaggio ("The Micro-Macro Dilemma in Organizational Research: Implications of Role-System Theory") suggests ways to think about the problem as it manifests itself in the study of organizations, anchoring his argument in a role theory terminology that differs significantly from Parsons's. Following William Julius Wilson's summary of his book, *The Truly Disadvantaged*, Morris Zelditch ("Levels in the Logic of Macro-Historical Explanation") argues that it is an error to formulate macro and micro as mutually exclusive alternatives. Multiplication of levels creates a house without stairs between the floors. Integration into one theoretical structure is a more fruitful strategy for sociology.

The second group includes the papers presented at the Plenary Session on micro-macro effects on gender stratification. Randall Collins, focusing on the First World in "Historical Change and the Ritual Production of Gender," argues that the greatest weakness in gender stratification theory is the failure to understand the sources of change, especially in industrial societies. Massive change in women's roles must come from political mobilization of cosmopolitan groups on behalf of universalistic ideals. Samuel Preston ("Parenthood, Work, and Women") responds that political mobilization explains the feminist movement better than gender stratification, to which the movement is only loosely related. Change in gender stratification was induced by sweeping technological and economic change. Rae Blumberg ("Women and the Wealth and Well-Being of Nations: Macro-Micro Interrelationships") focuses on the Third World, arguing that women produce more wealth than appears in national statistics; the Third World's major problems are exacerbated by policymakers' bypassing women as economic agents. Preston agrees with Blumberg that in sub-Saharan Africa the mother's income affects child survival far more than father's income, but he doubts that increasing women's control over income will lead to fertility reduction.

The third group of chapters links micro and macro issues to substantive problems in education, occupation, age, and family. Alan Kerckhoff ("Creating Inequality in the Schools: A Structural Perspective"), assessing three models for inequality in schools, shows why propositions about negative effects of social inequality in society and propositions about links between school processes and social inequality should be differentiated. Propositions about stratification effects on education substance and school criteria of evaluation and propositions linking within-school structures with pupil inequalities should also be differentiated. Barbara Reskin ("Labor Markets as Queues: A Structural Approach to Changing Occupational Sex Composition") uses the concept of queuing to explain why women have so disproportionately entered pharmacy, bank management, bartending, and a few other male occupations when they have made only modest progress in most and lost ground in a few. Sara McLanahan ("The Two Faces of Divorce: Women's and Children's Interests") discusses how sweeping macro changes in economic status fueled other macro changes in divorce and nonmarital births, which, in turn, affect mothers' and children's individual interests. Timothy Smeeding ("Mountains or Molehills: Just What's So Bad About Aging Societies Anyway?") argues that, save for severe underinvestment in children, individual behavioral responses to expected changes in supply and demand indicate that the funds to pay for the benefits needed are within our grasp.

Last, four chapters address micro-macro issues from a demographic perspective. The first two address metatheoretical problems. Karen Mason ("Multilevel Analysis in the Study of Social Institutions and Demographic Change") analyzes the role of social institutions versus the individual decision maker in promoting demographic change. William Mason ("Problems in Quantitative Comparative Analysis: Ugly Ducklings Are to Swans as Ugly Scatter Plots Are to . . . ?") addresses recent criticisms of quantitative, comparative, multilevel analysis. He concludes that more *public* effort is needed to check theoretical assumptions and that quantitative analysis (unlike qualitative analysis) offers a framework in which to sift arguments that can actually be rejected. The second two chapters put more emphasis on substantive problems. Marta Tienda ("Poor People and Poor Places: Deciphering Neighborhood Effects on Poverty Outcomes") discusses the nature of evidence required to establish the existence of neighborhood effects on poverty outcomes. Susan Watkins ("Markets, States, Nations, and Bedrooms in Western Europe, 1870-1960"), because she sees the individuals in the rational actor framework as too concerned with economic interests as they approach their "fertility relevant bedtimes," considers the effects of macro change on the way individuals interact with one another as a promising explanation of the decline of demographic diversity in Europe. Barbara Entwisle ("Micro-Macro Theoretical Linkages in Social Demography: A Commentary") enhances the impact of all four chapters with provocative comments.

These chapters point to a fruitful direction for the discipline. When scholars put work in the context of macro-micro relations, they are forced to think about the interrelations of population, organization, ecology, and technology (Duncan 1964) at various times and places (Lenski and Lenski 1978). Thinking about such matters simultaneously is a big order. It will require sociologists to conceptualize and measure much more complicated interactions than in the past. We shall be needing all of the quantitative and theoretical sophistication that we can muster.

I should like to thank the many persons who helped to make this volume a reality, especially William Form, who suggested the topic, and the members of the 1989 Program Committee, who developed the thematic sessions and selected participants: Michael Aiken, Jeffrey Alexander, Donna Eder, Glen Elder, Jr., John Hagan, Elizabeth Long, Victor Nee, Sam Preston, Beth Schneider, and Wade Smith. I also wish to thank William D'Antonio, ASA Executive Officer, and Jan Astner, who handled the huge load of work required to produce an annual meeting. Last, I owe special thanks to Judith Essig for invaluable assistance in manuscript preparation.

—Joan Huber

REFERENCES

Duncan, Otis Dudley. 1964. "Social Organization and the Ecosystem." Pp. 37-82 in *Handbook of Modern Sociology*, edited by R. E. L. Faris. Chicago: Rand McNally.

Goffman, Erving. 1983. "The Interaction Order." *American Sociological Review* 48:1-17.

Lenski, Gerhard and Jean Lenski. 1978. *Human Societies*. New York: McGraw-Hill.

1

Macro-Micro Links in
Gender Stratification

Joan Huber

The interrelationships of macro- and micro-level theory and data concern all social and behavioral sciences that study both individuals and collectivities like nations, firms, and large organizations. The basic problem is to explain how persons affect collectivities and how collectivities affect persons *over time*. However, to conceptualize and measure reciprocal effects over time is a formidable undertaking. We are only at the beginning of the beginning of this task (Campbell 1983). In practice, most scholars conceptualize the problem only along one direction, from micro to macro or from macro to micro, the approach of this chapter.

THE CONTEXT IN SOCIOLOGY

To set my remarks in context, I first briefly review the history of the problem in sociology. Few scholars debated macro and micro relations until the 1960s when Homans tried to reduce sociology to social behaviorism (Collins 1988a, p. 376). His attack on macrosociology was joined by interpretive sociologists who (with a few notable exceptions) tended not to share Homans's view of the requirements of scientific research. Their theories tended to be radically anticollectivist (Alexander 1987, p. 54) and they were being attacked for failing to take social structure into account. The actor was not seen as bringing a previously defined collective order into play

AUTHOR'S NOTE: *I am grateful to William Form for suggesting this topic and for criticizing this chapter, which previously appeared in the American Sociological Review 55:1-10.*

(Alexander 1988, p. 87). Much of the ensuing discussion was conducted by militant microsociologies as a war against macrosociology although they disagreed sharply over the type of microsociology with which to replace it (Collins 1988a, p. 386).

During most of this period, macrosociologists paid little attention to the controversy because, first, it seemed irrelevant. As Goffman (1974, p. 13) said, social organization and structure can be studied quite nicely without reference to social psychology. Macro theory must account for patterns of social relations not on the basis of motives but on the basis of external constraints and opportunities for social relations created by population composition and the structure of positions in the social environment (Blau 1987, p. 75).

Second, the controversy was muddied by disagreement about the meaning of the words *micro* and *macro*. Everyone agreed that *micro* refers to something small. Beyond this, sociologists divided into two camps.

One camp included interpretive sociologists, who tended to equate *macro* with "quantitative" and *micro* with "qualitative" sociology. This definition puts their own work, based on individual data, in the micro category but it implicitly excludes other work based on individual data (status attainment, for example) when those data are collected with methods that involve a quantitative and qualitative mix like that of survey research. To my knowledge, no other social and behavioral science scholars so use these words. As Berger et al. (1989) point out, it is wrong to use *micro* to mean a small structured action system and *macro* to refer to a large unstructured system without action. This treats the analytic aspects of micro and macro theories as being correlated, when in fact they are independent, and raises fruitless questions about relationships.

The other camp includes everyone else: macrosociologists, exchange theorists, life course theorists, and so on. Whatever else they disagree about, they tend to equate *micro* with individual and *macro* with collective level events, using the words much as economists do.

Some sociologists in this large residual category see the problem as one of showing how micro affects macro in a theoretically generalizing way (Collins 1988a, p. 244). For sociologists, the natural unit of observation has been the individual. Thus the analysis must move from the individual level of observation to the system level, where the problem of interest usually lies (Coleman 1987, p. 153). But how to move remains an unsolved problem that requires the integration of exchange theory and macro structure (Blau 1987, p. 84). The extent to which the problem is solvable remains to be seen.

Other sociologists have taken a macro-to-micro approach. One fruitful example is the life course perspective. It mixes history, social psychology, and demography with powerful quantitative techniques that can now handle both the timing and the sequencing of events (Blalock 1989). Life course theorists examine cohort and period effects on individuals with data taken from historical demography, social history, and recent longitudinal studies (Elder 1984). These studies necessarily focus only on the industrial era because they require data that can be analyzed quantitatively.

Like the life course theorists, I too am concerned with macro-to-micro effects—but not just in the industrial era. Since 1970, my favorite obsession has been gender stratification, how women's power and prestige relative to men's varies by time and place. The only way to develop an adequate theory is to compare the impact of ecological conditions and subsistence technologies on social organization and individual behavior over time. Only a theory that takes both preindustrial and industrial technology into account can put into context concrete problems that U.S. society faces today and demonstrate how these problems are reflected in individual lives.

PERIOD EFFECTS ON A 1967 COHORT

The events that I experienced led me to conclude that the macro-micro link is best approached as a substantive problem using comparative and historical data—which makes sense only in the context of a general theory. I begin by describing the direction in which my work was shoved by period effects on the 1967 crop of Ph.D.s.

Entering graduate school in the 1960s, I chose sociology because it examined societal constraints on individual behavior. Perhaps I wanted to know why I had been a housewife for 14 years when I liked books better than housework. I saw stratification as the heart of sociology. Duncan and Schnore's (1959) POET (population, organization, ecology, and technology) model included the variables with the most power to explain stratification comparatively and historically.[1]

By 1970, the black power movement and a new wave of the women's movement signaled that something had gone awry in stratification theory. Women and blacks were nearly invisible in it. In introductory sociology texts, women appeared primarily as mothers or prostitutes.[2] Blacks appeared in chapters euphemistically titled "Race Relations," as if racial interaction were symmetrical.

In response to these gaps in stratification theory, the concepts of institutional racism and sexism appeared, highlighting the ascriptive qualities of race and sex in contrast to those of class, which at least offered chances for mobility. Also, it now seems clear, especially since Karen Mason (1984) pointed it out, that class and socioeconomic status (SES) vary among individuals in all settings but gender stratification in a particular setting is a constant across individuals regardless of their economic status. But neither Marx nor Weber had said much about race and sex. What to do?

My response was triggered by a question that popped up at a college curriculum committee meeting in Urbana in 1972. I was earnestly defending the merits of women's studies courses when a learned linguist airily waved his hand and declared that women's studies was only a passing fad. The women's movement wouldn't last. I was shocked. But I had to ask, would it or wouldn't it? Why or why not? The basic theoretical question was, of course, what factors shape stratification patterns and what makes these patterns change?

The answers appeared piecemeal in the course of teaching introductory sociology and sex stratification. In 1972, I first used Lenski's (1970) text. It was based on his 1966 analysis that showed how the distribution of power and prestige was affected by use of a particular subsistence tool. His account, which covered all human societal types, gave theoretical underpinning to core sociological concepts by showing how ecology and technology affect stratification. The ecological evolutionary approach emphasizes strategy selection, which puts the study of production and expropriation in a new light. The approach assumes that persons (who enact strategies) are the units of behavior, but it permits analysis of populations in terms of strategy differences without erroneously inferring system-level behavioral dynamics from individual traits (Cohen and Machalek 1988).

A given ecology and technology permit a range of outcomes, limiting the ways that humans can organize themselves. Such factors as rainfall and temperature coupled with the use of a particular major subsistence tool affect the division of labor, which, in turn, affects social organization and stratification. One could thus present Joseph in Egypt as a world-class bureaucrat. His management skills were called into being by the invention of the plow, which created a food surplus so large that writing and counting had to be invented to keep track of it.

The ecological evolutionary context was a fine fit for my race lectures, based on van den Berghe's (1967) analysis of the confluence of ideational and technological factors that drove racism to historically unprecedented peaks of virulence in the nineteenth century: A wrongheaded interpretation of Darwinian theory—the notion that people in technologically advanced societies were more fit than others—was used to justify the exploitation of people in horticultural and herding societies all over the world. I also leaned on Fusfeld's (1973) account of the way that technological trends had affected black employment rates in the United States.

But sex stratification remained a puzzle. The first course I taught was more descriptive than theoretical, except for the part based on Oppenheimer's (1973) account of long-run effects of economic demand on women's entering the labor force. Actually, the literature on women's employment during the nineteenth and twentieth centuries was not the problem. Although skimpy, there was enough to suggest how the current women's movement paralleled what I came to call the men's movement.

In the West, both movements represented a response to men's and women's massive entry into the wage labor force. The men's movement emerged during the nineteenth century. Male workers, erstwhile peasants, serfs, and slaves, began to fight collectively for what they saw as their fair share. The current wave of the women's movement similarly emerged when women workers, erstwhile housewives, began to struggle for what they had come to see as their fair market share. The men's movement is called "the labor movement," but this is misleading. Women played almost no part in it. Indeed, one of the movement's objectives was to restrict the number of hours women could work for pay to give them more time at home to care for children. Such measures knocked women off the seniority ladder, thereby decreasing their ability to compete for high-wage jobs.

If the labor force literature was fairly satisfactory for theory, the fertility literature presented a real stumbling block. Demographers, suffering a terrible case of period effects, offered little help. As Ryder (1979, p. 359) put it, the baby boom had badly dented their theory of the demographic transition and they had retreated into the empty safety of empiricism.[3]

Help came, instead, from economics and anthropology. Economist Ester Boserup (1970) was first to link polygyny and women's productivity on a comparative basis (Lesthaeghe and Surkyn 1988b), demonstrating that women's ability to support themselves and their children was a critical factor in sub-Saharan polygyny. To my knowledge, anthropologist Ernestine Friedl (1975) was first to link work, fertility, and sex stratification in foraging and hoe cultures, thereby showing what factors caused variation in the gender distribution of power and prestige. Anthropologist Jack Goody (1976) extended Boserup's research, showing that property transmission is decisive in socioeconomic systems (Lesthaeghe and Surkyn 1988b), which suggested why gender stratification in plow societies differed so sharply from that of foraging or hoe cultures. Then Rae Blumberg (1978) put the approach into the Lenski (1970) ecological evolutionary context, which highlighted gender stratification variables across all societal types.

A MACRO THEORY OF GENDER STRATIFICATION

I summarize a general theory that has emerged from such research to show how it applies to a cluster of macro (social) and micro (personal) problems that men and women face today. The theory is not well known in either social science or women's studies.[4] It has, therefore, not received the kind of criticism it needs.

As Friedl (1975) suggested, the basic questions are these: Why do men and women do certain tasks, and which ones yield the most prestige and power? The answers suggest two principles of sex stratification that Friedl applied to foraging and hoe cultures. I then use these principles to relate production, reproduction, and stratification in societies based on herding, plow, and industrial technology (see Huber and Spitze 1988).

The first principle applies to the family. Producers in the family economy have more power and prestige than consumers. Historically, women's work has been constrained to mesh with pregnancy and lactation lest the society fail to reproduce itself and die out.

The second principle applies to the society. The most power and prestige accrue to those who control the distribution of valued goods beyond the family (Friedl 1975). Few men attain such positions. Almost no women have done so.

In foraging societies, men hunted the animals that were large enough to be distributed and consumed beyond the nuclear family. Women never hunted large animals because spending an uncertain period of time away from camp made nursing impossible. Because younger women were constantly pregnant or lactating to offset high death rates, the need to maintain population thus immobilized women, thereby excluding them from the most productive work.

In hoe cultures, men monopolized land clearing and, after the invention of metallurgy, warfare. Because warfare brings in more surplus than does land clearing, men outrank women more in advanced than in simple hoe cultures. But in both types, women's food production equals men's on average because the hoe is used near home. Because divorce has little effect on the subsistence of either of the spouses or their children, divorce rates are high, higher than in our own society (Friedl 1975). Women's ability to support themselves permits what Spitze and I (Huber and Spitze 1988, p. 488) have called "populist polygyny." Nearly everyone marries. Because women marry young, men marry old, and the death rate is high (as in sub-Saharan Africa), the sex ratio paradox tends to be resolved.

In herding societies, low rainfall, a short season, or mountains preclude growing crops. The need for water and grazing land makes war a major means of subsistence, enabling elites to control both economy and polity. Women lack access to major subsistence tools; warfare and herding are conducted far from home. These conditions permit what Spitze and I (Huber and Spitze 1988, p. 428) have called "elite polygyny." A few rich men have many wives while some poor men have none.

Desert conditions similarly affect baboon social organization (Collins 1988b, p. 38). In arid land where food is scarce and exposure to predators extreme, Hamadrayas baboons organize along military lines. Males dominate. Among Hamadrayas in forests where food is plentiful and trees offer protection from predators, males are not dominant and females mate promiscuously. Thus the environment rather than genetics seems to evoke different social patterns.

In Eurasia, the iron-shared plow vastly increased the food supply but depressed the status of ordinary people. Iron weapons enabled elites to extract heavily from peasants (Lenski 1970, p. 177). Women's share of food production decreased relative to that in hoe cultures. Larger fields further from home impede nursing (Blumberg 1978). The plow's effect on inheritance patterns also degraded women (Goody 1976). The plow makes land the chief form of wealth. Because land tends to be an impartible inheritance, the number of legal heirs must be limited. Monogamy prevails. Divorce is rare. Women's sexual behavior must be constrained lest a man's property go to another man's child. The richer her family, the greater the constraints placed on her—foot binding in China, suttee in India.

Industrialization first emerged in northwest European plow kingdoms. Men continued to use the most productive tools, which ensured that their wages would exceed women's. Other macro trends disrupted patterns adapted to plow cultures. Five trends that occurred in sequence were most disruptive.

First, infant mortality declined. This trend greatly reduced the number of births needed for population replacement.

Second, the spread of mass education redirected wealth flows within the family (Caldwell 1976). For the first time in history, economic returns on parental investment in children went to the children, making them a less attractive pension instrument (Parsons 1984). In the West, economic incentives to reproduce have vanished like the snows of yesteryear.

Third, spurred by the decline in infant mortality, the spread of mass education (compulsory in Europe by about 1880), and rapid economic growth between 1860 and 1910, fertility began its long decline in the West. Economic growth triggers demographic change by fueling ambition and opening opportunities (Lesthaeghe 1983).

Fourth, about 1910, the introduction of safe methods of artificial feeding wiped out the survival advantages of breast-fed babies. For the first time in human history, a mother could work away from her baby without endangering its life.[5]

Fifth, after the preceding four changes were well along, an increase in the demand for women workers induced a steady rise in women's labor force participation in this century, helping to launch a new women's movement.

Increases in economic demand trigger social movements by producing a demand for labor that cannot be met in the usual ways (Chafetz 1984; Chafetz and Dworkin 1986).

MICRO CONSEQUENCES OF MACRO CHANGES

Taking a long view, these macro-level changes soon transformed social patterns adapted to plow cultures into patterns better adapted to industrial work. Pervasive mass media allow for rapid value change and great homogeneity of values (Preston 1986, p. 178; Lesthaeghe and Surkyn 1988a). Friedl's (1975) two principles of stratification permit theoretical interpretation of the new and emerging patterns.

The first principle is that producers outrank consumers. Compared with men, women are more productive now than in plow societies. Early industrialization increased the U.S. female/male wage ratio by almost 50%. By 1885, it reached the 1970 value of about .56 (Goldin 1987, p. 214). Since 1970, the wage ratio again increased because, unlike the 1950s, women who are more educated are now more likely to be employed than are less educated women. The sex wage gap may nearly close for younger workers by century's end (Smith and Ward 1985).

As expected, women's increased productivity has eroded legal and customary restraints on their behavior. For example, marriage as an institution has declined since 1960[6] as indicated by postponement, fewer persons ever marrying, a lower ratio of time spent in wedlock, and shorter marital durations (Espenshade 1985).[7] Recent divorce rates imply that two-thirds of all first marriages may dissolve (Martin and Bumpass 1989). Divorce rates reflect spouses' ability to support themselves (Brinton 1983), although women's postdivorce income is less than 70% of its predivorce level (Stirling 1989).

The second principle is that the most power goes to those who control the distribution of valued goods beyond the family. In a modern context, this refers to elite positions in economy and polity. Few women hold such positions. Women still are hindered by behaviors and expectations related to fertility.

Feminist scholars have tended to focus on these expectations and behaviors while ignoring basic trends in fertility, apparently seeing it as a benign constant rather than as a variable. This is understandable considering the problems posed by rapid population growth in the Third World but it is an error nonetheless. It makes for myopic theories about women's status, as I point out below.

The major fertility-related expectation that restricts women is that of child rearing, which lowers occupational aspirations. The obverse is that people expect grown men but not grown women to work for pay. Only 12% of the respondents to a 1978 national survey thought a mother with school-age children should be employed; only a third thought a married woman, even if she had no children, should work for pay (Huber and Spitze 1983). Such expectations hinder women, for example, by making family migration largely unresponsive to the wife's work (Spitze 1986). Belief in a differential obligation to work for pay may be the aspect of women's work most resistant to change (Spitze 1988).

The major fertility-related behaviors that disadvantage women involve time spent in housework and child care. Women in the 1980s do less housework than in the 1960s and men do a little more, but men still do much less than women (Gershuny and Robinson 1988).

Fertility-related expectations and behaviors are in flux. Continuing macro trends in education, employment, and fertility churn the micro level relentlessly, leaving in their wake vast discrepancies in thought, feeling, and behavior. Such micro-level discrepancies were the object of Hochschild's (1989) recent study of the second shift in two-job marriages. A complex interplay of gender ideology, feeling, and behavior determines the division of labor. The supply of male commitment to share child care was far lower than female demand for it, making for high levels of marital tension. Such tension may spread because less educated women have begun to catch up with college women in adopting a feminist stance toward a gendered division of labor (Mason and Lu 1988).

In contrast to behaviors and expectations, actual fertility trends are in less flux. Except for the period of the baby boom, U.S. fertility has been declining for 200 years.[8] Will it level out at zero population growth or go down (Huber 1980)? If down, how far, how fast? Demographers don't know. The West may be experiencing a population implosion (Bourgeois-Pichat 1987). Childlessness is up (Jacobson et al. 1989). Marriage is down. Trends set in motion by the Industrial Revolution have put us into a new game.

From a macro-level perspective, immigration could improve demographic stability. At the micro level, however, the issues posed by large-scale immigration, would be divisive. Public concern with a growing immigrant community would increase as its share of total population growth rose. Many writers doubt there can be a politically acceptable immigration solution to allay fears of population decline (Espenshade 1986, p. 258). Thus the demographic situation suggests three sources of political concern.

POLITICAL CONCERNS

One is the vague fear that the human race might die out. The dinosaurs did. Why not us? Second, some pollsters and politicians worry that the nation is losing its will to live, especially its ability to conduct a really decent war. A third concern is with the funding of pension plans as the proportion of workers declines.

These political concerns will tend to reawaken interest in fertility and the problems posed by population decline. Such problems are not new. About a century ago, many northwestern European countries, concerned about population decline, instituted programs to make child rearing more attractive. Typically, such programs awarded modest grants to induce women to stay home and have babies. No one ever demonstrated the effectiveness of such programs. They would cost even more today because the proportion of educated women is larger and the loss of women's market productivity would be greater.

If the old approaches to the problem of population maintenance seem doubtful, what new ones might work? I briefly note three possibilities. All would significantly affect gender stratification.

One type would require a national state more coercive than any yet seen. The trends that lowered fertility would have to be reversed. By far the most important would be to limit women's education, say, to the completion of tenth grade, to reduce their ability to compete for high-wage jobs. However, the number of educated women is probably already too high to make such a measure politically feasible. Someone is sure to suggest outlawing contraceptive devices but such measures would probably be ineffective for the long run. In the West, the demographic transition occurred without fancy gadgets. People who don't want children figure out what to do.

A second approach would reconnect fertility and retirement security by allocating benefits entirely or partly on the basis of worker contribution to child rearing (Demeny 1987). This would shift responsibility for a macro problem to the micro level. Although the yuppie generation might find this solution radical, it is quite traditional, having served the human race from its beginnings. Currently, the persons who foot the bill for rearing the next generation of workers are in effect giving a free ride to those who for whatever reason do not share those expenses.

A third approach would spread costs over the body politic by making parenthood more attractive to persons who want to remain in the labor force. A basic problem with child rearing is that paid work and leisure are increasingly more attractive. Parents are on call 24 hours a day, perhaps one reason that children decrease marital satisfaction (McLanahan and Adams 1987). Parenting might be more acceptable if better day care and more attractive nursery schools professionalized motherhood as medicine now has been. Only 50 years ago, physicians were also on call 24 hours a day (Keyfitz 1986).

The disadvantage of such a program is its cost. The taxpayers would have to be committed to the idea that population maintenance is extremely important because programs to improve child care would benefit the children of the rich and poor alike. Historically, measures to benefit poor people have never been popular. Recently, measures to improve children's economic status have been swamped by successful efforts to improve the status of the aged, particularly those in middle-income groups (Preston 1984; Wilson 1987). However, because poor mothers typically rear a large share of the next generation of workers (Blake 1985), programs that improve early child care and education could potentially provide high returns on the investment. Improvements in what economists call child quality could increase the potential for macro-economic growth.[9]

Politically, the third approach seems most probable. No one seems to want women out of the labor force. Both men and women like the money that women earn. In turn, measures that make parenting more attractive would also improve women's market position. The more women's economic status resembles men's, the fewer the differences in men's and women's power and prestige. Thus the more that voters become concerned about low fertility, the better it will be for women. For the first time in human history, technology has made it possible for women's economic productivity to equal men's. Whether this possibility will ever be realized remains to be seen. In agricultural societies, women's reproductive capacity was the basis of their subordination. In industrial societies, their reproductive capacity may be the basis for their social equality.

CONCLUSIONS

In this chapter, I have tried to demonstrate how a macro-theoretical and historical approach to gender stratification illuminates (in a way that the micro-macro approach does not) how a series of macro-level trends during industrialization relate to one another and to people's trials and triumphs at the micro level. Thus the abortion issue, child care, rising divorce rates, social security financing, immigration, and tax schedules are linked in the context of a historical theory. Individual family members who confront these problems reflect evolutionary social changes in a microcosmic snapshot.

Thus changes in rates of social behaviors have resulted from a variety of macro trends. These rate changes typically reflect individual decisions in small groups like the family, personal dilemmas like abortion, conjugal conflicts over the division of household labor, and prejudices such as men's barring women from a work group. Macro trends are internalized as personal problems. The causal sequence is clear. Yet, once personal decisions are multiplied over a large population and stabilized (as in the desire for fewer children), collective problems emerge: How to sustain economic growth, how to provide for retirement pensions, how to provide personnel for the armed forces?

Clearly, the evolutionary perspective discussed here is strongest in explaining the origin, persistence, and interrelations of problems in gender stratification. This is an impressive achievement. But the approach offers few guidelines to explain and predict the short-term direction of social change. Neither does it explain why individuals select some choices over others. This is a challenge that structural theories must confront. At this stage in the development of sociology, the best short-term strategy is to press the micro-macro link for all it is worth to see how much structure and change it can explain and to push the macro-micro link for all it is worth to determine how well it can explain short-term change. Meanwhile, we need to gear up to confront the formidable task of explaining reciprocal effects over time.

NOTES

1. See Namboodiri (1988) for a cogent statement on the importance of ecology in social research.

2. The degree of change since that time is less than one might hope (Ferree and Hall 1989).

3. Demographers are becoming more theoretical. See, for example, H. Smith's (1989) suggestions for integrating theory and research on institutional determinants of fertility.

4. "Feminist theory" tends to be an idealist enterprise that takes little heed of organization, population, ecology, and technology.

5. The relation of breast-feeding to fertility, infant death, and women's work during industrialization has received little study. A skimpy literature suggests that the need for women's wages may curtail breast-feeding and thereby affect fertility and infant mortality. Strong evidence suggests that European fertility rose before 1880 because of a shortened period of nursing (Dyson and Murphy 1985). Infant mortality may have risen because of maternal factory work and unsafe bottle-feeding (Hogan and Kertzer 1986). Sussman (1982) reports the grim consequences of French wet-nursing practices at that time.

6. Even the health benefits of marriage have been questioned. Much excess mortality among the never-married results from selectivity. Poor health deters some persons from marrying (Kisker and Goldman 1987).

7. Divorce has decreased marital duration in this century but not as much as death did in the last century. Current U.S. mortality rates permit average marital durations of 45 years; the real average is 27 years (Watkins et al. 1987). In contrast, nineteenth-century French marriages averaged 20 years (Tabah 1980).

8. Below-replacement fertility has had a surprisingly long history in the United States (Sanderson 1987). A new study also reports that the sharp drop in black fertility in the rural South

from 1880 to 1940 resulted from voluntary measures rather than from disease or poor nutrition (Tolnay 1987).

9. It may be costly in the long run to ignore the effects of the mother's employment status and working conditions on child outcomes. Data recently gathered from the grown children of mothers first interviewed in 1967 permit the estimation of such outcomes for poor children, whose mothers were oversampled. The analyses suggest that the mother's working conditions affect such outcomes as verbal intelligence (Menaghan and Parcel 1989; Parcel and Menaghan 1989).

REFERENCES

Alexander, Jeffrey. 1987. "The 'Individualist Dilemma' in Phenomenology and Interactionism." Pp. 25-57 in *The Micro-Macro Link*, edited by J. Alexander, B. Giesen, R. Muench, and N. Smelser. Berkeley: University of California Press.

———. 1988. "The New Theoretical Movement." Pp. 77-101 in *Handbook of Sociology*, edited by Neil Smelser. Newbury Park, CA: Sage.

Berger, Joseph, Dana Eyre, and Morris Zelditch, Jr. 1989. "Theoretical Structures and the Micro-Macro Problem." In *Sociological Theories in Progress*. Newbury Park, CA: Sage.

Blake, Judith. 1985. "Number of Siblings and Educational Mobility." *American Sociological Review* 50:84-94.

Blalock, Hubert, Jr. 1989. "The Real and Unrealized Contributions of Quantitative Sociology." *American Sociological Review* 54:447-60.

Blau, Peter. 1987. "Contrasting Theoretical Perspectives." Pp. 71-85 in *The Micro-Macro Link*, edited by J. Alexander, B. Giesen, R. Muench, and N. Smelser. Berkeley: University of California Press.

Blumberg, Rae Lesser. 1978. *Stratification: Socionomic and Sexual Inequality*. Dubuque, IA: William C. Brown.

Boserup, Ester. 1970. *Women's Role in Economic Development*. London: George Allen & Unwin.

Bourgeois-Pichat, Jean. 1987. "The Unprecedented Shortage of Births in Europe." *Population and Development Review* 12(Suppl.):2-25.

Brinton, Mary. 1983. "Determinants of Group Cohesion in Contemporary Japan." Pp. 58-89 in *The Microfoundations of Macrosociology*, edited by Michael Hechter. Philadelphia: Temple University Press.

Caldwell, John. 1976. "Toward a Restatement of Demographic Transition Theory." *Population and Development Review* 2:321-66.

Campbell, Richard. 1983. "Status Attainment Research: End of the Beginning or Beginning of the End?" *Sociology of Education* 56:47-62.

Chafetz, Janet Saltzman. 1984. *Sex and Advantage*. Totowa, NJ: Rowman & Allenheld.

Chafetz, Janet Saltzman and Gary Dworkin. 1986. *Female Revolt*. Totowa, NJ: Rowman & Allenheld.

Cohen, Lawrence and Richard Machalek. 1988. "A General Theory of Expropriative Crime: An Evolutionary Ecological Approach." *American Journal of Sociology* 94:465-501.

Coleman, James. 1987. "Microfoundations and Macrosocial Behavior." Pp. 153-73 in *The Micro-Macro Link*, edited by J. Alexander, B. Giesen, B. Muench, and N. Smelser. Berkeley: University of California Press.

Collins, Randall. 1988a. *Theoretical Sociology*. San Diego: Harcourt Brace Jovanovich.

———. 1988b. *Sociology of Marriage and Family*. 2nd ed. Chicago: Nelson-Hall.

Demeny, Paul. 1987. "Re-linking Fertility Behavior and Economic Security." *Population and Development Review* 13:128-32.

Duncan, Otis Dudley and Leo Schnore. 1959. "Cultural, Behavioral, and Ecological Perspectives in the Study of Social Organization." *American Journal of Sociology* 65:132-45.

Dyson, Tim and Mike Murphy. 1985. "The Onset of Fertility Transition." *Population and Development Review* 11:399-440.

Elder, Glen. 1984. "Families, Kin and the Life Course." Pp. 80-135 in *Review of Child Development Research*. Vol. 7, edited by R. Parke. Chicago: University of Chicago Press.

Espenshade, Thomas. 1985. "Marriage Trends in America." *Population and Development Review* 11:193-245.

———. 1986. "Immigration and Low Fertility." *Population and Development Review* 12 (Suppl.):248-61.

Ferree, Myra Marx and Elaine Hall. 1989. "Gender and Race in Pictures in Introductory Sociology Books." University of Connecticut. (mimeo).

Friedl, Ernestine. 1975. *Women and Men: An Anthropologist's View.* New York: Holt, Rinehart & Winston.

Fusfeld, Daniel. 1973. Pp. 43-70 in *The Sociology of American Poverty,* edited by J. Huber and P. Chalfant. Boston: Schenkman.

Gershuny, Jonathan and John P. Robinson. 1988. "Historical Changes in the Household Division of Labor." *Demography* 25:537-52.

Goffman, Erving. 1974. *Frame Analysis.* New York: Harper & Row.

———. 1983. "The Interaction Order." *American Sociological Review* 48:1-17.

Goldin, Claudia. 1987. Pp. 185-222 in *Computer Chips and Paper Clips,* edited by H. Hartmann. Washington, DC: National Academy Press.

Goody, Jack. 1976. *Production and Reproduction.* Cambridge: Cambridge University Press.

Hochschild, Arlie. 1989. *The Second Shift.* New York: Viking.

Hogan, Dennis and David Kertzer. 1986. "The Social Bases of Declining Infant Mortality." *European Journal of Population* 2:361-85.

Huber, Joan. 1980. "Will US Fertility Decline Toward Zero?" *Sociological Quarterly* 21:481-92.

Huber, Joan and Glenna Spitze. 1983. *Sex Stratification.* New York: Academic Press.

———. 1988. "Trends in Family Sociology." Pp. 425-48 in *Handbook of Sociology,* edited by N. Smelser. Newbury Park, CA: Sage.

Jacobson, Cardell, Tim Heaton, and Karen Taylor. 1989. "Childlessness Among American Women." *Social Biology* 35:186-97.

Keyfitz, Nathan. 1986. "The Family That Does Not Reproduce Itself." *Population and Development Review* 12(Suppl.):139-54.

Kisker, Ellen Eliason and Noreen Goldman. 1987. "Perils of Single Life and Benefits of Marriage." *Social Biology* 34:135-52.

Lenski, Gerhard. 1970. *Human Societies.* New York: McGraw-Hill.

Lesthaeghe, Ron. 1983. "A Century of Demographic Change in Western Europe: Underlying Dimensions." *Population and Development Review* 9:411-35.

Lesthaeghe, Ron and Johan Surkyn. 1988a. "Cultural Dynamics and Economic Theories of Fertility Change." *Population and Development Review* 14:1-45.

———. 1988b. "Exchange, Production, and Reproduction: Women in Sub-Saharan Demographic Regimes." Vrije Universiteit Brussel. (mimeo).

Martin, Teresa Castro and Larry Bumpass. 1989. "Recent Trends in Marital Disruption." *Demography* 26:37-51.

Mason, Karen Oppenheim. 1984. *The Status of Women: Its Relationships to Fertility and Mortality.* New York: Rockefeller Foundation.

Mason, Karen Oppenheim and Yu-Hsia Lu. 1988. "Pro-Feminist Changes in Attitudes Toward Women's Familial Roles in the U.S., 1977-1985." *Gender and Society* 2:39-57.

McLanahan, Sara and Julia Adams. 1987. "Parenthood and Psychological Wellbeing." *Annual Review of Sociology* 13:237-57.

Menaghan, Elizabeth and Toby Parcel. 1989. "Mothers' Employment Conditions and Child Outcomes." Ohio State University. (mimeo)

Namboodiri, Krishnan. 1988. "Ecological Demography: Its Place in Sociology." *American Sociological Review* 53:619-33.

Oppenheimer, Valerie. 1973. "Demographic Influences on Female Employment and the Status of Women." Pp. 184-99 in *Changing Women in a Changing Society,* edited by J. Huber. Chicago: University of Chicago Press.

Parcel, Toby and Elizabeth Menaghan. 1989. "Maternal Working Conditions and Child Verbal Ability." Ohio State University. (mimeo)

Parsons, Donald. 1984. "On the Economics of Intergenerational Control." *Population and Development Review* 10:14-54.

Preston, S. 1984. "Children and the Elderly." *Demography* 21:435-57.

———. 1986. "Changing Values and Falling Birthrates." *Population and Development Review* 12(Suppl.):176-95.

Ryder, Norman. 1979. "The Future of American Fertility." *Social Problems* 26:359-70.

Sanderson, Warren. 1987. "Below-Replacement Fertility in Nineteenth Century America." *Population and Development Review* 13:305-13.

Smith, Herbert L. 1989. "Integrating Theory and Research on the Institutional Determinants of Fertility." *Demography* 26:171-84.

Smith, James P. and Michael Ward. 1985. "The Acceleration in Women's Wages." Ohio State University, Department of Economics Symposium.

Spitze, Glenna. 1986. "Family Migration Largely Unresponsive to Wife's Employment Across Age Groups." *Sociology and Social Research* 70:231-34.

———. 1988. "Women's Employment and Family Relations: A Review." *Journal of Marriage and the Family* 50:595-618.

Stirling, Kate. 1989. "Women Who Remain Divorced: The Long-Term Economic Consequences." *Social Science Quarterly* 70:549-78.

Sussman, George. 1982. *Selling Mothers' Milk.* Urbana: University of Illinois Press.

Tabah, Leon. 1980. "World Population Trends." *Population and Development Review* 6:355-89.

Tolnay, Stewart. 1987. "The Decline of Black Marital Fertility in the Rural South: 1910-1940." *American Sociological Review* 52:111-217.

van den Berghe, Pierre. 1967. *Race and Racism.* New York: John Wiley.

Watkins, Susan Cotts, John Bongaarts, and Jane Menken. 1987. "Demographic Foundations of Family Change." *American Sociological Review* 52:346-58.

Wilson, William Julius. 1987. *The Truly Disadvantaged: The Inner City, the Underclass, and Public Policy.* Chicago: University of Chicago Press.

Part I
Metatheoretical Issues

2

The Microfoundations of Social Structure: An Exchange Perspective

Karen S. Cook

In an article titled "Emerging Agendas and Recurrent Strategies in Historical Sociology," Skocpol (1984a, p. 385) writes: "Ours is an era when no existing macrosociological theory seems adequate, yet when the need for valid knowledge of social structures and transformations has never been greater." Few would disagree. Yet the cry for a revival of interest in social structure is not new. In the late 1960s, Smelser (1967, pp. 5-6, cited in Emerson 1972a, p. 58) argued that social structure constitutes the chief conceptual focus of the discipline, and Blau (1975) made social structure the theme of the 1974 American Sociological Association meetings. In this chapter, I discuss one theoretical approach to social structure based on a microsociological perspective. Before outlining this formulation, however, I situate it in the broader context of the micro-macro debate within sociology.

According to Smelser (see Emerson 1972a, p. 58), structural concepts result from progressions of conceptual abstraction beginning at the level of behavioral data. For some macrosociological theorists, however, abstract conceptions of structure exist independently of any conception of underlying behavioral data. These conceptions of structure are not consistent with Smelser's notion of a progression of conceptual abstraction from behavior to structure. The debate is more than definitional. For macrosociologists like Skocpol, structures form the central theoretical concept and are explicitly devoid of behavioral connotation. Microsociological conceptions of action are not necessary (in fact, do not add to the explanatory power of macrosociological perspectives). Let us refer to this position as radical macrosociological determinism, representing one end of a continuum. We will place radical microsociological determinism on the other end of the continuum, treating Homans's (1961) behaviorism, Blumer's symbolic interactionism, or Collins's interaction ritual chains as possible representatives. Between these poles, of course, lie many interesting attempts to explain structure and structural change that incorporate both models of action and structure, including such venerable efforts as Weber's and Parsons's.

Some macrosociologists have recently criticized this overreliance on purely structural explanations—or what I have called radical microsociological determinism. Hechter (1987, p. 6), for example, argues that ignoring individuals leaves structuralists with two serious problems. First, because the explanatory causal factors are contextual, they must always be treated as exogenous in the models. Hence structuralists have not succeeded in explaining the rise and fall of social structures from their own theoretical premises. The second problem is the insufficiency of explanations that ignore the potential consequences of differences in individual behavior. Structuralists profess no need to countenance individual behavior, but for many problems it is hard to see how the issue can be avoided (Hechter 1987, p. 6). Hechter (1987, p. 186), concluding his work on group solidarity, makes a rather bold claim for a macrosociologist: Without some highly elaborated model of individual behavior (of which rational choice is the leading candidate), sociologists cannot properly understand the behavioral consequences of different social structures; such an understanding requires the establishment of a link between structural constraints and individual dispositions.

In contrast to Hechter's critique of macrosociology in the late 1980s, Coser (1975) was responding to differing prevailing winds in the mid-1970s, to what I have called radical microsociological determinism (of the subjective variety). He applauded Blau's efforts at the 1974 ASA meetings to reemphasize that the analysis of objective social structures, rather than exclusive concern with variegated constructions of reality, is the cornerstone of the sociological enterprise. In Coser's (1975, p. 210) words,

> If we are not to give in to a social psychologism that would disregard an outside reality which sets bounds to the strivings and desires of individual actors and retreats into prepotent concerns with individual cognitions, perceptions, and subjective impressions, we have to return to the heritage of Marx, Simmel, and Durkheim, which is teaching us that individual striving is not sufficient to free us from the grip of societal constraints. . . . Lasting concern with the stubborn facticity of structural arrangements will have to continue to be in the very center of our inquiries.

Since that pronouncement in Blau (1975), structural analysis in sociology has been on the rise.

At least two highly visible versions of the revival of structural analysis have emerged in the past decade and a half: the strident structuralism of Skocpol and her contemporaries and the more methodological structuralism evidenced in some brands of formal network analysis (e.g., Berkowitz 1982). In prominent versions of both these schools of sociological inquiry, models of structure exist without an underlying model of action. But Coser (1975, pp. 210-211) warned of the pitfalls of this particular form of structural analysis:

> I would like to show that structural analysis, like love, crucial though it is, is not enough. Exclusive concern with structural factors could lead . . . to a neglect of social process. Structural factors . . . do not operate directly upon social behavior but are mediated through processes of social interaction among which social conflict is a major, though by no means the only one.

Coser provides several informative examples. In discussing the black power movements of the 1960s, Coser (1975) argues that the strategies and actions of actors on both sides of the controversy were determined by the actors' structural positions. Actors used opportunities provided by their positions to maximize their power and to make their values prevail. At the same time, they exploited their adversaries' structurally given vulnerabilities. Structure and process cannot be divorced in the analysis of social change. To account adequately for both structure and structural transformation, a theoretical framework must not only have a well-developed conception of structure but also some conception of the actor's nature (e.g., individual or corporate) and a model of the underlying social process(es) involved (i.e., exchange, conflict, cooperation, mobilization). A key concept in such a theoretical framework is power. Various theoretical orientations in sociology include aspects of such an account (e.g., conflict, Marxist, resource mobilization, exchange).

Given this redeclaration of sociology's fundamental task, I outline one approach to micro-level theorizing that forms the basis for explanations of the emergence of social structures and the mechanisms of structural change. The approach is social exchange theory, to which Homans, Blau, Coleman, and Emerson have made major contributions. I briefly summarize its key aspects and then discuss the link between exchange and structure. Subsequently, I contrast it with Collins's (1981) conception of the micro foundations of macrosociology, which offers a different perspective on the macrosociological underpinnings of social structure. I conclude with comments about the theoretical implications of adopting a macrosociological approach to the study of social structure and structural change.

SOCIAL EXCHANGE THEORY:
FUNDAMENTAL ASSUMPTIONS

The approach called social exchange theory has long historical roots in the social sciences. (For reviews of its development, outside the scope of this chapter, see Emerson 1981; Turner 1986; Collins 1988; Cook, Molm, and Yamagishi 1989). Here I define what is distinctive about this perspective as it relates to the development of a more complete conception of the micro foundations of social structure.

Conceptions of Actors, Action, and Interaction

While exchange behavior is viewed as choice behavior (both in the behavioristic formulation and in the theory's more cognitive versions), the fundamental building block is the *exchange relation*. From this concept and the related notion of *exchange networks* as connected sets of exchange relations (see Emerson 1972a, 1972b; Cook and Emerson 1978; Emerson 1981; Cook 1982, 1987), various types of social structures can be represented in theoretically meaningful but abstract ways. (The formulation of abstract propositions allows for the application of exchange principles across levels of analysis.)

My discussion draws on the Emerson-Cook research program, though other programs also now focus on exchange behavior and the network-level determinants of exchange processes (e.g., Molm and Markovsky, Willer and colleagues). The primary purpose of Emerson's original formulation was to address social structure and structural change within the framework of exchange theory. The goal was to construct a theory of social exchange in which social structure is the dependent variable (Emerson 1972b, p. 58). To achieve this goal, a framework was constructed first to provide a psychological basis for exchange theory (an extension and further refinement of an operant approach to behavior) and then to develop concepts and propositions to explain the emergence of specific types of exchange structures and mechanisms of structural transformation. The concept of an exchange relation and the principles that surround it provide a basis for studying the formation and change of social structures as enduring relations among specified actors, with the exchange relation as the structural unit (Emerson 1972b, p. 60). Actors can be persons, role occupants, or collective actors that confront the other party (or parties) as a single unit (Emerson 1972b, p. 61). The attempt to formulate principles at this level of abstraction facilitates the application of the theory to different levels and units of analysis (as in the work on dyads, families, organizational hierarchies, interorganizational relations, and nation-states).

In my view, the most fruitful developments (other than the fundamental work by Molm and others on the theory's behavioral foundations) center on the marriage of network structural concepts and social exchange theory. Thus I focus on these extensions. Emerson (1972b, p. 70) identified two distinct types of exchange structures: groups and networks. *Groups* were conceived as collective actors and *networks* as sets of exchange relations between either individuals or collective actors. Most of the recent theoretical developments have focused on networks (with the exception of some research on coalition formation).

Power, Dependence, and Network Connections

Within exchange theory, power and dependence are both defined at the relational level. *Power* is a function of one actor's *dependence* on another. It is determined by two factors: the value one actor places on the resources the other actor mediates in the exchange relation and the availability of that resource elsewhere. The latter factor allows for the link between network structure and dependence because networks represent exchange opportunity structures and thus access to alternative sources of valued resources. This insight has driven all of the recent work on power distribution in exchange networks (e.g., Cook and Emerson 1978; Cook, Emerson, Gillmore, and Yamagishi 1983; Yamagishi et al. 1988). This work specifies how various principles of network connection lead to predictions about power distribution in differently configured networks. It is significant because the network propositions are grounded in a theory of exchange that gives content to the relations between the actors. Coleman (1975, p. 80) has argued that one of the limitations of the application of theories of action to social structural analysis has been that the only form of interpersonal interaction considered has been that of exchange. In his 1975 essay, Coleman introduces the explicit consideration of sentiment relations in addition to interest relations to move the theory closer to accommodating a wider range of interactor relations. But, in Emerson's framework, sentiment relations are also viewed as exchange relations where resources may vary and be much less alienable and in which primacy of the relation is much higher than in exchange relationships that mediate a smaller range of valued resources. In addition, factors like balance and cohesion are viewed as variable dimensions of the exchange relation (see Emerson 1972a, 1972b; Cook, Molm, and Yamagishi 1989).

A related extension of the basic power-dependence formulation is Molm's (1987, 1988, 1989a, 1989b) recent work, which explicitly incorporates into the theory punishment power or power based on an actor's control over negative outcomes (in addition to positive outcomes as the basis of reward power). Emerson (1972b, p. 67) made it clear that actors in any exchange relation can be controlled by the relation, even in power-balanced relations: In his conception, power is fully operative in balanced relations—its use preserves the relation and makes the concept of cohesion possible. In a highly cohesive relation, both members are significantly controlled by the relation. As Molm's research indicates, the costs incurred in the use of power vary depending on whether it is power of reward or punishment. The principal limitation on an actor's use of power in Emerson's original framework was the actor's own dependence on the exchange relations in question. This remains true for punishment power except that the costs incurred appear to be much higher (as might be anticipated) and the situational determinants of the exercise of this form of power are different (e.g., often it must be instigated by a specific act on the part of the other party).

Mechanisms of Structural Change

In Emerson's version of social exchange theory, structural change processes were viewed as power-balancing mechanisms. Of course, this list of mechanisms did not exhaust the sources of structural change in exchange relations and the networks formed by connected relations, but it captured some of the key forces of change in these relational structures. Four power-balancing mechanisms were identified: (a) withdrawal from the relation or a devaluation of resources of value under the other actor's control; (b) network extension—location of new sources of valuable resources, an increase in the number of alternatives; (c) status giving, or an increase in the value of the resource valued by the other actor; and (d) network consolidation—coalition formation to reduce the other party's alternatives. The original formulation did not specifically predict the conditions under which one mechanism would be more likely to occur, except to argue that more costly forms of change would be less likely than less costly ones (with withdrawal from the relation portrayed as least likely, other things equal). Also, the third and fourth operations are argued to have a survival advantage in the long-range viability of social structures in that they increase relational cohesion; the other mechanisms decrease it (see Emerson 1972b, p. 68). This reasoning takes us closer to predictions concerning the factors that determine the preconditions of structural change but it needs further development.

Other sources of structural change were also identified in the theoretical framework including division of labor (a form of stratification based on specialization), which is discussed as a type of structural change emanating from unilateral monopoly. Subsequent research has focused primarily on coalition formation as a balancing mechanism in power-imbalanced networks and specification of the exact conditions under which this form of collective action is likely to occur (e.g., Gillmore 1983, 1987; Cook and

Gillmore 1984). Other forms of power-balancing mechanisms have been given less empirical attention, though the more applied literature has extensively considered the conditions of relational dissolution. In fact, an interesting set of findings emerging from research on abusive relationships is the extent to which actors are mutually controlled by the relation (or are codependent even though the relation is highly power-imbalanced). Actors in these situations often do not perceive that alternatives exist or that withdrawal from the relation is an option. What these underlying mechanisms of change have in common is that they represent adaptations to power in differently structured networks or dyadic situations.

Additional structural principles concerning the emergence of particular types of social structures (e.g., social circles and the principle of closure) and structural transformations are considered in some detail in Emerson's formulation. All suggest links to important research traditions in sociology but most have not yet been extensively investigated empirically within the exchange framework. Of interest is the brief discussion of stratified networks in which the emergence and maintenance of stratification within particular network structures functions as a balancing process. The independent variable in this discussion is resource distribution and acquisition, which governs the form of stratification to emerge involving both intraclass and interclass exchange (where class represents actors who occupy similar positions in the structure). Anthropologists have done more than sociologists to document these forms of exchange empirically (i.e., the nature and extent of interclass marriage exchange as well as patterns of food and commodity exchange).

FROM EXCHANGE TO STRUCTURE

Our review of some of the topics covered under the rubric of social exchange theory does not exhaust but suggests the basic approach to structure and structural change commonly found in this perspective. However, variants of exchange theory from Homans and Blau to Emerson differ significantly in the treatment of both the underlying conception of structure and the ways in which micro processes are viewed as connecting to macro-level events and structures. (Most recently, Blau 1987 has argued that the two levels require different concepts and principles; it is premature to assume that the problem of linking micro processes to macro structure can be solved.) Given space limitations, I note only that such differences exist. I will not compare these alternative exchange formulations.

Principles that have been developed to explain different forms of structural transformation and the emergence of particular structural prototypes (e.g., isolated dyads, systems of generalized exchange) describe ideal types and variables governing processes of exchange and power. What remains to be done is the empirical examination of the specific conditions under which these processes emerge and govern structural persistence and change.

What is unique to exchange theory is its broad vision of the nature of structure and the processes that create enduring patterns of interaction. Anthropologists most persistently documented specific forms of exchange and their historical or situational antecedents. Recently, some political scientists (e.g., Pizzorno, Marin 1987) have begun to examine what they refer to as systems of generalized political exchange.

Analyzing the articulation of capitalist and noncapitalist spheres in Papua, New Guinea, anthropologists Carrier and Carrier (1989) indicate specific ways in which historical antecedents bring about social change in a traditional society (in this instance, the historical antecedent is the capitalistic system imported into the cultural environment as a result of colonization). In describing the effects of these factors on exchange and kinship systems in New Guinea, Carrier and Carrier (1989, p. 233) indicate that the linking of Ponam and Manus to colonial capitalism sharply altered the relationships among kinship, exchange, and wealth because the productive resources that kin groups owned, the trade links kinship permitted, and the wealth local labor produced all lost importance. As imported manufactures displaced local goods and wage labor became an important source of wealth, practical kinship and affinal exchange relations shifted.

All of the examples in Carrier and Carrier's (1989, p. 235) field study of changing exchange and intergenerational relations illustrate how articulation affected kinship and exchange relations. Additional analyses demonstrate the broader impact on the society of these alterations in the fundamental relations of kinship and exchange. Structural change and persistence (referred to in this literature as preserving tradition) is the focus of much of the discussion. What is woven into the field study is a fairly elaborate set of descriptions of feedback mechanisms resulting in the modification of some aspects of the traditional culture and structure of the society that, however, persisted as structural constraints upon the possible forms that could emerge out of the old patterns of relations.

In its most basic form, the logic of the argument from exchange to structure in exchange theoretic terms is fairly straightforward. Actors engage in exchange relations to meet their needs. This applies to all classes of exchanges and to a wide variety of resource needs (emotional as well as material and social). Recurrent exchanges result in the formation of exchange relations over time, which, under certain conditions, are institutionalized. Even the specific form of the exchange relation that emerges may be determined either by the exchange opportunity structure (i.e., the network of available options) or by cultural and normative expectations (or some combination of the two). Interaction patterns may become ritualized (as in some of Collins's examples). However, this does not mean that there is no underlying logic to the continuation of these relations (or networks of relations) over time. As Homans so aptly demonstrated, institutionalized behavior patterns persist for a reason, not simply because they are enshrined in norms. Social change is manifest in the variations of these patterns of exchange behavior, which over time may also alter the normative (and sometimes institutionalized) conceptions of specific forms of exchange relations. This adds a dynamic quality to theory, in addition to the power mechanisms that underlie some forms of structural change in exchange systems. In fact, norm formation is explicitly included in Emerson's (1972b) original framework as a result of coalition formation. The norms are instituted by groups of actors as a mechanism of control. Intracategory exchange among the group members provides the basis for sanctioning. The norms are not assumed to preexist, but, once they emerge, they serve the functions documented in many varieties of sociological theory. Here Emerson also provided the rudiments of the inclusion of punishment power in his theory because sanctioning could involve the removal of or a reduction in positive reinforcements. (In different language, Hechter's 1987 theory of group solidarity advances a similar argument on sanctioning.)

In this section, I identify the various forms of exchange because they have different implications for emergent social structures and the potential for structural change. In addition to the fundamental distinction between groups and networks, distinctions have also been made between various forms of exchange. These provide a richer lexicon for the analysis of social structure. Elementary exchange is viewed by Emerson (1976, 1981) as the direct negotiation or transfer of resources of value (including the performance of valued behavior as in Molm's experimental paradigm) between two or more actors. This is the basic trade or contingent action form of exchange. Productive exchange is more complex because it entails the combination of resources or actions of value to produce an outcome of value to the actors involved. (Economists have developed various production functions to describe different ways in which resources are combined for productive purposes.) Productive exchanges (see also Stolte 1987a) differ from elementary exchanges in that frequently the resources gain value in the process of production, that is, there is a value-added process.

Another form of exchange discussed extensively in the literature (see especially Ekeh 1974) is generalized exchange. It is unique in that the exchanges involved do not take the form of either elementary exchange relations (which Ekeh refers to as restricted exchange) or productive exchange but instead involve generalized reciprocity because each actor in the chain provides resources of value (including also behaviors of value) to another actor to whom that actor is connected through an exchange opportunity, but the exchange is not directly negotiated or reciprocated. Instead, it involves some uncertainty in that the actor may only receive some act or resource of value in return from another actor in the network or chain. Thus both the timing and the potential value of the resources of value remain uncertain at the time the actor makes his or her contribution to the other actor. These systems have been analyzed extensively in anthropology and also by Ekeh because they form the basis of many helping and kin obligation networks. The emergence of the credit mentality required to establish such exchange systems and the link between the maintenance of such an exchange system and trust has been the focus of debate but less empirical investigation. (See Gillmore 1983, 1987, for a study of the link between generalized exchange and coalition formation.)

Theorists have only begun to sort out the precise conditions under which different forms of exchange emerge and serve to establish patterns of behavior that become the enduring structures we call social structures (friendship networks, international trade associations, or systems of generalized political exchange). Theory development in the next few years is likely to expand on the principles that distinguish the conditions under which these different forms of exchange are likely to emerge and the mechanisms that result in structural transformations moving from one form of exchange to another (similar to the development of the propositions relating to power-balancing mechanisms and their implications for structural change).

It is this structural diversity that cannot be found in economic versions of exchange theory because the market has for decades been the predominant institutional form under investigation. In neoclassical economics, it is the market that serves as the conceptual apparatus that links individual tastes and endowments to a set of prices and a distribution of goods, thus providing a straightforward way of linking individual-level behavior with macro-level outcomes. (And, as Coleman 1986, p. 36, notes, "modification of that theory to include monopolistic and oligopolistic markets, and to include markets with imperfections, such as transaction costs, expands the scope of this theoretical orientation.") But the individual-level model of action can be separated analytically from the structural focus of the theory. In fact, this is the strategy that Coleman (1986) suggests for sociology. A much broader conception of structural forms is required. Exchange theory and its recent marriage with network concepts offers a beginning to the development of a theory that includes structures like markets as one of a class of interesting structural forms (e.g., job markets and other topics of interest to sociologists in addition to networks like those examined by Harrison White 1970 in *Chains of Opportunity* and Granovetter 1973 in "The Strength of Weak

Ties," among more traditional exchange systems like those investigated by anthropologists involving food or commodity exchanges, Kula rings, and kinship structures). Furthermore, the addition of transaction cost notions to this literature has sensitized exchange theorists to the impact of such costs (e.g., of monitoring, sanctioning, and contracting on various types of exchange and the structures that emerge to limit costs such as hierarchical forms—see Williamson 1975; Miller forthcoming).

In addition to the variety of structural forms encompassed within the exchange perspective, another distinguishing feature is the prominence of power processes and the structural determinants of power relations. This concept is missing in most versions of microeconomic theory (see various debates on this omission including the exchange between Williamson and Perrow 1981). The significance of this concept was recognized by Blau, who made it central in his theoretical treatise on exchange, and by Emerson, who viewed exchange theory as an extension of his original power-dependence formulation. Inclusion of this concept allows exchange theorists to explain the persistence of various social structures that emerge to facilitate exchange in ways that economists cannot because efficiency is not the bottom line in social exchange theory whereas it is inconceivable that it would not be in economic theory. Thus structures emerge and are maintained for power-related reasons and not simply because they are the most efficient means for achieving individual or collective ends. They may also become institutionalized for power-related reasons and not simply because they are enshrined in norms, as Homans would argue.

If one uses Coleman's (1968, p. 360) criteria for an adequate social theory, it may be argued that exchange theory forms the rudiments of such a theory. The requirements are that the theory cannot remain at the macro level, and, when it descends to the individual level, it cannot return to the macro level through simple aggregation. The problem of developing such theoretical frameworks is a complicated one (see Coleman's 1986 discussion) but one Coleman has labeled the central theoretical problem in sociology. Exchange theory provides one approach to this problem although it is not without its weaknesses. In the next section, I contrast the exchange approach with a different attempt to produce a microsociological basis for social structure.

AN ALTERNATIVE PERSPECTIVE:
THE MICRO TRANSLATION OF MACRO EVENTS

To clarify some of the distinctive features of the exchange perspective, I briefly contrast it with the perspective advocated by Collins (1981), referred to as interaction ritual chains. For Collins (1981, p. 985), radical microsociology is important primarily because it gives a strong "impetus toward translating all macrophenomena into combinations of micro-events. A micro-translation strategy reveals the empirical realities of social structures as patterns of repetitive micro-interaction." Collins (1981, p. 985) argues against the utility of concepts like norms, rules, roles, and exchange in favor of a micro mechanism that "can explain the repetitive actions that make up social structure such that interactions and their accompanying cognitions rest upon noncognitive bases." This micro mechanism is labeled "interaction ritual chains." By micro-translating all social structure into such chains, microsociology offers macrosociology a new tool for "explaining both the inertia and the dynamics of macro structure."

There are two weaknesses in this perspective. First, as a radical microsociology perspective, it is explicitly reductionistic. According to Collins (1981, p. 987), "All macro-evidence is aggregated from micro-experiences" and "everyone's life, experientially, is a sequence of microsituations, and the sum of all sequences of individual experience in the world would constitute all possible sociological data." One can accept the notion that institutions and organizations are abstractions from the behavior of individuals without assuming that the only appropriate explanatory principles operate at the level of individual actors. Collins does accept the notion that a causal explanation need not be totally micro situational but refers to only a minute "residue" of several "types of macroreferences." What appears to be oversimplified in this form of microsociology is the mechanism or set of mechanisms that link individual-level behavior with macro-level outcomes. In this regard, the framework fails Coleman's (1986) second criterion for a viable social theory. This is the criterion that, when the theory returns to the macro level, it must not do so through simple aggregation.

Second, while Collins retains a market model, he replaces the driving mechanism with a form of emotional energy rather than any cognitive mechanism. In this sense, he has retained what exchange theory has viewed as problematic from the point of view of modeling social structures; that is, that many interesting forms of social structure simply do not fit a market model. This is precisely the reason for the inclusion into the theoretical framework of network concepts and principles. The rationale for dismissing the cognitive basis for a microsociology rests on the limitations of human cognition and rationality. Such limitations can be accepted without throwing out the notion that cognitive mechanisms operate at the micro level and are significant in the explanation of individual behavior and social interaction. Thus Collins overstates the case against cognitive bases in favor of emotional mechanisms. "The explanation," he concludes, "is . . . in the realm of feeling" (Collins 1981, p. 997). The framework seems to work well at explaining the persistence of ritualistic forms of behavior and existing institutions, but it is less compelling in its analysis of social structural change and the origins of social structure. In particular, power, a key concept in the exchange perspective, is curiously missing from the theory. Authority is described as a "type of routine in which particular individuals dominate micro-interactions with other individuals" (Collins 1981; p. 1012), but the power basis of this form of domination is not clear.

I have discussed Collins's version of microsociology in a very sketchy fashion simply to present it as an alternative to the exchange perspective. For this purpose, I have overdrawn the differences and ignored some of the similarities. What these two efforts share, however, is a commitment to the development of a microsociological framework that will provide the micro foundations of a theory of social structure.

CONCLUSIONS

I have argued against an approach to social structure that reifies macro structures and defines them as ontologically prior to individual behavior and social interaction. It is axiomatic within exchange theory that exchange and power processes result in certain patterns of social interaction that are the stuff of social structure. These structures can take a wide variety of forms, from dyads and small groups to large corporate bodies (e.g., international corporations) and extensive networks of actors, linked directly and indirectly through ties of various sorts. A fundamental distinction is made between corporate groups and networks. (*Networks* can include both individual and collective actors. *Corporate groups* can be composed of other collective actors or individuals.) A separate issue is how these patterns of interaction are reproduced and replicated over time and space. Collins's approach takes as its central problem the reproduction of structure. The exchange perspective views this problem in terms of the emergence and maintenance of institutionalized patterns of interaction. A major explanatory problem for exchange theories is the explication of the process by which certain exchange structures become institutionalized over time. (Much anthropological evidence suggests various conditions under which specific structures are reproduced and become institutionalized in the culture under examination.)

While social exchange theory provides a useful umbrella for the analysis of social structure and structural change, it is like a broken umbrella, missing some of its spokes. Current theoretical research programs represent attempts to fill in the missing spokes. Macrosociology stands to gain much from the eventual development of better and more complete microsociological perspectives, especially those that provide some purchase on explaining the emergence and persistence of social structures and the mechanisms of structural change. The overreliance on structural explanations devoid of behavioral bases and normative explanations, which overstate the case for socialization models of behavior in sociology, remains problematic for the advancement of the field. As Collins (1981, p. 1006) puts it, with respect to the oversocialized conception of actors, "the customariness of the behavior is just what remains to be explained, and to call this customariness a norm is merely to describe it." What remains unexplained is the emergence of the basic patterns of behavior (or the norms) in the first place. Where we differ is in the nature of the fundamental explanations offered. Though the terms *microsociology* and *macrosociology* may eventually drop out of the sociological lexicon (as some have advanced in recent economics textbooks for the similar distinction in that field), the underlying problem of integrating our theories when they have been developed to apply at different levels of analysis (e.g., to individuals, groups, organizations, markets, nation-states, the world system) will remain. To cope with this complex task, sociologists will have to be ever more explicit about their underlying assumptions and fundamental principles. In contrast to those who issue pessimistic assessments of the state of sociology, however, I view the current dialogue between microsociologists and macrosociologists as a very positive sign. As Muench and Smelser (1987, p. 185) concluded,

> Both microscopic processes that constitute the web of interactions in society and the macroscopic frameworks that result from and condition those processes are essential levels for understanding and explaining social life. . . . It seems to us that to strive for the better theoretical and empirical understanding of these processes constitutes a proper agenda for the coming years.

I agree.

REFERENCES

Anderson, Bo and David Willer. 1981. "Introduction." Pp. 1-21 in *Networks, Exchange and Coercion: The Elementary Theory and Its Applications,* edited by D. Willer and B. Anderson. New York: Elsevier.

Bacharach, Samuel B. and Edward J. Lawler. 1981. *Bargaining: Power, Tactics, and Outcomes.* San Francisco: Jossey-Bass.

Berkowitz, S. D. 1982. *An Introduction to Structural Analysis: The Network Approach to Social Research.* Toronto: Butterworths.

Blau, P. 1964. *Exchange and Power in Social Life.* New York: John Wiley.

———, ed. 1975. *Approaches to the Study of Social Structure.* New York: Free Press.

———. 1987. "Microprocess and Macrostructure." Pp. 83-100 in *Social Exchange Theory,* edited by K. S. Cook. Newbury Park, CA: Sage.

Karen S. Cook   43

Bonacich, Phillip. 1987. "Power and Centrality: A Family of Measures." *American Journal of Sociology* 92:1170-82.

Carrier, J. G. and A. H. Carrier. 1989. *Wage, Trade, and Exchange in Melanesia*. Berkeley: University of California Press.

Coleman, James S. 1975. "Social Structure and a Theory of Action." Pp. 76-93 in *Approaches to the Study of Social Structure*, edited by P. Blau. New York: Free Press.

―――. 1986. "Micro Foundations and Macrosocial Theory." Pp. 345-63 in *Approaches to Social Theory*, edited by S. Lindenberg, J. S. Coleman, and S. Nowak. New York: Russell Sage.

Collins, Randall. 1981. "The Microfoundations of Macrosociology." *American Journal of Sociology* 86:984-1014.

―――. 1988. *Theoretical Sociology*. San Diego: Harcourt Brace Jovanovich.

Cook, K. S. 1977. "Exchange and Power in Networks of Interorganizational Relations." *Sociological Quarterly* 18:62-82.

―――. 1982. "Network Structures from an Exchange Perspective." Pp. 177-99 in *Social Structure and Network Analysis*, edited by P. V. Marsden and N. Lin. Beverly Hills, CA: Sage.

―――, ed. 1987. *Social Exchange Theory*. Newbury Park, CA: Sage.

Cook, K. S. and R. M. Emerson. 1978. "Power, Equity, and Commitment in Exchange Networks." *American Sociological Review* 43:721-39.

Cook, K. S., R. M. Emerson, M. R. Gillmore, and T. Yamagishi. 1983. "The Distribution of Power in Exchange Networks: Theory and Experimental Results." *American Journal of Sociology* 89:275-305.

Cook, K. S. and M. R. Gillmore. 1984. "Power, Dependence, and Coalitions." Pp. 27-58 in *Advances in Group Processes*. Vol. 1, edited by E. Lawler. Greenwich, CT: JAI.

Cook, K. S., M. R. Gillmore, and T. Yamagishi. 1986. "Point and Line Vulnerability as Bases for Predicting the Distribution of Power in Exchange Networks: Reply to Willer." *American Journal of Sociology* 92:445-48.

Cook, K. S. and K. A. Hegtvedt. 1986. "Justice and Power: An Exchange Analysis." Pp. 19-41 in *Justice in Social Relations*, edited by H. W. Bierhoff, R. Cohen, and J. Greenberg. New York: Plenum.

Cook, K. S., K. A. Hegtvedt, and T. Yamagishi. 1988. "Structural Inequality, Legitimation, and Reactions to Inequity in Exchange Networks." Pp. 291-308 in *Status Generalization: New Theory and Research*, edited by Murray Webster, Jr., and Martha Foschi. Stanford, CA: Stanford University Press.

Cook, K. S., L. D. Molm, and T. Yamagishi. 1989. "Exchange Relations and Exchange Networks: Recent Developments in Social Exchange Theory." Paper presented at the Stanford Theory Conference, Stanford, CA.

Cook, K. S., J. O'Brien, and P. Kollock. Forthcoming. "Exchange Theory: A Blueprint for Structure and Process." In *Sociological Theory*, edited by G. Ritzer. New York: Columbia University Press.

Coser, Lewis. 1975. "Structure and Conflict." Pp. 210-219 in *Approaches to the Study of Social Structure*, edited by P. Blau. New York: Free Press.

Ekeh, Peter P. 1974. *Social Exchange Theory: The Two Traditions*. Cambridge, MA: Harvard University Press.

Emerson, R. M. 1969. "Operant Psychology and Exchange Theory." Pp. 379-405 in *Behavioral Sociology: The Experimental Analysis of Social Process*, edited by R. L. Burgess and D. Bushell, Jr. New York: Columbia University Press.

―――. 1972a. "Exchange Theory, Part I: A Psychological Basis for Social Exchange." Pp. 38-57 in *Sociological Theories in Progress*. Vol. 2, edited by J. Berger, M. Zelditch, and B. Anderson. Boston: Houghton Mifflin.

————. 1972b. "Exchange Theory, Part II: Exchange Relations and Networks." Pp. 58-87 in *Sociological Theories in Progress*. Vol. 2, edited by J. Berger, M. Zelditch, and B. Anderson. Boston: Houghton Mifflin.

————. 1976. "Social Exchange Theory." *Annual Review of Sociology* 2:335-62.

————. 1981. "Social Exchange Theory." Pp. 30-65 in *Social Psychology: Sociological Perspectives*, edited by M. Rosenberg and R. Turner. New York: Academic Press.

————. 1987. "Toward a Theory of Value in Social Exchange." Pp. 11-58 in *Social Exchange Theory*, edited by K. S. Cook. Newbury Park, CA: Sage.

Emerson, R. M., K. S. Cook, M. R. Gillmore, and T. Yamagishi. 1983. "Valid Predictions from Invalid Comparisons: Response to Heckathorn." *Social Forces* 61:1232-47.

Gillmore, M. R. 1983. "Sources of Solidarity and Coalition Formation in Exchange Networks." Ph.D. dissertation, University of Washington.

————. 1987. "Implications of General Versus Restricted Exchange." Pp. 170-189 in *Social Exchange Theory*, edited by K. S. Cook. Newbury Park, CA: Sage.

Granovetter, Mark. 1973. "The Strength of Weak Ties." *American Journal of Sociology* 78:1360-1380.

Grossman, Lawrence. 1983. "Cattle, Rural Economic Differentiation and Articulation in the Highlands of Papua New Guinea." *American Ethnologist* 10:59-76.

Heath, Anthony. 1976. *Rational Choice and Social Exchange: A Critique of Exchange Theory*. Cambridge: Cambridge University Press.

Hechter, Michael, ed. 1983. *The Microfoundations of Macrosociology*. Philadelphia: Temple University Press.

————. 1987. *Principles of Group Solidarity*. Berkeley: University of California Press.

Heckathorn, D. D. 1983. "Extensions of Power-Dependence Theory: The Concept of Resistance." *Social Forces* 61:1206-31.

Homans, George C. 1961. *Social Behavior: Its Elementary Forms*. New York: Harcourt, Brace and World.

Kuhn, Alfred. 1964. *The Study of Society: A Unified Approach*. Homewood, IL: Irwin-Dorsey.

Marin, B., ed. Forthcoming. *Generalized Political Exchange*. Berlin/New York: DeGruyter.

Markovsky, Barry. 1987. "Toward Multilevel Sociological Theories: Simulations of Actors and Network Effects." *Sociological Theory* 5:101-17.

Markovsky, Barry, David Willer, and Travis Patton. 1988. "Power Relations in Exchange Networks." *American Sociological Review* 53:220-36.

Miller, Gary J. Forthcoming. "Managerial Dilemmas: Political Leadership in Hierarchies." In *The Limits of Rational Choice*, edited by K. S. Cook and M. Levi. Chicago: University of Chicago Press.

Molm, Linda D. 1981a. "The Conversion of Power Imbalance to Power Use." *Social Psychology Quarterly* 16:153-66.

————. 1981b. "A Contingency Change Analysis of the Disruption and Recovery of Social Exchange and Cooperation." *Social Forces* 59:729-51.

————. 1987. "Power-Dependence Theory: Power Processes and Negative Outcomes." Pp. 171-98 in *Advances in Group Processes*. Vol. 4, edited by E. J. Lawler and B. Markovsky. Greenwich, CT: JAI.

————. 1988. "The Structure and Use of Power: A Comparison of Reward and Punishment Power." *Social Psychology Quarterly* 51:108-22.

————. 1989a. "Punishment Power: A Balancing Process in Power-Dependence Relations." *American Journal of Sociology* 94:1392-1418.

————. 1989b. "An Experimental Analysis of Imbalance in Punishment Power." *Social Forces* 68:178-203.

————. 1989c. "Structure, Action, and Outcomes: A Multilevel Analysis of Power." Paper presented at the annual meetings of the American Sociological Association, San Francisco.

Muench, Richard and Neil J. Smelser. 1987. "Relating the Micro and Macro." Pp. 356-87 in *The Micro-Macro Link*, edited by J. C. Alexander, B. Giesen, R. Muench, and N. J. Smelser. Berkeley: University of California Press.

Olson, Mancur. 1986. "A Theory of Social Movements, Social Classes, and Castes." Pp. 317-37 in *Approaches to Social Theory*, edited by S. Lindenberg, J. S. Coleman, and S. Nowak. New York: Russell Sage.

Perrow, Charles. 1981. "Markets, Hierarchies and Hegemony: A Critique of Chandler and Wiliamson." Pp. 371-86 and 403-4 in *Perspectives on Organization Design and Behavior*, edited by A. Van de Ven and W. Joyce. New York: Wiley Interscience.

Skocpol, Theda. 1984a. "Emerging Agendas and Recurrent Strategies in Historical Sociology." Pp. 356-91 in *Vision and Method in Historical Sociology*, edited by T. Skocpol. Cambridge: Cambridge University Press.

————, ed. 1984b. *Vision and Method in Historical Sociology.* Cambridge: Cambridge University Press.

Smelser, Neil J., ed. 1967. *Sociology: An Introduction.* New York: John Wiley.

Stolte, J. F. 1987a. "The Formation of Justice Norms." *American Sociological Review* 52:774-84.

————. 1987b. "Legitimacy, Justice, and Productive Exchange." Pp. 190-208 in *Social Exchange Theory*, edited by K. S. Cook. Newbury Park, CA: Sage.

Stolte, J. F. and R. M. Emerson. 1977. "Structural Inequality: Position and Power in Network Structures." Pp. 117-38 in *Behavioral Theory in Sociology*, edited by R. Hamblin and J. Kunkel. New Brunswick, NJ: Transaction.

Thibaut, J. and H. H. Kelley. 1959. *The Social Psychology of Groups.* New York: John Wiley.

Turner, J. H. 1986. *The Structure of Sociological Theory.* Chicago: Dorsey.

White, Harrison C. 1970. *Chains of Opportunity: System Models of Mobility in Organizations.* Cambridge, MA: Harvard University Press.

White, H. C., S. A. Boorman, and R. L. Breiger. 1976. "Social Structure from Multiple Networks. I. Blockmodels of Roles and Positions." *American Journal of Sociology* 81:730-780.

White, H. C. and R. L. Breiger. 1975. "Patterns Across Networks." *Transaction* 12:68-73.

Willer, David and Bo Anderson, eds. 1981. *Networks, Exchange and Coercion: The Elementary Theory and Its Applications.* New York: Elsevier.

Willer, David and Travis Patton. 1987. "The Development of Network Exchange Theory." In *Advances in Group Processes.* Vol. 4, edited by E. J. Lawler and B. Markovsky. Greenwich, CT: JAI.

Williamson, Oliver. 1975. *Markets and Hierarchy: Analysis and Antitrust Implications.* New York: Free Press.

Yamagishi, T. 1987. "An Exchange Theoretical Approach to Network Positions." Pp. 149-69 in *Social Exchange Theory*, edited by K. S. Cook. Newbury Park, CA: Sage.

Yamagishi, T., M. R. Gillmore, and K. S. Cook. 1988. "Network Connections and the Distribution of Power in Exchange Networks." *American Journal of Sociology* 93:833-51.

3

From Exchange to Structure

Michael Hechter

These days—perhaps more than ever—sociologists disagree about many things, but one thing about which nearly all can agree is that social structures constitute the discipline's keystone. The explanation of the genesis of these emergent-level phenomena has always been a central sociological concern.

There are, of course, two quite different ways to approach the problem. At one extreme, methodological *holists* argue that all existing social structures develop—through bargaining, diffusion, imitation, and a variety of other mechanisms—from prior structures. Whereas individuals act, they do not do so as independent agents.

At the other extreme, methodological *individualists* argue that the dynamic force for the genesis of social structures lies in the action of agents pursuing independent interests. In this tradition, structures can emerge either as unintended or as purposive solutions to the common demands that these individuals face.

The title of the session for which this response was written signals that the balance of our concern is weighted to the individualistic pole. Everyone who was on the panel has tried to develop explanations of the genesis of social structures from individualistic premises. Peter Blau, who was the first among us to make this attempt, subsequently abandoned the quest and claims that it may be a futile one. But the rest of us persist and are joined by a growing number of political scientists and economists. In fact, just during the course of this year, three new journals have been established that promise to carry this enterprise forward: *Rationality and Society* (in sociology), *Constitutional Political Economy* (in economics), and *The Journal of Theoretical Politics* (in political science).

Building an individualistic theory of social structure is no mean task because everywhere we look we find structure, whether in the guise of conventions, norms, informal organizations or formal ones. As structure appears to pervade social life, the holists' point—that all structures ultimately have structural roots—seems inescapable. To avoid the inescapability of structure, individualists are compelled to begin their explanations by positing a counterfactual social environment: the state of nature, that imagined territory populated by individuals free from any social obligations save perhaps those emanating from the nuclear family.

Because, in the individualist view, structure is seen to arise as a solution to commonly held desires, the state of nature must be considered to be a very unpleasant social environment, one that can only be improved by the invention of social structures of nearly any kind. From Hobbes onward, it has been recognized that voluntary exchange lies at the heart of any individualistic explanation of structural genesis. Yet, because most exchanges themselves appear to rest on institutional foundations (How else can Hobbes's agents be assured of one another's intentions to surrender sovereignty to a coercive state? How else can the rules underlying Adam Smith's free market be enforced?). A very large puzzle remains.

The real trick in building an individualistic theory of social structure is to explain how agents who are themselves unconstrained by any structure nevertheless will produce institutions that can sanction potential free riders. This has recently come to be known as the *second-order free-rider problem* (see Hechter et al. 1990). As notions of general equilibrium lie at the fount of individualistic theoretical wisdom, the earliest attempts to solve this problem used the theory of repeated games to identify the conditions favorable to the evolution of cooperative equilibria. Increasingly, however, these simple game-theoretic solutions are regarded as inadequate, for they rest on informational assumptions that are too stringent to have many real-world applications (Hechter 1990).

Where general equilibrium models run into trouble, sociologists have much to contribute. What does Cook's chapter offer in the way of possible solutions to the second-order free-rider problem? The chapter presents a strong case for exchange theory, especially that version of it stemming from a research program begun jointly with the late Richard Emerson. As she points out, most of the interesting empirical results to date show that exchange theory can predict how various principles of network connection between agents determine the distribution of power in different types of social structures. Yet can the same theory that is useful in the analysis of the *effects* of given social structures be turned then to account for the *genesis* of these structures? One lead mentioned in her chapter that may be promising concerns the four so-called power-balancing mechanisms. How this idea might be developed is, as Cook admits, still unclear.

To begin to address the origins of structures, one might ask: *Why do people engage in exchanges anyway?* The problem of values is essential for any exchange theory as it must be for any network theory. Yet what determines individual values? Unless this question is addressed, it is impossible to understand why people engage in exchange. Adam Smith's famous answer—that it is due to a natural propensity to truck and barter—evades the question altogether. The modern economist's answer relies on the concept of utility. People will engage in exchange, this argument goes, when they expect that doing so will yield a net increase in utility.

But when we ask what this utility consists of, economic theory gets tricky. The most common current response is that utility is a totally subjective state that is unknowable by observers *ex ante*. In this interpretation, the agent's behavior *ex post* offers the only basis for inferring his or her utility (which is known as the theory of revealed preference). This strategy—one that shares much with the behavioristic treatment of values—makes it easy to interpret behavior retrospectively but renders its prediction difficult. (To predict behavior under this conception, one would need to know the individuals's past ranking of goods and events and then to assume that this ranking remains constant in the future.)

Alternatively, it is possible to assume that utility is produced by combining time and personal endowments to produce fungible resources—like money, prestige, and power—that offer their recipients the means to any number of individually valued ends. This is an attractive conception, for no matter what an individual's subjective ranking of goods and events may be, everyone's utility is improved by increases in their stock of fungible resources. This fact has important consequences for the prediction of social outcomes. To the degree that people have interests that are unknown but statistically idiosyncratic, we can never predict aggregate behavior. However, to the degree that everyone's interests are both known and commonly held (for example, if everyone prefers more wealth to less), then there will be a high predictive capacity at the aggregate level.

Because all activities consume time, some people's time is worth more (in terms of its potential use for the production of fungible resources) than other people's time. If people can work as many hours as they desire, and if they are paid by time or piece wages, then wages determine the opportunity cost for all nonwork activity. Studies of time budgeting, therefore, can provide a key means of revealing individual interests *ex post*. If we assume that past interests are likely to hold in the future, this allows us to make a host of counterintuitive predictions—for instance, that people with high wages will sleep less than those with lower wages.[1] McCann (1972) once showed that southern Democratic congressional committee chairmen in the late 1960s had an amazingly long life expectancy. Once again, the explanation for this unusual finding might have something to do with the peculiar opportunity costs of these powerful politicians.

While the equation of values with fungible resources has proven useful in empirical research, it cannot provide the whole story. Reliance on this equation alone makes it difficult to say anything interesting about individual *trade-offs* between different kinds of fungible resources. Why are some people relatively more interested in prestige than money, and vice versa? What determines the substitutability of these different kinds of resources? Diminishing returns are an obvious starting point for any serious investigation of the matter, but only a starting point.

Moreover, if people were motivated solely by the prospect of capturing fungible resources, then how could we explain the behavior of risk-seeking entrepreneurs, charismatic heroes, and others who spurn the pursuit of these resources for other courses of action that apparently satisfy internal values or other subjective states?

There is, however, a far more fundamental objection to this external theory of values, and it is one that is directly relevant to our theme of structural genesis. Fungible resources—such as money, power, and prestige—are collective goods that are produced by people who are *already* embedded in social structures. This is so clear in the case of money that it bears no further mention. Like money, power and prestige are goods that are *collectively produced and maintained.* But once it is recognized that fungible resources are themselves a product of social structure, how can individualists legitimately employ them to explain how agents can overcome the second-order free-rider problem?

As Cook recognizes, explanations for structural genesis ultimately must rest on some substantive conception of values internal to individuals.[2] Without such a conception, individual motivation is condemned to be little more than a black box. Yet this is *not* a direction that is popular in the current individualistic research program, to say the least (see the interesting discussion of these issues at the conclusion of Lea et al. 1987).

Long ago, Emerson (1962), one of the fathers of exchange theory, pointed out that power emanated from dependence but that dependence, for its part, had two quite different roots. One root lies in the availability of other sources of goods. As Cook explains, this external condition has provided most of the leverage for empirical research in exchange theory. But the other root of power—its internal source—lies in the subjective value that agents place on given goods and events: this is what ultimately determines their interest in these goods and events. Until this fundamental insight is given its due, the individualistic tradition in social theory is unlikely to live up to its promise.

NOTES

1. See the National Bureau of Economic Research study by Jeff Biddle and Daniel Hamermesh mentioned in *The New York Times* (August 2, 1989, p. 1).

2. "In its most basic form the logic of the argument which gets us from exchange to structure in exchange theoretic terms is fairly straightforward. Actors engage in exchange relations in order to meet their needs. This applies to all classes of exchanges and to a very wide variety of resource needs (emotional as well as material and social)" (Cook, Chapter 2, this volume).

REFERENCES

Emerson, Richard. 1962. "Power-Dependence Relations." *American Sociological Review* 27:31-41.

Hechter, Michael. 1990. "On the Inadequacy of Repeated Game Theory for an Understanding of Real-World Collective Action." Pp. 240-249 in *The Limits of Rationality*, edited by K. S. Cook and M. Levi. Chicago: University of Chicago Press.

Hechter, Michael, Karl Dieter Opp, and Reinhard Wippler, eds. 1990. *Social Institutions: Their Emergence, Maintenance, and Effects*. New York: Aldine de Gruyter.

Lea, Stephen, Roger Tarpy, and Paul Webley. 1987. *The Individual in the Economy: A Survey of Economic Psychology*. Cambridge: Cambridge University Press.

McCann, James. 1972. "Differential Mortality and the Formation of Political Elites: The Case of the U.S. House of Representatives." *American Sociological Review* 37:689-700.

4

The Problem of Identity in Collective Action

Craig Calhoun

Bravery to the point of apparent foolishness is essential to many social movements, especially the most radical. It cannot be explained simply in terms of expected outcomes. The attempt to do so, in fact, forces arguments about radical social movements into false choices among explanations. Because the odds of a desirable outcome from some actions are so long, and the risks so great, those who engage in the actions are held to be (a) psychologically debilitated (i.e., crazy), (b) acting rationally but on radically inadequate information (e.g., completely unaware of historical precedents for what happens to peasants who lead revolts), or (c) forced to their seemingly brave behavior by the dictates of a structural logic that leaves them no room for individual will. None of these conclusions follows. The risk may be borne not because of the likelihood of success in manifest goals but because participation in a course of action has over time committed one to an identity that would be irretrievably violated by pulling back from the risk.[1]

The extent to which participants in collective action seek to build, legitimate, or express an identity, rather than pursue some more instrumental strategy, is important to recent accounts of "new social movements" (Cohen 1985; Melucci 1989). Struggles over feminism, gay rights, and ecology, in this argument, are not simply attempts to gain material changes but also and crucially struggles over signification; they are attempts simultaneously to make a nonstandard identity acceptable and to make that identity livable in

AUTHOR'S NOTE: *I am grateful to Peter Bearman and Phil O'Connel for comments on an earlier version of this chapter.*

the context of the movement itself. This is one reason why such movements are so intensely self-reflexive, so concerned with their organizational and associational forms, and so heavily focused on individual members' expressive actions (Melucci 1989, p. 60). These movements involve a turn away from the model of the labor movement that dominated classical conceptions of social movements. First, they do not involve a claim to offer a single, overarching transformation or liberation of society. Second, they are not focused primarily on processes of production or distribution of the wealth produced. Third, they do not regard access to state power as their major means or object of struggle. Rather, these movements "have shifted towards a nonpolitical terrain: the need for self-realization in everyday life" (Melucci 1989, p. 23, also p. 172).

This argument seems to me to overstate the difference between "new" and "old" social movements. In the nineteenth century too, people struggled over religion as well as labor, founded communes and cooperatives as well as unions and political parties, and defended local communities as well as class interests (Thompson [1963] 1968; Calhoun 1982). The dominant rhetoric of collective action during the last 200 years has obscured this, stressing instrumental interests, thus reflecting a general vocabulary and understanding of human identity current in the modern period (Taylor 1989). That same vocabulary and understanding, however, also lead us to overstate the extent to which the full range of collective action even in the heyday of the labor movement could be explained by reference to objective interests or even subjectively constructed interests focused narrowly on production and wealth. The constitution of identity, then, is a crucial concern for the study of social movements in all historical and cultural settings. Moreover, the issue of identity is not adequately dealt with in terms of *legitimation*, *expression*, or other terms that imply that it exists prior to and is the basis of a struggle. Identity is, in many cases, forged in and out of struggle, including participation in social movements.

Identity, in this sense, cannot be captured adequately by the notion of interest. Identity is a no more than *relatively* stable construction in an ongoing process of social activity. At a collective level, this is a large part of what E. P. Thompson ([1963] 1968) meant by describing class as a "happening" rather than a matter of structure and/or objective interests. Even at a personal level, however, identity is not altogether internal to an individual but is part of a social process. In the term Bourdieu (and Elias) have revived for sociological analysis, identity is a matter of *habitus*, of a process of regulated improvisation that is always intersubjective (Bourdieu 1976, 1980). The habitus gives one a sense of how to play the game—that practical social sensibility (which includes a concrete identity) that is a crucially missing ingredient in most game-theoretic accounts of social action.

An understanding of identity that goes beyond the notion of interest is especially important when we want to examine collective actions that involve high elements of risk and, for most participants, steps outside the routines of daily life: rebellions and radical protests, for example, not price fixing among gas stations. Though Melucci and Cohen argue against interest-based accounts, many of the new social movement examples they give do not seem intrinsically closed to a rational choice explanation but involve unconventional sorts of interests and especially processes of continual redefinition of interests because of reconstitution of identity. I want to put the stress on this latter sort of process, within a movement that would be hard to class as a "new" social movement and that certainly did involve interests and strategies, as at least part of its constitution.

My case is the Chinese student protest movement of 1989. I cannot offer a sustained narrative or analysis here (see Calhoun 1989a, 1989b, 1989c, 1989d, forthcoming-a). My fragmentary empirical reference is illustrative, certainly not definitive. But consider the problem: On the night of June 3 and the morning of June 4, students in Tiananmen Square knowingly risked death. They did so without belief that there was any near-term likelihood that their actions would improve their own or their fellows' circumstances or effect the political changes they sought in China. They did so despite the availability of apparent alternatives. Yet these were not habitual risk takers. Some of those who died that night had been too cautious to identify themselves publicly with the boycott of classes only a month before. Many of those who risked death that night have gone to great lengths to avoid attack or arrest in succeeding months. But, at the crucial moment, they were willing to be brave to the point of apparent foolishness. Why?

The question is not idle. Were it not for this extraordinary bravery, the Chinese protest movement would not be remembered as it is. Were it not for similar cases elsewhere, revolutions would not have been made, battles won, rescues attempted. An earlier sort of collective behavior analysis tended to assume that something had to be wrong with people for them to take such risks, that such steps outside social routine were evidence of some socio-psychological debility. This view has been countered by two others. One contends that rebels and protesters are quite rational and that good accounts of their activities can be given in terms of their interests and available options for action.[2] The other says that sociologists ought simply to stay away from psychological accounts and try to explain risky and unusual mobilizations in terms of the structural conditions that make them possible. Here we confront what is commonly, if not very clearly or helpfully, called the micro-macro divide.

This way of framing the problem implies that levels of analysis, rather than more substantive theoretical differences, are at issue. This makes it easy for sociologists to think they have solved the problem simply by combining micro and macro levels in analysis. Moreover, the equation of structure with macrosociology is challenged by the proliferation of "microstructural" analysis (e.g., in terms of personal networks), and Coleman (1990) has tried to show how a rational choice approach can deal with macrosociological problems. The more fundamental question to ask is not about levels of analysis but about basic organizing concepts. Can a language of interests adequately grapple with the identity and motivation of actors? Is a psychology implying irrationality the only alternative? Conversely, can structure be grasped adequately through "objective" measures rather than constructed, historically meaningful categories?

Both rational action and structural accounts also have been challenged by others that emphasize culture. Sewell, for example, has criticized both Coleman's rational choice-oriented account of how to link micro- and macrosociology (Sewell 1986) and Skocpol's structural theory of revolutions (Sewell 1985).[3] Sensibly, he has not suggested that we can dispense with all the arguments Coleman and Skocpol developed but that these are fundamentally insufficient without serious attention to cultural factors. Sewell's approach to culture is substantially structuralist and accordingly does not emphasize action, especially at the individual level. My claims about identity complement this sort of cultural argument, and in the last part of this chapter, I will develop briefly the suggestion that certain distinctive features of modern Western culture—notably an instrumental notion of self and neglect of the idea of honor—hinder our ability to grasp the centrality of the problem of identity in collective action. Recognition is especially problematic for structural approaches (e.g., Burt 1984) that treat structural factors only as *context* for action, not a dimension of a mutually constitutive whole (see Giddens 1985), and with rational action approaches (e.g., Coleman 1986, 1987, 1990; Hechter 1987; Friedman and Hechter 1988) that take the individual as unproblematically and a priori given as the "microsociological" foundation for macrosociological analysis.[4]

It is not adequate to conceive of a macrosociology entirely on microfoundations or to conceive of microsociology as set within the context of macro structure. Arguments over class point this up. I shall briefly consider the argument that Chinese students acted in ways shaped by class interest and then consider the classic dualism of Marx and Weber on this subject. Next I will try to show that seeing the construction of identity as an ongoing process undermines attempts to use either class or individual interests as Archimedean points for final explanations of social movements or similar actions. There can be no such fixed points. The identities and hence the interests of participants in collective actions are not objectively determined but subjectively constructed (albeit under conditions that are not subject to individual control, *pace,* Marx [1852] 1973). This construction is at once personal and collective; the two cannot be sharply distinguished. In the final section of the chapter, I will consider the way in which the idea of "honor" might help us to grasp something of the centrality of identity to action, offering a complement to that of interest.

PROTEST OF INTELLECTUALS

On April 27, in the early days of the "Beijing Spring," students marching on Tiananmen Square confronted soldiers. There had been no military violence yet, though many students were braced for some. The soldiers were young men from peasant families; the students came almost entirely from urban families, and those from "academic" universities were the products of a selection system that allowed only about 1.5% of their age mates such an educational opportunity. "Go home to your fields," the students shouted to the soldiers, "you have no business here."

The students began the protest movement of 1989 with a strong sense of themselves as young or prospective intellectuals and a strong sense of their own distinction from the peasants, members of the working class, and officials.[5] This was not just the product of China's extraordinarily detailed system of class designations, or even of 40 years of communist rule, which had recurrently made class background a matter of critical significance in determining treatment and life chances of individuals. It was a matter also and more deeply of basic personal identity. It had resonances with images of intellectuals going back thousands of years in Chinese history, and it was also manifest in the way people spoke, dressed, and carried their bodies. Who they were as individuals was bound up with and indistinguishable from their participation in a whole variety of social relationships that were colored and shaped by reciprocal recognitions of class identity.

From the self-strengthening movement of the 1890s, through the 1919 protests, the ebbs and flows of republicanism, and early stages of Chinese communism, intellectuals took on a stronger and stronger sense of their own crucial role in China's modernization.[6] In the 1980s, Deng Xiaoping and other communist leaders had courted intellectuals as important agents of reform. This new respect and tolerance was joined, however, with the older idea of the intellectual's responsibility to remonstrate with an emperor (though that responsibility had never matured into a right to be free from punishment for doing so). So when Chinese students in 1989 said that they were acting as "the conscience of the nation," and that this was not just a simple choice but a responsibility they had to live up to, they were speaking in line with a long tradition.

Students were different from other intellectuals not only in their youth and the lesser development of their ideas and skills but in the fact that they didn't have families to support or jobs to risk (at least in the immediate sense). They were, therefore, understood to be freer than their elders to act through public protest. More senior intellectuals offered advice, tried to protect young activists, and pushed for change in quieter ways (though a special respect was paid to those elders who did put themselves on the line in public protest). Of course, the student "fraction" of the intellectual class also had its own complaints: crowded, poorly constructed dormitories, inadequate stipends, a shortage of good jobs after graduation, and so on. Spatial concentration; subject, class, and cohort organization; and the web of communication among universities provided structural facilitation for mobilization.

So, can we explain the student protest movement of that spring simply in terms of the class consciousness of intellectuals? I think not, though that is a crucial dimension to any explanation. Certainly the students' class position exerted a causal influence on their consciousness and on their participation in the movement. Certainly some part of the content of their consciousness was focused on class—that is, on their identity as students and/or intellectuals and what that identity ought to mean in China. But the stronger Marxist sense of class consciousness as the correct self-understanding of a class as a whole, together with the compulsion to act on such understanding, will not help us very much.[7] Moreover, though relatedly, the consciousness of the students changed in important ways during the course of the protest, and the consciousness of Chinese intellectuals has been changed by it and by its repression. These processes of change cannot be grasped through an understanding of class consciousness that focuses on the recognition of class interests.

Students did see the movement for democracy through lenses colored by class. For example, when they spoke of the relationship of education to democracy, they always spoke of the need for them, and others like them, to "educate the masses of people." They did not speak of democracy as itself a process of public education as well as of self-government. On the other hand, the basic self-identification of the protesting students in Tiananmen Square—and not just their intellectual self-categorization but their lived identity—was transformed, and at least for a time radicalized, by six weeks of activism. Their consciousness expanded beyond class concerns to include national ones and in important ways universal ideals. In the same way, when the ordinary people of Beijing rallied to protect the student hunger strikers starting May 19, this was not only because they saw students speaking for ideals they shared but because the act of refusing sustenance and courting government reprisals impressed people that the students were not just seeking their personal gains but sacrificing themselves for the people as a whole.

In the midst of the struggle, it became possible to identify emotionally with a general category—the Chinese people—which under more ordinary circumstances would be rent by numerous divisions.

THE CLASSICAL DUALISM

Among other legacies from our founding fathers, Marx and Weber bequeathed us a classic version of the contest between methodological individualism and holism. This is one of the many dimensions packed into the heavily loaded and problematic conceptual distinction of micro- from macrosociology.

Despite appearances, Marx was not a consistent methodological holist. Rather, he followed Rousseau in an ambiguous and shifting position, both evaluatively and epistemologically. Some of his accounts of class treated it as a category of individuals and suggested that their collective action would be motivated by the various utilitarian gains it would bring them. In other texts, he treated classes as themselves individuals with needs, missions, and destinies. For the most part, Marx was contemptuous of those who conceptualized the proletariat as an aggregate of individuals, however, rather than a singular class. As he stressed in *The Holy Family,* class was neither an arbitrary analytic device nor an optional set of values individuals might chose or disregard at will: "It is not a question of what this or that proletarian, or even the whole proletariat at the moment regards as its aim. It is a question of *what the proletariat is,* and what, in accordance with this being, it will historically be compelled to do" (Marx [1845] 1975, p. 211). This was, in a sense, Marx's class-specific formulation of the general will, as objective and irreducible as Rousseau's somewhat broader version. The general will was distinguished from the will of all as sharply as the latter was from any minority viewpoint—perhaps more so.[8]

Weber had little patience for such an idea. He seems to have encountered it in Lukacs, who was particularly committed to this version of Marxist thought. Weber's summary dismissal was withering. A class, Weber argued, is not necessarily a group. To hold that "the individual may be in error concerning his interests but that the class is infallible about its interests" is pseudoscientific (Weber [1922] 1968, p. 93). For Weber, class could only be a more or less arbitrary and abstract categorization of individuals in terms of their life chances or market power.

Both Marx and Weber defined class in terms external to the consciousness of actors—position in the relations of production for Marx and market position for Weber. Both regarded class as describing a set of objective interests and treated rationality in terms of following those interests. For

Weber, objective interests based on class were important but far from predominant; they had to compete for individuals' attention with a range of other interests. For Marx, on the other hand, class interests were not only objective but fundamentally compelling. It is this last distinction that led Marx to expect radical action on the basis of class while Weber did not.[9]

The Marx-Weber argument—or dialogue of the deaf—has been rehashed and repeated many times in the history of sociology. This has sometimes led to interesting new insights, but it has also helped to keep us stuck in a debate that poorly and misleadingly formulates the central issues. On the Marxist side, the gulf between class-in-itself and class-for-itself has proved bridgeable only in faith and imagination and is at most of metaphorical utility. The conceptualization has sometimes been pernicious, as when it has been used to justify Leninist vanguard party substitutionism. Weber's account was perhaps more realistic but in many ways just as limited. It certainly grasped a central feature of typical action in capitalist societies. But it did not provide any serious account of the power of class—or other similar—ideas in people's lives. While it offered an approach to differences in consumer habits, it lacked purchase on the emotional commitments that underlie some of the great struggles of the modern era. Ironically, because Weber was perhaps the greatest of comparative historical sociologists, and the clearest about the importance of historically specific conceptualizations, his discussion of class, and the methodological individualism that underpinned it, reflected rather than situated or explained capitalism's characteristic individualistic ideology. Thus Weber did not use his category of value-rational action to address the creation of "classed" identities as well as religious, ethnic, or nationalist ones. Class, for Weber, was always a category based on objective market interests; implicitly thus it could be analyzed entirely through the notion of instrumental rationality. To focus on value rationality as the pursuit of ends indissoluable from self, on the other hand, raises precisely the problem of identity in social action.[10]

It is hard to make many advances in this argument as it is framed. Though both Marx and Weber were more subtle and complex than these summaries reveal, Marx postulated a "holistic" account of classes and Weber postulated methodological individualism. The two played out an antinomy, a mirror image, deeply embedded in nineteenth-century philosophy of science (Mandelbaum 1971). We remain largely caught in the same problematic formulation today. In Marxist discussions of class consciousness, for example (as Wright 1985, chap. 7, has recently observed), people tend to assert either that classes are units capable of consciousness (a position Wright associates mainly with Lukacs) or that class consciousness must refer only to statistical patterns of individual consciousness (the position Wright himself takes, within a methodological individualism drawn from the "analytic Marxist" version of rational choice theory).

Even the terminology of the dispute is oddly problematic, as though each term attempted to prejudge the case but in a way that rebounded on itself. What could individualism mean if not a sort of holism, the postulate that a given unit (the biological organism or the psychological or legal person) cannot be internally subdivided? If society, or class, is truly a whole, and, therefore, a phenomenon irreducible to its component parts, is it not then an individual?

Neither holism nor individualism in this sense is a sound starting point for analysis. Put simply, the problem is that neither perspective pays adequate attention to the *constructed* nature of both individuals and groups. A good opening to this has come in the growing influence of the network approach, which followed earlier social anthropologists in suggesting that the proper unit of analysis is neither individuals nor whole societies but the structure of social relationships (Nadel 1957). There is no reason, though, that the study of relationships should emphasize structure to the exclusion of action. In Giddens's (1985) terminology, we could say that the historical process of structuration is emphatically *not* a mediation between individual and society, for both individual and society are its products, or its contents, not its starting points. What is primary is the intersubjective process. This is nowhere more evident than in studying social movements and collective action.

IDENTITY AS A PROBLEM

By a problem of "identity," I mean the need for accounts of collective action to offer a coherent understanding of who participants are. This may seem simple enough, but in fact it is a difficult interpretive problem. There are ambiguities inherent in the relationship between the singularity of a personal identity and the multiplicity of social identities that may be borne by a person—to be me, for example, means in large part to put together the roles of father, husband, son, professor, neighbor, citizen. But each may also under some circumstances involve a more or less compelling claim to see myself in terms of membership in a collectivity. These ambiguities are enhanced by the question of representation—to what extent do a number of specific workers represent the working class? This is an issue not only for academic analysts but for participants in struggle, inclined to feel that they are the class (or people) in action. Third, and most important for this chapter, identity is not a static, preexisting condition that can be seen as exerting a causal influence on collective action; at both personal and collective levels, it is a changeable product of collective action.

These problems of identity are embedded in all the collective or plural nouns we use to describe the participants in collective action—*nations, classes, communities, trades, students, intellectuals, corporations, neighborhoods, peasants, women* or *men*, and so on. I do not want to focus on the commonplace observation that we need to identify the degree to which these terms (or their proper noun specifications) reflect the analyst's conceptualization versus the participants' self-identification. That much, I think, can be taken for granted, though a good many sociologists ignore it and its implications are sometimes very difficult to work out in practice.

What constitutes "groupness" is a more serious issue. When Weber remarked that "a class does not in and of itself constitute a group," he raised an important point. Externally formulated (especially in Weber's definition), "class" is a single-dimensional category. To know how much a class formed a group, we would need to know more about how influential this category was in determining patterns of association and action and how closely it overlapped with other categories of differentiation. At the same time, a class, like any other abstractly formulated category, may be more or less of a group in terms of its social relations and patterns of action; this is an empirical question. The big difficulty with class is that, in most theoretical accounts, including both Marx's and Weber's, it specifies a very large category—such as, for Marx, those who share a common position in the relations of production *at the level of capital accumulation.* Classes in the modern capitalist world thus are implicitly either national or international in scale. This means that it is very unlikely for them to have a high density of internal relationships when compared with smaller and/or more locally concentrated populations. If they (or even somewhat smaller substitutes) are to be solidary groups for purposes of collective action, they must depend on some other sort of organizational and/or cultural processes.

Accounts of "groupness" in terms of simple cultural commonality or external attribution are relatively weak, though I think this is the level at which nearly all researchers first identify at least all large groups (that is, we tend to first find cultural *categories* and then look to see how grouplike they are).[11] Structural analysts of various sorts have given strong accounts of groupness, perhaps most notably in the network tradition; Tilly's (1978) appropriation of Harrison White's idea of "CATNET" is perhaps paradigmatic in the collective action literature. More recently, Hechter (1987) and Coleman (1990) have offered serious and sustained accounts of groupness within the rational action perspective.

These treatments of groupness, however, are all essentially external in their understanding of the problem of identity. That is, they ask how, why, or to what extent certain aggregates of individuals should be understood to have acted as a group.[12] This is perhaps the basic question that recent accounts and theories of collective action have addressed. Basic as this question is, however, there is a deeper one. To address it, we have to grant that the notion of individual is just as problematic as that of group, though our Western cultural categories usually make us take it for granted. Thus, when Coleman (1990) sets out to analyze corporate actors as constructed individuals, it never occurs to him to question that human individuals are "natural" rather than socially constructed. My concern is not to rehash epistemological and ontological debates concerning the idea of individual, however, or to propose a radical cross-cultural incommensurability in understandings such that we are forced to an extreme particularism.[13] Rather, my question is whether basic ideas about personhood and identity—or, more precisely, personhood and identity themselves, lived phenomena, not just ideas about them—do not play a crucial role in collective action that is constitutive of the actor in a way that rational action theory and structuralism as currently practiced cannot recognize.

To engage in action is a process of living an identity that is always social; it is not the outcome of a decision-making or other process that is essentially individual. This is the difficulty with pushing analyses of the free-rider problem to a *reducto ad absurdum* in what Brustein (1989, p. 239) has called the "problem of first-order free riding"—that is, the possibility that individuals would opt out of society (or such primary groups as family) from the very beginning, making those groups as unlikely as Olson implied risky collective actions are. Like seventeenth- and eighteenth-century social contract reasoning, rational action theory taken to this extreme makes the existence of social institutions problematic but leaves the existence of individuals unexamined, as though those individuals were not socially constituted. This then poses the insoluble problem of trying to explain the creation of social institutions—family, community, and so on—as the products of the action of individuals imagined to exist externally to those institutions. Not only the social institution but the individual person is thereby misunderstood. We are not just influenced by social relationships during a socialization process and then left fully formed. We have our identity only within such relationships.

Not only is life always social, living is always a matter of action, not of statistically possessing an identity or set of attitudes prior to action. What one does defines who one is, both for others and especially for oneself. Risky and unusual collective action places one's identity on the line in an especially powerful way.

Put another way, very risky actions, like standing in front of a tank as it rolls down Chang'an Boulevard (to borrow 1989's most powerful media image of bravery to the point of foolishness), depend on a sense of who one is as a person and what it means to go on living with oneself that is inextricably social, as well as personal, and that is sufficiently powerful to outweigh what might ordinarily be paramount prudential concerns. When *I* stood in Tiananmen Square the evening of June 3, I felt a rush of adrenaline at early stages of the fighting, a macho impulse to be where the action was, and deep anger at the government's decision to attack the protesters. I also felt all sorts of good reasons for not being there, including personal safety, even though the army was not yet firing live ammunition. Prudential considerations won out, in large part, because my sense of who I was had not been put on the line. I was not Chinese; it was not my government or my army that was beginning to attack. I was not even a journalist whose professional identity involved commitment to getting a story or a photograph; I was more committed to being a husband and father. And my family and my main circle of friends and colleagues were thousands of miles away. But none of these aspects of my identity was fixed and immutable. By early June, I identified myself with the student protesters more than I had in mid-April, largely because I had been with them around the clock for six weeks. But I had not been on hunger strike, I had not made speeches, I had not put my career in jeopardy. In other words, I had not been through nearly so transformative a sequence of events and actions as had many Chinese students. Perhaps in some basic sense I was and am not as brave as they were. But on June 3, some students were brave enough to risk death who a month before had not been brave enough to be publicly identified with the boycott of classes.[14]

Perhaps another, older Chinese illustration will help. Qiu Jin was one of the first women to rise to importance among China's radical modernizers. She studied in Japan at the same time as Lu Xun (China's greatest modern writer and a protagonist of the May 4th intellectual movement). In Japan, Qiu Jin had developed a reputation as a fiery orator and drew large and admiring crowds among the other Chinese students. Her fame continued to grow when she returned to China in 1906. She played a key role in building a school and secret society in Datong and joined with her cousin and others in planning an insurrection. Eventually their plot was uncovered; before he was captured and executed, her cousin Xu Xilin succeeded in shooting the Manchu governor of Anhui province. She was warned by friends that the army was coming for her but chose to remain at her school, hoping to make a dramatic last stand with the arms that had been stockpiled there. She was captured and ultimately beheaded. Lu Xun, however, said that she had been "clapped to death." In other words, the crowds that had urged on her speeches and applauded her protestations against the government had implicitly pushed her to ever more radical positions. She could neither pause to consolidate her gains or escape when the troops came without humiliation and betrayal of her own sense of identity and direction. Lu Xun's comment stresses both the complicity of crowds in the increasing radicalism and ultimately often the deaths of their leaders and the way in which personal identity may be transformed in the course of public action so as to foreclose the options of moderation and retreat.[15]

The constant construction of identity that is the habitus is not entirely absorbed within the immediate situation. The habitus includes representations of historical memory. Qiu Jin, for example, contributes to contemporary Chinese protesters one of a number of scripts for action in the midst of radical struggle. The commonplace events of everyday action—shopping, flirting, asking questions in class, developing a style of dress—all have innumerable possible contemporary models. Even without innovation, the range of choice is wide and multiplied by print and electronic media, which extend the proliferation of examples beyond one's direct observation. But the number of available models for how to challenge the legitimacy of the government, or face the threat of military repression, or suffer execution, is fairly small. Moreover, those past protesters who backed down in the face of repression do not live on as heroic legends. Our daily lives are full of examples of caution, but our narratives of revolution and popular struggle contain mainly tales of bravery rather than prudent common sense. As the course of a movement takes participants beyond the range of usual experience, they are thrown back more and more on such heroic images in their struggle to find acceptable guidelines for action.

INTERESTS, HONOR, AND IDENTITY

One of the limits of a rational choice perspective is that it works best on the decisions that are the most routine (Davis 1973). Another is that its accounts hold best where actors can most readily be understood as individuals responding to situations in terms of some more or less calculable interests. This is not to say that rational action theory must be psychological in the sense of focusing on motivation as an internal state of mind. On the contrary, as Becker (1976) has shown, most of microeconomic theory, which overlaps closely with rational action theory, can be operated in aggregate (as distinct from individual case) terms without reference to such states of mind. All that is necessary is a situation in which certain goods are scarce; supply and demand then force the outcomes of rational choice models without any specific theory of action being needed. Difficulty will arise here first and foremost not in addressing rationality as such but when an attempt is made to specify demand for diverse and incommensurable goods (which depends, of course, on the rational choice theorist or economist admitting that there are diverse and incommensurable goods). The most common line of objection to rational action theory—that individuals are not so rational as it suggests—usually results in critics and proponents talking past one another. It is, in any case, not the central issue to be raised about the relationship of rational action to "consciousness."

The central issue, rather, is whether persons are constituted in terms of interests.[16] It is the notion of interest that provides the potential objectivity to evaluations of rationality, whether in Marxist terms of class interests or in utilitarian reckonings of individual and collective interests. It is the notion of interest, not of evaluation or rationality more generally, that is translated into the external terms of supply and demand by Becker's argument. But the notion of interest is both problematic and historically and culturally specific. That is, it is part of a way of thinking and an understanding of persons that is linked to the idea of discrete individuals constituted in terms of capacity for pleasures and pains—the view Bentham codified. This view is distinctive of modern Western culture, along with the idea of personhood as a state defined in terms of dignity rather than honor, universal (human) or civil rights rather than particular memberships.

The distinction between cultures emphasizing the axis of honor and shame and those emphasizing guilt and innocence is an old one in anthropology. I want to use it here not so much to argue that the Chinese (or any other non-Western people) are more motivated by honor in their collective actions than Westerners as to argue that we as Western analysts are peculiarly neglectful of the issue of identity raised by the matter of honor. Honor (and more generally issues of personal and collective identity) is important in understanding risky and/or unusual actions in the West as well as elsewhere. I think it is the case that the transformation of Western culture over the last few hundred years has made honor less salient a category and that this may be linked to differences in the radicalism of and/or risk taking in collective actions. My point here, however, is more general: We need to wrestle with the constitution and transformation of identity, and challenges to identity, in collective action.

The Western tradition has been distinctive (though not unique) in its reliance on ideas of guilt and innocence. This is one of the central cultural foundations for the modern version of individualism that rose along with capitalism and the state in Western Europe. The point is not that other societies lack notions of individual or self (as some extreme accounts have suggested) but that they organize personal identity differently. The Western individual is understood as the locus of a kind of responsibility that is epitomized in the notion of an eternal and eternally atomistic soul available for damnation or salvation.[17] We can be guilty, in biblical terms, precisely because we have eaten of the fruit of the tree of knowledge. From the biblical story of the Fall, Western thought might have stressed the shame of Adam and Eve at their nakedness but has instead focused on their sin and God's consequent curse. Our stress on knowledge as the basis of guilt and inno-cence is linked to a conceptualization of the individual (and on that basis the world) that is overwhelmingly and fundamentally conceived in terms of inside and outside a bodily boundary (see Taylor 1985b, 1989). The distinc-tive modern Western notion of the individual is rooted in this long-standing tradition. This involves positing the person as a bearer of rights and interests outside of and prior to any specific social relationships. The individual can only be responsible for his or her actions to the extent that he or she has knowledge of the consequences of an action and capacity to act otherwise, an idea of responsibility at odds with much more widespread notions of strict liability.[18] Some scholars have argued that even Western forms of causal reasoning and science are linked to this approach to individual responsibility.

Be that as it may, we have to make the effort to see other ways of conceptualizing the person if we are to develop a sound approach to the problem of identity in social action. Though no binary opposition of "them" and "us" could conceivably exhaust variation in this regard, the notion of honor is a good starting point. It stresses not only reputation, the opinions of others, but a particular way of evaluating oneself. This involves a much greater stress on archetypal patterns of behavior (Campbell 1964; Taylor 1989). The notion of honor does not break down into separable justifica-tions of specific acts so readily as does that of guilt and innocence, or a calculus of interests. In terms of the transmission of culture and of engage-ment in social action, it places a strong emphasis on following commendable models.

There are other distinctive features of social identity reliant on the notion of honor. As Peter Berger ([1970] 1984, p. 149) remarked some years ago, "The obsolescence of the concept of honour is revealed very sharply in the inability of most contemporaries to understand insult, which in essence is an assault on honour." One of the salient emotions driving student protesters in Beijing in spring 1989 was a recurrent sense of insult. Government descrip-tions of their protests as "turmoil," accusations that they were led or manip-ulated by a tiny band of foreign agitators, and charges that they were hooligans engaged in antisocial (or antisocialist) behavior all offended them deeply. On the night of May 19, I watched students dither in uncertainty about whether it was prudent to march yet again to Tiananmen Square only to be galvanized into immediate action by Li Peng's speech declaring martial law. Amid their tears and shouts, they repeated over and again their sense of anger and outrage at his insulting tone. "He lectures us like naughty chil-dren." "He speaks like a bad, old-fashioned teacher." "He is so arrogant." Earlier, students had felt a similar insult in the *People's Daily* editorial of April 26, which condemned their protests as unpatriotic. One of the central student demands became the call for an apology and an official recognition of student patriotism. To a Westerner, this seemed oddly abstract amid the more substantive calls for freedom of press or association and an end to corruption. But this may have been even more emotionally central to participants in the protest (though they were well aware that the other sorts of demands were more fundamental long-term goals).

As thinkers from Montesquieu to Dumont (1982) have suggested, honor is linked to a notion of the primacy of social hierarchy and is at odds with a conception of the world in which essentially equivalent individuals are primary. Not only personal reputation but the evaluation of collective niches in the hierarchy are crucial sources of honor (or shame): One's group must defend its honor against presumption from below and slights from above. Where such ideas are strong, notions like "human rights," which depend on abstracting the human individual from his or her social context (and perhaps even from his or her gender), are difficult to grasp or institutionalize. Yet, in pursuing democracy, Chinese students and intellectuals stressed the idea of human rights, which they saw (as had their forebears in 1919) as a quintessentially Western one. The Chinese protesters thus were in the paradoxical position of acting partly on the basis of a sort of identity at odds with one of their very goals. But paradox has never yet stopped a social movement.

An interest in honor is not adequately rendered—it seems to me, not in the strong sense that pertains to cultural difference and radical collective action—as an interest in something outside the individual. If we can use the term *interest* at all, it is an interest, rather, in a certain sort of identity. Let us compare the notion of rights that is familiar in the Western liberal tradition.

It is possible (though not uncontroversial) to render notions of individual rights in terms of external goods that people desire. One may even speak of life that way, though this may strain even a Westerner's habitual individualism; it sounds a little peculiar to speak of one's life as something external to or separable from one. We can translate the idea of honor into the language of possessive individualism (to borrow Macpherson's 1965 phrase) and treat it as a quantity of which we may possess more or less. This is, indeed, how we customarily try to deal with notions like the Chinese idea of "face." But it is a translation that is at odds with the original, for honor is not an external substance to be possessed. It is, rather, a quality of being. If it is honorable for a man to be manly, or honest, or intelligent, or Chinese, these are qualities not renderable as commensurable quantities. More of one does not make up for lack of another.[19]

Such qualities are simultaneously features of personal identity, within a habitus, and of archetypal images of "good" identity. If they are to be approached rationally, it is in Weber's sense of "value rationality," not instrumental rationality. But a set of honorable qualities is not entirely rationalizable; it is understandable mainly through a sense of practical knowledge derived from archetypes and experience. These qualities are also imperative in a way interests are not. An identity distinct from the objects of one's interests means that there is a basis for rational evaluation of those various interests as more or less desirable, but the identity, the basis of that evaluation, exists separately from them.

At one level, we can approach honor by saying that it gives individuals certain interests in rational action—for example, protecting their reputations. And we can use the role of honor in improving explanations of why people seem sometimes to pursue collective actions against what appear to be their more tangible or "material" interests. But, at another level, the role of honor in establishing identity reveals a limit to the individualist version of rational action theory. The difficulty arises when we try to treat the individual as an irreducible foundation for approaching social organization or action. Rational action theory calls on us generally to take individuals as we find them. We try to reason then either from a subjectivist notion of their interests as equivalent to their wants or from an objectivist notion that we can derive their wants from some external feature(s) of their identity—such as their class position.

Each of these approaches carries a pitfall of potential tautology. The first is the familiar one of revealed preference theory—that is, the denial of any significant difference between people's interests and the consequences of their actions. If, in such a view, people always act in their own best interests, then we don't really need a notion of interests. What is lost is not only the possibility of error but the impact of external structure—for example, that one might have wanted a completely different product that wasn't manufactured or that class differences in purchases reveal less people's preferences than their fate.

The second sort of tautology arises when the notion of interests is so deployed that we can no longer distinguish between it and the subject of the interests. If a class is defined (as the Marx/Lukacs notion of the proletariat as a whole being infallible about its interests comes close to doing) as that entity that pursues class interests—such as the proletariat as the agent of revolutionary transformation of capitalism—then one has lost analytic purchase as much as in revealed preference theory. But the problem here is not simply one of working at a "macro" rather than a "micro" or individual level. It could also arise at the individual level. No listing of a sum of positional identities solves the dilemma of how the individual reconciles them into a singular personal identity. A key reason to speak in terms of interests is to be able to ascertain whether or not a given subject is pursuing or achieving them or a given course of action is appropriate to them. The interests derivable from various positional identities may provide a relatively satisfactory account of a large part of the person's action under ordinary circumstances. What they cannot address is what the person will do when extraordinary circumstances place his or her very identity in question.

Even under more ordinary circumstances, it seems to me that using a language of interests can be problematic for talking about identity. What, for example, is added to the mere observation of one's existence by asserting that one has an interest in existing? Does one have an interest in being oneself? In a sense, I will argue, one does, but we need to be wary of an oversimplified notion of the self. For example, we should recognize, as Taylor (1985a) has suggested, that people may sometimes desire to change their desires. Indeed, it may be an important part of an idea of being good or virtuous to want one's desires to improve.

Consider, however, the test of extreme circumstances. Is it one's interests or one's very identity that is at issue when goods that one needs to live, or freedom from unbearable pain, are made available only contingent on the violation of one's fundamental sense of self—as, say, they might be to a prisoner asked under torture to reveal the whereabouts of comrades sought by her tormentors? Within a logic of guilt and innocence, we are apt to excuse the prisoner who gives the information because she had no reasonable choice in the matter. The prisoner's sense of herself as a person, however, may be deeply damaged by those events regardless of her knowledge that her action was forced. Being told that she is innocent may not stop her from reliving the nightmare of having betrayed her friends. A logic of honor is at work, then, and is substantially independent of intention and choice. Honor can be sullied through no fault of one's own. And so, as the example of the prisoner suggests, can one's identity be radically undermined by an action avoidable only at the cost of one's life.[20]

In this case, it would be hard to treat the dilemma before the person as one of a fixed individual possessor of interests confronting a competition between two of those interests. We might try to say that the person who chooses between life and honor makes an evaluation—correctly or incorrectly—of which choice holds the greater pain. But, in a sense, at the point of such a decision, there is no future in which the identity of the honorable individual is not radically altered. Each option negates the self in a fundamental way. By contrast, of course, a person lacking in honor would not find this choice difficult or suffer devastating consequences from choosing life. The difference between the two people would not be analyzable as a difference in interests except in the most tautological sense. It would be, precisely, the difference between *people*, that is, between identities. Moreover, it would be extremely difficult to relate ordinary identity—self-conceptions, the way people reconcile interests in everyday life—to the identity that emerges as salient under this kind of extraordinary situation. It is not just that the true test of honor lies in these extreme moments. It is also that the capacity to act according to high standards of honor may be nurtured by intense participation in certain courses of action, including some social movements.

CONCLUSION

During spring 1989, Chinese student protestors went through a series of actions and experiences that shaped and reshaped the identities of many. They moved from small statements like marching to boycotts of classes, signing petitions, and hunger strikes. They made speeches—simply to each other as well as on television—that affirmed the primacy or even irreducible priority of certain values. They linked these values—freedom, national pride, and personal integrity or honor—to their positional identity, seeing them as particularly the responsibility of intellectuals. But their actions were more than a reflection of positional interests. Students joined the protest movement largely in blocks of classmates, so their primary immediate social network supported the process of redefinition of identity. Indeed, it seems that those more centrally placed in everyday social networks—such as class monitors and other leaders at school—were more active in the movement and felt more obligated to hold themselves to high standards of committed behavior.[21]

Of course, various other factors in addition to honorable defense of identity determined expressions of bravery. Not least of all, I suspect, were detailed and largely arbitrary chains of events the night of June 3 that presented varying demands for heroism.[22] My point here is simply that accounting for actions so high in risk or cost as to be outside plausible instrumental rationality need not involve reliance on notions of psychological debility or more or less mystical leaps of substituting class interests for individual ones. Rather, even extraordinarily risky, apparently self-sacrificing action can be seen as rational. But the condition of a rational action account of such behavior, paradoxically, is precisely not to see it literally as self-sacrificing but to see it as self-saving. That is, the rational choice to take extraordinary risk may depend on the social construction, in the midst of unusual collective action, of a personal identity that makes *not* taking a given risk more certain to imperil the self of the actor than taking it. This sort of calculation cannot be understood in terms of an approach to rational action that takes actor's identities as fixed attributes of individuals or one that analyzes individual action solely in terms of interests derived from various external sources—such as class position. But it can be understood.

The student protesters of China's Beijing Spring certainly began their protest with a consciousness shaped by their class position and concrete material concerns (or interests). But the risks they took, the sacrifices they made, and the moral example they provided for the future of democratic struggles in China cannot be understood primarily in terms of that positional identity. This is not a matter of structural or holistic accounts being better than individualistic or micro-social ones. Rather, we have to see how, for some of the students, participation in the protest contributed, at least temporarily, to a transformation of personal identity. Not only did they identify with a larger whole—the Chinese people—or with democratic or other ideals. Crucially, these students understood who they themselves were on models of such high standards of courage and struggle that failing to accept the danger would have meant a collapse of personal identity or at least a bitter wound.

NOTES

1. We might apply Weber's ([1922] 1968, p. 25) distinction of value rationality and instrumental rationality: "Examples of pure value-rational orientation would be the actions of persons who, regardless of possible cost to themselves, act to put into practice their convictions of what seems to them to be required by duty, honor, the pursuit of beauty, a religious call, personal loyalty, or the importance of some 'cause' no matter in what it consists. In our terminology, value-rational action always involves 'commands' or 'demands' which, in the actor's opinion, are binding on him. It is only in cases where human action is motivated by the fulfillment of such unconditional demands that it will be called value-rational." Weber is somewhat unclear as to why this should be called *rational* action. He seems to have been seeking a way to acknowledge that people perfectly capable of making instrumentally rational judgments about the likely efficacy of their actions in achieving various outcomes sometimes do not do so because, for ethical, aesthetic, religious, or other reasons, they regard certain actions as ends in themselves.

2. I have offered a twist on this line of argument by suggesting that radical mobilizations may sometimes involve people acting in local situations—such as strongly solidary oppositional communities—that not only provide them with social foundations and selective incentives for collective action but systematically mislead them about their chances of success against more distant structures of power such as capital and state (Calhoun 1988a, 1988b).

3. One of the virtues of Sewell's dual challenge is that it points up implicitly something of how the rational action and structural positions tend to be flip sides of the same record. The rather overdrawn micro-macro debate between rational action analysts and structuralists concerns whether either can claim a primacy over the other. Do macro structures rest on micro foundations, for example, or are they autonomous? The structuralist claim to dominance, rather than mere autonomy, seems to rest most often on the rather intellectually unsatisfying grounds of a disciplinary division of labor with psychology (see, e.g., Blau 1987).

4. Coleman (1990) is very sophisticated and interesting in this regard but still assimilates corporate actors (his main vehicle for macrosociology) into individualism by understanding them as constructed individuals—and seeing human beings as "natural persons" rather than recognizing the process of social construction that establishes both the category of the individual and each particular person.

5. The term *intellectual* carries a broader reference in China than in the West. It means more or less all educated people. See Calhoun (forthcoming-a) for a more substantial treatment of the intellectual field influencing the student protests.

6. The May 4th movement was a particularly important prototype for student protest. In a narrow sense, it focused on the poor treatment China's weak government secured at the hands of its ostensible allies in the Versailles treaty. More broadly, it united a generation of modernizers intent on transforming Chinese culture. Ideologically, the slogan of the May 4th movement—democracy and science—sums up both the importance of the European Enlightenment model for modern Chinese intellectuals and their sense (like that of their European forebears) that they had a crucial role to play in enlightening and improving their country. Movement leaders mostly eschewed crude nationalism but did combine a search for democracy and cultural revival with the pursuit of a stronger China. See Schwarcz (1986) for a general discussion.

7. Marx, of course, did not see intellectuals as a "historic" class. But it's not clear that the proletariat is more cohesive or its members more single-minded.

8. Lest one think that Marxists have a monopoly on such anti-individualist formulations, recall Edmund Burke's argument that revolution is generally a mistake because it is an attempt to make history conform to inevitably individual ideas: "The individual is foolish, but the species is wise."

9. Weber's, rather than Marx's, understanding of class seems immanent, or at least natural, to "mature" capitalist society. This is why class struggle has characteristically been reformist and subject to competition from other lines of allegiance and competing goods. The stronger kind of solidarity that Marx envisioned for class struggle has been reserved so far for collectivities that fit his conceptualization of proletariat very imperfectly at best (Calhoun 1982, 1988a). Some later work broadly in the Marxist tradition has tried to confront the essentially historical and incompletely determined process of class formation (see Przeworski 1985; Katznelson and Zolberg 1986).

10. Baumann (1978, pp. 79-82) has suggested that Weber saw the prevalence of instrumental rationality as important to sociology because it gave social actors identical (or at least commensurable) ends. This made it possible for scientists to offer objective judgments of the rationality of various means. Value rationality was important, by contrast, precisely for taking account of residual but still powerful beliefs that dissented from the prevailing market-based instrumental rationality. These various "absolute" values could not simply be traded off against others, as, say, an official might seek to balance money, power, and prestige. They were, rather, ends indistinguishable from the self and thus problematic for Weber's search for a clear-cut basis for cross-personal evaluation (such as the market gave to instrumental rationality). Aesthetic, ethical, religious, or other bases for value rationality made people incommensurably different from each other. Elsewhere, Weber tends to limit rationality (and meaningful understanding) to those cases where a means/ends calculus is operative; rationality is reduced to instrumental rationality. Thus, for example, in his treatment of legitimacy, Weber ([1922] 1968, p. 33) groups value rationality with affective and religious legitimacy as "purely subjective"; the other sort of legitimacy is that based on "the expectation of specific external effects, that is, by interest situations."

11. Even a resolute structuralist like Peter Blau (e.g., 1977; Blau and Schwartz 1984), for example, must begin with some induction of the categories that he will then test for their salience in predicting in-group versus out-group rates of association. This induction is basically an untheorized role for culture in his anticulturalist argument (see Calhoun and Scott 1990).

12. Thus Hechter sees no qualitative distinction between voluntary, single-purpose associations and ongoing groups into which persons are born, like families or communities (see Wacquant and Calhoun 1989).

13. There is an enormous literature on these problems. The issue was perhaps most developed in the debate over rationality and cross-cultural analysis that followed the publication of Winch's *The Idea of a Social Science* (1958). This is summarized in two excellent anthologies, Wilson (1970) and Hollis and Lukes (1982). The issue has regained currency with the rise of so-called postmodernist social theories that argue for ethical and analytic particularism on somewhat distinct grounds (see Calhoun forthcoming-b).

14. McAdam (1986, 1988) has shown a similar process at work among participants in 1964's "Freedom Summer." More generally, he shows how participation in the longer-term civil rights movement nurtured an intense identification with that movement, supported by webs of relationships with fellow activists; these in turn encouraged participation in the specific high-risk and high-cost actions of Freedom Summer.

15. Qiu Jin's death, like that of many martyrs, fits well into Durkheim's (1895) account of altruistic suicide. See accounts by Rankin (1971) and Spence (1981).

16. Perhaps an even more basic issue is whether the construction of persons in a culture is based on a notion of the individual at all. All cultures have notions of personhood, but these may be very different than the Western individualistic one. Arguing this case does not seem essential here; it is a case, moreover, that would require a very developed account of what a person who is not an individual is—an account that I am not in a position to develop and would not have space for if I could. Several insightful discussions are contained in the book of essays sparked by Mauss's brilliant but neglected essay on the category of the person (Carrithers, Collins, and Lukes 1985).

17. In an essay focused on showing that the Chinese do in fact have a range of notions of the self, and that Mauss was wrong to make as sharp a distinction of Chinese from Western ideas of person as he did, Mark Elvin (1985), nonetheless, finds a significant distinction on just this point.

18. The current revival of strict liability doctrines often troubles us precisely because it is at odds with this deep-seated cultural understanding. Strict liability, by the way, is often closely related to notions of corporate or collective liability, as, for example, one kinsman or clansman may be held liable for the actions of another (see discussion in Moore 1972).

19. I am reminded of an old joke from the Jewish communities of pre-Holocaust Germany: God described his plans for the character of different nations to the archangel Gabriel. The Germans, he said, will be honest, intelligent, and National Socialists. "Oh no," said Gabriel, "that's too many good qualities for any one nation." God reconsidered, and so it is that each German has only two of those three qualities. There are honest Nazis, and there are intelligent Nazis, but people who are honest *and* intelligent are never Nazis.

20. This misfortune has befallen many Chinese people during the last 40 years. It is a central theme in the "literature of the wounded" in which victims of the Cultural Revolution recount, explore, and try to assuage their sufferings. Among the most central of these sufferings is living with the knowledge that one engaged in false or undeserved criticism of one's comrades. One can pride oneself for holding out a long time against pressure, or for trying to say only things that were strictly true, but this does not make the sense of violation go away. It is crucial that such violation is felt by those who criticized as well as by those they attacked. Several such personal narratives are recounted and discussed by Thurston (1988).

21. A somewhat distinct account of selective pressures is needed to account for the preponderance of students from outside Beijing in the square just before the crackdown. These had overcome greater obstacles (e.g., long-distance travel) to participate. They had a special need to demonstrate their own radical commitment because their comrades from Beijing had already proved theirs through the hunger strike and other earlier actions (and, in any case, had the benefit of membership in more prestigious and traditionally radical universities). Perhaps most important, it was much harder for them simply to leave as danger grew.

22. It is important to note also that students were not the only actors on the popular side of this drama. Insurgent workers and *laobaixing* (ordinary people) figure more prominently among the dead (if not so far among the martyrs of reconstructed history). Students were brave to be in the square, but the killing took place along the roads into Tiananmen, and the dead seem largely to have been local residents.

REFERENCES

Baumann, Zygmunt. 1978. *Hermeneutics and Social Science.* New York: Columbia University Press.

Becker, Gary. 1976. *The Economic Approach to Human Behavior.* Chicago: University of Chicago Press.

Berger, Peter. [1970] 1984. "On the Obsolescence of the Concept of Honor." Pp. 149-58 in *Liberalism and Its Critics,* edited by M. Sandel. New York: New York University Press.

Blau, Peter M. 1977. *Inequality and Heterogeneity.* New York: Free Press.

———. 1987. "Contrasting Theoretical Perspectives." Pp. 71-85 in *The Micro-Macro Link,* edited by J. C. Alexander, B. Giesen, R. Muench, and N. J. Smelser. Berkeley: University of California Press.

Blau, Peter M. and Joseph E. Schwartz. 1984. *Crosscutting Social Circles: Testing a Macro-structural Theory of Intergroup Relations.* New York: Academic Press.

Bourdieu, Pierre. 1977. *Outline of a Theory of Practice.* Cambridge: Cambridge University Press.

———. 1980. *Le Sens Pratique.* Paris: Editions de Minuit.

Brustein, William. 1989. "Review of M. Taylor, ed.: *Rationality and Revolution.*" *Contemporary Sociology* 18(2):239-40.

Burt, Ronald. 1984. *Towards a Structural Theory of Action.* New York: Academic Press.

Calhoun, Craig. 1982. *The Question of Class Struggle: Social Foundations of Popular Protest in Industrializing England.* Chicago: University of Chicago Press.

———. 1988a. "The Radicalism of Tradition and the Question of Class Struggle." Pp. 129-75 in *Rationality and Revolution,* edited by M. Taylor. Cambridge: Cambridge University Press.

———. 1988b. "Class, Place and Industrial Revolution." Pp. 51-72 in *Class and Space: The Making of Urban Society,* edited by P. Williams and N. Thrift. London: Routledge & Kegan Paul.

———. 1989a. "Democracy and Science, 1989: A Report from Beijing." *Society* 26:21-38.

———. 1989b. "The Beijing Spring, 1989: Notes on the Making of a Protest." *Dissent* 36:435-47.

———. 1989c. "Protest in Beijing: The Conditions and Importance of the Chinese Student Movement of 1989." *Partisan Review* 56:563-80.

———. 1989d. "Tiananmen, Television and the Public Sphere: Internationalization of Culture and the Beijing Spring of 1989." *Public Culture* 2:54-70.

———. Forthcoming-a. "The Ideology of Intellectuals and the Chinese Student Protest Movement of 1989." In *Intellectuals and Politics: Social Theory Beyond the Academy.* Newbury Park, CA: Sage.

———. Forthcoming-b. "Culture, History and the Problem of Specificity in Social Theory." In *Postmodernism and General Social Theory,* edited by S. Seidman and D. Wagner. New York: Basil Blackwell.

Calhoun, Craig and W. Richard Scott. 1990. "The Sociological Structuralism of Peter M. Blau."
    Pp. 1-34 in *Structures of Power and Constraint,* edited by C. Calhoun, M. Meyer, and
    W. R. Scott. Cambridge: Cambridge University Press.

Campbell, J. K. 1964. *Honor, Family and Patronage.* Oxford: Oxford University Press.

Carrithers, Michael, Steven Collins, and Steven Lukes, eds. 1985. *The Category of the Person:
    Anthropology, Philosophy and History.* Cambridge: Cambridge University Press.

Cohen, Jean L. 1985. "Strategy or Identity: New Theoretical Paradigms and Contemporary
    Social Movements." *Social Research* 52:663-716.

Coleman, James S. 1986. "Social Theory, Social Research, and a Theory of Action." *American
    Journal of Sociology* 91:1309-35.

———. 1987. "Microfoundations and Macrosocial Behavior." Pp. 153-73 in *The Macro-Micro
    Link,* edited by J. C. Alexander, B. Giesen, R. Muench, and N. J. Smelser. Berkeley:
    University of California Press.

———. 1990. *Foundations of Social Theory.* Cambridge, MA: Harvard University Press.

Davis, Jerome. 1973. "Forms and Norms: The Economy of Social Relations." *Man* 8:159-76.

Dumont, Louis. 1982. *Essays on Individualism.* Chicago: University of Chicago Press.

Durkheim, Émile. 1895. *Suicide.* New York: Free Press.

Elvin, Mark. 1985. "Between the Earth and Heaven: Conceptions of the Self in China." Pp.
    156-89 in *The Category of the Person: Anthropology, Philosophy, History,* edited by
    M. Carrithers, S. Collins, and S. Lukes. Cambridge: Cambridge University Press.

Friedman, Debra and Michael Hechter. 1988. "The Contribution of Rational Choice Theory to
    Macrosociological Research." *Sociological Theory* 6:201-18.

Giddens, Anthony. 1985. *The Constitution of Society.* Berkeley: University of California Press.

Hechter, Michael. 1987. *Principles of Group Solidarity.* Berkeley: University of California
    Press.

Hollis, Martin and Steven Lukes, eds. 1982. *Rationality and Relativism.* Cambridge: MIT Press.

Katznelson, Ira and Aristide Zolberg, eds. 1986. *Working Class Formation.* Princeton, NJ:
    Princeton University Press.

Macpherson, C. B. 1965. *The Theory of Possessive Individualism.* Oxford: Oxford University
    Press.

Mandelbaum, Maurice. 1971. *History, Man and Reason: A Study in Nineteenth Century Thought.*
    Baltimore: Johns Hopkins University Press.

Marx, Karl. [1845] 1975. *The Holy Family.* Pp. 5-211 in *Collected Works.* Vol. 4. London:
    Lawrence and Wishart.

———. [1852] 1973. "The Eighteenth Brumaire of Louis Bonaparte." In *Surveys from Exile.*
    Harmondsworth: Penguin.

McAdam, Doug. 1986. "Recruitment to High-Risk Activism: The Case of Freedom Summer."
    American Journal of Sociology 92:64-90.

———. 1988. *Freedom Summer.* New York: Oxford University Press.

Melucci, Alberto. 1989. *Nomads of the Present: Social Movements and Individual Needs in
    Contemporary Society.* Philadelphia: Temple University Press.

Moore, Sally Falk. 1972. "Legal Liability and Evolutionary Interpretation: Some Aspects of
    Strict Liability, Self-Help and Collective Responsibility." Pp. 51-108 in *The Allocation of
    Responsibility,* edited by M. Gluckman. Manchester: Manchester University Press.

Nadel, S. F. 1957. *The Theory of Social Structure.* London: Cohen and West.

Olson, Mancur. [1965] 1971. *The Logic of Collective Action.* Rev. ed. New York: Schocken.

Przeworski, Adam. 1985. *Capitalism and Social Democracy.* Cambridge: Cambridge University
    Press.

Rankin, Mary B. 1971. *Early Chinese Revolutionaries: Radical Intellectuals in Changhai and
    Chekiang, 1902-1911.* Cambridge, MA: Harvard University Press.

Schwarcz, Vera. 1986. *The Chinese Enlightenment: Intellectuals and the Legacy of the May Fourth Movement of 1919.* Berkeley: University of California Press.

Sewell, William, Jr. 1985. "Ideologies and Social Revolutions: Reflections on the French Case." *Journal of Modern History* 57:57-85.

————. 1986. "Theory of Action, Dialectics and History: Comment on Coleman." *American Journal of Sociology* 93:166-72.

Spence, Jonathan. 1981. *The Gate of Heavenly Peace.* New York: Penguin.

Taylor, Charles. 1985a. "Self-Interpreting Animals." Pp. 45-76 in *Human Agency and Language: Philosophical Papers I.* Cambridge: Cambridge University Press.

————. 1985b. "The Person." Pp. 257-81 in *The Category of the Person: Anthropology, Philosophy, History,* edited by M. Carrithers, S. Collins, and S. Lukes. Cambridge: Cambridge University Press.

————. 1989. *The Sources of the Self.* Cambridge, MA: Harvard University Press.

Thompson, E. P. [1963] 1968. *The Making of the English Working Class.* Rev. ed. Harmondsworth: Penguin.

Thurston, Anne. 1988. *Enemies of the People: The Ordeal of Intellectuals in China's Great Cultural Revolution.* Cambridge, MA: Harvard University Press.

Tilly, Charles. 1978. *From Mobilization to Revolution.* Reading, MA: Addison-Wesley.

Wacquant, Loic and Craig Calhoun. 1989. "Interêt, Rationalité, et Histoire: à propos d'un debat Americain sur la thèorie d'action." *Actes de la Recherche en Sciences Sociales* 78:41-60.

Weber, Max. [1922] 1968. *Economy and Society,* translated by G. Roth and K. Wittich. Berkeley: University of California Press.

Wilson, Bryan. 1970. *Rationality.* Oxford: Basil Blackwell.

Winch, Peter. 1958. *The Idea of a Social Science.* London: Routledge.

Wright, Eric Olin. 1985. *Classes.* London: New Left.

5

The Micro-Macro Dilemma in Organizational Research: Implications of Role-System Theory

Paul DiMaggio

How do the actions of individual agents produce and reproduce the constraining structures evident at more aggregated levels of analysis? This question's answer has come to constitute the Holy Grail of social science theory. This chapter will not produce the Holy Grail but will pursue the more modest objectives of developing a useful way of thinking about the problem as it manifests itself in the study of organizations and suggesting a few lines of attack.

The micro-macro distinction refers to continuous variation among phenomena along the dimensions of time, space, and number (Collins 1981). More macro-analytic levels comprise events or structures that are more long lasting, embrace more people, and are more spatially extensive than relatively micro levels. Thus the micro-macro distinction is not the same as the opposition between psychological and structural explanation. The argument that a member of a four-person exchange system who has access to two persons only through a third is less autonomous than one who has access to each directly is structural but relatively micro. A model that posits relationships between distributions of personality attributes in a large population and system outcomes is psychological but macro. For similar reasons, to identify agency with micro analysis and structure with macro analysis is also misleading.

AUTHOR'S NOTE: *For helpful comments on this chapter, I am grateful to Emmanuel Lazega, Woody Powell, and participants in Yale's Complex Organizations Workshop.*

Why is the "micro-macro dilemma" a dilemma? If we are concerned with generically micro or macro processes outside of an organizational context and specify our scope conditions carefully, it is not. Blau's theory of inequality and heterogeneity (1977), for example, provides extraordinarily valuable insights into macro processes. We need only worry about the micro side if we apply it to organizations, at which point it becomes necessary to explain why parameters are more consolidated or certain attributes more salient in some organizations than in others. Most good research emphasizes a single analytic level but takes into account factors operating at other levels. Hackman and Oldham (1980), for example, focus on relationships between task characteristics and worker attitudes but are careful to specify the organization-level conditions that must be satisfied if work redesign is to do any good.

Social scientists erect three kinds of bridges across the micro-macro divide. The first is what Collins (1981) calls *micro-translation*, which requires only that the researcher offer plausible accounts of how macro-structural models are consistent with what we know about micro-level processes. For example, to explain the relationship between organizational size and organizational differentiation, one must be able to describe the ways in which growth in the number of employees produces practical problems to which managers respond by designing smaller, more numerous work groups (Blau and Schoenherr 1971).

A second form of articulation, by *aggregation*, is more demanding in that it requires modeling macro outcomes as cumulations of micro events. Demographic models exemplify this strategy when they account for changes in distributions of organizational attributes as the result of varying rates of birth, death, and transition among organizations with and without such attributes; so do models that explain societal income inequality as a function of interrank wage differentials within organizations and the distribution of organizations with differing numbers of ranks (Thurow 1975).

A final type of articulation comprises *systems* explanations. These are more complex still because they treat macro outcomes as interactions, rather than simply summations, or lower-unit actions: for example, modeling levels of job segregation between men and women as the result not just of differential rates of movement in and out of jobs but also of the effects of changes in such levels on the rates at which men and women are attracted to or driven out of gender-typed positions (Jacobs 1989). Population-ecology models that include density and competition parameters (e.g., indicating the effect of the size of a generalist population on the death rates of specialists) exemplify systems explanations, as do studies that compare many organizations and treat parameters of models of *intra*organizational processes as variables affected by organization-level attributes (Hannan and Freeman 1989; Blau and Alba 1982).

ORGANIZATIONS AS THE SOLUTION TO SOCIOLOGY'S MICRO-MACRO DILEMMA

Interest in articulating micro and macro analysis evolved out of the reaction to tight-fit models of social systems represented by both Parsonsian and Marxian versions of functionalism, the weaknesses of which are by now well known. The consequence of the reaction, as Alexander (1987) has argued, was increasing distance between theory and research and a proliferation of sectarian theoretical solutions. Much of the grand theory of the 1980s attempted to escape the postfunctionalist impasse by returning to the first Parsonsian problem—that of the theory of action—and developing accounts of the fit between micro and macro that are loosely coupled and consistent with what research tells us about the world. A peculiarity of this otherwise admirable work is that it almost invariably ignored the organizational level of analysis, which would seem to be a natural point of micro/macro interchange.

Outside the realm of grand theory, the quest for a solution to micro-macro dilemmas took quite a different form, as organizational analysis became a privileged site for addressing linkages between societal conditions and individual behavior. Indeed, the most exciting fields within sociology have been those in which organizations have been used to address the micro-macro dilemma via *translation*. Twenty years ago, for example, sociologists who studied the state (whether influenced by Parsonsian functionalism or the Miliband/Poulantzas debates) often asserted a general fit between the behavior of governments and national developmental imperatives or the interests of capital. By contrast, contemporary political sociology conceives of the state as a set of corporate actors, loosely coupled agencies with distinct interests, competing or cooperating with other organizations in particular policy areas (Skocpol 1985; Laumann and Knoke 1988). Analyzing the state in organizational terms enables such scholars to understand historical and cross-national variability in political response to "social problems" and political mobilization and to develop arguments that reflect the multiple paths of development represented in the world system.

A similar shift can be seen in the sociology of culture. Early practitioners emphasized links between macro-societal or historical variation and the content of art and literature, positing connections, for example, between the rise of consumer capitalism and the content of magazine biographies (Lowenthal 1961). By contrast, the production of culture approach, which was rapidly assimilated into the common sense of the field, views cultural products as outputs of organizations or industry systems and explains change by investigating decision-making and filtering processes at the organizational and industrial levels of analysis (Peterson and Berger 1975; Hirsch 1972). The advantages are substantial: The focus on organizations enables researchers to specify the mechanisms that produce varying styles, contents, and levels of innovation and explain thematic variation among different communication media and art forms.

Organizational analysis contributed to political and cultural sociology by pushing research in a more "micro" direction. By contrast, in social stratification, the organizational turn represented a shift toward more "macro" units of analysis. Whereas in 1970 the dominant paradigm drew on human-capital theory and social psychology to model status attainment as the product of individual attributes and dispositions, in recent years, labor market segmentation models have emphasized the ways in which industrial characteristics and employer attributes constrain the allocation of opportunity (Baron 1984; Kalleberg 1989; Granovetter and Tilly 1988).

Migration to the organizational level of analysis in these and other areas of sociology has done much to address the micro-macro dilemma. More powerful theories and empirical explanations have been produced, standards of micro-translation are higher, and theory and research are more clearly linked.

ORGANIZATIONS AS THE PROBLEM

If this were all there was to it, we could declare victory and retire. More interesting and sophisticated approaches to theory and research, however, yield more interesting and sophisticated questions as well as answers. By shifting their attention to organizations, scholars in effect trade one micro-macro dilemma for two: micro and organizational ("meso") levels and meso and macro.

An oil field metaphor may be useful here. Most of the organizational solutions to the micro-macro problem have assumed, first, that people and organizations behave purposefully and, second, that attributes of persons and organizations are fairly good proxies for their strategies, utility functions, or structural positions.

To do so is efficient—it means one can use readily available data, for one thing—and, given the high payoff of organizationally focused micro-macro

translations, it has been an excellent way to proceed. In effect, the functionalist legacy and the isolation of organizations from the sociological mainstream left high-grade oil in big pools near the surface. Once the easy oil has
been pumped, however, researchers confront the double articulation problem
as more difficult questions push toward complex, less elegant models linking
micro and meso, and meso and macro, analytic levels.

Take, for example, research on organizations and social stratification.
Early work established causal paths between organizational attributes and
individual outcomes, but, in doing so, it raised new questions, too complex
to be addressed by adding organizational variables to status-attainment
models, about organizational and environmental factors responsible for
variation in employment practices that influence employees' life chances.
Many such questions pointed to problems of interlevel articulation, either
meso-macro (e.g., Why do some organizations but not others have internal
job ladders?) or micro-meso (e.g., Why are some employees more likely than
others to be in jobs that are part of job ladders?) (Cohen and Pfeffer 1986;
Baron et al. 1986; Braddock and McPartland 1987).

Another example comes from political sociology, which has benefited
from two critical innovations, both of which brought renewed attention to
the organizational level of analysis: resource-mobilization theory (Zald and
McCarthy 1979), with its emphasis on social movement organizations to
explain the contingent relationship between individual dissatisfaction and
political change, and state-centered theory (Skocpol 1985; Block 1987),
which focuses on the interests and activities of state managers and their
agencies to explain the contingent relationship between elite wishes and state
policies.

These approaches brought us far beyond social psychological models of
political dissent and instrumentalist or structural/functionalist versions of
state theory. But their initial formulations could not easily explain, for
example, why agencies differ in their capacity to take advantage of structural
opportunities for autonomy or why some social movement organizations are
more effective than others that are equally resourceful. One result has been
research like Laumann and Knoke's trail-blazing study, *The Organizational
State* (1988), which focuses on the connections between political events and
patterns of interorganizational relations in two policy domains, those of
health and energy. The authors' strategy was to go beyond micro-macro
translation in two ways: first, by emphasizing meso-macro articulation (of
organizational networks and policy outcomes) and, second, by developing a
systems rather than a translation explanation. Their method was expensive
and time-consuming, but such costs are necessary to get to the hard oil.

INSTITUTIONS, NETWORKS, AND
NADEL'S PARADOX

I have argued that, in one stage of scientific progress, the Parsonsian functionalist legacy is the problem and organizations are the solution. In the second, once the considerable benefits of translation to the organizational level are gained, organizations become a problem, requiring the solution to two, rather than one, dilemmas of articulation—micro-meso and meso-macro. Paradoxically, at this stage, the Parsonsian legacy again becomes a resource.

I refer to a particular part of that legacy, role-systems theory, a critical element in Parsons's solution to the problem of order—that is, of articulating the micro behavior of locally situated persons and groups to the macro regularities of the social system (1951; Parsons and Shils 1951; Alexander and Giesen 1987). I shall argue that, although his use of role-system theory was flawed, Parsons's work points both to problems in the way that much organizational research ordinarily proceeds and to some useful alternatives.

Parsons began his quest with crisp and still timely critiques of the Hobbesian and utilitarian solutions to the problem of order (1937). Neither, he argues, explains why most people pursue legitimate interests in legitimate ways, how persons of varying "needs dispositions" manage to coexist, and why those to whom little is allocated accept the rules of the game.

Parsons's own solution speaks to micro and macro levels and to the connections between them. His micro story uses object-relations theory to explain why people are disposed to win the approval of others and to value normative behavior for its own sake. His macro story highlights value consensus and the division of labor. More important for our purposes is the "status/role complex," by which individuals with varied needs dispositions are matched to differentiated positions. A status is a social position, and a role is the pattern of behavior associated with a status. "Roles," write Parsons and Shils (1951, p. 23), are "institutionalized when they are fully congruous with the prevailing culture patterns and are organized around expectations of conformity with morally sanctioned patterns of value-orientations shared by members of the collectivity."

Three aspects of the status/role complex command our attention. First, insofar as roles are institutionalized—that is, to the extent that role labels represent widely shared typifications with associated legitimating accounts—they are powerful sources of standardization and order, eliminating transaction costs by facilitating routine, scripted interactions and serving to reproduce existing macro structures. Second, insofar as behavior is governed by roles, Parsons's notion points to the context dependence of individual behavior: The same person may behave, think, or feel quite differently depending on the role that a situation evokes.

Third, inherent in this view of roles is a *duality of culture and structure*: Role relations consist of "classificatory criteria . . . which orient the actor to the object by virtue of the fact that it belongs to a universalistically defined *class*" *and* "relational criteria . . . by which the object as a particular object is placed in a specific significant *relation* to ego and thus to other significant objects" (Parsons 1951, p. 89). In other words, a status/role complex is both a shared typification and a location in a relational network.

Thus individual behavior produces macro regularities as a consequence of the dual constraints of culture (or institutionalized typifications) and relational networks. Because "roles" are the locus at which institutions and relational networks intersect, they are crucial elements in articulating micro and macro levels of analysis. Unfortunately, Parsons retreated from the brink of this insight, in effect reducing the cultural aspect of roles, first, to its normative dimension and then, for most purposes, to six stylized "pattern variables" (DiMaggio and Powell 1991). Social relations were deemphasized and likewise stylized, deprived of their particularity, and consigned to an arid ego-alter model.

Whereas Parsons noted the institutional/relational duality in role systems only to flee into theoretical formalism, in his *A Theory of Social Structure* (1957), S. F. Nadel confronted it directly. Like Parsons, Nadel viewed roles as the fundamental building blocks of social structure: "Societies are made up of people," he wrote, but research attention must focus on "ways of acting governed by rules and hence in some measure stereotyped." But, whereas Parsons stressed the "rights and obligations" attendant to roles, Nadel focused upon the social relations that defined them. Roles, he wrote, are an analytic means of aggregating social relations by which "we arrive at the structure of a society through abstracting from the concrete population and its behavior the pattern, or network of relationships" (Nadel 1957, p. 12).

Nadel's discussion of role systems is remarkably prescient. By bringing indeterminacy in role systems to the center of analysis, he anticipates Goffman (1967) and ethnomethodology. His landmark contribution, however, was to point to the possibility of a formal mathematical approach to analyzing social relations (developed by White et al. 1976 and Boorman and White 1976) as a means of characterizing and comparing social structures.

Despite this emphasis, Nadel (1957, p. 28) was troubled by the cultural aspect of roles as "class concepts," with related norms existing not just in "performance" but also as bits "of knowledge . . . or perhaps only in an image that people carry in their heads." To find transposable regularities in role systems and compare their structures, it is essential to reduce relations to a common metric. Yet, insofar as they fail to capture qualitative variation among roles, such metrics may be misleading, because roles always "include qualities, and hence *differentiae* of an irreducible nature. . . . Each relationship contains unique features which render it incomparable to the others, offering nothing in the way of a common criterion or dimension." How then "can we extract . . . any embracing order while still paying attention to these qualitative characteristics?" (Nadel 1957, p. 102).

Nadel's solution—to abstract role relations along the dimensions of authority and control over resources—is less convincing than his characterization of the problem. What I call *Nadel's paradox* is precisely this dilemma: A satisfactory approach to articulating micro and macro levels of analysis requires simultaneous attention to both cultural and relational aspects of role-governed behavior. But cultural aspects (i.e., those institutionalized in cognition) are intrinsically qualitative, pushing researchers toward taxonomic specificity, whereas concrete social relations require mathematical reduction involving high levels of abstraction.[1]

Early work on social roles, reflecting Parsons's normative emphasis, hewed to the cultural and taxonomic, with the severe limitations of any purely descriptive, particularizing enterprise. Subsequent work has employed network analysis to focus on relational aspects of roles with more fruitful results. But network approaches are constrained by their inability to abstract culture away in its entirety and thus smuggle cultural understandings in by the back door (in choices of relations about which to ask or evocative, field-based interpretations of structural patterns) or substitute stylized rational actor assumptions for the view of behaviors as guided by institutionalized rules.

Outside of network analysis, researchers in sociology, in general, and organizational sociology, in particular, have rarely pursued the potential of role theory as a bridge across the micro-macro border (but see Barley 1989). Part of this neglect is a consequence of intellectual history. Parsons's version carried heavy excess baggage, and the reaction against functionalism was so strong that the wheat was discarded with the chaff. Nadel's role theory suffers none of these limitations but, perhaps because he was a British anthropologist writing in Parsons's shadow, his book has never attained its deserved place in the social theory canon.

IMPLICATIONS OF ROLE THEORY FOR RESEARCH

There is more than historical accident in the neglect of role theory, however, for the notion of "roles" has never really been discarded. Rather, it receives ceremonial recognition in introductory texts without influencing much of what researchers actually do. The reason for this is a lack of fit between the insights of role theory and standard approaches to research, in at least three respects.

First, whereas role theory suggests that the fundamental actors are "persons-in-role" (i.e., that role-related behavior, and not behavior per se, is patterned and thus predictable), the units of analysis in most of our studies are persons (often in a particular role—survey respondent—that does not bear directly on their organizational performance). It follows from role theory that, to predict people's behavior, we should understand the full set of roles they occupy and the extent to which each of these is likely to bear on the behavior we wish to predict. Most research takes more of a shotgun approach.

Second, research focuses on actors and their attributes, about which it is easy to collect data, whereas our theories are all about interaction and institutions (Abbott 1988). Attributes are taken as proxies for interaction patterns or role incumbencies, but this is rarely theorized (Blau 1977 is an exception) and (except in network studies) rarely confirmed. Although network analysis has become more common in organizational research (see, e.g., DiMaggio 1986; Laumann and Knoke 1988; Galaskiewicz 1985), it remains weakly institutionalized in standard statistical packages and required research methods curricula.

Third, role theory distinguishes between roles that are institutionalized and those that are not and calls attention to the content of roles and the scripted quality of role behavior. There are several implications: (a) Efforts to use individual attributes to predict behavior should link them to plausibly institutionalized roles; (b) the degrees to which particular roles are (1) institutionalized and (2) associated with particular individual attributes varies at the organizational level and influences the predictive power of such role location and attributes; (c) unacknowledged interorganizational variation of this kind may produce model heterogeneity; and (d) we should study the cognitive aspect of institutionalized roles directly whenever possible.

Nadel's paradox admits no easy solution: The nexus between relational and classificatory aspects of role systems is ineluctably complex. Shared typifications are diffused, altered, and reinforced through social interaction, and social ties are more enduring when they are institutionalized in named roles. But degrees of institutionalization, and of correspondence between role names and relational patterns, vary among roles and role systems in ways that must be discovered and explained, not established by theoretical fiat.

In the rest of the chapter, I illustrate these abstract points by discussing concrete ways of using cultural or relational aspects of roles (or both) to bridge both the micro-meso and meso-macro boundaries. I treat the two articulation problems separately because, although formally similar, they are distinctive. For one thing, organizations are not intendedly rational in the same sense that people are. Persons often have reasonably clear and standardized ideas of what they want; organizations' operative goals, by contrast, tend to be contested and ambiguous. For many purposes, assuming individual rationality is a useful heuristic; organizational rationality is always a variable.

Neither are organizations "actors" in the same way that people are. Individuals ordinarily remember what they have done from one day to the next, monitor their own behavior closely, and make some attempt to be consistent. By contrast, only some of what people do in organizational roles is authorized, not all authorized actors know what others are doing, and authorized actors are often unaware of what unauthorized ones are up to. As Cohen and March (1974) demonstrate, this makes time extremely important: Decisions depend on sequence and work load, which in turns affects the persons and interests represented. If intrapersonal consistency is often a useful assumption, organizational consistency is always a variable.

Finally, persons' attributes and organizational roles are more strongly institutionalized than organizations' attributes and roles in organizational fields. Labels we give people—occupation, educational attainment, gender, and race—are more numerous, are more sharply defined, and carry more cultural baggage than those we give organizations within an industry. Organizations' employees occupy formal positions that are likewise highly institutionalized, whereas our vocabulary for talking about the positions of organizations in their fields is relatively impoverished. Thus data on individual attributes and positions often capture more about how people behave and how others treat them than do organizational attributes. Organizations more frequently have distinct identities and structural positions that are irreducible to their measurable attributes.

Institutions, Networks, and the Micro-Meso Dilemma

Let us begin with the first boundary dilemma, the articulation of individual behavior with organizational outcomes. Organizations are peculiar in that they consist of formal roles, often highly institutionalized, as well as informal social positions, which may or may not correspond to these formal roles. Moreover, they tend to be highly bounded, and thus behavior in them is often more elaborately institutionalized than behavior in organizational fields.

Logics and strategies. One effect of psychology's cognitive revolution is to complicate the view that rules governing roles are characteristically role specific. It seems more likely that role behavior is constituted negotiatively out of a small number of orientations to action and a finite number of action scripts operating at the taken-for-granted level of cognition. Institutions work at two levels: upon the availability and legitimacy of particular orientations and scripts and upon roles as switching systems invoking particular scripts and orientations. Consequently, research on organizational role systems must attend not just to how people understand roles but to the institutional stuff available for role construction within the organization and in its environment.

A group of notions that capture the ways in which action scripts are bundled not only in discrete roles but in institutional predispositions that influence role performance comes out of recent work on "logics of action" (Friedland and Alford 1991), "strategies" (Swidler 1986), and the "habitus" (Bourdieu 1990). Each of these suggests that "culture" is an inventory of interdependent category schemes, scripts, and expectations upon which people draw as they devise their interpretations of and responses to environmental stimuli. Such ideas are particularly well developed in research on social cognition (ably summarized in Kiesler and Sproull 1982).

Sometimes strategies can be inferred from sequences of behaviors (Abbott 1988). In research on the relationship between cultural capital, educational attainment, and marital selection, John Mohr and I (DiMaggio and Mohr 1985) learned that the correlation between cultural capital and husband's educational attainment was very high for young women from upper-middle-class homes who dropped out of college but trivial for married women with education beyond the B.A. We interpreted this interaction as reflecting two strategies related to distinct conceptions of the gender division of labor.

How can such ideas be used in research on organizations? Consider management efforts to implement organizational change by altering the structure of work groups to enable employees to exercise more autonomy in designing the work flow, assigning tasks, hiring members, and allocating productivity-based bonuses. Research tells us that success is contingent upon various factors consistent with rational actor models: satisfaction with existing compensation levels and employment security, confidence in management, and executives' capacity to defuse opposition from middle managers (Hackman and Oldham 1980; Kanter 1983). But rational actor models are limited: At the individual level, both opponents and supporters of work redesign can offer plausible rational accounts to bolster their positions; at the organizational level, the fate of redesign reflects more than a simple aggregation of individual preferences.

At the individual level, employees' willingness to support redesign is likely to be linked to underlying schema or strategies of action. Those who view the employment relationship as antagonistic or whose orientation toward rationality is primarily individualistic are likely to oppose it. Those with collectivist orientations toward rationality may support change if they see the employment relationship as non-zero sum but oppose it if they see it as antagonistic. Employees who view their jobs as steps in careers may find participation attractive; those who anticipate remaining in their jobs may oppose or support it based on other premises.

So far, none of this departs from conventional social psychological theory (e.g., of reference groups) or method. But once we focus on roles rather than persons, we deviate from attitude studies in three ways. First, rather than assume that employees have stable attitudes, we posit that most employees have access to a range of linked interpretations and dispositions that are triggered by specific roles, which act as switching systems among strategies of action. The same person may view change in different ways in her capacity as a union member or as a member of a particular work group. Thus measurement of dispositions must be role specific. And in order to know how individual dispositions are linked to organizational outcomes, we must know something about the key roles and action settings in which dispositions are transformed into action. If union settings evoke collective, antimanagement scripts and work groups trigger individualistic or collective/cooperative schema, then the relative weight of union-based and workplace events in influencing successful adoption will affect the manner in which sentiments emerge. Moreover, where roles are new or poorly defined, available role scripts will be generalized as resources in struggles over the definition of new positions (Stark 1986).

Second, to articulate micro and macro levels, we must examine not only individual sentiments but distributions of sentiments. A key question about distributions is whether they are sufficiently one-sided so as to stifle dissent. As Granovetter and Soong (1988) argue, at some threshold (itself a variable), each person is unwilling to oppose openly what he or she perceives to be the popular view. If supporters believe that enough others oppose work redesign, for example, they will keep quiet; and if they have a lower silence threshold than opponents, they may come to believe that opposition is more widespread than it is and lose the day even if they are in a numerical majority.

Third, because work redesign deinstitutionalizes employee roles, worker response will vary with the extent to which roles have been institutionalized in the first place. To the extent that roles are strongly institutionalized, adoption will be difficult; to the extent that they are not, adoption will be more likely. This is consistent with the common observation that work redesign is more effective in new plants than in old ones; although that observation is unsurprising, it is one that rational actor, resource-dependence, or simple attitude models would have trouble predicting.

More generally, this perspective shifts from seeing attitudes as individual traits that exert influence through aggregation to viewing cognition as consisting of repertoires that are invoked by roles and interact with properties of the organization. One of the few examples of this kind of argument is Basil Bernstein's contention, based on a substantial research program, that British working-class school failure is produced by an interaction of student cognitive styles and features of classroom organization (1973; see also Greenwood and Hinings 1988).

Intraorganizational ecology. Organizational change reflects the movement of different kinds of persons in and out of organizations. Demographic processes in organizations influence career opportunities (and thus incentive structures), patterns of conflict and coalition, and definitions of organizational roles (Pfeffer 1983). Such processes are constrained by such institutionalized aspects of roles as age grading and gender specificity (Lawrence 1988).

Demographic intuitions apply to research on rates of organizational change. As Zucker (1987) has argued, organizations vary in the extent to which processes and structures are institutionalized at the organizational, as opposed to the environmental, level. When roles are strongly institutionalized within an organization and weakly institutionalized outside, persistence is likely to be high. When they are weakly institutionalized within but strongly institutionalized in the environment, change may be more rapid.

It follows from this that organizations' susceptibility to normative isomorphic pressures is a positive function of rates of entry to (and degree of external recruitment for) and exit from salient organizational roles. Moreover, the degree to which practices in subunits are institutionalized and thus resistant to change may be a negative function of entry and exit rates. For example, software companies with high or moderate rates of executive turnover may be more likely, all else being equal, to remain at the forefront of their field (Walker 1985).

Much may be gained by applying ecological methods and models to studying the movement of persons through organizations. The distribution of different types of persons in an organization may vary in its consequences for organizational action depending on the rate at which different kinds of persons are recruited and depart. As Jacobs (1989) has shown, women enter male-gender-typed occupations at brisk rates but leave them almost as frequently. Population models represent a natural way to study such processes (Hannan and Freeman 1978) and may also be useful in illustrating links between formal organizational roles and positions in relational networks. Consider, for example, the implications of high turnover rates among women executives for organizational policies that are especially salient to women. To the extent that effective advocacy relies on strong informal relations among potential advocates and gatekeepers, turnover is hypothesized to undermine the potential for change, regardless of the *proportion* of women in particular roles. Because newcomers are marginal and exits may destabilize regions of informal networks where leavers are prominent, high turnover rates are likely to prevent mobilization.

Studies of intraorganizational networks. Intraorganizational network research has already yielded a rich harvest. As role theory suggests, the direct measurement of relational patterns often permits one to predict behavior more effectively than using attributes of persons as proxies. Ibarra (1989) found that participation in innovations by employees of a midsized advertising agency was much better predicted by network centrality than by several measures of personal characteristics, career experience, or formal position. Barley's study of the effects of technological change on occupational role relations within two hospital radiology departments (1989) revealed distinct structural patterns that were poorly captured by job titles alone. Walker (1985) found network location a better predictor of software firm managers' cognitions about product development than formal role and other individual attributes.

Relatively little work has used data on social relations to predict or explain change at the organizational level of analysis. One of the few examples, Romo's study of a residential adolescent mental health care facility (1986), found that patterns of structural cleavage revealed by block models portended a major "blowup" and identified staff and patients who would leave the facility.

There are several directions in which such research might move. One involves the relationship between network structure and organizational effectiveness: Romo, for example, argues that certain patterns of organizational relations are untenable and conflict producing (1986). Anheier and Romo (1988) identify distinct relational configurations that produce "structural stalemate," "factionalism," or prolonged "organizational failure" (Meyer and Zucker 1989).[2] Nelson (1989) contends that high-conflict organizations have more unreciprocated and ambiguous role relations and weaker correspondence between relationally and formally defined roles. Such arguments are highly plausible, but more comparative research and theoretical development are necessary to develop these insights.

Second, research may explore connections between relational and cultural aspects of role systems. The extent to which relationally defined roles and shared typifications are mutually supportive or inconsistent, and the conditions under which each is the case, are empirical matters of substantial importance. One might hypothesize that roles are more strongly institutionalized when analysis of informal organizational networks yields structurally equivalent groups consisting of persons with similar role labels and less strongly institutionalized when structural locations crosscut individual attributes and organizational positions. Following Blau (1977) and research on homophily in organizational friendships (McPherson and Smith-Lovin 1987; Marsden 1988), the former is more likely the greater the extent to which member attributes are consolidated and correlated with formal titles.

Third, comparative structural research can address the ways in which informal networks condition relationships among conventional variables in organizational models. Two hypotheses follow from the foregoing discussion. (a) Rational actor models predict change less well in organizations with stalemate-inducing relational structures than in those with structures that facilitate mobilization (Kanter 1983). (b) The effects of individual attributes and formal roles on behavior and sentiments are stronger in organizations in which such variables are closely articulated to network position than in those in which they are not.

Institutions, Networks, and the Meso-Macro Dilemma

In this section, we turn to organizational sociology's second micro-macro dilemma: how the behavior of organizations articulates with the structure and performance of organizational fields, industries, or societies themselves. Meso-macro linkages are particularly important in articulating organizational sociology to the discipline as a whole, because they generate many of the macro structures with which general sociology is concerned: structures of social mobility, patterns of political stability and disorder, and rates and direction of cultural change.

Meso-macro differs from micro-meso articulation in several respects. Because organizations "act" through multiple personnel, the "actorness" of organizations is more complex than that of persons. And organizational positions are less well institutionalized than individual attributes and formal roles; organizational fields often have fewer players than formal organizations, and relations among them are more likely to reflect vividly experienced organizational profiles than institutionalized role labels (White 1981; Blau 1982). In other words, the relational aspects are relatively more important than the cultural aspects of role systems in organizational fields as compared with role systems in organizations.

Positions in organizational fields. Research on interorganizational networks (IONs) has yielded impressive results, revealing that patterns of relations among organizations influence the strategies they pursue, the people they recruit, and their opportunities for growth and survival (e.g., DiMaggio 1986; Mizruchi and Schwartz 1987; Singh et al. 1991). Such studies have ordinarily failed to exploit data on the full variety of ties that constitute network structures and thus have failed to determine the positions of organizations in them, however.

There are three fundamental kinds of interorganizational relations. First, and most often emphasized in ION research, are formal ties between organizations *as corporate actors*: joint ventures, board interlocks, membership in fieldwide associations, resource exchanges, or formal liaison arrangements. Second, *informal ties* include the full range of social relationships among consequential members of the organization, whether or not these relations are formally sanctioned. The few studies that have used data on informal relations have usually focused upon ties among chief executives. Third, *personnel flows* constitute an important form of interorganizational relation that, despite Baty et al.'s early work (1971), has rarely been employed in empirical research. It seems likely that, for many purposes, the position of an organization in its field is a consequence not only of formal ties with other organizations, or even of its CEO's network, but of the full set of informal relations and personnel flows as well. To my knowledge, no ION study has used information on all three kinds of ties.

The importance of formal relations is self-evident and amply documented. The bearing of informal relations is more complex and has been neglected, except for studies of networks of professionals (Galaskiewicz and Wasserman 1988) and executives (DiMaggio and Romo 1984). Such relations are particularly interesting because of the organizational consequences of relations that may be entered into for personal, as well as corporate, motives. Although he did not use formal network methods, Useem (1984) developed this insight in his study of relationships among top corporate managers in the United States and United Kingdom. Executives participate in formal and informal fieldwide associations for a combination of motives, in the process accruing social capital that both enhances their own status and acquires information for companies with which they are affiliated. Despite tension between the "classwide logic" sustained by such activities and the "company logic" of short-term competitive profit seeking, the network produces a collectively rational elite that works to maintain public policies that business supports. Galaskiewicz (1985) measured informal ties directly and found that the network proximity of CEOs to a local business elite predicted an important expression of "classwide logic," corporate philanthropic giving.

Another example is the case of local branches of multinational enterprises. Such firms participate in two organizational fields, one defined by the MNCs of which they are a part and one defined by the host country environment (Arias 1988; Westney 1988).[3] The subsidiary as a whole is enmeshed in close, vertical relations with the parent company as well as in a range of formal relations with agencies of the host country state. Chief executives are usually parent country nationals or, occasionally, well-socialized host country nationals educated in parent country graduate programs and closely tied to staff of the parent firm. But data on formal relations and CEO ties by themselves may be of limited use in predicting the subsidiary's autonomy with respect to the MNC parent and its ability to navigate the host country's political environment. Information on the local networks of host country managers and staff may be essential to understanding the position of the subsidiary in the local environment as well as its autonomy with respect to the parent MNC. One might hypothesize, for example, that subsidiaries with staff who are integrated into local elite networks exercise more autonomy in relation to both the host country and the parent company than do subsidiaries without such links.

As Blalock (1984, p. 358) has argued, network analysis may complement contextual research on interlevel effects by identifying distinct positions within which context effects will differ. This insight has direct application to studies that use industry dummy variables to model organizational behavior. "Industry" is likely to mean something very different to dominant firms, on the one hand, and small producers, on the other; thus models that rely on industry dummies are likely to suffer from heterogeneity. By identifying distinct positions in organizational fields, network analysis provides a means of overcoming the heterogeneity dilemma.

Organizational fields as units of analysis. Questions about the behavior of fields as a whole require field-level measurement and comparison of what we might call industrial role systems (see White 1981). With such measures, one may assess the relationship between the structure of the field and such dependent variables as rates of innovation, solidarity versus conflict in attempts to influence the state, and social control at the industrial level.

Several pioneering studies have been completed, including Laumann and Knoke's (1988) comparison of IONs in the health and energy policy domains. Comparative research has also been conducted on local hospital networks (Fennell et al. 1987), West African development consortia (Anheier 1987), research organizations (Shrum and Wuthnow 1988), county rural-development organization sets (Knoke and Rogers 1979), the history of the U.S. intercorporate network (Mizruchi 1982), arts industries (DiMaggio and Romo 1984), and national intercorporate networks (Scott 1987).

These studies vary in questions asked, data collected, and methods of analysis; in particular, the absence of consensus on theoretically salient dimensions of field structure impedes cumulation. Nonetheless, they provide enticing evidence for the utility of a comparative structural approach. Laumann and Knoke (1988) discovered broad similarities between the health and energy fields, both in relational structure and in the predictors and consequences of relations at the organizational and dyadic levels. Anheier (1987) discovered an interaction between state policies and network structures that facilitated effective resource mobilization in one consortium and stymied it in another. DiMaggio and Romo (1984) found consistent patterns of hierarchy in a field of relatively homogeneous organizations, a complex and highly differentiated structure in a more heterogeneous field, and historically rooted anomalies in the structure of a third.

Few studies have collected data on enough IONs to permit hypothesis testing. Further development of comparative analysis of organizational fields requires not just more data, however, but systematization of theoretical dimensions. Ultimately, one would hope to assess the effects of fieldwide structures upon intrafield processes, after the fashion of Blau and Schwartz's (1984) comparative analysis of factors influencing intermarriage patterns in U.S. SMSAs. Such an approach might enable researchers to test hypotheses using structural (and other) field-level variables to explain such aggregate outcomes as rates of organizational foundings and deaths, levels of innovation, patterns of inequality, and effectiveness in pursuing legislative or administrative action.

CONCLUSION

In one sense, organizations have offered a solution to sociology's micro-macro dilemma: by shifting from theories employing almost entirely macro or micro references to theory and research at the organizational, or "meso," level of analysis, scholars have used organizations as a micro-macro link to revitalize dormant or exhausted research areas. In accomplishing this, they have usually adopted the strategy of treating organizations and the people in them as rational, consistent entities. This is an efficient approach, and the intellectual payoff has been high.[4]

Once the dust has cleared, however, the initial triumphs (which almost always leave much variance unexplained) are followed by further drives into the heartland of explanation. This next stage requires engagement at a more complex level of theory, in which systems explanations succeed translations, and utilitarian assumptions are displaced by closer attention to institutional, collective, and emergent factors in organizational behavior. Studies in population ecology (Carroll 1988; Hannan and Freeman 1989), comparative analyses of causal processes within multiple organizations or fields (Lincoln et al. 1986; Laumann and Knoke 1988), contextual effects models (Lincoln and Zeitz 1980; Blalock 1984), and network analysis have already made substantial progress along these lines.

I have followed up three hunches that may yield additional help in understanding relations among units at different levels of analysis. (a) Organizational sociology faces two distinct articulation problems, micro-meso and meso-macro. (b) In addressing these dilemmas, we have something to learn from classical role-systems theory. (c) Bridges can be built by interpreting roles both as institutionalized typifications and as locations in relational networks.

It may appear misleading to anchor this argument in role-theory terminology because I have differed on so many points with Parsons's account. Specifically, I have argued that many roles, especially within inter-organizational fields, are weakly institutionalized, that cognitive typifications operate not only at the level of named roles but at many other levels, and that cognitive and relational aspects of role systems often stand in decided tension.

Nonetheless, three fundamental intuitions that follow from the role theory of Parsons, and especially Nadel, remain sound. First, macro structure derives from distributions of shared typifications and regularities in social relations. Second, patterns of articulation between shared typifications and interactional regularities are of special importance. Third, social reproduction and change are produced by systemic effects of social interactions of persons-in-roles rather than by aggregations of persons and their attributes. Whether or not the illustrative hypotheses provided in this chapter prove fruitful in exploiting these insights, if it stimulates readers to consider the problems that drive them in designing research, it will have achieved its purpose.

NOTES

1. *Qualitative* is used in two senses in social science writing: in opposition to *quantitative* (e.g., ethnography versus survey analysis) and in opposition to *formal* (discursively specific as distinct from formal and abstract). Because social scientists operate in a cultural tradition that includes an untheorized binary opposition between "hard" and "soft," the two senses are often conflated, but they should not be. I use *qualitative* only in the second sense. There is no reason that measurement of scripts, premises, and cognitive maps cannot be as precise and as quantitative as measurement of social relations; but there is good reason, as Nadel argues, that the former is unlikely to be as abstract.

2. The notion of stalemate was developed by Anheier in his dissertation and further elaborated by Anheier and Romo. Conversations with both of them over the years, and with Scott Boorman, have influenced my thinking about comparison among networks.

3. These thoughts were stimulated by informative conversations with Maria Arias, whose dissertation on the relationship between interfirm networks and human resources practices in Ecuador's pharmaceutical industry promises to be a model for research of this kind.

4. The distinction between rational and institutional models of action in systems models of macro phenomena is less simple and the disagreement is less fundamental than many suppose. Human behavior is often routine and often purposeful. Insofar as strategies of action are institutionalized in practical consciousness, behavior may be both routine *and* (in effect) purposive. Thus far, few would disagree. The trouble starts when one gets down to cases, that is, specifying sets of objective functions for particular actors.

In any instance, one must ask at least three questions. First, how broad are the proposed model's scope conditions? The narrower the scope, the more likely are particular rationality assumptions to suffice. (It is more reasonable to posit short-term wealth optimization as a universal objective in studies of investors than in research on businessmen as a group, more so for executives than for all corporate employees, more reasonable for corporate employees than for managers and staff of nonprofits or public agencies, and so on.) Second, how many objective functions are to be posited? The more differentiated the motives attributed to different kinds of actors, the more likely are models to work. A model of labor-management relations in unionized firms, for example, will have greater explanatory power if it posits different objectives for managers and workers (perhaps treating the utility functions of the latter as interdependent) than if it assumes that all actors try to optimize the same thing. Third, to what sorts of actors are purposes being attributed? As I argue below, it is more plausible to attribute purpose to persons than to organizations.

I doubt many researchers would find these observations terribly controversial. With respect to the problem of organizational rationality, J. Coleman, who is perhaps most closely identified with the view that organizations should be seen as rationally oriented corporate actors, makes only the modest claim that "it may well be that, for some investigations, corporate bodies such as formal organizations are usefully regarded as purposive actors, though in other research and theory in sociology, the coherence of their action would itself be taken as problematic" (Coleman 1986, p. 1312).

Because debates about rational models often proceed at high levels of theoretical (and at times polemical) abstraction, however, they tend to drive people into opposite camps. Outside the field of ideological battle, opponents and proponents of rational actor models may vary more in their optimism about what such models may achieve than in their theoretical presuppositions. Ultimately, this is a matter to be settled empirically: To the extent that rational actor models offer genuinely robust empirical results, their tractability makes them desirable.

REFERENCES

Abbott, Andrew. 1988. "Transcending General Linear Reality." *Sociological Theory* 6:169-86.
Alexander, Jeffrey C. 1987. *Twenty Lectures: Sociological Theory Since World War II.* New York: Columbia University Press.
Alexander, Jeffrey C. and Bernhard Giesen. 1987. "From Reduction to Linkage: The Long View of the Micro-Macro Debate." Pp. 1-42 in *The Micro-Macro Link,* edited by J. C. Alexander, B. Giesen, Richard Muench, and N. J. Smelser. Berkeley: University of California Press.
Anheier, Helmut. 1987. *Private Voluntary Organizations, Networks, and Development in Africa: A Comparative Study of Organizational Fields in Nigeria, Senegal and Togo.* Ph.D. dissertation, Yale University.
Anheier, Helmut K. and Frank Romo. 1988. "Structural Stalemate: Elements of a Theory of Structural Failures." Paper presented at the Sunbelt Social Network Conference VIII, San Diego.

Arias, Maria. 1988. "Human Resource Management Structures and Policies in the Ecuadorian Pharmaceutical Industries." Ph.D. dissertation prospectus, Yale University.

Barley, Stephen. 1989. "The Alignment of Technology and Structure." Manuscript. Cornell University, School of Industrial and Labor Relations.

Baron, James N. 1984. "Organizational Perspectives on Stratification." *Annual Review of Sociology* 10:37-69.

Baron, James N., Allison Davis-Blake, and William T. Bielby. 1986. "The Structure of Opportunity: How Promotion Ladders Vary Within and Among Organizations." *Administrative Science Quarterly* 31:248-73.

Baty, Gordon, William Evan, and Terry Rothermel. 1971. "Personnel Flows as Interorganizational Relations." *Administrative Science Quarterly* 11:207-23.

Bernstein, Basil. 1973. *Class, Codes and Control.* Vol. 3. Boston: Routledge & Kegan Paul.

Blalock, Hubert. 1984. "Contextual-Effects Models: Theoretical and Methodological Issues." *Annual Review of Sociology* 10:353-72.

Blau, Judith and Richard Alba. 1982. "Empowering Nets of Participation." *Administrative Science Quarterly* 27:363-79.

Blau, Peter M. 1977. *Inequality and Heterogeneity.* New York: Free Press.

———. 1982. "Structural Sociology and Network Analysis: An Overview." Pp. 273-79 in *Social Structure and Network Analysis,* edited by P. Marsden and N. Lin. Beverly Hills, CA: Sage.

Blau, Peter M. and Richard Schoenherr. 1971. *The Structure of Organizations.* New York: Basic Books.

Blau, Peter M. and Joseph E. Schwartz. 1984. *Crosscutting Social Circles: Testing a Macrostructural Theory of Intergroup Relations.* Orlando, FL: Academic Press.

Block, Fred. 1987. *Revisiting State Theory: Essays in Politics and Postindustrialism.* Philadelphia: Temple University Press.

Boorman, Scott A. and Harrison C. White. 1976. "Social Structure from Multiple Networks, II: Role Structure." *American Journal of Sociology* 81:1384-1446.

Bourdieu, Pierre. 1990. *The Logic of Practice.* Stanford, CA: Stanford University Press.

Braddock, Jomills Henry, II, and Alexander M. McPartland. 1987. "How Minorities Continue to Be Excluded from Equal Employment Opportunities: Research on Labor Market and Institutional Barriers." *Journal of Social Issues* 43:5-39.

Carroll, Glenn, R., ed. 1988. *Ecological Models of Organization.* Cambridge, MA: Ballinger.

Cohen, Michael and James G. March. 1974. *Leadership and Ambiguity: The American College President.* New York: McGraw-Hill.

Cohen, Yinon and Jeffrey Pfeffer. 1986. "Organizational Hiring Standards." *Administrative Science Quarterly* 31:1-24.

Coleman, James S. 1986. "Social Theory, Social Research, and a Theory of Action." *American Journal of Sociology* 91:1309-35.

Collins, Randall. 1981. "The Microfoundations of Macrosociology." *American Journal of Sociology* 86:984-1014.

DiMaggio, Paul. 1986. "Structural Analysis of Organizational Fields." *Research in Organizational Behavior* 8:335-70.

DiMaggio, Paul and John Mohr. 1985. "Cultural Capital, Educational Attainment, and Marital Selection." *American Journal of Sociology* 90:1231-61.

DiMaggio, Paul and Walter W. Powell, eds. 1991. "Introduction." In *The New Institutionalism in Organizational Analysis.* Chicago: University of Chicago Press.

DiMaggio, Paul and Frank P. Romo. 1984. "Domination and Stratification in Organizational Fields." Paper presented to the annual meeting of the American Sociological Association.

Fennell, Mary, Christopher Ross, and Richard Warnecke. 1987. "Organizational Environment and Network Structure." *Research in the Sociology of Organizations* 5:311-40.

Friedland, Roger and Robert Alford. 1991. "Bringing Society Back In: Symbols, Practices and Institutional Contradictions." In *The New Institutionalism in Organizational Analysis,* edited by W. W. Powell and P. DiMaggio. Chicago: University of Chicago Press.

Galaskiewicz, Joseph. 1985. *Social Organization of an Urban Grants Economy: A Study of Business Philanthropy and Nonprofit Organizations.* Orlando, FL: Academic Press.

Galaskiewicz, Joseph and Stanley Wasserman. 1988. "Mimetic and Normative Processes Within an Interorganizational Field: An Empirical Test." Paper presented at the annual meeting of the American Sociological Association.

Goffman, Erving. 1967. *Interaction Ritual.* New York: Doubleday.

Granovetter, Mark and Roland Soong. 1988. "Threshold Models of Diversity: Chinese Restaurants, Residential Segregation, and the Spiral of Silence." *Sociological Methodology* 10:69-194.

Granovetter, Mark and Charles Tilly. 1988. "Inequality and the Labor Process." Pp. 175-221 in *Handbook of Sociology,* edited by N. Smelser. Berkeley: University of California Press.

Greenwood, Royston and C. R. Hinings. 1988. "Organizational Design Types, Tracks and the Dynamics of Strategic Change." *Organization Studies* 9:293-316.

Hackman, Richard and Gregory Oldham. 1980. *Work Redesign.* Reading, MA: Addison-Wesley.

Hannan, Michael T. and John H. Freeman. 1978. "Internal Politics of Growth and Decline." Pp. 177-99 in *Environments and Organizations,* edited by M. W. Meyer. San Francisco: Jossey-Bass.

———. 1989. *Organizational Ecology.* Cambridge, MA: Harvard University Press.

Hirsch, Paul M. 1972. "Processing Fads and Fashions: An Organization-Set Analysis of Cultural Industry Systems." *American Journal of Sociology* 77:639-59.

Ibarra, Hermi. 1989. *Network Location and Participation in Innovations.* Ph.D. dissertation, Yale University.

Jacobs, Jerry. 1989. *Revolving Doors.* Stanford, CA: Stanford University Press.

Kalleberg, Arne L. 1989. "Linking Macro and Micro Levels: Bringing the Workers Back into the Sociology of Work." *Social Forces* 67:582-92.

Kanter, Rosabeth Moss. 1983. *The Changemasters.* New York: Simon & Schuster.

Kiesler, Sara and Lee Sproull. 1982. "Managerial Response to Changing Environments: Perspectives on Problem Sensing from Social Cognition." *Administrative Science Quarterly* 27:548-70.

Knoke, David and David L. Rogers. 1979. "A Blockmodel Analysis of Interorganizational Relations." *Sociology and Social Research* 64:28-52.

Laumann, Edward O. and David Knoke. 1988. *The Organizational State: Social Choice in National Policy Domains.* Madison: University of Wisconsin Press.

Lawrence, Barbara. 1988. "New Wrinkles in the Theory of Age: Demography, Norms and Performance Ratings." *Academy of Management Journal* 31:309-37.

Lincoln, James R., M. Hanada, and Kerry McBride. 1986. "Organizational Structures in Japanese and U.S. Manufacturing." *Administrative Science Quarterly* 31:338-64.

Lincoln, James R. and Gerald Zeitz. 1980. "Organizational Properties from Aggregate Data." *American Sociological Review* 45:391-408.

Lowenthal, Leo. 1961. *Literature, Popular Culture, and Society.* Englewood Cliffs, NJ: Prentice-Hall.

Marsden, Peter V. 1988. "Homogeneity in Confiding Relations." *Social Networks* 10:57-76.

McPherson, J. Miller and Lynn Smith-Lovin. 1987. "Homophily in Voluntary Organizations." *American Sociological Review* 52:370-379.

Meyer, Marshall and Lynne G. Zucker. 1989. *Permanently Failing Organizations.* Newbury Park, CA: Sage.

Mizruchi, Mark S. 1982. *The American Corporate Network, 1904-1974.* Beverly Hills, CA: Sage.

Mizruchi, Mark S. and Michael Schwartz, eds. 1987. *Intercorporate Relations: The Structural Analysis of Business.* New York: Cambridge University Press.

Nadel, S. F. 1957. *A Theory of Social Structure.* London: Cohen and West.

Nelson, Reed E. 1989. "The Strength of Strong Ties: Social Networks and Intergroup Conflict in Organizations." *Academy of Management Journal* 32:377-401.

Parsons, Talcott. 1937. *The Structure of Social Action.* New York: McGraw-Hill.

———. 1951. *The Social System.* Glencoe, IL: Free Press.

Parsons, Talcott and Edward Shils. 1951. "Values, Motives and Systems of Action." Pp. 47-275 in *Towards a General Theory of Action.* New York: Harper & Row.

Peterson, Richard A. and David Berger. 1975. "Cycles in Symbol Production: The Case of Popular Music." *American Sociological Review* 40:158-73.

Pfeffer, Jeffrey. 1983. "Organizational Demography." *Research in Organizational Behavior* 5:299-357.

Romo, Frank P. 1986. *Moral Dynamics: A Blockmodeling Study of Conflict in a Mental Hospital.* Ph.D. dissertation, Yale University.

Scott, John. 1987. "Intercorporate Structures in Western Europe: A Comparative Historical Analysis." Pp. 208-33 in *Intercorporate Relations: The Structural Analysis of Business,* edited by M. S. Mizruchi and M. Schwartz. New York: Cambridge University Press.

Shrum, Wesley and Robert Wuthnow. 1988. "Reputational Status of Organizations in Technical Systems." *American Journal of Sociology* 93:882-912.

Singh, Jitendra V., David J. Tucker, and Agnes G. Meinhard. 1991. "Institutional Change and Ecological Dynamics." In *The New Institutionalism in Organizational Analysis,* edited by W. W. Powell and P. DiMaggio. Chicago: University of Chicago Press.

Skocpol, Theda. 1985. "Bringing the State Back In: Strategies of Analysis in Current Research." Pp. 3-37 in *Bringing the State Back In,* edited by P. B. Evans, D. Rueschemeyer, and T. Skocpol. New York: Cambridge University Press.

Stark, David. 1986. "Making a New Form of Industrial Association: Materials for a Case Study of an Internal Subcontracting Unit in a Hungarian Factory." Paper presented to Groupe de Sociologie Politique et Morale, E.H.E.S.S.-C.N.R.S., Paris.

Swidler, Ann. 1986. "Culture in Action." *American Sociological Review* 51:273-86.

Thurow, Lester. 1975. *Generating Inequality.* New York: Basic Books.

Useem, Michael. 1984. *The Inner Circle: Business and Politics in the U.S. and U.K.* New York: Oxford University Press.

Walker, Gordon. 1985. "Network Position and Cognition in a Computer Software Firm." *Administrative Science Quarterly* 30:103-30.

Westney, D. Eleanor. 1988. "Isomorphism, Institutionalization, and the Multinational Enterprise." Paper presented at the Academy of International Business Meetings, San Diego.

White, Harrison C. 1981. "Where Do Markets Come From?" *American Journal of Sociology* 87:517-47.

White, Harrison C., Scott A. Boorman, and Ronald L. Breiger. 1976. "Social Structure from Multiple Networks, I: Blockmodels of Roles and Positions." *American Journal of Sociology* 81:730-80.

Zald, Mayer N. and John D. McCarthy. 1979. *The Dynamics of Social Movements.* Cambridge: Winthrop.

Zucker, Lynne G. 1987. "Institutional Theories of Organization." *Annual Review of Sociology* 13:443-64.

6

The Truly Disadvantaged: A Synopsis

William Julius Wilson

One of the purposes of *The Truly Disadvantaged* (1987) was to challenge the dominant themes on the "underclass" reflected in the popular media and in the writings of conservative intellectuals not by shying away from using the concept of underclass, not by avoiding a description and explanation of unflattering behavior, but by attempting to relate the practices and experiences of inner-city ghetto residents to the structure of opportunities and constraints in American society. The book argues that the vulnerability of poor urban minorities to changes in the economy since the early 1970s had resulted in sharp increases in joblessness, in the concentration of poverty, in the number of poor single-parent families, and in welfare dependency, despite the creation of Great Society programs and despite antidiscrimination and affirmative action programs.

Also, *The Truly Disadvantaged* emphasizes that the effects of changes in the economy are most clearly felt in the concentrated poverty areas of the ghetto. The exodus of higher-income families, together with the sharp rise in joblessness, has transformed the social structure of these neighborhoods in ways that severely worsen the impact of the continuing industrial and geographic changes of the American economy since the 1970s: periodic recessions, wage stagnation, and the restriction of employment opportunities for the low-wage sector. Today the dwindling presence of middle- and working-class households in the ghetto makes it more difficult for the remaining residents of inner-city ghetto neighborhoods to sustain basic formal and informal institutions in the face of high and prolonged joblessness and attendant economic hardships. And, as the basic institutions decline, the social organization of inner-city ghetto neighborhoods disintegrates, further depleting the resources and limiting the life chances of those who remain mired in these blighted areas.

A term used in *The Truly Disadvantaged* to describe this process is *social isolation,* which implies that contact between groups of different class and/or racial backgrounds is minimal and/or intermittent and thereby enhances the effects of living in a highly concentrated poverty area. These "concentration effects," reflected in a range of outcomes from labor force attachment to social dispositions, are created by the constraints and opportunities that the residents of inner-city ghetto neighborhoods face in terms of access to jobs and job networks, involvement in quality schools, availability of marriageable partners, and exposure to conventional role models. Accordingly, the book argues that the factors associated with the recent increases in social dislocation among the ghetto underclass are complex and cannot be reduced to the easy explanations of "a culture of poverty," advanced by those on the right, or of racism, posited by those on the left. Although the inner-city ghetto is a product of historic discrimination and although present-day discrimination no doubt contributed to the increasing social and economic woes of the ghetto underclass, to understand the sharp increase in these problems since 1970 requires the specification of a complex web of other factors, including shifts in the American economy.

The Truly Disadvantaged concludes by recommending a comprehensive set of reforms that would both address the complexity of the problems in the inner-city ghetto and attract the attention and support of broad segments of the American population.

REFERENCE

Wilson, William Julius. 1987. *The Truly Disadvantaged.* Chicago: University of Chicago Press.

7

Levels in the Logic of
Macro-Historical Explanation

Morris Zelditch, Jr.

My task is to bring a micro perspective to bear on Wilson's macro-historical explanation of racial stratification in *The Truly Disadvantaged* (1987). Most of you probably expect this to lead to some controversy. I'm afraid I'm going to disappoint you. This is not only a fine book on its own terms, it is one that I agree with at almost every point. It is true that this book is controversial: Some sociologists will dispute repetition of an earlier Chicago assumption that ghettos are socially disorganized. Even more will dispute its deracialization hypothesis—that past, not present, discrimination explains inner-city poverty, dependency, family disorganization, and crime. More yet will object to its conclusion that systemwide, not racially targeted, policies are what the inner city now needs. And at least some will dispute a metatheoretical logic in which culture is epiphenomenal. But, whatever else is controversial about this book, it is not the contrast of micro versus macro, because its "macro-historical explanation" is actually a mix of both kinds of factors.

THE STRUCTURE OF WILSON'S ARGUMENT

Although complex in detail, Wilson's argument simplified is that history creates a structure of inequality linked to contemporary behavior by a combination of opportunities, constraints, and social psychology. The exogenous determinants of racial stratification are a past history of discrimination as well as economic changes that have restructured occupations and relocated industries and political processes that have restratified the black population. The endogenous processes caused by these factors, like the exogenous factors, also include a number of macro-level variables: demographic factors, such as migration, age profiles, and the available marriage pool, and economic factors, such as employment and income distributions. But they also include a "social isolation" argument, which is in part a matter of resource constraints and in part a matter of models. The "social isolation" of blacks in the inner city means the absence of contact and interaction with individuals and institutions of mainstream society (Wilson 1987, 1960), caused by the out-migration of better-off blacks. It has a contextual effect on the jobless in the inner city, depriving them not only of resources but also of models, whose presence formerly buffered unemployment effects. Without models,

> joblessness as a way of life, takes on a different social meaning; the relationship between schooling and postschool employment takes on a different meaning. The development of cognitive, linguistic, and other educational and job-related skills necessary for the world of work in the mainstream economy is thereby adversely affected. In such neighborhoods, therefore, teachers become frustrated and do not teach and children do not learn. A vicious cycle is perpetuated through the family, through the community, and through the schools. (Wilson 1987, 1957)

Wilson does self-consciously reject social psychology in *The Truly Disadvantaged:* But what he actually does is reject one social psychology in favor of another. Closely examining the culture of poverty hypothesis, he finds it unsatisfactory in part because it presupposes a dispositional social psychology. The "culture of poverty" is supposedly transmitted by early learning. It is transformed into transituational "personality" traits of individuals. Such traits determine subsequent behavior at the individual level and are magnified into group differences by common subcultural experience. Once learned, these group differences are unaffected by economic fluctuations because they become self-fulfilling and to change them requires massive resocialization. This hypothesis has been widely discredited but to reject it is not to reject social psychology in favor of macro explanation. The alternative is a different, more situational social psychology. This social psychology is an indispensable link in Wilson's argument, because it is the link between structure and action.

STRUCTURE AND ACTION

A similar mix of levels is common in many other macro explanations. I do not mean that it is true of all of them: For example, it is not true of population ecology (Hannan and Freeman 1977), in which social psychology is neither explicit nor implicit. Population ecology has no actors. Populations and the elements of which they are composed are acted on rather than acting. They do not manage the environment, they are managed by it; they do not even adapt to it, they are selected for it. What is different about *The Truly Disadvantaged* is that the objective of the theory is to explain and predict actions by actors; its social psychology is the necessary link between structure and action. But this is a very common pattern of sociological argument.

For example, the argument of Merton's (1938) "Social Structure and Anomie" has the same structure. Like Wilson, Merton rejects a social psychology. What he means is that he rejects an individual differences explanation of rates of deviance. But the alternative is a different social psychology, one in which holding out unattainable goals to any actor causes aberrant behavior. Because this social psychology is a constant across individuals, what explains variation in behavior is not social psychology but the situation of the actor. This, in turn, is determined by structure. Hence, variations in deviance are explained either by differences between structures or by differences in location of actors within them. But, as in Wilson, without the social psychology, the argument is incomplete, because without it there is no link between structure and action.

Even in more systemic theoretical strategies, which often explicitly deny action, the structure of the argument is similar, as in the functional theory of stratification or the theory of class conflict. In the former, performance of and recruitment to roles depends on rewards motivating actors (Davis and Moore 1945); in the latter, the transformation of a class in itself into a class for itself depends on subjective consciousness of class (Marx [1852] 1955).

It is possible to deny, as is common in the case of class conflict, that there is any social psychology involved. The disadvantage of doing this is that the social psychology, though it is indispensable in completing the argument, goes unexamined. In Wilson, for example, though the social psychology underlying the culture of poverty hypothesis is examined closely, that underlying the modeling hypothesis is not. This particular link in the argument is a vulnerable one, which could stand some explicit test.

But this is not the main point I want to make. I have so far tried to persuade you, first, that Wilson's macro-historical explanation of racial stratification in *The Truly Disadvantaged* is actually a mix of micro and macro elements, because it employs social psychology to link structure to action. Second, I have tried to show that the logic of this argument is common in sociology, occurring wherever structure is linked to action, because the link is necessarily a social psychology of one kind or another. If this much is accepted, it follows, third, that the dichotomy dividing micro from macro is false, both in Wilson's *The Truly Disadvantaged* and in sociology more generally. But suppose that structure/action is not the real distinction?

OTHER USES OF "MICRO" AND "MACRO"

One problem with debating "*micro* versus *macro*" is the large number of meanings that have been attached to these terms. They can mean not only structure versus action but also small versus large, actor versus system, or individual actor versus group actors. It is often tacitly supposed that it makes no difference which meaning is given to the terms because they are correlated. But even the smallest system has both structure and action, both actors and system; and a system of groups, like a system of individuals, can be either small or large. The argument that social psychology is the necessary link between structure and action does not logically imply that "*micro* versus *macro*" is a false dichotomy in all uses of the terms. Nevertheless, regardless of how one uses the terms, it remains true that the dichotomy between *micro* and *macro* is false.

I do not mean that size, level, or nature of the actor make no difference. A small system behaves differently than a large one; actors behave differently than systems; the "actorness" of an individual is different than the "actorness" of groups. What I mean is that the differences do not give rise to qualitatively different kinds of theories. Size is a variable within, not a difference between, theories. Actor and system are levels within, not different kinds of, theory. The difference between individual and collective actors raises more complicated issues, because its significance depends on whether or not the units of analysis in the theory in which they figure are actors. All theories are by definition capable of multiple interpretation. Some, like Emerson's theory of power-dependence relations (1962), are capable of both micro and macro interpretations. Emerson's theory can be applied to both individuals in families and organizational interrelations (see Berger et al. 1989). In such cases, the theory itself is neither micro nor macro, it is abstract. It is the interpretations that are micro or macro, and, whether micro or macro, the two interpretations have the same underlying theoretical structure. If, like Hannan and Freeman's population ecology, there are no actors in the theory, it is still capable of multiple interpretation, but none of the interpretations will be recognizably micro. On the other hand, in theories like Cyert and March (1963), in which the actorness of groups is questioned, none of the interpretations will be macro. One might reasonably insist, in these two cases, that there are qualitatively different kinds of theories for micro and macro phenomena. But neither theory has yet had very wide application; they will certainly not solve the kind of problem Wilson has set for himself. Until such theories take sociology over, it remains fair to say that the dichotomy between *micro* and *macro* is false no matter how one uses these terms.

CONCLUSION

There is little that is "micro versus macro" in *The Truly Disadvantaged* because the structure of its argument mixes the two levels in one explanation. It mixes them because the argument requires a social psychology to link structure to action. Like *The Truly Disadvantaged,* much of the rest of sociological explanation also mixes the two, whether or not self-consciously macro historical. The two are mixed wherever structure is linked to action, actors are linked to systems, a single theoretical structure is applied to groups as well as individuals, or size is linked coherently to its effects. Whatever meaning is given to *micro/macro*, the dichotomy is false in the sense that together they form a single theoretical structure rather than two qualitatively different kinds of theory.

Exceptions to this rule arise only if one theoretically rejects either structure or action, actors or system, or individuals or groups or, in the case of size, if one demarcates small from large at some arbitrarily fixed point on the real number line. Despite its symbolic value in defining a unique subject matter for sociology, the effect in each case is to so narrow its scope that it is unable to pursue such tasks as explaining rates of inner-city poverty, dependency, family breakdown, and crime.

One recent trend in the micro/macro debate has in fact been toward integration. While not yet common in the case of size, where particular theories incorporating both small and large exist, such as Olson's logic of collective action (1965), but there is no general strategy, integration is increasingly common in the case of structure and action (Giddens 1979). It is even more common in the case of actor and system (Alexander et al. 1987). In the case of persons/groups, Berger, Eyre, and Zelditch (1989) have pointed out that the "interactor" strategy that results from linking structure to action and actors to systems, if formulated abstractly, becomes capable of application to both. The opposite trend, of course, has been to bifurcate micro from macro, formulating them as mutually exclusive alternatives. There are perhaps four variants of the latter trend: In two, micro and macro compete for dominance of the whole of sociology, reducing explanation of all its phenomena to either micro (Collins 1981) or macro (Meyer et al. 1987). In the third, it is the scope of sociology that is reduced (as in Hannan and Freeman 1977). In the fourth, instead of reducing levels, one multiplies them. Sociology becomes organized around them; three are increasingly common—micro, meso, and macro, each of which is thought to have a distinct theoretical structure. If the dichotomy between micro and macro is false, none of the four is likely to be fruitful. The reduction of explanation is the wrong way to create a single theoretical structure—reduction of scope excessively narrows the subject; multiplication of levels creates a house without stairs between the floors. Integration into one theoretical structure is likely to be a more fruitful strategy for the future of sociology.

REFERENCES

Alexander, Jeffrey, Bernhard Giesen, Richard Muench, and Neil Smelser. 1987. *The Micro-Macro Link.* Berkeley: University of California Press.

Berger, Joseph, Dana Eyre, and Morris Zelditch, Jr. 1989. "Theoretical Structures and the Micro-Macro Problem." Chapter 1 in *Sociological Theories in Progress.* Newbury Park, CA: Sage.

Collins, Randall. 1981. "The Microfoundations of Macrosociology." *American Journal of Sociology* 86:984-1014.

Cyert, Richard M. and James G. March. 1963. *The Behavioral Theory of the Firm.* Englewood Cliffs, NJ: Prentice-Hall.

Davis, Kingsley and Wilbert Moore. 1945. "Some Principles of Stratification." *American Sociological Review* 10:242-49.

Emerson, Richard. 1962. "Power-Dependence Relations." *American Sociological Review* 27:31-41.

Giddens, Anthony. 1979. *Central Problems in Social Theory: Action, Structure, and Contradiction in Social Analysis.* Berkeley: University of California Press.

Hannan, Michael and John Freeman. 1977. "The Population Ecology of Organizations." *American Journal of Sociology* 83:929-64.

Marx, Karl. [1852] 1955. "The Eighteenth Brumaire of Louis Bonaparte." Pp. 243-344 in *Selected Works,* edited by K. Marx and F. Engels. Moscow: Foreign Languages.

Merton, Robert K. 1938. "Social Structure and Anomie." *American Sociological Review* 3:672-82.

Meyer, John, Francisco O. Ramirez, and John Boli. 1987. "Ontology and Rationalization in the Western Cultural Account." Pp. 12-37 in *Institutional Structure: Constituting State, Society, and the Individual,* edited by G. Thomas et al. Newbury Park, CA: Sage.

Olson, Mancur. 1965. *The Logic of Collective Action.* Cambridge, MA: Harvard University Press.

Wilson, William Julius. 1987. *The Truly Disadvantaged: In the Inner City, the Underclass, and Public Policy.* Chicago: University of Chicago Press.

Part II
Perspectives on Gender Stratification

8

Historical Change and the
Ritual Production of Gender

Randall Collins

The greatest weakness for theory of gender and stratification is dynamics, our systematic understanding of the sources of change. Any theory needs comparative leverage, hence most theorizing uses wide-ranging macro-historical comparisons. The subordination of women to men was typically severe in agrarian or peasant societies, much less so in some types of stateless horticultural societies, relatively favorable in hunting and gathering societies, and unfavorable in pastoral tribes. One hundred years ago, Engels developed his theory of sexual and economic property around a crude perception of these differences. With better understanding of the anthropological data, we now have more refined theories like those of Rae Blumberg (1984) and Janet Chafetz (1984), which focus on the correlation between gender power and the economics of production, property, and reproduction as well as theories that connect gender stratification to variations in ecological setting and cultural categories (Sanday 1981).

The home ground of these theories is their anthropological comparisons. Their weakness is when bureaucratic industrial societies enter the picture. Most of the key variations fade away at this time. Participation in subsistence food production, compatibility of women's work with lactation and child care, high death and birth rates, and matri- or patrilineality or locality of kinship structures distinguish very few differences within modern societies. Hence this line of theory leaves us with the proposition that women's status depends upon their economic position, which is now based mainly on occupational attainment. Because the historical conditions that used to determine women's economic subordination have dropped out, we should expect modern societies to converge on gender equality. Following this line of argument, Joan Huber (1986) has given us an optimistic extrapolation.

There remains a gap in explaining the slow pace of change in gender stratification in the nineteenth and twentieth centuries. Part of the theoretical problem comes from the method of comparing a set of static snapshots of different types of societies. We see what structures are correlated with each other but we do not thereby turn up a mechanism of change. My own comparative theory of sexual stratification (Collins 1971; 1988, pp. 168-73) has the same problem. I emphasized men's appropriation of women's sexuality as a weapon in marriage politics. Hence long-term historical variations can be explained as the rituals of sexual display and control, which are a means of signaling status and making alliances in political conflicts. But my theory comes up against the same problem as the economically based theories. When we arrive at industrial and bureaucratic societies, the source of variation and the causes of women's subordination drop out.

For my theory, the key variable is the location at which violence is organized. Differences in kinship systems are important as long as kinship constitutes military alliances in tribal societies. The feudal or patrimonial state of agrarian societies continues to have a role for marriage politics because the structure of the state is the alliance among fortified households. But the rise of the bureaucratic state severed this identity between state and aristocratic families with their households full of servants.

All the structural reasons for marriage politics drop out in modern societies, leaving us with a purely private sexual marketplace, personal displays of status, and the individualized emotions that go along with them. We end up with modern cults of love, eroticism, and psychological reflection on our private lives. This implies more erotic freedom but it leaves open the question of gender stratification. Again we don't know what should impede the change toward economic equality of men and women since the old sources of male dominance have dropped out—in this instance, military or political structures that hinged on controlling women as sexual property.

We now have considerable research on gender within modern societies. Much of this is descriptive, documenting existing inequalities. Some research shows a slow structural drift in some aspects. There have been very considerable increases in female education but long periods of static inequality in incomes. A recent study, for instance, shows that occupational segregation in the United States by sex was largely static from 1900 to 1970 and then declined in the 1970s and early 1980s (Jacobs 1989). One can disaggregate such data in various ways. Some researchers propose optimistic scenarios. Smith and Ward (1984) project that economic equality between younger men and women will come about in the near future, based on women's increasing level of education and assuming that economic returns on education will be the same for women as they have been for men. But the extrapolation of selective trends in the absence of a general theory is always risky, and expectations of impending gender equality may well be unwarranted.

The other type of contemporary empirical research now available is microsociological. Here we find the micro details of gender stratification, such as conversation analysis, which shows that men tend to interrupt women more than vice versa. Again there is a theoretical problem. Micro analysis is almost literally a snapshot of a small duration, and microsociologists almost never make comparisons across time. This is a methodological reason why micro analysis cannot handle change. There is also a deeper theoretical reason. Empirical micro research overwhelmingly documents the conservatism of face-to-face interaction. The ethnomethodologists' major finding is that people depend on the taken-for-granted nature of social order and dislike having it questioned. Conversation analysis shows that there is a strong preference for agreement on the overt level of talk. Goffman's interaction ritual theory, which comes out of Durkheim, is a model of how people produce local solidarity and conformity. Recently, Ann Rawls (1987) referred to this structure of ordering as the interaction level sui generis. The mechanisms of everyday life tend to reproduce things as they were—group cleavages, personal identities, dominance relations, and the cultural ideologies that reflect them.[1]

SOURCES OF CHANGE:
TOP-DOWN MOVEMENT MOBILIZATION
OR BOTTOM-UP AGGREGATE SHIFTS?

Accounting for changes in gender stratification is a micro-macro problem. The micro level, contrary to some claims about the fluidity of the negotiated order, is conservative and self-reproducing. When changes come, they seem to be driven by the macro side. It is not my intention to reify the macro structure, because it consists of nothing empirically but an enormous chaining of micro situations across time and space. But, given the forces of micro conservatism, changes have to ripple from one situation to the next, harnessing local conformity into a tide that shifts the relationship among different parts of the system. There are two possible ways this can come about. From the top down, changes may be set in motion by political conflicts or elite movements among the upper and upper-middle classes. From the bottom up, changes might be driven by more glacial movement in aggregations, like labor force participation of women or the interconnections between sexual relationships, marriage, childbearing, and household work.

The bottom-up changes are bound to be slower. This is partly because any large and decentralized aggregate moves more slowly than a smaller and more focused network can move. Bottom-up changes also encounter forces of inertia that limit their effects. For example, the long-term shift of women into the paid labor force in the twentieth century has not altered gender stratification very much. Instead, it resulted in creating gender-stereotyped occupations such as that of secretary and other segregated positions of the lower-middle bureaucracy, nurses, and the pink-collar ghetto of women's services. It is not clear that recent token integration of women into management and the dominant professions has changed this much, as we see in the elaboration of new segregated forms like the "mommy track" in law firms.

The creation of new occupations is not just technically neutral. Their forms depend on the balance of power. Theory about professionalization now incorporates much information about the processes of monopolization that take place here. Favorable occupational niches become closed—which is what we mean by a strong profession—when a highly mobilized group gets the state to license and enforce its monopoly (Larson 1979; Murphy 1988; Burrage 1990). The negative counterpart of this is an enforced closure of jobs that have limited power and rewards. A good example is the downgrading of the occupation of secretary at the end of the nineteenth century when it became a segregated, dead-end position for women. The lesson in this seems to be that bottom-up changes will have the minimum possible impact on the preexisting structure of stratification. The main advantage goes to occupational changes that are allied with politics, such as the elite reform movements that raised the status of medicine and law in the United States at the turn of the twentieth century or, at a more model level, the labor unions that won closed shop contracts.

I am proposing, then, that the main force of change in gender stratification will be found at the level of political mobilization. In the simplest version, the state enforces changes by legislation. But this overt aspect of politics is probably secondary to the mobilizing process itself. Political mobilization is the most rapid kind of macro permeation of micro life, sweeping people up into a new collective consciousness. It is apparent that the career aims of middle-class women went through a dramatic upward shift in the 1970s. Without this breakthrough in aspirations, the demographic and educational trends were doing little more than moving women into roles in the paid work force that were most similar to traditional female culture: helping roles in bureaucracies, nurturant roles in medicine, sexual display roles as cocktail waitresses and entertainers.

Political mobilization also affects its audience—in this instance, men. An interest group movement can rarely succeed without sympathizers. At the height of feminist mobilization, large numbers of men had to be drawn into opposition to gender segregation or at least feel morally intimidated to go along with the change. For this reason, legislative goals like the Equal Rights Amendment have been largely symbolic indicators of how well the mobilization is doing. If the mobilization of new career aspirations and the accompanying wave of moral sentiment in its favor is strong enough, then the occupational situation changes and the passage of legislation just puts its stamp of approval on it, serving mainly to coerce recalcitrant traditionalists. If the mobilization fades out, however, or is too narrowly oriented to legislation, like the women's suffrage movement early in the century, then legal changes become mostly a dead letter.

Even a mobilization in this full sense, consisting not only of political feminism but the larger shift of life-style aspirations and audience effects, is not enough to guarantee major changes. Mobilizations typically produce countermobilizations, a backlash that mirrors many of the structural features of the original movement and that is especially likely to neutralize sympathizers and to reverse or at least complicate the process of moral intimidation. The sociological problem is to theorize this process and make the patterns predictable. To do so, we must move to a theory of politics.

RITUAL POLITICS AND INTEREST POLITICS

There are two large dimensions of political struggle, both of which have their counterpart in everyday life. The kind of political mobilization in the broadest sense referred to above may be called *ritual politics*. The other type is a vertical dimension of struggle that I will call *interest politics*.

The focus of ritual politics is explicitly on ideals and moral issues. It invokes standards of justice, altruism, and rightness rather than appealing to self-interest. The abortion issue is a good example. There is a ritual mobilization on both sides, one of which takes the fetus as a sacred object, a Durkheimian symbol of a traditional life-style. The other side is attached to the ideals of women's freedom and the life-style options associated with it. I am not suggesting that there are no real interests in addition to these ideals that are connected with these movements. But ritual politics is never successful if it does not mobilize large numbers of people who have no direct interest in the question, whom it does not touch personally but who sympathize with or against the moral ideal.

Is there a structural basis for ritual politics? The theoretical model I have invoked is Durkheimian, which implies that the main dimension is between universalistic ideals, which we would expect to find in cosmopolitan networks, and, on the other side, particularistic ideals and reified symbols that arise from bounded localistic groups. It is a political conflict between

Durkheimian organic solidarity and mechanical solidarity, with the proviso that there are not different historical stages but antagonistic social structures found within the same society. Of the older research on this dimension of political attitudes, much is concerned with issues such as prejudice on one side and support for civil liberties on the other. There is also much evidence bearing on everyday life interactions along these dimensions. Cosmopolitan networks and complexity of work interactions foster internalized child-rearing techniques and associated ideals of self-expression, whereas localistic group structures and simplified work experiences are associated with punitive child rearing and an emphasis on external conformity (Bronfenbrenner 1966; Kohn 1977). The two sides of the abortion controversy are associated with this same structural continuum (Luker 1984).

This ritual dimension of politics, with cosmopolitans at one pole and defenders of local solidarity at the other, is one of two dimensions of politics. There is also a vertical dimension of power struggle, *interest politics*. For our purposes, we can simplify this as the conflict between order givers and order takers, or haves and have-nots, subsuming all the aspects of economic and organizational struggle with which Marxian and Weberian sociology are concerned. These material interests have a crucial role in reproducing the structure of society, yet they are not so apparent as one might expect in dramatic social change. The reason is that material interests are very difficult to organize politically on a massive scale. Interest conflicts are chronic, but they most typically involve local groups or private, individual interests. Trade unions, professional associations, financial and business groups, and frequently the units and individuals within them maneuver opportunistically for their own advantage and strike whatever alliances and bargains are temporarily expedient. In the aggregate, however, material interests are often too jumbled to provide a coherent force for political change. Their structure is likely to result in inertia, except on the rare occasions when there is a massive economic or organizational breakdown (Goldstone 1990). Even then, we can doubt whether sheer interest group politics can force a massive enough coalition to act coherently unless it amalgamates with a ritually mobilized group. This is why class politics has always been most successful when it was tied to ethnic or religious mobilization.

For this reason, the ritual dimension of politics—mobilization around symbolic issues—usually holds center stage. Even in normal times, politicians who have a sufficient basis of support in a coalition of interests become really popular or unpopular only in relation to a ritual mobilization. Much of ordinary politics takes place at the particularistic end of the ritual dimension, including cults of personality and attacks on rival personalities. Election campaigns consist to a considerable degree of contests of opposing scandals, as politicians attempt to carry out a collective degradation ceremony for violating some minor taboo at each other's expense. Another kind of ritual mobilization consists of patriotism, especially in times of war or other international conflicts. This too is at the particularistic end of the ritual spectrum. It invokes national solidarity, as well as loyalty for its own sake, and reifies symbols of our heroes against foreign villains. The most successful movement of ritual solidarity of the 1980s has been the antidrug crusade. This is a witch-hunt for tabooed objects, which manages both to attack the symbol of the 1960s radical counterculture and to scapegoat today's black lower class. Ritual mobilization of this kind creates a massive emotional wave that sweeps everyone into supporting the movement or at least prevents their saying anything against it. This is what I refer to as moral intimidation, a key aspect of success in ritual politics.

It might appear that ritual politics is usually dominated by particularistic symbols. But highly particularistically oriented rituals, such as personality cults and scandals, can be used by either right or left, because they have little content except for elevating or discrediting particular politicians. What we are concerned about here is a deeper split on the ritual dimension, the war of universalizers against particularizers. The feminist movement is located toward the universalistic pole. This is especially true of its sympathizers, the men who favor women's rights. Women, of course, have a place on the nonritual dimension of conflict too, as they have straightforward material interests and struggles over power in everyday life. But not only are material interests less easily organized than ritual movements, women's material interests are especially hard to mobilize. Housewives, secretaries, divorcées, single parents are structurally among the most privatized and fragmented of all interest groups. Structural change in favor of their interests, therefore, depends especially on the tidal wave of a movement on the ritual dimension.

Universalizers and particularizers tend to hate each other, in an inarticulate way. They don't speak the same language. Each regards the other as both stupid and evil. Most academics are on the universalistic side, because it is the business of the modern research university to produce universalistic ideas. We dislike bigots and also look down on them. It is perhaps not so well recognized that particularizers, the defenders of localistic tradition and conformity, equally dislike universalizers. The extreme form of this dislike was the Nazi ideology. This was an explicit attack on cosmopolitans and on the rootlessness of modern society, which the Nazis particularistically identified with the Jews. A milder form of the same theme is extremely widespread in our own society. The same combination of moral outrage and disdain for incompetents is expressed in complaints about "pointy-headed liberals on bicycles," although the rhetoric may vary from charges of "godlessness" to complaints about society's having lost its values. Universalistic symbols offend against particularistic symbols. The more abstract viewpoint undercuts them at their symbolic core by treating them as reifications.

Particularistic symbols are not merely carried by dwindling pockets of small town traditionalism. Most people do not like living in the unfocused conglomerates of today's bureaucratic capitalist society (Bellah et al. 1985). Moreover, the very freedom and privacy this structure affords enables people intentionally to construct their own pockets of *Gemeinschaft*. They can re-create religious cults or withdraw into private circles of friends and family; they can use the techniques of modernity to create intense flashes of high ritual density, ranging from psychotherapy groups to pop concerts. Contrary to what Durkheim expected and Weber feared, history does not seem to be inevitably on the side of the universalizers. But neither are we going to see a rollback to the world of small conformist communities. Even the Nazis, who wanted to confine women to *Kueche* and *Kinder,* ended up with more women than ever in the labor force because women were needed for the war economy (Millett 1970, pp. 159-66). Instead, we have an ongoing ritual conflict between people who gravitate toward one pole or another of our social structure.

Can we find a pattern in this conflict? The particularistic side is truly a backlash, a countermobilization. Ordinarily, the dynamic starts from the universalistic side. In turn, this offends traditionalist symbols and sets off a particularistic countermovement in their defense.[2] What then produces universalistic mobilization? The basis of universalism is cosmopolitan networks, especially those that process literate communications. In many instances, universalism is related to mass education, especially higher education. At one time, it was thought that exposure to mass media was also universalizing. But education and the media can have quite ambiguous effects, especially during a countermobilization. The expansion of conservative Christian education has been the organizational base for particularistic countermobilization since the 1970s. Techniques such as encounter groups, once pioneered by cosmopolitan psychologists, have been adopted by traditionalists, along with their own media networks. Television seems to have an especially ambivalent effect. Though the news professionals and members of the entertainment industries tend to be cosmopolitans and universalizers, nevertheless, television as a visual medium depicts particular, concrete individuals. The content of TV entertainment provides viewers with surrogate families in situation comedies. TV adventure heroes display the highly particularistic virtue of being people who can be trusted in a fight. One might say that violence on TV, in sports or in cop shows, always generates a particularistic loyalty, a ritual focus upon the crude symbolism of "us" against "them." If TV turns the world into a global village, the emphasis should be not on the global but on the village.

WHAT HAS HAPPENED TO THE
UNIVERSALISTIC GENDER MOBILIZATION?

The mobilization for gender equality seems to be stalled today in the middle ranges, and the particularistic countermobilization seems to be stalled at about the same level. This also seems to be the case with most of the other universalistic movements of the 1960s and 1970s, especially the movements for racial and ethnic equality. Both feminist and antifeminist movements have become institutionalized in a narrower sense. There is a structural irony here. This stagnant condition seems to produce a particularizing of universalistic issues. An analogy is ethnic politics. It can take the form of a universalizing movement, under the banner of justice for all. It can also settle into the kind of practical compromise that once characterized New York City politics, when every slate had to include one Irishman (not an Irishwoman), one Italian, and one Jew. The ethnic groups and the genders have shifted but the structure is familiar today. Instead of a broad movement for racial and gender equality, we have institutionalized a new particularism. Pork barrel politics has merely expanded to include a few slots at the trough for representatives of ethnic and women's pressure groups. This is probably an inevitable result of having lost the momentum of a massive mobilization around these universalistic ideals.

For these reasons, I would not expect to see any major swing in gender stratification in the near future. Top-down, ritually mobilizing movements do not seem likely to bring major change in the visible future. In their absence, bottom-up trends in education, labor force participation, or family patterns are not likely to add up to real structure change. It is a safe bet that most women are going to remain in the white-collar working class of secretaries, nurses, and lab assistants, in the pink-collar ghetto, the service working class, and the women's consumer industries for quite some time to come.

THE THEORETICAL TASK

Do we have enough theory to make a long-term prognosis? There are some big blank spots. Do mobilizations have a rhythm, a period of time at which they expand to maximal intensity and participation and then fade? We need to look at more macro comparisons on this point and especially at the relationship between mobilizations and countermobilizations. (Some evidence and analysis is now becoming available in Chafetz and Dworkin 1990.)

Another pattern we need to understand better is the way movements on the same side of the ritual spectrum feed off each other. The upsurge of feminism in the 1970s spun off from the antiwar movement, which in turn built upon the black civil rights movement and its sympathizers. All of this was entwined with movements of university reform and many other mobilizing features of the 1960s. This is structurally similar to the way nineteenth-century feminism spun off from the antislavery movement and was organizationally connected to many other reform movements of that time.

Conjunctures among movements seem to be crucial for generating the truly massive life-style mobilization that changes social structures. Theoretically, we have little sense of what brings about such conjunctures. The next big wave of feminism may have to wait a long time for the next conjuncture. Even that may not do it, for not all mobilizations move in the same direction. Working-class mobilization as in the 1930s could come again. We may see a white-collar version of class conflict in the next few decades as capitalism gets itself into its inevitable cyclical troubles. But it would not necessarily be profeminist. Here are two chilling examples. As Rae Blumberg points out (personal communication), in Algeria, the left-wing anticolonial movement was very conservative on women's rights. This was because the French colonial administration had pushed for women's emancipation. Hence, wearing the veil was a symbol of leftism. Similarly, in Iran, the revolution against the authoritarian regime of the shah used antifeminist mobilization to build its momentum. This worked especially well because the shah's wife was a leading force for women's emancipation.

The cross-cutting effects of class mobilization can be a significant problem for gender equality. Upper- and upper-middle-class women everywhere have been the leaders in women's movements. This was the case as far back as movements for women's marital and property rights in ancient Roman times (Collins 1986). Populist revolts against the elite thus have a structural affinity for traditionalist antifeminism. Nevertheless, the political lineup can sometimes swing the other way. The late eighteenth-century radicals in France and England were on the left both on the dimension of vertical power struggle and at the pole of ritual universalism and included the early modern feminists.

The main structural basis of universalistic mobilizations in the past has been cosmopolitan organizations, those specializing in broad networks of people and the processing of ideas. At various times in history, universities, scientific associations, newspapers, even churches have played this role. But all of these institutions are quite capable of swinging to the particularistic side. There have been both Christian liberals and bigots, just as universities can be places for class snobbery or for local pork barrel politics—as we seem to be becoming now—as well as places where idealistic movements are bred. For this reason, the brute fact of a trend to increasing levels of higher education does not make me confident that it will result in another wave of universalistic mobilization. It can just as well result in petty interest groups like those of the 1980s generation or, for that matter, ideological conservatives like the American students of the 1920s. In recent decades, the process of credential inflation (Collins 1979) makes students cynical about whatever they might learn in a cosmopolitan setting.

But this sort of ambivalence has characterized all the great universalistic institutions of the past—churches, journalism, law. We are left with another theoretical problem for sociology: to find the conditions under which this universalizing potential is unleashed, rather than its opposite. I suspect it has to do with the overall structural relationships with the other major institutional spheres. The answer may lie in an as yet undiscovered principle about the conflict of macro structures.

Massive changes in the occupational structure often rest upon social movements, which change aspirations, create sympathizers, and morally intimidate the opposition. Such movements are an aspect of ritual politics on the universalistic side. But modern social structure also facilitates countermobilizations on the particularistic side. We have had two waves of feminist mobilization since 1850, each time in conjuncture with other social movements. It appears we will have to wait for another big conjuncture in the future before a third wave is mobilized to challenge the structure again.

NOTES

1. Some lines of micro theory do not agree on this point. Symbolic interactionism in particular has stressed that life is fluid, indeterminate, open to reinterpretation, and some theories in the micro-macro debate have stressed the importance of human agency as supplying the dynamics of social change. My point, however, is that the truly refined detail of micro analysis (research on what actually happens, second by second or minute by minute, in interaction) overwhelmingly shows conservatism and reproduction of social forms, not their challenge, reinterpretation, and change. By contrast, the empirical research of symbolic interactionism is not at this extreme end of the micro continuum but tends to focus instead on medium-scale changes over the definition of occupational roles, deviance, self-images, and the like.

2. Chafetz and Dworkin (1987) present evidence in the case of first and second waves of feminist movements for this pattern. In their interpretation, countermovements are based on realistic threats to males' power and income and by extension to the income of wives who depend upon their husbands' income. They also recognize threats to status. In the micro reality of everyday life, however, status is constructed by styles of ritual participation. "Status threats" are thus struggles over which form of ritualism will dominate. In addition, Chafetz and Dworkin's key mediating factor between economic interests and antifeminism is *encapsulated roles*, that is, women whose social relationships are circumscribed as housewives and mothers or whose occupational contacts are in highly segregated spheres. These encapsulated roles are precisely

the kind of network situations, bounded localistic groups, that should produce commitment to particularistic symbols. By the same token, women's *expansion of role networks* due to urbanization and education, the key factor in Chafetz and Dworkin's model of feminist mobilization, is the kind of network structure that produces symbolic universalism.

REFERENCES

Bellah, Robert, Richard Madsen, Anne Swidler, William Sullivan, and Steven Tipton. 1985. *Habits of the Heart.* Berkeley: University of California Press.

Blumberg, Rae Lesser. 1984. "A General Theory of Gender Stratification." Pp. 23-100 in *Sociological Theory 1984,* edited by R. Collins. San Francisco: Jossey-Bass.

Bronfenbrenner, Urie. 1966. "Socialization and Social Class Through Time and Space." Pp. 362-76 in *Class, Status and Power,* edited by R. Bendix and S. M. Lipset. New York: Free Press.

Burrage, Michael. 1990. "Patterns of Occupational Development: A Search in the Histories of Professional and Manual Workers in France, Russia, the United States, and Britain." Pp. 1-23 in *Professions in Theory and History,* edited by M. Burrage and R. Torstendahl. London: Sage.

Chafetz, Janet Saltzman. 1984. *Sex and Advantage: A Comparative Macro-Structural Theory of Sexual Stratification.* Totowa, NJ: Rowman & Allanheld.

Chafetz, Janet Saltzman and Anthony Gary Dworkin. 1987. "In the Face of Threat: Organized Antifeminism in Comparative Perspective." *Gender & Society* 1:33-60.

———. 1990. "Action and Reaction: An Integrated, Comparative Perspective on Feminist and Antifeminist Movements." Pp. 33-67 in *Cross-National Research in Sociology,* edited by M. Kohn. Beverly Hills, CA: Sage.

Collins, Randall. 1971. "A Conflict Theory of Sexual Stratification." *Social Problems* 19:3-21.

———. 1979. *The Credential Society.* New York: Academic Press.

———. 1986. "Courtly Politics and the Status of Women." Pp. 297-321 in *Weberian Sociological Theory.* Cambridge: Cambridge University Press.

———. 1988. *Theoretical Sociology.* San Diego: Harcourt Brace Jovanovich.

Goldstone, Jack. 1990. *State Breakdown: Revolution and Rebellion in the Early Modern World, 1640-1848.* Berkeley: University of California Press.

Huber, Joan. 1986. "Trends in Gender Stratification, 1970-1985." *Sociological Forum* 1:476-95.

Jacobs, Jerry. 1989. "Long-Term Trends in Occupational Segregation by Sex." *American Sociological Review* 95:160-73.

Kohn, Melvin. 1977. *Class and Conformity.* Chicago: University of Chicago Press.

Larson, Magali Sarfatti. 1979. *The Rise of Professionalism.* Berkeley: University of California Press.

Luker, Kristin. 1984. *Abortion and the Politics of Motherhood.* Berkeley: University of California Press.

Millett, Kate. 1970. *Sexual Politics.* New York: Doubleday.

Murphy, Raymond. 1988. *Social Closure.* Oxford: Clarendon.

Rawls, Anne. 1987. "The Interaction Order Sui Generis: Goffman's Contribution to Social Theory." *Sociological Theory* 5:136-49.

Sanday, Peggy Reeves. 1981. *Female Power and Male Dominance.* New York: Cambridge University Press.

Smith, James P. and Michael Ward. 1984. *Women's Wages and Work in the Twentieth Century.* Santa Monica, CA: Rand.

9

Women and the Wealth and Well-Being of Nations: Macro-Micro Interrelationships

Rae Lesser Blumberg

WOMEN AS SECRET AGENTS OF DEVELOPMENT

In this chapter, I contend that women may be likened to secret agents in the creation of the wealth and well-being of nations. It is not that the women are acting clandestinely. I use the analogy because women are responsible for much more of both wealth and welfare than is shown in standard national statistics or seen by those conceiving and carrying out the policies and programs of planned development. I also suggest that women's most secret (i.e., unrecognized) role as controllers of independent income within households may be their most crucial role in creating both micro- and macro-level wealth and well-being. My arguments rest on a bed of hypotheses culled from two theories: my general theory of gender stratification (Blumberg 1984) and my evolving theory of gender and development (Blumberg 1989a, 1989c).

I further argue that a number of the Third World's major problems are being unwittingly exacerbated by policymakers' bypassing and undercutting women as economic agents. Their neglect of women, I suggest, stems from their prevailing paradigms and perceptions, which cut their vision of females as *producers* of wealth and well-being and nearly blind them to women as wielders of independently controlled income within the household. Because of these blinders, key actors in Third World economic development treat all Third World men as if they were sole providers and all Third World households as if they were monolithic, resource-pooling entities, united in common survival strategy. The African food crisis and the population crisis are discussed briefly as two problems intensified by development elites' mistakenly monolithic model of the household and their murky view of women as agents of development.

GENDER THEORIES

Hypotheses from a General Theory of Gender Stratification

My theory involves 25 hypotheses about gender equality, a few of which I repeat as this chapter's basis. Because other writings explicate evidence for many of the propositions that follow (Blumberg 1978, 1984, 1988a, 1989a, 1989c), I document mainly those hypotheses that I have not previously explored empirically. My most recent field research was conducted in summer 1989 in all three regions of Ecuador—highlands, coast, and Amazon (Blumberg and Colyer 1989; Blumberg 1990a). Whenever possible, I use my newest findings to illustrate the theoretical arguments.

(1) The independent variable that is both most demonstrable and most important in determining the degree of female equality is women's economic power relative to men's. Relative gender economic power (defined as control of key economic resources such as income, property, and other means of production) is posited as the most influential (though not the sole) independent variable affecting overall gender stratification at a variety of nested micro- and macro levels ranging from the couple to the state.

I argue that economic power's key role stems from both theoretical and empirical reasons. If, following Lenski (1966), we consider the major types of power to be economic, political, force, and ideological, we can trace women's position compared with men's historically and across the range of human societies. (a) The power of force clearly is the least achievable for women, who are more likely to be its victims than its wielders. This is true at both the individual level (e.g., wife beating) and the group level of organized force (police or military power). Males have one-third to one-half more upper body strength, disadvantaging females in hand-to-hand encounters, and men hold almost universal sway in organized group violence. (b) For political power, there is no solid evidence of a single society where women had as much as a 50-50 split. (c) For the power of ideology, we know of a few societies that proclaim gender equality but there are no data about societies that deem women superior. (d) Only with respect to economic power does women's position run the gamut: There are societies where women control almost no economic resources, holding even their personal effects and ornaments at the suffrance of whatever man controls them—father, husband, and, finally, son. But there are others (mainly hunting and gathering and prestate horticultural societies) where women's economic power is fairly equal to men's. And there are a few (e.g., the Iroquois of colonial North America) where women control the lion's share of the economy, especially at the micro levels of family and community.

(2) Once they emerge historically, macro levels control micro levels more than vice versa.

(3) Consequently, a woman's leverage from a given amount of micro-level economic power is subject to a possible negative discount rate to the extent that the macro levels of a society uphold economic, political, legal, religious, and ideological policies that disadvantage women. In short, the more male-dominated and repressive of women are the macro levels, the larger the negative discount rate on how much leverage a woman might get from any micro-level economic resources she might bring into the household. (That countries vary in the extent to which their macro levels disadvantage women can be ascertained by comparing, say, Sweden with Saudi Arabia or Iceland with Iran.)

(4) Conversely, at the level of the couple, we also encounter micro-level discount rates affecting a woman's relative economic power. These rates emerge from such factors as relative commitment to the relationship, relative attractiveness, each partner's gender role ideology, relative assertiveness, and the man's perceived dependence on the woman's economic resources and income. What is distinctive about these micro-level discount rates is that they can be either negative or positive (e.g., the beautiful, bored, nonemployed young wife doted over by a rich husband may have far more leverage over the relationship than might be expected from her minuscule economic resources).

(5) Adjusting a woman's overall economic power by these macro- and micro-level discount factors gives us her net economic power, relative to that of counterpart males (Blumberg and Coleman 1989). In other words, if both a woman and a man bring in a metaphorical dollar to the household, the macro- and micro-level discount factors that apply to their particular situations would determine how many cents of that dollar remain for each to be converted to net economic power. In contemporary societies, more cents of the woman's dollar than the man's would be nibbled away by various macro- and micro-level discount factors, although the extent would vary not only from couple to couple but also by class, ethnicity, historical era, society, and even phase of the life course.

An Ecuadorian example illustrates these points. In summer 1989, I researched two ethnic groups with quite different discount rates affecting women's relative economic power. *Mestizos* (Spanish-Indian people with a

Spanish-derived culture) are the numerically larger, dominant group, although a tiny group of whites exercises more control of the country's political economy. The subordinate group are Indians, mainly Quichua speakers, who live in the Andean highlands and the Amazon lowlands. More than 450 years after Spanish conquest, the Indians still retain features of their traditional culture. Thus their gender stratification is more egalitarian than the mestizos'. Women are more likely than men to be monolingual Quichua speakers and retain traditional dress, a fact that several social scientists attribute less to women's conservativism than to the fact that assimilation would bring greater gender subordination (Alberti 1986; Poeschel 1988; Blumberg and Colyer 1989). Nonetheless, Indian women's micro-level position in family and community is subtly reduced by the impact of negative macro-level discount factors filtering from the top of the mestizo/white social structure. Still, Indian spouses farm more or less as partners and the traditional ideology is much closer to male-female equality than among the mestizos. Therefore, for every *sucre* an Indian woman brings into her household, she still gets close to a whole sucre's worth of net economic power. In contrast, the discount rate is more negative among the mestizos. Women are not seen as producers (Weiss 1985). Therefore, a mestiza's sucre would bring her much less net economic power, because it is unseemly for her to have it in the first place. This leads to a fascinating social class contrast. The Indian stratification pyramid is more truncated, below that of mestizos and whites. Yet a well-off Indian farm woman is as likely to be economically active as a poor one. In contrast, there is a strong social class effect in economic activity among rural mestiza woman (Alberti 1986; Blumberg and Colyer 1989). The better-off mestizo families can better keep women economically dependent, whereas, among the poor, women are more likely to be economic contributors. In contrast to the Indians' generally strong family systems regardless of class, a growing proportion of mestizo households at the bottom are female-headed. In short, the ethnically distinct discount rates on gender stratification affect Indian and mestizo men and women differently, with marked social class differences among mestizos but not Indians.

(6) The degree of control over surplus allocation is held to be more important than the degree of control over resources needed for bare subsistence (withholding food from hungry children is not an option, which is why poor women don't gain greater power from their undeniably essential contributions).

(7) Mere work is not a source of economic power in itself; that is, being economically active or even owning economic resources does not translate into economic leverage if it gives no control over economic resources. For what can this key independent variable of net economic power be cashed in?

I contend that the most crucial dependent variables involve control over one's person and life chances rather than measures of prestige or status.

(8) A woman's net economic power relative to a man's at the same micro level predicts her leverage in a variety of micro-level life options and decisions. With greater control of economic resources, her fertility should conform more closely to her expected utilities rather than to those of her husband, extended family, or the state. Similarly, she should have more say in household decisions.

(9) In gender-stratified systems, when women's relative economic power falls, their level of equality, such as leverage over fertility and household decisions, tends to fall faster than it rises when their relative economic power increases.

In sum, this first set of propositions establishes the importance of women's relative net economic power and the fact that it is a volatile, dynamic entity that can be affected by everything from ethnic to cultural discount factors.

Hypotheses from an Emergent Feminist Theory of Gender and Development

The next two sets of hypotheses come from my still evolving feminist theory of gender and development (Blumberg 1989a, 1989c, 1990b, forth-coming-a, forthcoming-b). The first set refers to micro-level male/female issues and the second set refers to the nearly all-male elite that devises and implements development policies in today's Third World. As specified below, consequences of these hypotheses are manifest at both micro and macro levels. While the hypotheses from the general theory of gender stratification established the importance of income under women's control, the hypotheses from my evolving theory of gender and development (Blumberg 1989c) assert that women's control of income is more prevalent than often assumed and that women's preferences concerning earnings and spending income under their control have social and economic impact.

Male/female micro-level hypotheses. (1) There is a worldwide continuum of the extent to which households have internal economies based on gender and age. Household members differ in rates of economic activity, degrees of control over economic resources, and levels of responsibility for providing for dependents. More particularly,there are worldwide continua the extent to which married women (a) control economic resources and (b) have provider responsibilities. These two continua are correlated but not perfectly. For example, most Muslim Hausa women in Northern Nigeria live in seclusion but engage in income-generating pursuits within their compounds.

Because only the husbands have formal provider obligations, these women (except in periods of intense privation) can use their income for, say, business expansion or daughters' dowries (Hill 1969; Simmons 1976; Norman et al. 1982; Schildkrout 1982, 1984; Coles 1983; Jackson 1985; Blumberg 1988b).

(2) Geographically, the household internal economy is strongest in much of sub-Saharan Africa. Especially where polygyny prevails or marriages are unstable, men and women may maintain separate purses for most income streams and expenditures (Guyer 1980, 1988; Staudt 1987; Fapohunda 1988). Often women have strong provider obligations, especially to their children, and most women are economically active, mainly in low-resource farming and market trade.

Conversely, the gender-differentiated internal household economy fades to insignificance where there are almost no jobs or market trading opportunities that let women earn income on their own account. Places lacking both informal and formal sector income-generating possibilities for women are fairly rare worldwide. One example involves rural areas of the Yemen Arab Republic, where half the young men are off working in the Persian Gulf, sending remittances home to the family's senior male, while women act as unpaid family labor in agriculture (Howe 1985; Carloni 1987). A second example involves remote colonization projects in tropical lowlands, where women typically are cut off from income-generating opportunities (Blumberg and Colyer 1989; Scudder 1979).

Another Ecuadorian example involves a region of the Amazon (Napo) opened to settlers by oil company penetration roads begun in 1968. The government gave colonists 50 hectare plots, 250 meters wide by 2000 meters deep, leading to settlement patterns that left many colonists as far as 10 to 12 miles from the unpaved main road, reached by mule trail through the rainforest. Women may remain isolated for weeks or months with tenuous access to markets and income.

But, despite strong cultural and regional variation, the worldwide central tendency on the extent to which households are characterized by an internal economy rests closer to the sub-Saharan than to the Yemen Arab Republic or Ecuadorian rainforest end of the continuum. This is because of the impact of social class and the fact that the world majority is poor and most often engaged in low-resource farming or urban informal sector activities.

(3) In social class terms, with some ethnic or cultural exceptions, the further down in the class structure or economic sector (a) the higher the proportion of female-headed households (Blumberg with Garcia 1977; Buvinic et al. 1978), (b) the higher the proportion of women who are economically active, and (c) the higher the proportion of household subsistence they provide (see Deere 1977 on Peru; Matlon 1979; Norman et al.

1982; Blumberg 1988b on Nigeria; Mencher 1988 on India; and Roldan 1988 on Mexico).

(4) Where women have provider obligations and generate income, they tend to spend differently than do male counterparts. (a) They hold back less for themselves, devoting more to family subsistence (Mencher 1988 on India; Roldan 1988 on Mexico; Guyer 1988 on Cameroon). (b) Women are also more likely than men to spend that income on children's nutrition, health care, or education (see references in Blumberg 1989b).

Another example comes from Ecuador's coastal region, which is overwhelmingly mestizo and where women tend to be much less involved in farming than they are in the Andean highlands or the Amazon rainforest. In the poor coastal province of Manabi, men typically migrate for six months of off-farm work after the harvest. But a new development project provides an alternative economic activity for this period: processing cassava into flour and starch for the shrimp industry, Ecuador's largest export earner after oil. Fourteen men's associations were forced to process cassava into flour. Two women's associations process it into starch, a much more labor-intensive process. Hence women get a much lower return to their labor. Because their earning opportunities were so limited before (two months harvesting coffee; selling an occasional pig, chicken, or eggs), their economic situation improved more than men's. The men were pleased with their increased income and reported spending it on many things, including a better family diet. The women in the one association that had operated for the full 1988 season were ecstatic about their earnings. Their spending priorities were much more family-focused, mainly on children's food, health care, school expenses, and clothes, with a few household goods and clothes for the woman. In two surprise visits to the women's processing plant, we found that the children some women brought to the plant that day were notably well dressed and well fed, by local standards (Blumberg and Colyer 1989; Blumberg 1990b).

(5) Women with provider responsibilities will attempt to allocate their labor toward activities that put income and food under their control and, to the extent culturally feasible, away from activities that do not, even if the latter are somewhat more profitable for the household or husband. (This hypothesis has more empirical support than any other in the gender/women, and development literature, including an econometric study in Cameroon— Jones 1983—showing women choosing to work on their own sorghum rather than their husbands' more profitable rice unless compensated well above opportunity costs for their labor.)

(6) Because women almost always earn less than men, their opportunity costs are, by definition, lower.

(7) Third World economic change (ranging from the continuing economic/debt crisis to increased male migration and female-headed households) has tended to increase women's provider obligations faster than their economic situation improves. In some instances, women are hit harder than men by the painful austerity measures known as "structural adjustment programs" that most debt-ridden governments in developing countries have adopted under pressure from the International Monetary Fund and World Bank (see Joekes et al. 1989; Boyle 1988; Longhurst 1987).

(8) To the extent that women's lower earnings and increased obligations mean they have greater unmet income needs as well as lower opportunity costs, they may prove more responsive than male counterparts to even modest easing of constraints on their production or increases in prices and returns. An example from Cameroon indicates that, in a village where a new road made the marketing of perishable fruits and vegetables possible and more profitable, women responded more than men, devoting much more time to increased production, even though they already worked double the men's 32 hours a week and their newly profitable vegetable crops produced a much lower return than the men's now marketable plantains and bananas (Henn 1988).

The Ecuadorian cassava processing project provides another example. As noted, women express greater enthusiasm for their new work and income, even though their starch provides them a lower level of return than the men's flour. (In fact, their income increased proportionately more from cassava earnings than did the men's.) One project official also found women more productive than the men at a lower level of investment—a complete flour processing plant costs about 20% more than a starch processing plant. In short, women made more efficient use of resources (Blumberg and Colyer 1989; Blumberg 1990b).

(9) Thus there appears to be a synergy bonus when economically active, income-controlling women with provider responsibilities obtain—and get economic returns from—development aid targeted to their areas of economic expertise. This is because the women tend not only to use it to advantage concerning the project's economic goals but also to use resulting income under their control to enhance important social goals of development, from improved children's nutrition and welfare to decreased fertility.

(10) But this synergy effect works in the negative direction as well. Development efforts that ignore or undercut women's expected returns to labor on which the project depends may lower returns all around. The women may reallocate their labor in ways that are less efficient or prejudicial to the project's achieving its goals. Moreover, if their income falls, they face all the negative social consequences indicated above, such as lower input into

fertility and household resource allocation decisions and lowered ability to meet their children's food, health, and other needs.

Even this limited selection of hypotheses and documentation hints at the productivity and economic responsiveness of Third World women. Indeed, a stronger case can be made for Third World women's economic importance (Blumberg 1989b, 1989c, and 1990b try to do so empirically; Carloni 1987 provides another synthesis). But even though a large, empirically grounded literature on women in development has appeared since Boserup's (1970) path-breaking book engendered the field, it has had less than spectacular impact on the practices of key actors in the development community. Development practices concerning the incorporation of women have changed much more slowly than the policies of major development agencies. Within three years of the appearance of Boserup's book, for example, the U.S. Congress had amended the 1973 Foreign Assistance Act (via Section 113, the "Percy Amendment") to mandate that U.S. bilateral assistance henceforth integrate women into their country's economic development and improve their status. Soon, virtually all the main development entities, including the World Bank, the largest, had adopted policies in favor of including women in the activities and benefits of planned development. But implementation lagged behind intentions. The next set of hypotheses considers why this may be so.

Development elites' blinders with respect to women as producers. The second set of hypotheses from my evolving theory on gender and development pertains to those who guide development planning, paradigms, policies, and practice (see also Blumberg 1990b). An overwhelmingly male group, it includes development elites from the governments, universities, and top enterprises of First and Third World countries as well as key actors in the multilateral international development agencies and banks. These elites see a very different world than that described above. They fail to fully see women's economic productivity and, especially, their role as controllers of income within the household because at least three sets of blinders obscure and distort their view of women as agents of economic and social development.

(1) One blinder is imposed by their development paradigm's view of the monolithic household: Both mainstream development elites and their left and radical critics posit the household as the basic unit of analysis for development, and they see it as a unitary, resource-pooling entity, a black box. Indeed, the mainstream, neoclassical paradigm describes any household by a single production function. In other words, this model ignores regional, cultural, and ethnic variations, and elites do not perceive an internal economy of the household based on gender and age. Correspondingly, they ignore

intrahousehold inequality (Folbre 1988). To them it doesn't matter who within a household gets development information, does the work, or receives the rewards. Conversely, according to the hypotheses proposed above and much supporting data (Blumberg 1989b, 1989c; Dwyer and Bruce 1988), it does matter. Both women's productivity and power are negatively affected when their incentives are ignored or undercut.

(2) Another blinder is imposed by an inappropriate "farmer and his wife" agrarian perspective: Key elites in Third World rural development disproportionately are drawn from First World industrial countries or were trained there. These countries have agrarian (plow-based) farming systems, with a largely male labor force. Thus development assistance is aimed at "the farmer and his wife." The farmer gets technical aid, credit, and agricultural extension. The wife gets home economics. This means that, even in countries where the farming system is horticultural (hoe based, often with shifting cultivation) and women may be critically important as farmers, these elites may not see the difference. The situation in much of Africa, Natalie Hahn (personal communication, 1986) argues, is better described as "the African farmer and her husband." Indeed, men are the predominant labor force in only about a fifth of the 376 hoe societies included in Murdock's (1967) sample of 1,170 preindustrial societies.

(3) The third blinder is imposed by standardized statistics that leave much of women's productive activities un- or undercounted: A large literature now shows how standard national and international statistics undercount women due to a stress on monetized, formal sector data, whereas much of women's economic activities are in the ill-measured areas of low-resource farming and the urban informal sector (Anker 1983; Beneria 1982; Blumberg 1981; Deere 1977; Dixon 1982; Dixon-Mueller 1985; Fong 1980; Garrett 1976; United Nations 1978; Wainerman and Recchini de Lattes 1981). Many of these references also show how the phrasing of census and household survey questions about women often leads to their being wrongly listed as economically inactive.

Eliminating this third blinder may be more difficult than the first two, however. Any reforms that lead to counting more of women's economic activities along with those of men in now undercounted areas of the economy, such as low-resource farming and the informal sector, would add to a country's gross national product and GNP per capita. As it happens, however, much foreign aid (e.g., loans at below-market rates) is given out precisely on the basis of GNP per capita. So, unless all poor Third World countries simultaneously reformed their measurements, those that reduced undercounting would be penalized. In short, removing this third blinder is made problematic due to what one may term the *political economy* of national statistics.

(4) Therefore, based on the three blinders noted above, especially the black box model of the household and the androcentric, agrarian-derived model of how to raise rural productivity, development elites continue to target farming assistance to men and home economics to women. This remains overwhelmingly the case, even in horticultural, "separate purse" sub-Saharan Africa, where women raise as much as 80% of the locally produced food (Sivard 1985, pp. 5, 17).

Even if these triple blinders magically vanished, two further inertia factors also must be overcome before development elites personally make attention to gender a top priority, even when it is the official policy of their organizations. First, development elites may be reluctant to push programs aimed at directly increasing women's resources because of feelings of cultural inappropriateness, augmented, most likely, by what stratification theory tells us is the reluctance of dominant groups to give up power and privilege (witness the June 1989 crackdown in China). And loss of patriarchal advantage is especially difficult for cultural or psychological as well as structural reasons. Second, the reward system for professionals and managers working in development organizations is based more on success in moving money than the success of the programs and projects they mount (Tendler 1974; Fortmann 1985). Thus they are unlikely to suffer negative career repercussions if a program or project ultimately proves unsuccessful.

Given all these paradigmatic, perceptual, and institutional obstacles, it is not surprising that progress has been uneven and often slow in physically incorporating women into the activities and benefits of planned development.

TWO MACRO PROBLEMS WORSENED BY LEAVING WOMEN OUT

All of the preceding propositions have important macro-level implications.

The African Food Crisis: Exacerbated by Neglecting Needs and Incentives of Primary Producers—Women Farmers

We now know that women raise more than half the food produced in the Third World. Yet, even when women are primary food producers, as in much of sub-Saharan Africa, technical resources such as extension and credit still remain almost universally directed to the male household head. This is sometimes done explicitly under the rationale of the black box household model or the inappropriateness of women's receiving these services from male extension or credit officers. Otherwise, ignoring women farmers seems to be more a case of inaction than deliberate action. But regardless of the reasons, without access to the factors for agricultural intensification, women cannot improve their production. Moreover, they may not want to if their incentives are ignored or if the returns of their labor are diverted to their husbands via cooperatives or marketing schemes that enroll only the male household head. This is particularly true in the large parts of sub-Saharan Africa where a widespread system of separate purses prevails, where husband and wife or wives maintain most of their income as *his* or *her's* rather than *their* funds. Polygyny still is common in much of Africa and cowives almost always maintain separate purses from each other as well as from their husbands. In fact, in no other world region is the black box household model almost always such a poor and counterproductive fit. The continuing prevalence of patrilocal residence and patrilineal descent and inheritance also enhances the unsuitability of the black box model of the household in most of sub-Saharan Africa. Women need income not only to provide for their own children and personal needs but also to permit them to keep up obligations and exchanges with their own natal kin (see also Staudt 1987). This is crucial to women's security in case of divorce, desertion, widowhood, or other emergency, because the kinship system puts them at a structural disadvantage.

The complex causes of the African food crisis include factors ranging from ecological degradation under population pressure to war to entrance into the world economy under unfavorable terms. But surely the problem of worsening food shortfalls cannot be solved without considering the interests of the women farmers who actually produce the bulk of the food. Worse yet, if women's returns to food crops that traditionally generated income under their control are undermined by macro-level development policies that misdirect assistance to the head of the black box household, women may reallocate their labor so that food production may actually fall. The women-in-development literature is filled with examples of African development projects and goals that suffered because they relied on rural women for labor but provided them with no direct return. The women soon resorted to underproduction or even sabotage (see examples in Blumberg 1989b).

Thus these sets of hypotheses from my theories on gender illuminate what has, until now, been a neglected yet important factor in the persistent African food crisis. Specifically, they show how macro-level policies and practices (both of governments and of international development agencies) can founder on the reefs of ignored micro-level gender considerations. Conversely, macro-level policies that make information and resources available to women food producers and enhance both the yields and the income under their control could be helping not only regional food availability but also the well-being of these women's children, another bonus foregone when macro-level policies target only men or the black box household.

The Population Crisis: Gender Stratification and Fertility

During the Reagan administration, U.S. support for many population programs faltered or fell hostage to the political clout of the "pro-life" lobby. The numbers of humans relentlessly increased. Yet very few of the population planning elite were dealing with the full implications of the fact that women still have all the babies. The hypotheses above suggest that women with more independent economic leverage will use it to control fertility outcomes more in accordance with their own utilities, whatever they may be, rather than those of their mate, extended family, or state. Many fertility variables are at play other than completed family size. A woman's life chances are also much affected by her age at first birth, birth spacing, the sex ratio of the children, her age at last birth, her total number of children ever born, and the "means of intervention" (Davis and Blake 1956), from abstinence to traditional or modern contraception to abortion—including whether it is back alley and life threatening or legal and safe.

To be sure, not all women with leverage over their fertility will want fewer children. Where children provide sorely needed labor or income and are a woman's best hope for crisis aid and old age security, her desired fertility may be even higher than her husband's. Women in much of rural Africa, for example, still want and need more than six children (United Nations 1987). Why? With more of her children in school, and her older sons and, often, her mate migrating to the city, a woman urgently needs labor for her farm. With deforestation and increasing drought and desertification, fetching water and firewood can each take three to four hours a day and occupy an extra child or two. But, by and large, impressive documentation shows that most women in most developing countries use added leverage over fertility to curb it (United Nations 1987; also see literature review in Blumberg 1989b).

Interconnections between female income, education, and fertility. There is also another way in which women with independent economic resources are able to influence fertility: through their daughters' education, because the relationship between female schooling and fertility is generally inverse. Women with economic leverage tend to spend or promote their husbands' spending on education for daughters as well as sons, with one main exception, treated below.

In general, higher levels of development mean more access to education. Higher proportions of the age cohort can be accommodated in schools and, despite continuing regional and cultural variation, the disparity between boys and girls in school tends to shrink. But, in a number of Third World countries, preliminary evidence shows that girls are most likely to be sent to and kept in school when parents can see an economic return. And there also is preliminary evidence that mothers with economic leverage are more likely than their husbands to push a daughter's education.

The major exception to the promotion of daughters' education by women with income is when a woman's daughter's schooling will deprive her of labor needed for her own subsistence and income pursuits. Nigeria's Muslim Hausa wives are a good example. They live in the world's strictest seclusion but almost all of them engage in own-account economic pursuits without leaving their compounds. They use preadolescent, unsecluded daughters to sell their wares. Where there is no convenient substitute for their daughters' help, these women entrepreneurs are reluctant to send their girls to school (Schildkrout 1982, 1984; Coles 1983; Jackson 1985; Blumberg 1988b).

How female education generally reduces fertility. As the final report on the World Fertility Survey (United Nations 1987) shows, it is not just education but *education for girls* that offers some of the most impressive payoffs in fertility reduction in most of the Third World. Educating girls has a multidimensional impact on fertility. Below are six different paths whereby female education reduces fertility.

First, these girls tend to marry later, thus reducing exposure to pregnancy. Second, they almost always want fewer children. Third, they are more likely to use modern contraceptives. Fourth, their education dramatically reduces child mortality—and decreased infant mortality is an important predictor of lower fertility. Fifth, in most countries, educated females are more likely to enter the paid labor force and, sixth, have higher earnings. Combining the first four points, we can say that, for educated females, higher fertility is both less feasible and less desirable. Combining the fifth and sixth points, we can say that educated females are more likely to earn the income that will enhance their leverage over their own subsequent fertility, thus increasing the fertility-reducing impact of the first four points (see Blumberg 1989b).

And lower Third World fertility has a large payoff. First, Hess's (1988) regression study provides strong empirical evidence that reducing fertility contributes to economic growth in contemporary Third World countries. Using two-stage least square regressions for a sample of 49 countries over two time periods encompassing the 1960s and 1970s, Hess found that lower fertility directly increased the per capita growth rate in real national output. He also found that the most important factors lowering fertility were female educational opportunity and economic mobility as well as family planning program effectiveness (Hess 1988). All three factors involved females, and they proved more important than factors that did not, such as urbanization, per capita income, and infant mortality. We can speculate that every dollar spent for boys' education not matched by a dollar for girls may be lost to a Third World country by the subsequent higher fertility of those girls.

Second, lower fertility not only decreases the use of our planet's resources but also decreases the production of greenhouse gases contributing to global warming. While more of these gases are being produced from automobile combustion in the developed capitalist countries than from any other single activity in any part of the globe, extra people in poor Third World countries also precipitate further deforestation, another major culprit in the ominous trend toward heating up the earth.

In short, female-controlled economic resources and education are intertwined in complex ways that reduce fertility. In today's world, it is significant that lower fertility not only promotes income growth in Third World countries, it also helps ease the strain on our overburdened and apparently overheating planet.

Reducing constraints on women's creation of wealth and well-being. Planetary considerations also may be invoked (as, thus far, economic and welfare arguments have had limited success) as a rationale for reducing some of the special and daunting constraints under which Third World women toil. Time budget studies show that poor women work longer hours than men and that much of their time is spent in several primary activities that take inordinate and needless time. These include fetching firewood and water, hand processing basic staples before cooking, and then cooking with inefficient fuel, fires, or stoves (Blumberg 1989b).

For example, in poorer Third World countries, it is estimated that over half the nation's energy budget goes up in the smoke of women's daily cooking fires. And with drought, deforestation, and increasing population pressure, it takes longer to gather increasingly marginal fuels, which are inherently less energy efficient and require longer and more closely watched cooking. Yet it remains difficult to get funding for projects that ease women's fuel wood, water, and hand-processing drudgework. One study (Howe 1985) found that, in the Yemen Arab Republic (YAR), women in the average household spent 11.5 hours per day providing water, fuel wood, and cooking. Computer simulation indicated that merely bringing water into village spigots (not houses), and providing butane cooking gas, would reduce women's burden from 11.5 hours to 1.7 hours per household per day. Adult women in the household could increase the time they spent in agricultural production by 50% while adolescent girls' time could be freed enough for them to go to school (Sivard 1985, pp. 39-41). The YAR has the world's lowest combined female literacy (3%) and schooling rates (8%). The macro-economic consequences of thus reducing women's drudgework, Howe (1985) found, range from sharply cutting food imports (currently, agricultural output is increasingly falling behind food consumption) to reducing the foreign exchange drain of hiring expatriate health and education workers due to a lack of educated women.

Since this report was presented to the YAR government in 1985, there has been interest but little action. The YAR is not alone. With a few exceptions, amelioration of these "women's work" constraints on female productivity and school attendance remains a hard sell in the development community. And so women continue to work—and generate income, food, and babies— under easily remedied constraints to their productivity or stewardship of world resources.

CONCLUSIONS

Recognizing women's full contributions to world wealth and well-being is the first step toward a "win-win" approach with impact from household to planet. With regard to production, even with a system of national statistics that seriously undercounts women's productive activities, 1985 ILO estimates indicate that women comprise 41% of the measured labor force in developed countries and 32% in developing ones. Since 1950, the growth rate of female labor force participation has outstripped the rise for males by two to one (Sivard 1985, p. 12). And this refers only to the measured labor force. Not only has this increase in economic participation typically resulted in female-controlled income, some of whose micro and indirect macro effects I have explored, it also has contributed directly to the wealth of nations.

In the United States, the one country where, to date, women's contribution to national wealth has been measured econometrically, it was substantial: Between 1890 and 1980, women aged 15-64 increased their formal labor force participation from 20% to 60% while the ratio of female to male full-time earnings rose from $.46 to $.60. These two factors were associated with a growth in per capita GNP that exceeded the growth in male earnings by 28% (Goldin 1986, p. 557). In this same period, women's teaching for low wages made possible the mass education that added another 12% to 23% to the national income (Carter 1986, p. 598).

With regard to reproduction, women, in addition to having all the babies, continue to do most of the housework, to fetch water and fuel wood, and to provide first line health care. As a time drain, these activities keep millions of girls out of school—and their mothers down. Moreover, if women's unpaid household labor were counted and given economic value, in 1985, it would have added an estimated $4 trillion, or one-third of the world's annual economic product (Sivard 1985, p. 5).

With regard to education, there has been some progress since 1950 in narrowing the percentage gap in primary and secondary school enrollments between boys and girls, even though, in sheer numbers, the shortfall of girls enrolled is bigger than ever. In the Third World, 76 girls are enrolled in primary and secondary school for every 100 boys (Sivard 1985, p. 22).

Giving women access to the factors that improve their productivity, from credit to technical assistance, could be the first step toward this ultimate "win-win" scenario. Their greater productivity would enhance economic goals of development, at both micro and macro levels. And, to the extent that their enhanced productivity also brings more income under their control, we would expect that their children and families' well-being would gain, while, in most countries, fertility would drop. Then, if the burden of needlessly time-consuming reproductive activities were eased and more emphasis placed on educating their daughters, we could expect further benefits to production, family welfare, and most emphatically, fertility reduction. And all of this would take place in the context of reducing ecological stress and the rate of resource depletion and planetary warming.

To conclude as a partisan citizen rather than an objective social scientist (if such a creature exists), let me ask: How could anyone be opposed? How can something so important be left to the triply blindered eyes of the development elites? How can we not add our voices to the cry that dealing women in is as important as reducing the number of NATO tanks or backing democracy where it is emerging, and maybe more so, when we consider the alternatives.

REFERENCES

Acharya, Meena and Lynn Bennett. 1983. *Women and the Subsistence Sector: Economic Participation in Household Decision-Making in Nepal.* Working Paper no. 526. Washington, DC: World Bank.

Alberti, Amalia. 1986. "Gender, Ethnicity, and Resource Control in the Andean Highlands of Ecuador." Ph.D. dissertation, Stanford University.

Anker, Richard. 1983. "Female Labour Force Participation in Developing Countries: A Critique of Current Definitions in Data Collection Methods." *International Labour Review, 122* (6, Nov.-Dec.).

Beneria, Lourdes, ed. 1982. "Accounting for Women's Work." *Women and Development: The Sexual Division of Labor in Rural Societies.* New York: Praeger.

Blumberg, Rae Lesser. 1978. *Stratification: Socioeconomic and Sexual Inequality.* Dubuque, IA: William C. Brown.

———. 1981. "Females, Farming and Food: Rural Development and Women's Participation in Agricultural Production Systems." Pp. 24-100 in *Invisible Farmers: Women and the Crisis in Agriculture,* edited by B. C. Lewis. Washington, DC: Agency for International Development.

———. 1984. "A General Theory of Gender Stratification." Pp. 23-100 in *Sociological Theory 1984,* edited by R. Collins. San Francisco: Jossey-Bass.

———. 1988a. "Income Under Female vs. Male Control: Hypotheses from a Theory of Gender Stratification and Data from the Third World." *Journal of Family Issues* 9:51-84.

———. 1988b. *The Half-Hidden Economic Roles of Rural Nigerian Women and National Development.* Draft. Washington, DC: World Bank.

———. 1989a. "Toward a Feminist Theory of Development" Pp. 161-99 in *Feminism and Sociological Theory,* edited by R. Wallace. Newbury Park, CA: Sage.

———. 1989b. *Making the Case for the Gender Variable: Women and the Wealth and Well-Being of Nations.* Washington, DC: Agency for International Development, Office of Women in Development.

———. 1989c. Gender, Control of Household Income, and Planned Development: 20 Hypotheses. Draft. Washington, DC: Agency for International Development/GENESYS.

———. 1990a. "Power, Class, Ethnicity and Gender in the Ecuadorian Highlands and Amazon." Paper presented at the Symposium on Power, Class, Ethnicity and Gender in the World System, San Diego State University.

———. 1990b. *Gender Matters: Involving Women in Development in Latin American and the Caribbean.* Draft. Washington, DC: Agency for International Development, Bureau for Latin America and the Caribbean.

———. Forthcoming-a. *Women and the Wealth of Nations: Theory and Research on Gender and Global Development.* New York: Praeger.

———. Forthcoming-b. *Women, Development and the Wealth of Nations: Making the Case for the Gender Variable.* Boulder, CO: Westview.

Blumberg, Rae Lesser and Marion Tolbert Coleman. 1989. "A Theoretical Look at the Gender Balance of Power in the American Couple." *Journal of Family Issues* 10:225-50.

Blumberg, Rae Lesser and Dale Colyer. 1989. *Assessment of Ecuador's Agricultural Sector: Social Institutions, Gender, and Rural Living Conditions.* Working Paper no. 12. Quito, Ecuador: Agency for International Development.

Blumberg, Rae Lesser with Maria Pilar Garcia. 1977. "The Political Economy of the Mother-Child Family: A Cross-Societal View." Pp. 99-163 in *Beyond the Nuclear Family Model,* edited by L. Lenero-Otero. London: Sage.

Boserup, Ester. 1970. *Women's Role in Economic Development.* New York: St. Martin's.

Boyle, Philip. 1988. "The Socioeconomic Effects of Structural Adjustment on Women." Washington, DC: Agency for International Development.

Buvinic, Myra, Nadia Youssef, and Barbara von Elm. 1978. *Women-Headed Households: The Ignored Factor in Development Planning.* Washington, DC: International Center for Research on Women.

Carloni, Alice Stewart. 1987. *Women in Development: A.I.D.'s Experience, 1973-85.* Vol. 1. Program Evaluation Report no. 18. Washington, DC: Agency for International Development.

Carter, Susan B. 1986. "Comment" on "The Female Labor Force and American Economic Growth" by Claudia Goldin. Pp. 594-604 in *Long-Term Factors in American Economic Growth,* edited by S. Engerman and R. Gallman. Chicago: University of Chicago Press.

Coles, Catherine. 1983. *Urban Muslim Women and Social Change in Northern Nigeria.* Working Paper no. 29. Madison: University of Wisconsin.

Davis, Kingsley and Judith Blake. 1956. "Social Structure and Fertility: An Analytic Framework." *Economic Development and Cultural Change* 4:211-35.

Deere, Carmen. 1977. "The Social Relations of Production and Peruvian Peasant Women's Work." *Latin American Perspectives* 4:48-69.

Dixon, Ruth. 1982. "Women in Agriculture: Counting the Labor Force in Developing Countries." *Population and Development Review* 8:539-66.

Dixon-Mueller, Ruth. 1985. *Women's Work in Third World Agriculture*. Geneva: International Labour Organization.

Dwyer, Daisy and Judith Bruce, eds. 1988. *A Home Divided: Women and Income in the Third World*. Palo Alto, CA: Stanford University Press.

Fapohunda, Eleanor. 1988. "The Nonpooling Household: A Challenge to Theory." Pp. 143-54 in *A Home Divided: Women and Income in the Third World*, edited by D. Dwyer and J. Bruce. Palo Alto, CA: Stanford University Press.

Folbre, Nancy. 1988. "Toward a New Paradigm of Household Economics." Pp. 248-62 in *A Home Divided: Women and Income in the Third World*, edited by D. Dwyer and J. Bruce. Palo Alto, CA: Stanford University Press.

Fong, Monica. 1980. "Victims of Old-Fashioned Statistics." *Ceres: FAO Review on Agriculture and Development* 13:29-32.

Fortmann, Louise. 1985. "A Matter of Focus: The Inclusion of Women in USAID Agricultural Projects, 1976-84." Working Paper no. 91. Washington, DC: Agency for International Development.

Garrett, Patricia. 1976. "Some Cultural Constraints on the Agricultural Activities of Women: The Chilean Hacienda." Madison: University of Wisconsin, Land Tenure Center.

Goldin, Claudia. 1986. "The Female Labor Force and American Economic Growth." Pp. 557-604 in *Long-Term Factors in American Economic Growth*, edited by S. Engerman and R. Gallman. Chicago: University of Chicago Press.

Guyer, Jane. 1980. "Household Budgets and Women's Incomes." Working Paper no. 28. Boston: Boston University, African Studies Center.

———. 1988. "Dynamic Approaches to Domestic Budgeting: Cases and Methods from Africa." Pp. 155-72 in *A Home Divided: Women and Income in the Third World*, edited by D. Dwyer and J. Bruce. Palo Alto, CA: Stanford University Press.

Henn, Jean Koopman. 1988. "Intrahousehold Dynamics and State Policies as Constraints on Food Production: Results of a 1985 Agroeconomics Survey in Cameroon." Pp. 315-30 in *Gender Issues in Farming Systems Research and Extension*, edited by S. Poats, M. Schmink, and A. Spring. Boulder, CO: Westview.

Hess, Peter N. 1988. *Population Growth and Socio-Economic Progress in Less Developed Countries: Determinants of Fertility Transition*. New York: Praeger.

Hill, Polly. 1969. "Hidden Trade in Hausaland." *Man* 4:392-409.

Howe, Gary Nigel. 1985. *The Present and Potential Contribution of Women to Economic Development in the Yemen Arab Republic*. Washington, DC: Agency for International Development, Office of Women in Development.

Jackson, Cecile. 1985. *The Kano River Irrigation Project*. West Hartford, CT: Kumarian.

Joekes, Susan, Margaret Lycette, Lisa McGowan, and Karen Searle. 1989. "Women and Structural Adjustment." Prepared for the Meeting of the Women in Development Expert Group of the OECD Development Assistance Committee.

Jones, Christine. 1983. *The Impact of the SEMRY I Irrigated Rice Production Project on the Organization of Production and Consumption at the Intrahousehold Level*. Washington, DC: Agency for International Development, Bureau for Program and Policy Coordination.

Lenski, Gerhard. 1966. *Power and Privilege*. New York: McGraw-Hill.

Longhurst, Richard, Samura Kamara, and Joseph Mensurah. 1987. "Structural Adjustment and Vulnerable Groups in Sierra Leone." *IDS Bulletin* 19.

Matlon, Peter. 1979. *Income Distribution Among Farmers in Northern Nigeria: Empirical Results and Policy Implications*. Washington, DC: Agency for International Development and Michigan State University.

Mencher, Joan. 1988. "Women's Contribution to Household Maintenance in Two Regions of South India." Pp. 99-119 in *A Home Divided: Women and Income in the Third World*, edited by D. Dwyer and J. Bruce. Palo Alto, CA: Stanford University Press.

Murdock, George. 1967. "Ethnographic Atlas: A Summary." *Ethnology* 6:109-236.

Norman, David, Emmy Simmons, and Henry Hays, eds. 1982. *Farming Systems in the African Savanna: Research Strategies for Development*. Boulder, CO: Westview.

Poeschel, Ursula. 1988. *La Mujer Salasaca.* 2nd ed. Quito: Ediciones Abya-Yala.

Roldan, Martha. 1988. "Renegotiating the Marital Contract: Intrahousehold Patterns of Money Allocation and Women's Subordination Among Domestic Outworkers in Mexico City." Pp. 229-47 in *A Home Divided: Women and Income in the Third World*, edited by D. Dwyer and J. Bruce. Palo Alto, CA: Stanford University Press.

Schildkrout, Enid. 1982. "Dependence and Autonomy: The Economic Activities of Secluded Hausa Women in Kano, Nigeria." Pp. 55-81 in *Women and Work in Africa*, edited by E. Bay. Boulder, CO: Westview.

———. 1984. "Schooling or Seclusion: Choices for Northern Nigerian Women." *Cultural Survival Quarterly* 8:46-48.

Scudder, Thayer. 1979. "Evaluatory Report on Mission to Sri Lankan Settlement Projects." Special Study presented to Asia Bureau. Washington, DC: Agency for International Development.

Simmons, Emmy. 1976. *Economic Research on Women in Rural Development in Northern Nigeria.* OLC Paper no. 12. Washington, DC: American Council on Education, Overseas Liaison Committee.

Sivard, Ruth. 1985. *Women: A World Survey.* Washington, DC: World Priorities.

Staudt, Kathleen. 1987. "Uncaptured or Unmotivated? Women and the Food Crisis in Africa." *Rural Sociology* 52:37-55.

Tendler, Judith. 1974. *Inside Foreign Aid.* Baltimore: Johns Hopkins University Press.

United Nations. 1978. "Effective Mobilization of Women in Development." Report to the Secretary General. UN/A/33/238. New York: Author.

———. 1987. *Fertility Behaviours in the Context of Development: Evidence from the World Fertility Survey.* (ST/ESA/SER.A/100). New York: U.N. Department of International Economic and Social Affairs.

Wainerman, Catalina and Zulma Recchini de Lattes. 1981. *El Trabajo Feminino en el Banquillo de los Acusados: La Medicion Censal en America Latina.* Mexico City: Population Council.

Weiss, Wendy. 1985. "Es El Que Manda: Sexual Inequality and Its Relationship to Economic Development in the Ecuadorean Sierra." Ph.D. dissertation, Bryn Mawr College.

10

Parenthood, Work, and Women

Samuel H. Preston

A decade ago, a plenary session on stratification at the ASA annual meetings no doubt would have featured the process by which sons inherit their fathers' occupational standing. The session for which this chapter was written was about relations between men and women. The shift in focus reflects the upsurge in interest in this unsettled domain as well as the excellent work sociologists have accomplished in charting its perturbations. We are presented with two fine examples of these studies, one addressed to developing countries and one to developed.

I begin with remarks on Professor Blumberg's chapter, which has several parts. One discusses how development policy has ignored women's role as producers of wealth. Part of the problem, as she points out, is the obsession with per capita income as the central measure of economic development. Things count only if they enter the monetized economy. Dams and factories appear more worthwhile than home-produced food and clothing. A second problem is that development policies treat the household as a unitary black box within which conflicts are magically resolved and resources benignly allocated.

Both of these perceptual afflictions are traceable to lazy thinking at the higher reaches of development policy. It is easier to assume that households are maximizing a single utility function than to deal with the messy realities beneath. It is easier to assign value to those activities that have an established market price than to those that do not. But both problems can be overcome, and it is good to see someone insist that we try. Blumberg is not a voice in the wilderness but joins a growing chorus of people who are attempting a fundamental reorientation of development policy, one that perhaps started with the "basic needs approach" promoted by economists and social scientists at the University of Sussex in the 1970s. The idea is to measure progress by how well societies meet the basic needs of their members for food, education, longevity, and jobs and to institute those policies that are most directly designed to meet those needs. This approach has been quite popular in international organizations, and the development policies of Canada, England, and the Scandinavian countries have been substantially recast along these lines.

When basic needs are at issue, it quickly becomes obvious that it is women in developing countries who are most directly responsible for satisfying most of them. A group of us at the University of Pennsylvania prepared a U.N. monograph several years ago on micro-level correlates of child mortality in 15 developing countries. The most important variable that emerged in this study was the mother's level of schooling, which had roughly twice the importance for child survival as the father's education (United Nations 1985). Economists are perplexed by this finding because it is father's education that is more closely associated with household income. But better educated mothers are apparently able to arrange resources in such a way as to enhance child survival at a particular level of household income, and this ability is confirmed by several more direct studies. In one country, Nigeria, we were able to look at the separate impact of mother's and father's income on child survival. Consistent with Blumberg, we found an impact four times larger for mother's income. It seems clear that a higher fraction of women's earnings than men's earnings were being spent on children, which agrees with ethnographic accounts of child-raising norms in West Africa.

Yet women who worked outside the home in Nigeria and in most of the other countries had higher child mortality than women who didn't work. If a woman worked, her children were better off the more she earned, but they were best off if she didn't work. Studies in the United States and Britain at the turn of the century clearly demonstrate the same phenomenon, which is almost certainly related to the greater difficulties of breast-feeding faced by employed women in situations where there are no reasonable substitutes for breast milk (e.g., Preston and Haines 1991). It is also related to conditions in the home that urge mothers of young children into the labor force in societies where there are strong sanctions against mothers' working. But the finding does give one pause in thinking that work outside the home is an unalloyed benefit, at least for infants.

The African situation is quite important to the rest of Blumberg's chapter, which presents some empirical generalizations about women's relative status. Africa presents a paradox. On the one hand, separate purses are often maintained by husbands and wives; women are, to an unusual extent, economically active outside the home; and women are principally responsible for subsidizing child rearing. African women are unusually autonomous compared with, say, Indian women. On the other hand, men typically control the property, and among the property they control are women, for whom a large bride-price is typically paid at marriage. The fact that men provide less in the way of support for the household than elsewhere and contribute less of their own labor to it is not an obvious advantage for women.

Blumberg suggests that allowing women to have more income under their control, as in much of Africa, will ultimately lead to a reduction in fertility. But fertility is higher in Africa than it is anywhere else in the world. Esther Boserup, Jack and Pat Caldwell, and Odile Frank and Geoffrey McNicoll all suggest that the typical African family structure, which places reproductive decisions in the hands of husbands and the economic burden on the shoulders of wives, is exceptionally conducive to high fertility. The husband's prestige is enhanced by having large numbers of children, and he bears little of their cost. The woman, on the other hand, is highly dependent on her children in old age because the husband, who may take additional wives, will provide little. Consequently, she is eager to ensure a sufficient number of surviving children to provide protection through the life cycle.

So it's unclear to me that the African model of gender relations is one to which other societies might aspire. Gender stratification is clearly a multi-dimensional concept, as Blumberg recognizes. Who controls property is perhaps as important as who can work outside the household; and how many resources men and women contribute to one another, and to their joint enterprise, is perhaps the key to understanding the relative positions of men and women. We also need to understand the conditions that men and women face *outside* the married state to interpret the nature of the marital bargains that are struck. Once we have a clear picture of these circumstances, we then face the even more daunting task of accounting for how they arose and how they might change. Blumberg provides a very useful preliminary road map to this terrain, and her exciting program of research is filling in some of the vital details.

Let me now turn to the chapter by Randall Collins. This is a provocative and stimulating attempt to understand recent changes in gender stratification in developed countries. It is embedded, about as deeply as a brief chapter can be, in a well-articulated theory of social change. In fact, the theory gets quite a bit more attention than does gender. The distinctions drawn between interest politics and ritual politics, and within the latter between universalistic and particularistic impulses, are very clearly developed and put to excellent use.

The basic argument as it relates to gender is that massive social changes in the roles of women relative to men will have to come from the top down, from political mobilization of cosmopolitan groups on behalf of universalistic ideals. Collins admits to not fully understanding how such mobilization occurs and suggests that the answer may lie in some as yet undiscovered principles about the conflict of macro structures. The feminist movement of the 1960s and 1970s, which is seen as a spin-off of the antiwar and black civil rights movement, had now become stalled, he argues, by the inevitable particularistic reaction.

"Bottom-up changes"—those aggregate changes that reflect millions of choices about work, children, and marriage that are made by women in their own households—are seen as having little potential to alter gender stratification. They are disorganized and marginalist, lacking the power to fuel a major social movement.

It seems to me that Collins's arguments work better as an explanation of the feminist movement and countermovement than as explanations of changes in gender stratification, to which the feminist movement is only loosely related. By *gender stratification,* I refer to the distribution of activities and resources between men and women perceived through such measures as labor force participation, earnings, wealth, and hours spent in child care and home building as well as through interactional indicators such as those supplied by conversational analysis.

Collins is skeptical about the potential for bottom-up processes to produce large-scale social change. Part of the reason, I think, is that he may be talking about short-term changes, and another part of the reason is that he has omitted any discussion of technology and economy. Changes in technology—the way we produce things that we value—have unquestionably been the dominant source of economic change in the past century, and these have in turn been a principal source of social change. This is probably seen most clearly in the process of urbanization. We didn't go from being a 20% urban society to being an 80% urban society because of a political movement. The millions who moved to cities overcame the Jeffersonian ideal of the yeoman farmer and a national political system that favored rural areas and agricultural interests. They were driven instead by technical changes that reduced the prices of agricultural products relative to manufactured goods and reduced the fraction of income spent on food. It was a bottom-up, micro-level convulsion, powered by a macro-level change in productive technology.

Much the same process, I believe, has been at work to shift the balance of gender relations. I'm about the 500th person to point out that the emergence of service industries has been a relative advantage for women. As of 1986, only 22% of the U.S. labor force was in manufacturing and construction and 3% in agriculture (U.S. Bureau of the Census 1989). The remaining 75% of the labor force was in the service sector, nearly triple the fraction in 1900. Blumberg notes that males have, on average, one-third to one-half more upper body strength, which was clearly a greater advantage in plow-based agriculture and in the heavy manufacturing industries that dominated the early stages of the Industrial Revolution. It was much less of an advantage in textiles, and if one looks at textile towns in the nineteenth century, one finds precursors of today's patterns. Women had much higher labor force participation rates, they married later and less frequently, and they had fewer children. Coal-mining towns, where women had few labor force opportunities, had nearly universal marriage and exceptionally high fertility (Ogle 1890; Charles and Moshinsky 1938). There are echoes of these same patterns today, with manufacturing areas having a more rigid sexual division of labor than service areas. Washington, D.C., presents an extreme example of the latter. Women in Washington, nearly all of whom work for pay, are currently bearing, on average, only 0.7 children in the course of their lives.

Women have responded to their improved opportunities outside the home by increasing their work effort and adjusting family behaviors, especially with regard to marriage and fertility. These increased opportunities were in turn a product of the same kinds of technological changes that fueled the earlier phase of industrial growth: faster growth of productivity in manufacturing than in services and consumers' tendencies to spend larger fractions of their higher incomes on services than on manufactured goods.

For a while, this explanation of increased work by women seemed inadequate, because the ratio of female full-time earnings to male full-time earnings was stuck at about .6; how could a constant relative wage for women be responsible for the large increases in women's labor force participation in the past several decades? But Goldin (1990) has shown that this constancy was something of a mirage. Because so many women were pouring into the labor market, the average experience of women workers actually declined and artificially depressed average earnings. Once the experience distribution was controlled, women's earnings were rising relative to men's, and now even the uncontrolled averages are rising.

Increased earnings for women have meant not only increased power and autonomy within the family, as a large number of studies have shown, but also a greater ability to live independently and to avoid some of the bad marital bargains that women in the past were forced to accept.

I am not claiming that technological change and rising income are the whole story of the changes that have occurred in relations between the sexes. But they are the basic foundation on which these changes are built. It is impossible to imagine the current sexual division of labor in the family and the work force arising in an agrarian setting or in mining towns.

What long-term economic change fails to account for satisfactorily is the timing of changes in labor force participation, fertility, and marriage. As Collins notes, these changes have been fitful, quite slow in the early decades of the twentieth century, rapid in the 1920s, and exceptionally fast since 1965. I don't think that the details of this history can be adequately interpreted without introducing other factors, which I'll call ideational—neither, for that matter, can current international differences in gender stratification among highly advanced countries, ranging from the very equalitarian pattern of Sweden to the much more rigid sexual division of labor in Japan.

What ideational factors have been at work in the United States? Collins is certainly correct that a major force has been the slow and irregular march of universalism and egalitarianism, the notion that individuals are entitled to at least begin the game on a level playing field. Another factor is individualism, the idea that individuals should be able to pursue their conception of self-fulfillment minimally constrained by social expectations and entanglements. The feminist movement of the last two decades has unquestionably invoked the rhetoric and ideals of universalism and individualism to help create a different climate for women's daily lives.

But we are still left with questions of timing, as Collins notes. Why did these ideals, vividly cast since the Enlightenment, suddenly prove so much more powerful in the past several decades? I would suggest—*speculate* may be a better term—that one answer is to be found in the changing social construction of parenthood. In preparing a monograph on child health at the turn of the century, I am struck, as others have been, by the enormity of the burden that was laid at the feet of parents, especially mothers. Children were a national treasure, needed to carry forward the national purpose, including the fighting of battles. Great concern was expressed by officials, social scientists, journalists, and physicians about the quality of American children, particularly after a high fraction of World War I recruits were rejected on medical grounds.

Child raising itself had become far more arduous after the 1880s, when the germ theory of disease was accepted. Before, the sources of disease lay essentially outside the home, in rivers, cesspools, and slaughterhouses. Then, afterward, the principal sources of disease were to be found inside the home, on bottles, hands, flies, food, and one another. Mothers were urged to become warriors against filth, and constant vigilance was required. Feeding formulas were sometimes so complicated that pediatricians couldn't understand them. The discovery of vitamins in the 1910s added an additional burden. The public health movement, as historian Richard Meckel (1990) has effectively documented, was from 1900 to 1930 principally a movement for better mothering.

By and large, mothers seemed to buy the heroic view of their role, and the Children's Bureau pamphlet *Baby Care* became the largest selling publication in the history of the Government Printing Office. Of course, they were expected to do much more than keep their children alive: they were expected to educate, to instruct in religious doctrines, and above all to instill the character traits that would enable children to grow into productive citizens and workers. Nobody seemed to question the importance of what they were doing. This was an era before per capita GNP had become the central indicator of social performance. Women were pigeonholed and restricted, but what most were doing was socially valued, even sacred.

Things changed. Immunization and antibiotics moved much of the responsibility for child health outside the home and into the medical establishment. Household appliances meant that many fewer hours a day needed to be spent on the tedium of homemaking. The postwar economic boom meant that fewer financial sacrifices were required to raise a family. Women predictably took advantage of these changes by doing more of what everyone told them they should be doing: having babies and raising families.

But they had too many babies. By the 1950s, their babies were flooding school systems and raising taxes, becoming juvenile delinquents and threatening public order, straining labor markets and undermining economic prosperity, and eventually posing the threat of ecological collapse. Their children were not even of military value, because the next war would be fought with missiles rather than rifles.

The message that population growth was too rapid in the United States and other countries was spread very widely in the 1960s and encountered almost no dissent outside of the Catholic church. The large majority of women seemed to accept the notion. By 1970, 69% of a national sample of reproductive-aged women agreed with the statement: "United States population growth is a serious problem." Those who agreed with it intended to have nearly one fewer child than those who didn't (Rindfuss 1972). For some women, of course, the population explosion was merely a convenient rationalization for doing what they wanted to do anyway; and working outside the home was an increasingly attractive alternative. But this was a situation where very few legitimate reasons for childlessness or low fertility had been available, as Judith Blake has described, so even as a rationalization the doctrine may have affected behavior. For other women, and men, the depreciation of parenthood must have been demoralizing. Parenting had come to be seen as sufficiently easy that women who stayed at home with their children were considered by many to be lazy. Worse, the products of their endeavors were no longer national treasures but despoilers of the common.

Into this breech rushed the women's movement, which redefined the responsible life of a woman to include activities outside the home—perhaps even to be centered on such activities. I'm not suggesting that the movement had no other roots, only that it resonated to the extent that it did because of role confusion that had been engendered by a changing social construction of parenthood. This changed construction shows up clearly in surveys that ask what people think about *other* people's family-related behaviors. The valuable study by Veroff et al. (1981) asked representative samples of adults in 1957 and 1976 the identical question, "Suppose all you knew about a woman was that she did not want to get married. What would you guess she was like?" The proportion answering with only negative characteristics— selfish, immature, peculiar—declined from 53% to 34% between these years. Even more dramatically, Thornton and Freedman (1982) report on the results of asking the same group of Detroit women in 1962 and 1980 whether they agreed with the statement: "Almost all married couples who can *ought* to have children." In 1962, 84% agreed with the statement; but, by 1980, only 43% agreed with it.

I'm taking something of a rational choice approach here, arguing that there is some process by which the social interest comes to be defined and then to be reflected in norms of appropriate behavior as well as in laws and policies such as those related to abortion, contraception, divorce, and employment. These are macro structures that influence the behavior of individuals and in turn they respond to that behavior in the aggregate.

However complex the process by which these macro structures are created, it's clear that, as Collins suggests, social scientists are playing a central role therein. We form one of the important macro structures whose behavior we have examined at our meeting. Given the importance of what we do, we can be grateful that the chapters by Blumberg and Collins were so responsibly and thoughtfully constructed.

REFERENCES

Charles, Enid and Pearl Moshinsky. 1938. "Differential Fertility in England and Wales During the Past Two Decades." Pp. 106-60 in *Political Arithmetic,* edited by L. Hogben. New York: Macmillan.

Goldin, Claudia. 1990. *Understanding the Gender Gap: An Economic History of American Women.* New York: Oxford University Press.

Meckel, Richard. 1990. *Save the Babies: American Public Health Reform and the Prevention of Infant Mortality, 1850-1929.* Baltimore: Johns Hopkins University Press.

Ogle, William. 1890. "On Marriage Rates and Marriage Ages, with Special Reference to the Growth of Population." *Journal of the Royal Statistical Society* 53:253-80.

Preston, Samuel and Michael Haines. 1991. *Fatal Years: Child Mortality in Late Nineteenth Century America.* Princeton, NJ: Princeton University Press.

Rindfuss, Ronald. 1972. "Recent Trends in Population Attitudes." Pp. 465-74 in *U.S. Commission on Population Growth and the American Future.* Vol. 6, *Aspects of Population Growth Policy.* Washington, DC: Government Printing Office.

Thornton, Arland and Deborah Freedman. 1982. "Changing Attitudes Toward Marriage and Single Life." *Family Planning Perspectives* 14:297-303.

United Nations. 1985. *Socioeconomic Differentials in Child Mortality in Developing Countries.* New York: Author.

U.S. Bureau of the Census. 1989. *Statistical Abstract of the United States.* Washington, DC: Government Printing Office.

Veroff, Joseph, Elizabeth Douvan, and Richard Kulka. 1981. *The Inner Americans: A Self-Portrait from 1957 to 1976.* New York: Basic Books.

Part III
Perspectives on Social Issues

11

Creating Inequality in the Schools:
A Structural Perspective

Alan C. Kerckhoff

A central issue in discussions of the macro-micro distinction is the degree to which the former influences the latter. How do the larger social entities sociologists study affect individual lives? Do individuals develop in distinctive ways because of their locations in social structures? One place where such lasting influences are assumed to occur is in school. But schools have internal structures, and all pupils do not occupy the same positions in the structure. A charge sometimes brought against our schools is that their internal structures segregate pupils into groups that have unequal opportunities to learn and that, through these unequal opportunities, the schools actually create inequality among their pupils.

I will tentatively conclude that schools *do* create inequality, but I will arrive at that conclusion only after offering a specific conceptual framework and sharply delimiting the issues to be discussed. To put the matter in a broader context than the chapter's title might imply, I will outline three models of inequality in the schools and assess the logical and empirical bases for them.

Before turning to the three models, however, it is important to be clear about a fundamental point. We must recognize that, in all contemporary industrial societies, a primary function of the schools is to introduce into the society a *stratified* flow of young adults. Whatever else may be the function or purpose of the schools, they are supposed to *grade* their pupils. The term *grade* is so familiar to us that we sometimes lose sight of the fact that it

AUTHOR'S NOTE: *This chapter is based on work supported by the National Science Foundation under grant SES-8711211.*

means to classify something into differentiated categories that are hierarchically ordered. We grade pupils in the same way we grade eggs or beef. We evaluate their qualities and judge their relative merits according to a set of generally agreed upon criteria. Schools are supposed to *teach*, of course, but a school that does not *evaluate* its pupils has done only part of the job. Neither the school system itself nor the society at large knows what to do with an undifferentiated set of products.

Thus inequality is one of the essential characteristics of pupils emerging from our schools. We expect, even require, them to be unequal. The rest of society requires the differentiation the schools carry out. A wide range of outcomes and later decisions depend on the schools' effectiveness in carrying out that task. Schools use "a set of institutional rules which legitimately classify and authoritatively allocate individuals to positions in society" (Meyer 1977, p. 59). They function, to use Joel Spring's (1976) apt phrase, as "the sorting machine" for the rest of the society.

Much recent criticism of the schools is essentially a rejection of their sorting function. Many critics seem to believe that all pupils should leave the school system on an equal basis, that the schools should do everything possible to produce a uniform product, and that inequalities are clear evidence that the schools have failed. However ideologically appealing that position may be, it clearly contradicts the history and current organization of our school system. The system is structured so as to turn out a stratified set of products, and a great deal would have to change in our society if it ceased to do so.

For the purposes of this chapter, then, the issue is not *whether* the schools produce a certifiably unequal set of products. It is not even whether the schools *should* produce unequal products. Rather, the issue is how those inequalities come about. In oversimplified terms, the question can be posed as the difference between the schools *creating* inequalities and *identifying* inequalities. Whichever it is, one of the schools' primary charters is to legitimize the society's stratification system by providing an institutional certification of inequalities that have long-term implications in people's lives (Meyer 1977). Given those long-term implications, it is not surprising that inequality in the schools has attracted so much attention.

THREE MODELS OF INEQUALITY
IN THE SCHOOLS

To conclude that the schools create inequalities rather than simply identifying them, it is necessary to show that the inequalities observed as pupils leave the schools are greater than (or at least different than) any inequalities observed as they enter the schools. It is *also* necessary to show that those differences are due to something that happens in the schools.

There seems to be little disagreement about the fact that pupils are unequal at the time they enter the schools as well as when they leave the schools. Although all students enter regular school for the first time at roughly the same age, they exhibit a wide range of knowledge and skill at those tasks carried out in school. And, not only do student performances vary widely at the end of schooling, the amount of schooling obtained is equally varied.

I will suggest three models of inequality in the schools, all of which recognize inequalities at both entry and exit but differ in the ways they interpret those inequalities. The three models are differentiated according to the kinds of structural assumptions that undergird them. I will refer to these as the "genetic-socialization model," the "school structure model," and the "power imposition model." They are "nested" models in that each subsequent one assumes and builds on the previous one. I will outline the basic ideas involved in each of them and then turn to some of the research literature to assess the degree to which the empirical evidence provides support for them.

The *genetic-socialization model* might be thought of as a pure, unstructured view of inequality in the schools. It recognizes that there are genetic differences among individuals in their ability to learn. It also recognizes that the school is not the only source of learning. Other agencies, especially the family, influence the individual in ways that are relevant to performances within the school (Heyns 1974; Alwin and Thornton 1984). There are at least two kinds of influence from these other sources. One is wholly parallel with the primary influence from the school; it consists of teaching basic knowledge and skills. The other is an influence on the attitudinal and motivational characteristics of the individual, characteristics that make pupils differentially open to the lessons the school attempts to teach. Whatever influences the school may have, therefore, the outcomes are bound to vary depending on the genetic makeup of the individual and the other socialization influences to which he or she is exposed.

According to this model, the school attempts to teach all pupils as much as they are willing and able to learn, but it is certain to be more successful in some cases than others. That may be unfortunate, but it is a basic fact of life, something outside the control of the school. All the school can do is provide opportunities to learn. The grades given to pupils, then, are simply symbolic recognition of the pupils' varying degrees of success in mastering the material presented to them. Because there is an assumed association between success in school and the individual's ability to function in the adult world, grades and test scores are reported to others as the school's best estimate of the individual's potential in later life.

The *school structure model* also recognizes the genetic and other socialization sources of pupils' abilities to perform within the school context. It differs from the genetic-socialization model, however, by taking into account the ways in which the organization of the schools can affect the pupil's performances and progress through the system. Rather than viewing the school as a homogeneous, open opportunity arena for learning, it sees the internal structure of the school as providing unequal opportunities and thereby directly influencing the amount of inequality among the pupils.

Recognition of differences among its pupils at the time they begin their education leads the school to treat pupils in different ways depending on their entry characteristics. In structural terms, this is most clearly reflected in the separation of pupils into ability groups or tracks and the adjustment of curricula and teaching methods to fit the pupils' recognized differences. The classification and selective treatment both reinforce the initial differences and introduce new sources of inequality.

To the extent the original and newly created kinds of differentiation are carried forward during their educational careers, pupils are likely to become progressively more stratified in educational performances as they pass through the system. This model is also sensitive to the school's effects on the attitudinal and motivational bases of learning. The varying degrees of success in school, symbolized by the test scores and grades pupils receive, affect not only their ability to learn additional material but also their attitudes toward the institution and their motivation to do well.[1]

In its abstract form, the school structure model assumes the schools are blind to what is going on outside the school. Whatever the sources of entry inequality, organizing pupils into ability groups and tracks and adjusting curricula and teaching practices are founded wholly on academic performance or objective measures of potential and the need to match offerings to pupils' readiness. The actions of the school are well-intentioned attempts to cope with the task of providing an education to pupils of different ability levels.

The power imposition model, in contrast, sees school processes as strongly influenced by the world outside the school, especially by the society's stratification system. Social stratification is recognized in both of the other models, but, in those models, the strata are simply seen as the origins and destinations of the schools' pupils. The stratification system is "out there," beyond the boundaries of the school. In the power imposition model, the stratified nature of the larger society penetrates the organization and functioning of the school itself. The school is no longer seen as an autonomous institution with a socially relevant educational mission. Rather, it is seen as a mechanism by which powerful segments of the society perpetuate their dominant position. What happens in the school is not guided by purely educational values and principles but by the self-interests of powerful groups and by principles of social control.

The treatment of pupils within the school is assumed to follow rules that are designed to increase the probability that the children of the powerful segments of the society will succeed and those of the less powerful segments will not. Ability groups, tracks, and differentiated curricula are mechanisms by which that goal is pursued.[2]

The school structure model and the power imposition model are similar in that both assume that there will be changes in pupils' positions in the academic hierarchy as they move through the school system, and both seek explanations of those changes by reference to the organizational structure of the school. They differ, however, in the kinds of changes they expect as well as the reasons for expecting them.

The school structure model views the changes as unintended consequences of the school's attempt to cope with pupils with varied preparation and potential. The changes are associated with pupils' positions in the school structure, but school positions are only loosely associated with the pupils' levels in the power structure of the society. Pupil assignments to positions in the school structure are based on academic criteria, not on social stratification criteria. The power imposition model, in contrast, views those changes as due to school structures that are designed to serve the purposes of powerful external forces. The changes are thus expected to be strongly associated with pupils' levels in the power structure of the society because the school is organized so as to reproduce that power structure, and pupil assignments to positions in the school structure are based on their levels in the power structure.

CAN THE THREE MODELS BE TESTED?

Although the three models contain familiar elements, they do not correspond closely to any of the theoretical positions most discussed in the literature. For instance, one could agree with Bourdieu (1977) that the "cultural capital" of the upper classes is highly valued by the schools or with Bernstein (1975) that the schools use linguistic patterns favored by the middle class without adopting one rather than another of the three models. Even the genetic-socialization model can encompass those theorists' positions. All three of the models would be consistent with the observation that the kinds of lessons taught in our schools are more easily learned by those with the dominant "habitus" who use "elaborated linguistic codes."

Many critics of the schools object to the fact that the lessons taught in the schools and the criteria of evaluation used by the schools are those of the society's dominant culture. That is one version of the power imposition view of the schools. There is little doubt, I think, that pupils from high-status homes generally do have an advantage in the schools. Even if we reject the notion of genetic differences, their opportunities outside the school increase the probability they will succeed by the standards used in the schools. The criteria of evaluation used by the schools are heavily influenced by the society's dominant culture, and those who have fuller access to that culture will generally perform more effectively and be more favorably evaluated in the schools. It is not unreasonable to claim that that constitutes "creating inequalities," but that is not the way the phrase is used here.

This discussion takes the current criteria of evaluation as given and asks whether the schools do anything that increases the amount of inequality of success by those criteria.[3] It is important to distinguish between advantages and disadvantages pupils may have due to their social milieus, on the one hand, and actions taken by the schools that may increase those advantages and disadvantages, on the other. The schools may well be vehicles of social reproduction. All three of the models suggested here are consistent with that possibility. But the question posed by comparing the three models is whether the schools make an *independent* contribution by increasing the amount of inequality among pupils by the time they leave school. And, if the schools do make an independent contribution, as expected in the school structure model, does that contribution serve to perpetuate the power structure of the society? The power imposition model requires that it does.

How can we tell? To assess the relative merits of the three models, we need to chart the positions of pupils in the educational hierarchy over time to see if they change or remain constant. If they change, we need to see if we can find connections between those changes and specific factors imping-ing on the pupils during their stay in the schools. The basic conceptualization underlying this approach is of a stream of pupils entering, passing through, and emerging from an institutional setting in which they experience a structured set of influences. The most basic data needed, if we are to test the models, then, are measures of changes in the pupils' positions in the aca-demic hierarchy as they move through the system.

The genetic-socialization model is the baseline model. If we observe no change in pupils' positions in the academic hierarchy as they pass through the system, or if the changes are unsystematic, the genetic-socialization model is the most parsimonious way to account for the outcomes. If differ-ences in school performance are due wholly to genetic endowment and socialization experiences external to the school, there should be very little shift in the relative positions of pupils. The school simply certifies that the differences exist.

One pattern of systematic change is consistent with the genetic-socialization model, however. If some pupils are genetically superior and if some pupils have greater learning opportunities outside the school, there may be a progressive divergence in school performance among pupils wholly independent of any differential treatment of pupils in the school. Bright pupils and those with more stimulating outside experiences can be expected to be advanced initially and to continue to move ahead more rapidly than others.

If a pattern of diverging performances is observed, so that those who are advanced on entry become more so as they move through the system (Coleman et al. 1966), a test is needed to determine if that pattern can be attributed to genetic and nonschool socialization factors or to differential experiences within the school. To attribute that outcome to the school, we must be able to show that pupils with equal entry performance levels change in different ways depending on where they are located in the school structure. The simple fact of change during the school years is insufficient to show that the schools are responsible for the change.

If, as the school structure model suggests, it is found that pupils *do* shift positions in the academic hierarchy as they pass through school, and those shifts *can* be attributed to school structure, the power imposition model asks which pupils shift position and in what direction. It expects children with powerful parents to move up and those with weak parents to move down. They should do so independent of their initial performance levels. And, if pupils' positions in the school structure are found to be associated with changes in performance levels, the power imposition model would expect social stratification bias in pupil placements in those positions.[4]

WHAT DO WE KNOW ABOUT THE
CREATION OF INEQUALITY?

To test the models, we need measures of pupils' levels in the academic hierarchy over time. Most research that lends itself to this kind of analysis has used some kind of test score as the index of those levels. The three models call for different kinds of patterns of test scores as pupils pass through the system. The fundamental question is this: Do the positions of pupils in the academic hierarchy change as they pass through the system and, if they do, can the changes be attributed to something the schools *do*?

The models are sufficiently abstract that it is possible to subsume under them any number of possible "treatments" to which the schools subject their pupils. In general, though, those treatments can be classified into organizational and interpersonal influences. The organizational features include ability groups, curricular differences, tracks, and between-school differences in learning opportunities. The interpersonal sources of influence are largely pupil relations with teachers and peers. (These two kinds of sources of influence are not necessarily independent, of course.) For our purposes, I will limit myself to the organizational features and, within that category, I will concentrate on within-school divisions of pupils.[5]

The analysis of the flow of pupils through the institutional structure of the schools ideally calls for data on cohorts of pupils over the full period of their schooling. Unfortunately, rather than such a continuous moving account, we have, at best, a series of snapshots or short-term longitudinal records. It is possible to piece together some tentative impressions from the available research, but there is still room for debate over interpretation.

Sociologists have paid less attention to the issues raised here in the early school years than they have to those at the secondary and post-secondary levels. The available elementary school research is often concerned with interaction patterns in the classroom or other fairly small-scale and short-term aspects of the educational system rather than the broader, population flow analysis called for here. Yet, there has been enough relevant research to provide some impressions of the patterns involved.

There is considerable evidence that first grade pupils are highly varied in their initial performance levels, and the differences are at least somewhat associated with their social origins. Similarly, pupils vary greatly in change (growth) of performance during the first few years of school, and social origins are also related to the patterns of change (Entwisle et al. 1986; Barr and Dreeben 1983).

Studies of the effects of school structure on pupil performance in elementary school have not produced wholly consistent results, but, to the extent any pattern can be found in those results, they suggest that homogeneous grouping may lead to an increase in the average test performance of pupils in the "high" groups and a decrease in the performance of pupils in the "low" groups (Weinstein 1976; Rowan and Miracle 1983; Barr and Dreeben 1983). There is some evidence that the different outcomes are due to instructional variations across the ability groups (Gamoran 1986).

Although some analysts have reported an SES bias in assignments to ability groups in elementary schools (Rist 1970), the most careful recent multivariate analyses have suggested that the effects are quite modest at best (Haller and Davis 1981; Rowan and Miracle 1983). Most of the SES effects seem to be indirect, due to the association between SES and earlier achievement.

There is a more extensive literature on curricular and tracking effects within secondary schools.[6] Here also we find quite varied reports of the effects of pupil grouping, but the most recent research, based on large diverse samples and using a wide range of statistical controls, seems to support the idea that grouping does affect pupil performance. Three kinds of general observations seem justified based on the research on secondary school tracking.

(1) Track placement does lead to differentiated pupil achievement even when an extensive set of antecedent factors are taken into account (Kerckhoff 1986; Gamoran 1987; Vanfossen et al. 1987; Gamoran and Mare 1989; Sorensen and Hallinan 1986). In settings in which all pupils are tracked, those in higher academic tracks gain more than those in lower tracks. Placement in a lower track is often found to have a negative effect on achievement. Where comparisons can be made between those who are and are not tracked, those in high tracks gain, and those in low tracks lose, in performance measures compared with comparable pupils not placed in tracks (Kerckhoff 1986). In addition to its effects on individual pupils, therefore, tracking has the effect of increasing the variance in outcomes.

(2) The reasons for the gains and losses are not wholly clear, but they seem in large part due to differences in curricula in the different tracks (Hotchkiss and Dorsten 1987; Gamoran 1987). It is difficult to separate the curricular and pedagogical effects, however, and observers disagree about the degree to which teacher expectations and efforts in the different kinds of courses influence the outcomes.

(3) The effects of track placement, as such, appear to be weaker the more information is included about pupils' prior academic experiences and performances (Alexander and Cook 1982). The single structural feature, track placement, needs to be considered as only one visible aspect of the overall school experience. It may be that track placement is an overly crude index of organizational differentiation within schools, and, as such, it is not as important as the distributions of courses within tracks. I will suggest later, however, that to conclude that track placement, as such, has no real significance will probably miss some important effects.

One of the controversies within the literature on tracking has to do with the process of pupil placement in tracks (Cicourel and Kitsuse 1963; Rosenbaum 1976). To the extent it can be claimed that pupils are actually *assigned* to tracks by the school, there is little question that the differential effects of track placement can be attributed to school process. To the extent placements are *chosen* by pupils, however, one might question whether the school has actually created the resulting shifts in outcome. There is no consensus about which of these interpretations of track placement is more valid.

Yet, even if placement is based on pupil choice, the fact remains that the school provides the options, the options are not equal, and they evidently lead to different pupil outcomes. In addition, there is very little movement of pupils between tracks from year to year (Schafer and Olexa 1971; Alexander and McDill 1976; Rosenbaum 1976; Hallinan and Sorensen 1983), which suggests that, however pupils enter tracks, track placement is not very responsive to individual differences in academic progress.

It is thus possible to reach a tentative conclusion that the way schools process pupils, providing different experiences to different categories of pupils, does affect the distribution of academic performances. To that extent at least, it is reasonable to conclude that the schools do, indeed, *create* inequality. Output inequality appears to be greater and different than input inequality, and the differences can, at least in part, be attributed to school process.

If the literature on tracking is accepted as indicating that there are school structure effects, is there also evidence to support the power imposition model? Are the effects differentially felt by more and less powerful segments of the society? There is a less solid basis for conclusions here, although it is here that the discussion gets most heated.

The most directly relevant question in testing the power imposition model within an analysis of the effects of tracking is whether track placement is made on the basis of pupils' positions in the social stratification system rather than on, or in addition to, their positions in the academic performance hierarchy. That is, is there a status bias in distributing pupils in the school structure?

There is considerable evidence that pupils from lower-status backgrounds are more likely to end up in the lower tracks. Once we control for prior level of academic performance, however, the evidence that social status has much effect on track placement is mixed at best. While some analysts conclude that there is little evidence of status bias (Rehberg and Rosenthal 1978; Heyns 1974; Rowan and Miracle 1983; Alexander and Cook 1982), others provide convincing evidence that some status bias does exist, though it is quite modest in degree (Vanfossen et al. 1987; Gamoran and Mare 1989).

Review of the three models and the empirical research literature thus provides support for the school structure model of inequality in the schools. The schools do more than identify levels of academic performance. They actually increase the variance in the levels of performance by the way pupils are processed through the system. On the basis of relatively weak assessments of pupil potential, divisions are made within the student bodies of individual schools, and those divisions receive unequal educational experiences that, in turn, alter the distributions of academic performances. There also seems to be some evidence to support the power imposition model, although the evidence is more limited and the effects are not as strong as some theorists would expect.

LIMITATIONS OF OUR KNOWLEDGE

The literature reviewed here is the kind usually alluded to when analysts refer to the effects of school structures on inequality. We need to move well beyond our current knowledge of those effects, however, if we are fully to understand the role schools may have in creating inequality in our society. Some of the needed improvements consist of further refinements of the kinds of analyses already being carried out; some depend on broadening the kinds of questions we investigate. I will suggest five areas of needed improvement in our research.

Cumulative Effects

As noted earlier, the ideal analysis would be based on following cohorts of pupils throughout their stay in the school system, but we do not have the necessary data to carry out such an analysis. One of the reasons that kind of analysis is so important is that structural effects are likely to be cumulative. Our studies already show some statistically significant effects of the internal structures of the schools, but we have only been able to observe these effects over relatively brief periods. Even small short-term effects, if continued over a longer period of time, can amount to very large effects (Jencks 1985). Observing the cumulative effects across the school years may be especially important in assessing the validity of the power imposition model. Our current data show some effects, but they are not very strong. If these effects occur throughout the school experience and are thus cumulative over a 12- (or more) year period, however, they may prove to be much more important than they now appear to be.

Crude Measures of School Structure

The literature on the effects of secondary school structure on student achievement has been based almost entirely on analyses of the effects of tracks and, more specifically, on the difference between the college preparatory track and all others. Most high schools provide more than two options, however, and there are important distinctions among them. It is both possible and worthwhile to include at least three, rather than two, tracks in our analyses—academic, general, and vocational (Gamoran 1987; Vanfossen et al. 1987).

Even if three or more tracks are included in the analysis, however, we will still oversimplify the actual structural variations available in the schools. There is considerable variation in courses taken by pupils in any track. The configurations of courses taken have demonstrable effects on the amount of inequality among pupils, and they vary systematically by pupils' social backgrounds (Hotchkiss and Dorsten 1987; Gamoran and Mare 1989). We need to do further research using these more sensitive measures.

Interaction Effects of Structural Differences

Almost all of our research has used a relatively simple additive model of structural effects. Track position is introduced into the analysis as just another independent variable, coequal with measures of SES, earlier achievement, and so on. It is highly likely, however, that any particular structural feature (track or individual course) will have somewhat different effects on the later performances of pupils with different antecedent characteristics. There is already evidence that track or ability group placements have different effects on performance in English and mathematics, and the effects differ by the race and sex of the students (Gamoran and Mare 1989; Kerckhoff 1986). It will complicate our investigations considerably to take such interactions into account, but we will learn much more about structural effects by doing so.

Compensatory Effects

All of the attention here, and most of the attention in the literature, is directed toward identifying structural effects that *increase* the amount of inequality in the schools. The implication is that, if we did away with these structural differentiations, there would be less inequality among pupils at the end of the school experience. Yet, many educators believe that pupil grouping is necessary to compensate for the disadvantages experienced by some pupils.

There already exists some evidence to support the idea that the ways schools process pupils may serve a compensatory function. One study found that teachers teaching pupils in different ability groups spent more time with those in the lower group in an attempt to bring them up to the level of the higher group (Rowan and Miracle 1983). There is also some indication that, given the same antecedent characteristics, black pupils have a higher probability of being in the college preparatory track in high school (Gamoran and Mare 1989). Whatever the generality of those findings, the basic point to be made here is that we need to be sensitive to the possibility that some school structures may serve to compensate for initial inequalities. We should not just look for those that increase inequalities.

Other Kinds of Inequalities

The literature on tracking has been largely focused on effects measured in terms of achievement test scores. There are other outcomes that may be at least as important, however, outcomes observed both within and outside the academic arena. In addition to achievement test scores, track placement also affects later course selection (Alexander and Cook 1982), high school graduation (Gamoran and Mare 1989), and a whole range of social psychological variables (Vanfossen et al. 1987) that can be expected to influence what pupils do after they leave high school. Also, the distribution of courses taken in high school has a strong effect on college attendance and early occupational attainment (Hotchkiss and Dorsten 1987).

The reasons for these effects are not wholly clear. It may simply be a matter of what and how much pupils learn. Or it may be due to the effects of placement on pupils' self-confidence and ambition levels. If pupils' positions in the school structure are visible to the world outside the school, however, the reason for the effects may be partly independent of any specific pupil characteristics. Postsecondary school administrators and employers seek whatever indications they can obtain of the potential performance of applicants. The evidence reviewed here suggests that pupil placement in the school structure affects achievement scores and thus it may indirectly affect educational attainment, occupational attainment, and income. But it is also possible that school structure placement has a *direct* effect on those outcomes. Information about pupils' positions in the school structure may act as a "signal" (Rosenbaum 1986) to decision makers and gatekeepers.

Position in the school structure may thus have effects that go well beyond anything that can be measured by an achievement test. The location of individuals in the society's stratification system depends very heavily on their occupational attainments, and those, in turn, are strongly influenced by educational attainments. If school structures alter the distributions of educational attainments, they also alter the lifetime attainments of their pupils.

CONCLUSION

I have chosen to delimit the focus of this discussion because I think that too much of our theorizing about the schools mixes levels of analysis and often produces propositions that are not subject to focused investigation. We need to differentiate between propositions about the negative effects of social inequality in a society and propositions about the linkage between school processes and social inequality. Within the latter, we need to differentiate between propositions about how the society's stratification system affects the substance of education and the schools' criteria of evaluation and propositions linking within-school structures with inequalities among pupils.

This is not to say that one of these is more important than the other but only that they are different and that they require different methodologies of investigation. This discussion simply sets aside general questions about what is desirable for the society as a whole and about what affects the substance and evaluative criteria the schools emphasize and instead focuses only on the effects of school structures on the distributions of inequalities among pupils.

Although the evidence is not as clear as some critics of the schools might claim, it indicates that the way the schools process pupils by using various forms of grouping tends to increase inequalities among pupils. It also seems likely, though it is less well established, that some of that increase is in the form of exacerbating the kinds of initial inequalities among pupils that result from their different positions in the stratification system.

The evidence is not all in, however. Not only are the patterns we have observed less than wholly consistent, we have yet to conduct comprehensive assessments of the effects of school structures on the distribution of inequality. We need to specify the relevant school structures more fully and to chart their cumulative effects (both positive and negative) across the full range of school years. It may be some time before we have wholly adequate data to conduct such an analysis, but it should be possible to move in that direction progressively as the opportunities are presented. Our greatest need for this kind of analysis is at the elementary school level, but further work is needed at all levels.

NOTES

1. These organizational features are assumed to exist in all schools, but the school structure model also allows for between-school differences. Not only do some parts of any school's program provide better educational opportunities, some schools are better overall than others. The idea of school structure thus refers to differences between schools as well as to differences between programmatic units within schools.

2. According to this model, the differences between schools also show the way powerful elements control the system, restricting the best opportunities to those schools attended by their children.

3. Another possible interpretation of "creating inequalities in the schools" could be based on the view that ability is a social construction (Rosenbaum 1986; Simpson and Rosenholtz 1986). That approach emphasizes the roles of the schools in the social construction of ability as a socially significant concept used to justify many kinds of differentiation within the society. Although the schools no doubt do have a critical role in that process, that is not what I mean by creating inequalities in the schools.

4. Another version of the external structure model is concerned with sex differences. It argues not so much from the perspective of the position of a pupil's parents in the power structure as from the position of a pupil's sex in the power structure. It thus leads to the hypothesis that shifts in position in the academic hierarchy should be such that girls move down and boys move up as they pass through the system.

5. The most widely discussed recent analysis of differences in outputs between schools is that presented by Coleman and his colleagues (Coleman et al. 1982; Coleman and Hoffer 1987; Hoffer et al. 1985) in their comparison of public and private schools. Methodological critiques of that research have questioned whether selection into the two types of schools was adequately taken into account, but the findings suggest that much of the difference in performance by public and private school pupils can be attributed to curricular and disciplinary differences between the two types of schools. Such findings are consistent with the school structure model. An analysis of the same data set examined effects of specific characteristics of the organizational features of the schools (proportion of pupils in the academic track, a gifted student program, advanced placement courses) without reference to the public-private distinction (Gamoran 1987). Consistent with earlier research (Alwin 1976), it failed to find consistent effects of such between-school differences on pupil achievement. The picture is quite unclear, therefore, with respect to the effects of between-school differences, and those reviewing the available evidence can reach contradictory conclusions (Mackenzie 1983; Rowan et al. 1983).

6. Fortunately, for our purposes, schools are not wholly consistent in the ways they process pupils, and their inconsistencies provide sufficiently varied patterns to permit an assessment of the effects of within-school structures on pupil performance. The association between measured ability or achievement and track placement is far from perfect. There are thus pupils with the same early performance levels who have experienced different placements in the school structure. It is thus possible to test the independent effects of measured ability or achievement and track placement.

REFERENCES

Alexander, Karl L. and Martha A. Cook. 1982. "Curricula and Coursework: A Surprise Ending to a Familiar Story." *American Sociological Review* 47:626-40.

Alexander, Karl L. and Edward L. McDill. 1976. "Selection and Allocation Within Schools: Some Causes and Consequences of Curriculum Placement." *American Sociological Review* 41:963-80.

Alwin, Duane F. 1976. "Assessing School Effects: Some Identities." *Sociology of Education* 49:294-303.

Alwin, Duane F. and Arland Thornton. 1984. "Family Origins and the Schooling Process: Early Versus Late Influence of Parental Characteristics." *American Sociological Review* 49:784-802.

Barr, Rebecca and Robert Dreeben. 1983. *How Schools Work.* Chicago: University of Chicago Press.

Bernstein, Basil. 1975. *Class, Codes and Control.* London: Routledge & Kegan Paul.

Bourdieu, Pierre. 1977. *Outline of a Theory of Practice.* Cambridge: Cambridge University Press.

Cicourel, Aaron and John Kitsuse. 1963. *The Educational Decision-Makers.* Indianapolis: Bobbs-Merrill.

Coleman, James S. and Thomas Hoffer. 1987. *Public and Private High Schools: The Impact of Communities.* New York: Basic Books.

Coleman, James S., Thomas Hoffer, and Sally Kilgore. 1982. *High School Achievement: Public, Catholic and Private Schools Compared.* New York: Basic Books.

Coleman, James S. et al. 1966. *Equality of Educational Opportunity.* Washington, DC: Government Printing Office.

Entwisle, Doris, R., Karl L. Alexander, Doris Cadigan, and Aaron Pallas. 1986. "The Schooling Process in First Grade: Two Samples a Decade Apart." *American Educational Research Journal* 23:587-613.

Gamoran, Adam. 1986. "Instructional and Institutional Effects of Ability Grouping." *Sociology of Education* 59:185-98.

———. 1987. "The Stratification of High School Learning Opportunities." *Sociology of Education* 60:135-55.

Gamoran, Adam and Robert D. Mare. 1989. "Secondary School Tracking and Educational Inequality: Compensation, Reinforcement, or Neutrality?" *American Journal of Sociology* 94:1146-83.

Haller, Emil J. and Sharon A. Davis. 1981. "Teacher Perceptions, Parental Social Status and Grouping for Reading Instruction." *Sociology of Education* 54:162-74.

Hallinan, Maureen T. and Aage B. Sorensen. 1983. "The Formation and Stability of Instructional Groups." *American Sociological Review* 48:838-51.

Heyns, Barbara. 1974. "Social Selection and Stratification Within Schools." *American Journal of Sociology* 79:1434-51.

Hoffer, Thomas, Andrew M. Greeley, and James S. Coleman. 1985. "Achievement Growth in Public and Catholic Schools." *Sociology of Education* 58:74-97.

Hotchkiss, Lawrence and Linda Eberst Dorsten. 1987. "Curriculum Effects on Early Post-High School Outcomes." Pp. 191-219 in *Research in the Sociology of Education and Socialization,* edited by R. Corwin. Greenwich, CT: JAI.

Jencks, Christopher. 1985. "How Much Do High School Students Learn?" *Sociology of Education* 58:128-35.

Kerckhoff, Alan C. 1986. "Effects of Ability Grouping in British Secondary Schools." *American Sociological Review* 51:842-58.

Mackenzie, Donald E. 1983. "Research for School Improvement: An Appraisal of Some Recent Trends." *Educational Researcher* 12:5-17.

Meyer, John W. 1977. "The Effects of Education as an Institution." *American Journal of Sociology* 83:55-77.

Rehberg, Richard A. and Evelyn R. Rosenthal. 1978. *Class and Merit in the American High School.* New York: Longman.

Rist, Ray C. 1970. "Student Social Class and Teacher Expectations: The Self-Fulfilling Prophecy in Ghetto Education." *Harvard Educational Review* 40:411-51.

Rosenbaum, James E. 1976. *Making Inequality: The Hidden Curriculum of High School Tracking.* New York: John Wiley.

———. 1986. "Institutional Career Structures and the Social Construction of Ability." Pp. 139-71 in *Handbook of Theory and Research for the Sociology of Education,* edited by J. Richardson. New York: Greenwood.

Rowan, Brian, Steven T. Bossert, and David C. Dwyer. 1983. "Research on Effective Schools: A Cautionary Note." *Educational Researcher* 12:24-31.

Rowan, Brian and Andrew W. Miracle, Jr. 1983. "Systems of Ability Grouping and the Stratification of Achievement in Elementary Schools." *Sociology of Education* 56:133-44.

Schafer, Walter E. and Carol Olexa. 1971. *Tracking and Opportunity: The Locking-Out Process and Beyond.* Scranton, PA: Chandler.

Simpson, Carl H. and Susan J. Rosenholtz. 1986. "Classroom Structure and the Construction of Ability." Pp. 113-38 in *Handbook of Theory and Research for the Sociology of Education,* edited by J. G. Richardson. New York: Greenwood.

Sorensen, Aage B. and Maureen T. Hallinan. 1986. "Effects of Ability Grouping on Growth in Academic Achievement." *American Educational Research Journal* 23:519-42.

Spring, Joel. 1976. *The Sorting Machine: National Educational Policy Since 1945.* New York: McKay.

Vanfossen, Beth, James Jones, and Joan Spade. 1987. "Curriculum Tracking and Status Maintenance." *Sociology of Education* 60:104-22.

Weinstein, R. S. 1976. "Reading Group Membership in First Grade: Teacher Behaviors and Pupil Experience Over Time." *Journal of Educational Psychology* 68:103-16.

12

Labor Markets as Queues:
A Structural Approach to Changing
Occupational Sex Composition

Barbara F. Reskin

The historic persistence of sex segregation (Gross 1968; Beller 1984) made women's dramatic gains during the 1970s in such diverse male occupations as pharmacy, bank management, bartending, and typesetting noteworthy. Why did women disproportionately enter these and a few other male occupations when they made only modest progress in most and lost ground in a few? To answer this question, Patricia Roos and I conducted a two-part study: multivariate analyses of the changing sex composition in all detailed census occupations and in-depth case studies of 14 occupations in which women's representation increased at least twice as much as it had in the labor force as a whole (see Table 12.1). This chapter draws on those case studies: bank managers (Bird 1990), bartenders (Detman 1990), systems analysts (Donato 1990a), public relations specialists (Donato 1990b), pharmacists (Phipps 1990a), insurance adjusters/examiners (Phipps 1990b), typesetters/compositors (Roos 1990), insurance salespersons (Thomas 1990), real estate salespersons (Thomas and Reskin 1990), bakers (Steiger and Reskin 1990), book editors (Reskin 1990), print and broadcast reporters, and accountants.[1] Although the case studies revealed that widely different factors

AUTHOR'S NOTE: *I am grateful to Ross Boylan, Lowell L. Hargens, Heidi Hartmann, and Patricia A. Roos for their comments on earlier drafts of this chapter and to James N. Baron and Ronnie Steinberg for helpful discussions of the issues it addresses. The larger study that gave rise to the ideas in this chapter is a collaborative project with Patricia A. Roos. The case studies on which this chapter is based appears in our book,* Job Queues, Gender Queues: Explaining Women's Inroads into Male Occupations *(1990).*

Barbara F. Reskin — 171

Table 12.1 Percent Females in Feminizing Occupations, 1970, 1980, 1988

Occupation	1970 %	1980 %	1988 %	1970-88 Increase %
Financial managers	19.4	31.4	42.4	23.0
Accountants/auditors	24.6	38.1	49.6	25.0
Operations/systems analysts	11.1	27.7	39.6	28.5
Pharmacists	12.1	24.0	31.9	19.8
Public relations specialists	26.6	48.8	59.1	32.5
Editors and reporters	41.6	49.3	n.a.	n.a.
Insurance sales	12.9	25.4	29.7	16.8
Real estate sales	31.2	45.2	48.5	17.3
Insurance adjusters/examiners	29.6	60.2	72.2	42.6
Bartenders	21.2	44.3	49.6	28.4
Bakers	25.4	40.7	47.8	22.4
Bus drivers	28.3	45.8	48.5	20.2
Typesetters/compositors	16.8	55.7	73.9	57.1
Labor Force	38.0	42.6	45.0	7.0

precipitated these occupations' feminization, the process of change can be encompassed in a single perspective—queuing. This chapter begins by outlining the queuing approach. It then shows how the determinants of occupational feminization conformed to queuing processes. Finally, it argues that the queue model as I have developed it offers a structural approach to understanding change in job composition.

QUEUING: AN OVERVIEW

Simply stated, a queuing perspective views labor markets as composed of labor queues and job queues that reflect, respectively, employers' ranking of possible workers and workers' ranking of jobs.[2] The idea of the *labor* queue originated in Lester Thurow's (1969) work on race differences in unemployment and was elaborated by Hodge (1973) and Lieberson (1980). Rotella's (1977) analysis of the feminization of clerical work, Lieberson's (1980) study of racial and ethnic inequality, and Strober's (1984) theory of sex segregation implicitly invoked *job* as well as *labor* queues. The queuing perspective presented here views occupational composition as resulting from the simultaneous operation of job and labor queues (also see Reskin and Roos 1990). Employers hire workers from as high in the labor queue as possible, and workers accept the best jobs available to them, so the most desirable jobs go to the most preferred workers, less attractive jobs go to workers lower in the labor queue, and the most lowly workers end up jobless or in jobs others have rejected.

Three structural properties characterize both job and labor queues: (a) the ordering of their elements, (b) whether or not their elements overlap, and (c) their shape. By *elements,* I mean the constituent units—groups of potential workers or jobs. Thus the *ordering of elements* simply indicates in what order workers rank possible jobs and employers rank prospective workers. I pass over how workers order jobs in the labor queue as something both sociologists and workers understand. In ordering the labor queue, employers consider potential productivity and cost.[3] However, the indirect effect of workers' sex on employers' estimations of the former and its direct influence on how employers rank workers result in labor queues that encompass and often act as *gender queues.*

The absolute and relative numbers of elements in a queue determine its *shape.* Thus the number of prospective workers in each subgroup in a labor market sets the shape of the labor queue, and the number of jobs at each level in the job queue fixes its shape. Panels A and B of Figure 12.1 show how the shape of labor and job queues can vary while their order remains constant. This variation influences each group's probable access to occupations of varying desirability. (Put differently, it shows how a queue's shape influences each occupation's chance of recruiting workers from particular groups.) For example, in a society with relatively few workers in the preferred group (A2) and few desirable jobs (B2), preferred groups will monopolize good jobs. A mismatch in the relative numbers of jobs and workers at corresponding levels of the respective queues means that some workers will get better or worse jobs than persons from their group normally command. In consequence, when good jobs sharply outnumber highly ranked workers as in panels A2 and B1, employers must fill the better jobs with workers from lower in the labor queue than they usually hire. In contrast, when the *job queue* is bottom heavy, only the highest-ranked workers get desirable jobs, and workers moderately high in the labor queue are forced to settle for less. As Lieberson (1980, p. 297) has shown, both the *absolute* and the *relative* sizes of each group in the labor queue affect lower-ranked workers' chances of getting desirable jobs. The larger a subordinate group relative to the size of the preferred group, the more costly it is for employers to deny its members good jobs (Hodge 1973).

Whether or not *elements overlap* denotes the strength of rankers' preferences for one element over another. Among some employers, group membership is the overriding consideration in ordering the labor queue, and rankers favor persons from the group they prefer, regardless of qualifica-

Panel A. Hypothetical labor queues ordered by race for predominantly white and predominantly black labor markets, respectively

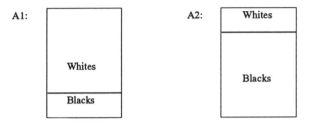

Panel B. Hypothetical job queues ordered by nonmanual-manual work for predominantly nonmanual and predominantly manual occupational structures, respectively

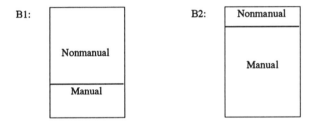

Figure 12.1. Illustration of Variation in the Shape of Labor and Job Queues

tions. For other labor queues, employers are indifferent to group membership except to break ties between otherwise equally qualified prospects. Figure 12.2 illustrates variation in the intensity of raters' preferences with respect to workers' race in three hypothetical labor queues. The space between the races in panel A depicts the ranking for employers who invariably hire the lowest-ranked white worker over the best black worker; the overlapping groups in panel B depict the situation in which raters' aversion to blacks is slight. Panel C illustrates an intermediate situation in which employers prefer white workers over equally qualified blacks but will set aside racial biases to hire very talented blacks over mediocre whites. Where preferences are weak, substantial job-level integration exists. In contrast, when preferences are overriding, all members of the favored group precede all members of the disfavored group in the labor queue, and the labor market is totally segmented.

Workers' job preferences also vary in intensity. Some workers may categorically prefer any job in a high-ranked occupation to working in a lower occupation (expressed, for example, in rejecting manual jobs in favor of nonmanual work). Alternatively, they may be more attuned to specific job

Panel A. Racial group membership is an overriding consideration to rankers. Employers hire applicants as qualified as possible, but hire unqualified whites before hiring highly qualified blacks.

Blacks	Blacks	Blacks	Whites	Whites	Whites
Low	Moderate	High	Low	Moderate	High

Level of Qualification

Panel B. Racial group membership is a minor consideration to rankers. Employers hire the most qualified applicants, but within levels of qualification, give white applicants an edge over equally qualified blacks.

Blacks	Whites	Blacks	Whites	Blacks	Whites
Low	Low	Moderate	Moderate	High	High

Level of Qualification

Panel C. Racial group membership is an intermediate consideration to rankers. Employers will prefer a more qualified white over a less qualified black, but will hire very qualified blacks over unqualified whites.

Blacks	Blacks	Whites	Blacks	Whites	Whites
Low	Moderate	Low	High	Moderate	High

Level of Qualification

Figure 12.2. Illustration of Variation in the Intensity of Raters' Preferences with Respect to Race

characteristics than their overall rank, occasionally eschewing jobs in occupations usually reserved for the preferred group and appropriating more desirable jobs within lower-ranked occupations that usually go to less preferred groups. Strong preferences mean that workers invariably prefer one type of job (e.g., professional or nonmanual work) over another.

Changes in any of these structural features of queues—employers' rankings of workers or workers' ranking of jobs, the intensity of either groups' preferences, and the relative distributions of workers or jobs—can transform occupations' composition. Below, I show how they did so in the 1970s and 1980s.

FACTORS PROMOTING
OCCUPATIONAL FEMINIZATION

I turn now to the factors that led the occupations we studied to feminize. Although this chapter emphasizes the role of these factors in explaining women's inroads into customarily male occupations, they also accounted for women's ghettoization *within* feminizing occupations into a few specialties, work settings, and industries. In order of importance for women's entry were job deterioration (reflecting changes in the ordering of the job queue), job growth (reflecting changes in the shape of the job queue), emergence of a sex-specific demand for women (reflecting changes in the ordering of the labor queue), and declining preference for men or aversion to women (reflecting changes in strength of employers' preferences). Women's increasing share of the labor queues for specific occupations or jobs (denoting a change in the shape of the labor queue), although it contributed to their inroads into male occupations, was itself in part a response to the increasing demand for women.

Occupational growth. Although scholars recognize the potential of occupational growth to open male occupations to women (Oppenheimer 1970; Doeringer and Piore 1971; Bielby and Baron 1984; Fields and Wolff 1989), it does so only when it depletes the supply of acceptable candidates from the preferred group. In growing male occupations in which qualified male prospects were plentiful—that is, desirable occupations for which workers could easily qualify such as driving trucks—employers had no need to resort to women. Only when occupations grow faster than the traditional labor supply must employers resort to nontraditional sources of labor. This is especially likely for jobs whose high entry requirements limit the number of qualified male prospects. Among the occupations we studied, this played a role in the feminization of accounting and systems analysis. As the computer industry served an increasingly broad range of users, the demand for systems analysts skyrocketed, creating almost 100,000 new jobs during the 1970s. Accounting registered even greater growth as expanding American corporations rationalized business functions, small firms became more dependent on accounting services, and complex tax laws made accountants indispensable to many taxpayers. Both occupations required credentials that took time to acquire, and in each the supply of qualified men proved inadequate, forcing employers to look lower in the labor queue for qualified workers. Thus occupational growth meant that employers reached women who had acquired the necessary credentials in the labor queue before filling all job openings. Rapidly growing occupations provide men with mobility opportunities (e.g., Strom 1987, p. 74), so an invasion by women is less threatening, especially if they are confined to female ghettos.

Job deterioration. Most of the occupations we studied feminized after their work process or rewards changed to render them less attractive than competing possibilities open to men. In every occupation we studied, men's real earnings declined during the 1970s. For example, bartenders' earnings dropped after a 1966 amendment to the Fair Labor Standards Act allowed employers to pay tipped employees subminimum wages. Several changes reduced the earnings in residential real estate sales: New tax laws prompted brokers to transfer sales agents from employees to independent contractors to whom they paid no salaries or benefits. The erratic housing market left agents with low-income spells, and real earnings declined appreciably in residential sales. As a result, many male agents left residential real estate, and few entered to replace them.

Technological change, occupational transformation, and deskilling. Technological change often means the transformation and sometimes the deskilling of jobs. The resulting job deterioration has historically been the agent of feminization. A middle-aged male machinist summarized the pattern: "I've seen it happen more than once. Work gets simple enough, and they turn it over to the girls" (Astrachan 1986). The feminization of insurance adjusting/examining, typesetting/composing, and baking all justify his concern. Indeed, insurance adjusting epitomizes how transforming an occupation's work process feminized it. Throughout the 1960s, adjusters—virtually all of whom were male—worked in the field where they enjoyed the right to schedule their work, the use of a company car, and reasonable prospects for upward mobility. To increase profits in response to a decade of high inflation, firms shifted adjusting into the office, where "inside" adjusters handled claims by telephone and VDTs, had limited autonomy and promotion prospects, and earned low wages. With the transformation and clericalization of adjusting, the number of male adjusters dropped by 6,447 between 1970 and 1980, while an additional 73,744 women became adjusters.

Automation and computerization also figured into the feminization of typesetting/composing by adversely affecting work content and rewards. Electronic advances computerized the work of typesetters and compositors, transforming it to clerical work. However, given the propensity to devalue women's work (Phillips and Taylor 1980; Reskin 1988), we must be cautious in assuming that transformed jobs in typesetting/composing and adjusting/examining were necessarily less skilled than those involving the methods male workers formerly used to produce the same product.

Technical advances that allowed manufacturing bakeries to ship unbaked goods to retail outlets created less skilled, often part-time, minimum-wage jobs "baking off" these products in retail settings. These jobs attracted few men, but, as Hartmann (1989) has noted and Beechey and Perkins (1987) have shown for Britain, employers structure jobs with the object of filling them with one sex or the other. For example, employers deliberately structured bake-off baking to use an inexperienced female labor pool rather than creating full-time jobs that would have attracted more men.

Thus technological change can create jobs for women in customarily male occupations when it reduces rather than raises skill requirements (Hacker 1979). However, technically based deskilling does not inevitably lead to feminization (Roos 1986; Cockburn 1988; Rose 1988; Walsh 1989). Whether it does so depends on male workers' ability and desire to retain the jobs.

Industrial change. Some occupations changed because of events in the industries that housed them. For example, following deregulation of the banking industry, banks tried to compete with savings and loan institutions by providing more services and easily accessible branches. This created thousands of new service-oriented management jobs in personal banking. However, they lacked prestige and the opportunity to acquire skills for promotion so they did not attract many men. Industrial change in book publishing resulted from conglomerization that commercialized the industry and robbed the job of editor of its primary attractions: a cultural image and the chance to shape American literature. As the number of qualified male applicants dropped, employers gave women the editorial jobs they had long sought. Industrial change in retail pharmacy made it less attractive to men as drugstore chains (as well as pharmacy outlets in discount stores, supermarkets, and health maintenance organizations) replaced independent pharmacies, thus eliminating the most lucrative aspect of pharmacy, the chance to be an entrepreneur.

In sum, men eschewed these declining occupations, and the ensuing labor shortages—sometimes exacerbated by occupational growth—drove employers to look lower in the labor queue, where they found women. As Joan Smith (1989) paraphrased Carter and Carter (1981), "Women [got] a ticket to ride *because* the gravy train has left the station."

Sex-specific demand for women. Antidiscrimination regulations of the 1960s and early 1970s restricted employers' freedom to downrank women because of their sex. In particular, a 1971 revised presidential executive order barred federal contractors from discriminating against women and required affirmative action to eliminate the effects of past discrimination.

Despite limited enforcement, in a few industries, the Office for Federal Contract Compliance helped women enter male occupations. For example, women's headway in bank management resulted partly because Office for Federal Contract Compliance programs targeted the banking industry.

Regulatory agencies fostered women's gains in public relations by requiring employers to provide equal employment data on employees' sex across broad occupational groups. Employers improved their EEO statistics by placing women in public relations jobs, line positions most men shunned because they seldom offered a path to top-management posts.

Action by individual women or women's organizations also raised the costs employers risked for preferring men. Litigation or pressure by employee groups enhanced women's access to jobs as newspaper and magazine reporters, book editors, insurance agents, bank managers, and bartenders. For example, in 1971 women successfully challenged state "protective" laws that prohibited women from tending bar under Title VII of the Civil Rights Act. This was by far the most important reason for the feminization of bartending. Credit for women's progress in broadcast reporting goes to women's groups who challenged renewal-license applications to the Federal Communications Commission from stations that did not employ women in professional capacities and to pressure from women employees at the networks (Lewis 1986; Sanders and Rock 1988). Thus a few of the occupations we studied feminized because employers reordered or weakened the gender queue within the labor queue, placing women ahead of men for jobs in which they risked costly sanctions for preferring men. Integration prompted by regulatory agency pressure is unstable as long as the beneficiaries remain downranked in the labor queue (Collins 1983).

Changing social attitudes and declining discrimination. Until a generation ago, the public tolerated sex discrimination, but the civil rights movement and the feminist movement challenged white men's birthright to first place in the labor queue. Together, these movements reshaped attitudes about the propriety of excluding people from jobs because of their color and sex. Changed public sentiments prompted employers to espouse equal employment practices, regardless of whether their own attitudes had changed, and gave women permission to aspire to occupations formerly off limits to them. Large numbers of women, anticipating equal treatment, began to prepare for traditionally male jobs.

The only occupation in which new attitudes directly contributed to feminization was bartending. Women's exclusion had depended partly on male unionists' claims that mixing drinks would corrupt women (Cobble forthcoming). The women's liberation movement and the "sexual revolution" as well as changing courtship practices and delayed marriage of the late 1960s and 1970s appear to have transformed public attitudes about women's corruptibility and hence their need for protection. In the other feminizing occupations, changing attitudes did not spur employers to hire large numbers of women. In general, public sentiments about the kinds of work appropriate for women change after rather than before occupational feminization (Rotella 1977). For example, broadcasters long barred women from reporting the news because their voices allegedly lacked authority. What opened news reporting to women was not more enlightened attitudes by radio and television stations but the risk of losing their broadcast licenses.

Given the sources of feminization in the occupations we studied, it should come as no surprise that occupational-level desegregation did not bring job-level integration. In almost every occupation we studied, informants indicated that discrimination restricted women's access to the best jobs. For example, the personnel manager explained to a young female bank manager that her rapid career rise had leveled out because "the chairman and president want . . . people that they are comfortable with, and they are not . . . comfortable with women" (Bird 1990).

Women's labor supply and preferences. With women's continued influx into the labor force during the 1970s, their share of the labor queue grew. However, what enlarged the female labor pools on which feminizing occupations drew was shortages of qualified male applicants that resulted from men's disdain for available jobs and from occupational growth. In short, women's growing proportion in the recruitment pools for sex-atypical occupations was largely a *response* to having a shot at jobs higher in the queue.

Women's beliefs that affirmative action and equal employment regulations ensured their access to jobs encouraged thousands to study to be pharmacists, systems analysts, accountants, and financial managers. Moreover, women's presence in sex-typical jobs in many industries that were home to feminizing occupations made them available for recruitment into male jobs. "Generating" a supply of female candidates often simply involved transferring women from sex-typical to sex-atypical jobs. For example, banks promoted women from clerk or teller to manager, publishers promoted women from secretary or editorial assistant to editor. In intensively female industries, such as banking, insurance, publishing, and real estate, as in the labor force as a whole, women were queued up—positioned to take advantage of a demand for their labor.

Explaining women's willingness to take customarily male occupations is easy: The available jobs paid better and offered better chances for advancement than female-dominated occupations that demanded comparable credentials. Although women's increasing need to support themselves and their dependents no doubt exacerbated their need for sex-atypical jobs, women were equally responsive to the attraction of higher wages during World War II when fewer women headed households. However, the contraction of female occupations in the 1970s pushed women toward male occupations (Blau 1989). Moreover, the greater attractiveness of these male occupations compared with those customarily open to women probably would have sufficed to draw women from female jobs even if the female labor force had not grown during the 1970s. Thus, while women's growing share of the labor queue played a role in their entry into formerly male jobs, without increased demand, the increased supply of female labor would not have feminized these male occupations.[4]

QUEUING MODELS AS STRUCTURAL APPROACHES TO OCCUPATIONAL COMPOSITION

Queuing emphasizes how employers rank groups of potential workers as well as how workers rank jobs. Because rankings simply boil down to preferences, is *queuing* not simply a fancy way to say that workers' and employers' preferences affect their labor market decisions? What does the queuing perspective add to the neoclassical economic approach to occupational segregation?

The neoclassical economic approach assumes (a) that workers' labor market decisions represent attempts to maximize their lifetime earnings, (b) that differences in the sexes' distributions across jobs stem primarily from women's family responsibilities, (c) that employers act to maximize revenues, and (d) that, in the short run, discriminatory "tastes" sometimes divert employers from their economic best interests, but, in the long run, competitive disadvantages that accrue from indulging economically irrational tastes lead discrimination to decline over time (Becker 1957). Thus traditional economic analysis treats sex segregation as the *aggregate* outcome of the mostly rational choices of *individual* workers and employers.

A queuing approach to changing occupational sex composition differs in several ways. First, queuing emphasizes the *collective* nature of sex segregation that results from *socially structured rankings* by *groups in conflict*. In contrast to the neoclassical perspective, queuing highlights the roles played by power and conflict between groups with contradictory interests in shaping occupations' composition. As I show below, the queuing perspective elucidates the role of group power in determining occupational access.

Second, it takes seriously the effects of noneconomic factors on workers' rankings of occupations and employers' rankings of prospective workers. It reminds us that working conditions, autonomy, social standing, career opportunities, and sex composition influence how workers appraise jobs and that employers' prejudices, stereotypes, and desire to preserve their own and other men's advantages influence how they rank workers.

Third, the queuing perspective assumes that the sexes rank most occupations similarly, so it predicts women's influx into accessible male occupations in view of their superior rewards. In explaining occupational feminization, it directs our attention to changes in employers' need for women and to declining barriers to women's access to traditionally male jobs. In other words, the queuing perspective redirects us from characteristics of female workers to structural properties of labor markets that in turn are shaped by the preferences of employers and male workers.

POWER AND COALITIONS IN ORDERING
THE LABOR QUEUE

In examining how conflict affects occupations' composition, we must bear in mind three points: First, three groups with competing interests have a stake in which sex predominates in an occupation—employers (who are overwhelmingly male), male workers, and female workers. Second, the greater social and economic power of employers and of men give them a substantial advantage in the struggle over what sex heads the queue for desirable occupations. Third, the outcome of the struggle over what sex dominates an occupation—occupations' sex compositions—represents a de facto coalition between competing groups.

Employers. Given their orientation toward minimizing costs and maximizing labor docility, employers should prefer female workers for all jobs. That so few have done so reminds us that other considerations affect male employers' labor decisions. Foremost among these is the personal stake of both male employers and male workers in excluding women from male-labeled jobs to preserve sex differentiation and hence male privilege in all spheres. Because sex differentiation both legitimates and facilitates unequal treatment, physically segregating the sexes at work and assigning them different tasks preserves male dominance by legitimating unequal wages, insulating men from female competition, supporting men's dominance in other public realms and the home, and shoring up myths of essential sex differences and male superiority (Reskin 1988). As Cockburn (1988, p. 41) put it, "Behind occupational segregation is gender differentiation, and behind that is male power."

Other considerations inclining employers to preserve good jobs for men include (a) the ability of male workers—and sometimes customers—to penalize employers for hiring women for "men's" jobs (Bergmann and

Darity 1981; Strober 1988); (b) organizational inertia that makes following standard practices the course of least resistance; (c) custom—in other words, jobs' sex labels—combined with the uncertainties attendant on radically altering employment practices (Cohn 1985; Strom 1987; Figart and Berg-mann 1989, p. 36); (d) gender solidarity with male workers;[5] and (e) fore-stalling later threats to their own jobs. As long as employers can operate profitably, preserving male jobs can be a fairly cheap amenity, especially if their competitors also practice male preference (Stolzenberg 1982; Strober 1988). Thus, in reserving male-dominated jobs for men, employers at once appease male workers, who could make hiring women costly; simplify organizational decisions; and shore up the gender hierarchy from which they benefit.

Male workers. Male workers' disadvantaged economic position vis-à-vis employers and their advantaged sex status divide their interests. They stand to gain in the long run from acting collectively with *all* workers, but, in the short run, men are vulnerable to job and wage competition from women who must settle for lower wages. Equal job opportunities for women can also cost men domestic benefits they derive from sex inequality in the workplace and can threaten the gender hierarchy from which working men benefit (Hart-mann 1976; Reskin 1988). Thus, for the most part, male workers do better in the short run by monopolizing male jobs than by welcoming female coworkers with whom they could collectively fight for better pay. Only when large numbers of women already have their foot in the door, or when labor shortages or outside agencies have imposed integration, are male workers freed to pursue their class interests collectively with female workers (Hirsch 1986; Milkman 1987; Cobble forthcoming). Under such conditions, male unions have tried to organize women and advocated equal pay.

Coalitions between employers and male workers. Male workers' monop-oly of most occupations stems from the de facto coalition between male employers and male workers. Although I use the term *coalition* figuratively, employers' power to hire workers and assign them jobs means that ordinarily male workers can resist women's entry only with their male bosses' active contrivance (Baker 1964; Hartmann 1976; Cockburn 1988). The result of this coalition between male workers and employers is also seen in feminizing occupations in women's confinement to the least desirable jobs, thereby providing male workers a refuge from integration in still-male jobs (Cock-burn 1988). For example, when outside pressure forced a large publishing firm to promote women to jobs as editorial assistants, it created a new, higher rank into which it promoted male former editorial assistants (Osterman 1979).

Despite the forces that preserve sex segregation, it broke down in the occupations we studied when male employers or male workers withdrew from their coalition. Employers never violated a coalition by directly substituting women for men, but they set aside customary practices, their own sex biases, and concern with the reactions of male workers when their firms' survival depended on cutting labor costs or averting unionization. In the occupations we studied, increased competition and the concomitant need to cut costs as well as vulnerability to work disruptions by unions precipitated this action. For example, industrywide demand for increased profits during the high-inflation 1970s prompted insurance companies to cut costs by standardizing the work of insurance adjusters and examiners. As I noted above, heightened competition for customers following deregulation forced banks to provide more customer services while trying to increase productivity and keep the lid on wages. In typesetting and composing, the International Typographical Union's frequent recourse to strikes spurred newspaper publishers to develop a printing technology that the union could not control, and then they hired women for the newly clericalized typesetting and composing jobs. It is important, however, that, in occupations that became less attractive to men for reasons not tied to employers' actions (book editing, real estate sales, retail pharmacy, and bartending), employers did not counter by improving male jobs. Employers' economic interests prevailed, and they replaced men with cheaper women.

In sum, the case studies suggested that employers put women ahead of men in labor queues *only* when labor costs became a pressing concern or when action by women or government regulators raised the cost of male preference.[6] Faced with economic exigencies, employers' willingness to donate profits to support white male privilege went by the wayside, and they struck a bargain with women workers.

Coalitions between male employers and female workers. Why women should enter into de facto coalitions with male employers is no mystery. Disadvantaged relative to both male workers and male employers, women stand to gain from cooperating with either group. Employers are more likely to accept a coalition with women when their numbers are large. Cobble's (forthcoming) comparison of women's efforts early in this century to preserve the right to serve drinks with their efforts to tend bar illustrates the importance of numbers. Women waitresses' moderate representation within union locals gave them the clout to block proposed restrictions against their serving alcoholic drinks. In contrast, women's small numbers doomed their efforts to tend bar until they could invoke the Civil Rights Act. In the 1970s, women capitalized on their numbers in the book publishing, newspaper, broadcasting, and banking industries to challenge their exclusion from male jobs or their confinement in low-status posts. Large numbers mean that women can better spot their concentration in the least desirable jobs and more effectively protest it. Thus women's increased share in labor queues for male occupations contributed to their gains both by increasing the odds that employers would get down to women in the hiring queue and by making them more powerful adversaries.

Resistance by male workers. Male workers' stake in monopolizing the best jobs encourages them to oppose employers' efforts to integrate women. To this end, they may try to reduce women's productivity by denying them training and information or withhold their own labor (Doeringer and Piore 1971; Bergmann and Darity 1981).[7] Whether men win the battle depends on their power base. For example, early in the Industrial Revolution, before strong unions existed, employers could easily feminize jobs (Kessler-Harris 1982, p. 266; Cohn 1985; Milkman 1987; Cockburn 1988). However, once unions were well established, they could preserve their domains. They did so in bartending, baking, and typesetting and composing as well as many other occupations throughout most of the century.

Obviously, men did not ultimately prevent women's entry in the occupations we studied. In most of those occupations, by abandoning jobs, male workers gave employers the go-ahead to hire women. Sometimes men do not see women as a threat. For instance, although men fought women's integration into clerical jobs in the British railroads (Cohn 1985), they did not resist women's movement in similar jobs in the United States because integration occurred slowly, and Pullman reserved the best jobs for men (Hirsch 1986, p. 33). In rapidly growing occupations, men did not resist women's entry because growth ensured that good jobs were plentiful, and within-occupation segregation assured men's access to the best jobs.

Thus the case studies of accounting and systems analysis revealed no systematic efforts to exclude women. Male incumbents in high-turnover occupations like book editing, bartending, and residential real estate sales had no stake in what happened in the long run. High turnover also means workers were too poorly organized to resist integration. Finally, in re-organizing work, employers had an effective tool in phasing out men. By changing the work process to incorporate female-labeled tasks, employers could disguise the fact that they were filling what had been men's jobs with women (Davies 1975, p. 282; Rotella 1977, pp. 162, 165) and recast them as women's work. For instance, after transforming the work of ad-justers, industry trade journals construed the ideal insurance adjuster as a woman.[8]

However, men did effectively resist women's employment in the most desirable specialties within desegregating occupations, such as production baking, commercial real estate, and industrial pharmacy—partly by informal pressures that discouraged women's entry. I suspect, however, that women's continued exclusion depended more on employer discrimination in job assignment and promotion practices than on male workers' actions.

CONCLUSIONS

In summary, the queuing model proposed here holds that (a) employers rank prospective workers in terms of their potential productivity as well as their personal characteristics, but that they are also influenced by current employees and others who can impose costs for hiring or failing to hire women; (b) shortages—whether from job growth or from a job's inability to attract enough customary workers—prompt employers to hire workers from lower in the labor queue; (c) male workers affect women's access to jobs through their ability to preempt jobs, their power to enforce their monopoly over desirable jobs, and their ability, in abandoning jobs, to bestow them on workers lower in the labor queue; and (d) women's search for better jobs leads them to individually and collectively challenge their exclusion from men's jobs and to move into male lines of work that become open. The case study data support these predictions. I caution readers that our selection of case studies of occupations in which women's gains were exceptionally large limits the generalizability of these findings. However, most occupations included specialties or work settings that had feminized at varying rates, so the case studies provide variation on the dependent variable. Nonetheless, the bases for women's movement into occupations not marked by rapid feminization may have differed. Patricia Roos and I addressed this question in statistical analyses of all 503 detailed occupations (Reskin and Roos 1985).

The case studies support two empirical generalizations both of which are consistent with the operation of queuing processes. First, in most of the occupations we studied, after they had become less attractive to men, employers hired disproportionate numbers of women. Second, within these nominally desegregating occupations, women tended to be relegated to female enclaves, while men retained the most desirable jobs.[9] These findings confirm Bielby and Baron's (1986) contention that greater balance in the sex composition of *occupations* does not necessarily imply decreased segregation of *jobs* and also establish the fallacy of inferring declines in sex segregation from occupational-level data. Yet social analysts cannot ignore such data, because policymakers and the media use them to assess change, and, as W. I. Thomas said, situations men define as real are real in their consequences. Exaggerated conclusions about women's progress in male occupations support claims that governmental agencies no longer need to intervene in the workplace to ensure equal treatment. Thus it is incumbent on researchers to determine whether or not the trends that superficial comparisons imply are genuine.

If a queuing approach illuminates the factors that facilitate feminization and influences its forms within occupations, what does it say about women's prospects for future movement into customarily male occupations? Potential sources of change arise from the structural properties of queues: their shape, ordering, and the intensity of raters' preferences. Changes in the shape of the job queue are not likely to bring much additional sex integration. Economists predict less job growth in the 1990s than the 1980s, and the most growth is expected in female-dominated service occupations (Beller and Han 1984). Changes in the shape of the labor queue are more likely: Women's labor force participation is projected to keep growing, with women accounting for two-thirds of labor force growth up to the year 2000 (U.S. Department of Labor, Women's Bureau 1989). Thus we can expect a reshaping of specific labor queues (e.g., for managerial occupations) toward greater balance between the sexes. As women's share of these queues increases, employers are more likely to hire them, especially for growing occupations (Lieberson 1980). Moreover, women's growing numbers enhance their likelihood of protesting men's monopoly of the best jobs as well as their ability to enforce their claims on these jobs.

However, for changes in the shape of the labor queue to substantially reduce segregation, employers must reorder the labor queue. How likely are employers to rerank female and male workers? With the increasing social repugnance toward discrimination in the 1970s, the intensity of employers' preferences for men probably declined, even if their ordering of the labor queue remained stable. During the 1980s, with the Reagan administration's greater tolerance for inequality, discrimination appears to have become more acceptable. Counteracting this force for preserving men at the head of the queue are the probable effects of employers' observing women successfully performing customarily male jobs. Scattered and anecdotal evidence suggests that women newcomers try harder and may be better qualified than the average man (Lorence 1987; Bielby and Bielby 1988). Experience with them should assuage employers' anxieties about women's ability (Reskin and Padavic 1988), and, in industries in which international competition intensifies, employers may gladly subordinate gender considerations to productivity—and insist that their managers follow suit.

Women's movement into decision-making posts provides another reason that some hiring agents may reorder labor queues or reduce the intensity of preference for men for the best jobs. Kulis and Miller (1989) found that women faculty made larger gains in sociology departments that women headed than in those men led; women's increasing role in hiring workers for customarily male jobs may contribute to reshaping the labor queue so that the sex of prospective workers diminishes in importance.

I expect little impetus for change from the other primary force for reordering the labor queue—that is, regulatory agencies. The limited effects of affirmative action on women's employment in some male occupations in the late 1970s disappeared after the Reagan administration derailed enforcement efforts (Burbridge 1984; Leonard 1988). Subsequently, the Supreme Court's 1989 affirmative action decision in *Martin v. Wilks* has further undermined employers' incentive to desegregate jobs. Historically, external pressure by proponents of integration has been necessary for the enforcement of anti-discrimination and affirmation action regulations. Ironically, the gains that some women made in the 1970s and 1980s from those efforts reduce the likelihood of such pressure in the 1990s. The increasing number of women in midlevel managerial jobs supports a "politics of optimism" that masks the need for collective action (Blum and Smith 1988) while at the same time creating a gulf between women who have entered customarily male managerial jobs and those still stuck in traditionally female ghettos. Even if women can overcome their differences to voice a renewed appeal for regulatory activity, barring changes in the political climate, that appeal is likely to fall on deaf ears.

I leave for last the structural change that contributed most to women's movement into these case study occupations: men's reordering the job queue. By downranking jobs in some customarily male occupations, men effectively abandoned them to women. Obviously, we neither can nor do we wish to make male jobs worse in order to open them to women. Ironically, it is this factor that seems most likely to contribute to future *nominal* desegregation. For example, take physicians: Declines in the profitability, entrepreneurial opportunities, and social status of practicing medicine are implicated in young men's waning interest in studying medicine (Leslie 1987, pp. 39-40). Between 1975 and 1985, the number of male medical students dropped by over one-third; women represent an increasing segment of medical students and have posted disproportionate gains in medicine during the 1980s (U.S. Department of Labor, Bureau of Labor Statistics 1989) and will almost certainly continue to do so in the 1990s. I expect the same result in other occupations (e.g., the clergy, social science) for the same reason: They no longer attract enough qualified men.

A generation ago, Gross (1968, p. 198) said of the persistence of occupational segregation, "the more things change, the more they stay the same." That summation provides a regrettably apt conclusion to this chapter. Despite the economic progress some women have made relative to their sisters, and although employers today construe different jobs as "women's work" than they did when Gross wrote about segregation in 1968, jobs remain sex segregated, and the structure of white male advantage remains largely intact. Without structural change on several fronts to ensure the access of *all* women and *all* people of color to *all* jobs, we risk ending the twentieth century with a labor force almost as segregated by sex as when the century began.

NOTES

1. I conducted the last two unpublished studies. Unless otherwise noted, assertions about these occupations are based on the case studies whose full citations are in the references. For a description of the case study method, see Reskin and Roos (1990).

2. This analysis takes for granted the existence of multiple labor markets, each composed of a labor queue of potential workers and a job queue of available jobs.

3. Incumbent workers can affect the ordering of the labor queue, for example, through seniority rules that restrict employers' hiring prerogatives.

4. Of course, through labor queues, "supply-side" factors influenced which of the almost 45 million women in the labor force in 1980 moved into formerly male jobs that had become more open to women during the 1970s and which ones were consigned to female occupations.

5. This should be especially common among bosses who share a similar background with male workers, previously held the jobs in question, and currently work with or remain friendly with their former coworkers. Two examples are blue-collar supervisors or sales managers.

6. Unless it is backed by threats from regulatory agencies, pressure from women rarely suffices to persuade employers to assign women to male jobs, partly because it elicits opposition from male workers.

7. Employers can rarely forestall resistance by feminizing entire work teams. Seniority rules may prevent their replacing men, they may doubt whether enough qualified women are available, and they may be unable to train women because male unions control training or because training is too long and expensive.

8. Kessler-Harris (1986) and Strober and Arnold (1987) also recounted how banks exploited sex stereotypes to justify hiring women for banking jobs as well as to exclude them from the same jobs.

9. For further evidence on this point, see Chapter 3 in Reskin and Roos (1990).

REFERENCES

Astrachan, Anthony. 1986. *How Men Feel.* New York: Anchor.

Baker, Ross. 1964. "Entry of Women into Federal Job World—At a Price." *Smithsonian* 8:82-91.

Becker, Gary. 1957. *The Economics of Discrimination.* Chicago: University of Chicago Press.

Beechey, Veronica and Tessa Perkins. 1987. *A Matter of Hours: Women, Part-Time Work and the Labour Market.* Cambridge, MA: Polity.

Beller, Andrea. 1984. "Trends in Occupational Segregation by Sex, 1960-1981." Pp. 11-26 in *Sex Segregation in the Workplace: Trends, Explanations, Remedies,* edited by B. Reskin. Washington, DC: National Academy Press.

Beller, Andrea and Kee-ok Kim Han. 1984. "Occupational Sex Segregation: Prospects for the 1980s." Pp. 91-114 in *Sex Segregation in the Workplace: Trends, Explanations, Remedies*, edited by B. Reskin. Washington, DC: National Academy Press.

Bergmann, Barbara R. and William Darity. 1981. "Social Relations, Productivity, and Employer Discrimination." *Monthly Labor Review* 104:47-49.

Bielby, Denise D. and William T. Bielby. 1988. "She Works Hard for the Money." *American Journal of Sociology* 93:1031-59.

Bielby, William T. and James N. Baron. 1984. "A Woman's Place Is with Other Women: Sex Segregation Within Organizations." Pp. 27-55 in *Sex Segregation in the Workplace: Trends, Explanations, Remedies*, edited by B. Reskin. Washington, DC: National Academy Press.

———. 1986. "Men and Women at Work: Sex Segregation and Statistical Discrimination." *American Journal of Sociology* 91:759-99.

Bird, Chloe. 1990. "High Finance, Small Change: Women's Increased Representation in Bank Management." Pp. 145-66 in B. F. Reskin an P. A. Roos, *Job Queues, Gender Queues: Explaining Women's Inroads into Male Occupations*, Philadelphia: Temple University Press.

Blau, Francine D. 1989. "Occupational Segregation by Gender: A Look at the 1980s." Revised version of a paper presented at the meetings of the American Economics Association, New York.

Blum, Linda and Vicki Smith. 1988. "Women's Mobility in the Corporation: A Critique of the Politics of Optimism." *Signs* 13:528-45.

Burbridge, Lynn. 1984. *The Impact of Changes in Policy on the Federal Equal Employment Opportunity Effort*. Washington, DC: Urban Institute.

Carter, Michael J. and Susan Boslego Carter. 1981. "Women's Recent Progress in the Professions or, Women Get a Ticket to Ride After the Gravy Train Has Left the Station." *Feminist Studies* 7:476-504.

Cobble, Dorothy Sue. Forthcoming. " 'Drawing the Line': The Construction of a Gendered Workforce in the Food Service Industry." In *Work Engendered*, edited by Ava Baron. Ithaca: Cornell University Press.

Cockburn, Cynthia. 1988. "The Gendering of Jobs: Workplace Relations and the Reproduction of Sex Segregation." Pp. 29-42 in *Gender Segregation at Work*, edited by S. Walby. Milton Keynes: Open University Press.

Cohn, Samuel. 1985. *The Process of Occupational Sex-Typing: The Feminization of Clerical Labor in Great Britain*. Philadelphia: Temple University Press.

Collins, Sharon. 1983. "The Making of the Black Middle Class." *Social Problems* 30:369-82.

Davies, Margery W. 1975. "Women's Place Is at the Typewriter: The Feminization of the Clerical Labor Force." Pp. 279-96 in *Labor Market Segmentation*, edited by R. Edwards, M. Reich, and D. Gordon. Lexington, MA: D. C. Heath.

Detman, Linda. 1990. "Women Behind Bars: The Feminization of Bartending." Pp. 241-56 in B. F. Reskin and P. A. Roos, *Job Queues, Gender Queues: Explaining Women's Inroads into Male Occupations*. Philadelphia: Temple University Press.

Doeringer, Peter B. and Michael J. Piore. 1971. *Internal Labor Markets and Manpower Analysis*. Lexington, MA: D. C. Heath.

Donato, Katharine M. 1990a. "Programming for Change? The Growing Demand for Women Systems Analysts." Pp. 167-82 in B. F. Reskin and P. A. Roos, *Job Queues, Gender Queues: Explaining Women's Inroads into Male Occupations*. Philadelphia: Temple University Press.

————. 1990b. "Keepers of the Corporate Image: Women in Public Relations." Pp. 129-44 in
    B. F. Reskin and P. A. Roos, *Job Queues, Gender Queues: Explaining Women's Inroads
    into Male Occupations.* Philadelphia: Temple University Press.
Fields, Judith and Edward Wolff. 1989. "The Decline of Sex Segregation and the Wage Gap."
    Economic Research Report #89-04. New York: New York University, Starr Center for
    Applied Economics.
Figart, Deborah M. and Barbara Bergmann. 1989. "Facilitating Women's Occupational Integra-
    tion." Paper prepared for the U.S. Department of Labor, Commission on Workforce
    Quality and Labor Market Efficiency, American University.
Gross, Edward. 1968. "*Plus ça Change* . . . . The Sexual Segregation of Occupations over Time."
    Social Problems 16:198-208.
Hacker, Sally L. 1979. "Sex Stratification, Technology and Organizational Change: A Longi-
    tudinal Analysis." *Social Problems* 26:539-57.
Hartmann, Heidi I. 1976. "Capitalism, Patriarchy, and Segregation by Sex." *Signs* 1:137-70.
————. 1989. "Comments." Paper presented at the meetings of the American Sociological
    Association, San Francisco.
Hirsch, Susan E. 1986. "Rethinking the Sexual Division of Labor: Pullman Repair Shops,
    1900-1969." *Radical History Review* 3:26-48.
Hodge, Robert W. 1973. "Toward a Theory of Racial Differences in Employment." *Social Forces*
    52:16-31.
Kessler-Harris, Alice. 1982. *Out to Work.* New York: Oxford University Press.
————. 1986. "Women's History Goes to Trial: EEOC vs. Sears, Roebuck and Co." *Signs*
    1:767-79.
Kulis, Stephen and Joanne Miller. 1989. "The Changing Sex Composition of a Contracting
    Profession: Academic Sociology in the Early 1980s." Paper presented at the meetings of
    the American Sociological Association, San Francisco.
Leonard, Jonathan S. 1988. "Women and Affirmative Action in the 1980s." Paper presented at
    the meetings of the American Economic Association.
Leslie, Connie. 1987. "Making Doctors Human." *Newsweek on Campus,* September, pp. 39-40.
Lewis, Cherie Sue. 1986. "Television License Renewal Challenges by Women's Groups." Ph.D.
    dissertation, University of Minnesota.
Lieberson, Stanley. 1980. *A Piece of the Pie.* Berkeley: University of California Press.
Lorence, Jon. 1987. "A Test of 'Gender' and 'Job' Models of Sex Differences in Job Involve-
    ment." *Social Forces* 66:121-42.
Milkman, Ruth. 1987. *Gender at Work.* Urbana: University of Illinois Press.
Oppenheimer, Valerie. 1970. *The Female Labor Force in the United States.* Population Mono-
    graph Series, no. 5. Berkeley: University of California.
Osterman, Paul. 1979. "Sex Discrimination in Professional Employment: A Case Study."
    Industrial and Labor Relations Review 32:451-64.
Phillips, Anne and Barbara Taylor. 1980. "Sex and Skill." *Feminist Review* 6:79-88.
Phipps, Polly A. 1990a. "Occupational and Industrial Change: Prescription for Feminization."
    Pp. 111-28 in B. F. Reskin and P. A. Roos, *Job Queues, Gender Queues: Explaining
    Women's Inroads into Male Occupations.* Philadelphia: Temple University Press.
————. 1990b. "Occupational Resegregation: A Case Study of Insurance Adjusters and Exam-
    iners." Pp. 224-40 in B. F. Reskin and P. A. Roos, *Job Queues, Gender Queues: Explaining
    Women's Inroads into Male Occupations.* Philadelphia: Temple University Press.
Reskin, Barbara F. 1988. "Bringing the Men Back In: Sex Differentiation and the Devaluation
    of Women's Work." *Gender & Society* 2:58-81.

Reskin, Barbara F. and Irene A. Padavic. 1988. "Supervisors as Gatekeepers: Male Supervisors' Response to Women's Integration in Plant Jobs." *Social Problems* 35:401-15.

Reskin, Barbara F. and Patricia A. Roos. 1985. "Collaborative Research on the Determinants of Changes in Occupations' Sex Composition Between 1970 and 1980." National Science Foundation Grant no. 85-NSF-SES-85-12452. Manuscript.

———. 1990. *Job Queues, Gender Queues: Explaining Women's Inroads into Male Occupations.* Philadelphia: Temple University Press.

Roos, Patricia A. 1986. "Women in the Composing Room: Technology and Organization as Determinants of Social Change." Paper presented at the annual meetings of the American Sociological Association, New York.

———. 1990. "Hot Metal to Electronic Composition: Gender, Technology, and Social Change." Pp. 275-98 in B. F. Reskin and P. A. Roos, *Job Queues, Gender Queues: Explaining Women's Inroads into Male Occupations.* Philadelphia: Temple University Press.

Rose, Sonya O. 1988. "Gender Antagonism and Class Conflict." *Social History* 13:191-208.

Rotella, Elyce. 1977. *From Home to Office: U.S. Women at Work, 1870-1930.* Ann Arbor: UMI Research Press.

Sanders, Marlene and Marcia Rock. 1988. *Waiting for Prime Time.* Urbana: University of Illinois Press.

Smith, Joan. 1989. "The Impact of the Reagan Years." Paper presented at the first Annual Women's Policy Research Conference, Washington, DC, May 19.

Steiger, Thomas and Barbara F. Reskin. 1990. "Baking and Baking off: Deskilling and the Changing Sex Make up of Bakers." Pp. 257-74 in B. F. Reskin and P. A. Roos, *Job Queues, Gender Queues: Explaining Women's Inroads into Male Occupations.* Philadelphia: Temple University Press.

Stolzenberg, Ross. 1982. "Industrial Profits and the Propensity to Employ Women Workers." Paper presented at the Workshop on Job Segregation by Sex, Committee on Women's Employment and Related Social Issues, National Research Council, Washington, DC.

Strober, Myra. 1984. "Toward a General Theory of Occupational Sex Segregation." Pp. 144-56 in *Sex Segregation in the Workplace: Trends, Explanations, Remedies,* edited by B. Reskin. Washington, DC: National Academy Press.

———. 1988. "The Processes of Occupational Segregation: Relative Attractiveness and Patriarchy." Paper presented at the meetings of the American Educational Research Association, New Orleans.

Strober, Myra and Carolyn Arnold. 1987. "The Dynamics of Occupational Segregation Among Bank Tellers." Pp. 107-48 in *Gender in the Workplace,* edited by C. Brown and J. Pechman. Washington, DC: Brookings Institute.

Strom, Sharon Hartman. 1987. " 'Machines Instead of Clerks': Technology and the Feminization of Bookkeeping, 1910-1950." Pp. 63-97 in *Computer Chips and Paper Clips.* Vol. 2, edited by H. Hartmann. Washington, DC: National Academy Press.

Thomas, Barbara J. 1990. "Women's Gains in Insurance Sales: Increased Supply, Uncertain Demand." Pp. 183-204 in B. F. Reskin and P. A. Roos, *Job Queues, Gender Queues: Explaining Women's Inroads into Male Occupations.* Philadelphia: Temple University Press.

Thomas, Barbara J. and Barbara F. Reskin. 1990. "A Woman's Place Is Selling Homes: Women's Movement into Real Estate Sales." Pp. 205-24 in B. F. Reskin and P. A. Roos, *Job Queues, Gender Queues: Explaining Women's Inroads into Male Occupations.* Philadelphia: Temple University Press.

Thurow, Lester. 1969. *Poverty and Discrimination.* Washington, DC: Brookings Institute.

———. 1972. "Education and Economic Equality." *The Public Interest* 28:66-81.

192 PERSPECTIVES ON SOCIAL ISSUES

U.S. Department of Labor, Bureau of Labor Statistics. 1989. *Employment and Earnings.* Washington, DC: Government Printing Office.

U.S. Department of Labor, Women's Bureau. 1989. "Fillers from the U.S. Labor Department." In *Women and Work* (August 21). Washington, DC: Government Printing Office.

Walsh, John P. 1989. "Technological Change and the Division of Labor: The Case of Retail Meatcutters." *Work & Occupations* 16:165-83.

13

The Two Faces of Divorce:
Women's and Children's Interests

Sara S. McLanahan

No other change during the twentieth century has had a greater impact on the American family than the emerging economic independence of women (Bergmann 1986; Bianchi and Spain 1986; Fuchs 1988). Since the early 1900s, the labor market has become increasingly favorable toward women in terms of both greater employment opportunities and higher wages. In response, women have been entering and remaining in the labor force in ever greater numbers, and their personal earnings have been growing steadily. While job segregation and the gender wage gap continue to exist, there can be little question that women are more equal to men today in terms of their economic opportunity and earnings capacity than they were at the turn of the century.[1]

The macro-level changes in women's economic status have led to micro-level changes in women's family formation behavior. Greater personal income has provided women with the option of maintaining independent households and raising children alone. As a result, they have become more selective about when and whom they marry and more willing to leave unhappy marriages.[2] These individual decisions, when aggregated, constitute a sweeping macro change. Indeed, one might argue that the family has adapted to changes in women's economic status by reorganizing itself into

AUTHOR'S NOTE: *This research was supported in part by The Russell Sage Foundation, by a grant from the National Institute for Child Health and Human Development (HD19375-05), and by a grant from the U.S. Department of Health and Human Services to the Institute for Research on Poverty. I would like to thank Irwin Garfinkel and Judith Seltzer for their comments on a previous draft.*

increasingly smaller units, the most prominent of which is the mother-child dyad. Mother-only families have increased by over 250% since 1960, growing from 9% of all families with children in 1960 to nearly 23% in 1987.[3]

The macro changes in divorce and nonmarital births, in turn, have further fueled the increase in women's independence. For example, individual expectations about declining family stability have increased women's propensity to pursue employment outside the home.

In keeping with the theme of the volume, this chapter will focus on the effects of macro changes in family formation on women's and children's individual well-being. Specifically, it will explore the potential conflict between mothers' and children's individual interests. I begin by looking briefly at the costs and benefits of marital disruption for women.[4] Next, I summarize my own research on the long-term effects of family disruption on children. Finally, I examine society's interest in maintaining family stability and discuss what, if anything, should be done to reconcile the conflict between women's independence and children's well-being.

WOMEN'S INTEREST IN DIVORCE

Are women better off living independently and raising children on their own, or are the gains associated with independence offset by losses in other areas of personal welfare? Certainly divorce has substantial economic costs for women. About 26% of divorced mothers live below the poverty line, and an even larger proportion of these women have experienced a substantial drop in their standard of living. Estimates of the postdivorce income drop for women vary from a high of 70% (Weitzman 1985) to a low of 30% (Duncan and Hoffman 1985a, 1985b; see also Duncan and Hoffman 1988). In addition to economic problems, single mothers have primary responsibility for making family decisions, for performing domestic work, and for meeting the emotional needs of their children. It is not surprising that numerous studies have shown that single mothers report higher levels of anxiety and depression than married mothers (see Weiss 1979; Guttentag et al. 1980).

Nevertheless, many people would argue that, on balance, the increase in divorce and decline in marriage at the macro level symbolize a gain in women's status. Neoclassical economists would say that women's behavior speaks for itself. Assuming that individuals know and seek to maximize their well-being, it follows that women who divorce (or never marry) find more satisfaction living separately than they did in their marriages. Many feminists would agree. Women's economic dependence on men has long been viewed as a cornerstone of gender inequality, and freedom from the institution of marriage is seen by some as a necessary if not sufficient condition for women's emancipation and empowerment.[5] Thus, while the costs of divorce are unequally distributed between women and men, the absolute costs have declined for women.[6]

The empirical evidence lends support to the notion that, on average, divorce improves the well-being of women. In a recent national survey—the National Survey of Families and Households (see Sweet et al. 1988)—individuals who had divorced in the past five years were asked whether they had wanted their divorce and whether they were better or worse off after the divorce. Women were 2.5 times as likely as men to report having wanted a divorce. Furthermore, the overwhelming majority of women reported substantial improvements in the quality of their social lives and sexual relationships, in their career opportunities, and in their overall level of happiness after divorce. Over half reported improvement in their standard of living.[7]

CHILDREN'S INTEREST IN DIVORCE

What about children? Are they also better off living apart from their biological fathers or has the increase in family instability lowered their well-being? While many people would like to believe that women's economic freedom translates directly into gains for children, there are logical as well as empirical reasons for questioning such an assumption.

First, there is no reason to expect the interests of women and children to be the same at all times. Mothers and children are separate individuals, and although many women have been taught to believe that motherhood is their primary purpose in life, it is doubtful that identification with the mother role has ever been complete, even in the most traditional societies. Given the extension of individual rights to women during this past century, and given the increase in women's opportunities outside the home, it is reasonable to assume that, in some instances, the interests of mothers and children diverge.

Second, assuming that conflicts of interest arise from time to time, children have very little power over their parents' decisions. While the state protects children against extreme parental abuse, and while most parents consider their children's well-being in making important decisions, there is no reason to believe that parents give greater weight to their children's interests than to their own. In cases where parents place a higher value on their personal interests, children have very little power to alter the decision.

Finally, in its current form, the institution of marriage almost ensures that parents' and children's interests will diverge at some point. Whereas at one time marriages were held together by an economic bond that was based on the common interest of all household members, marriages today are increasingly based on sexual attraction and the pursuit of individual fulfillment. Sexual attraction and personal satisfaction are private goods that may or may not coincide with the needs of the larger family unit. Where marriage and divorce are subject to the ebb and flow of sexual attraction and personal happiness, there is a greater likelihood that children's and parents' interests will diverge.

Consider the following examples: A father drinks heavily and refuses to contribute to the support of the family, emotionally or financially. At times, he is abusive toward the mother and child, and family life is generally chaotic. In this instance, the interests of the child and the mother are similar; both are better off living apart from the father. Now consider a case in which the father provides economic support to the family and emotional support to the child but no longer loves the mother. He may have fallen in love with someone else, or perhaps he has just grown indifferent to the mother (the sex of the parents may be reversed). In this instance, the mother may conclude that she is better off living apart from the father, whereas the child is probably better off if the parents stay together.

What does the empirical evidence tell us about the life chances of children from nonintact families? It is interesting that public perceptions about the consequences of divorce and single parenthood for children have undergone several transformations during the past three decades, responding in part to the dramatic increase in the rate of marital disruption during the 1960s and 1970s.

During the 1950s and 1960s, the prevailing view was that single parenthood was indicative of individual pathology, and the children of such unions were expected to exhibit similar psychological problems. This view was seriously challenged in the early 1970s by Herzog and Sudia (1972), who, in their lengthy review of the literature, noted that most of the existing studies contained serious methodological flaws, including a failure to control for differences in race and socioeconomic status. Herzog and Sudia ushered in a new perspective on divorce and single parenthood, which was accompanied by studies focusing on the strengths as opposed to the weaknesses of single-parent families. A common assertion during this period was that parents' personal fulfillment was a necessary component of good parenting and children were better off living with one happy parent than with two unhappy parents. It is also interesting that the shift in consciousness coincided with and served to legitimate the dramatic increase in divorce that occurred during the 1960s and 1970s.

More recently, the pendulum has swung back toward a more critical view. While not making assertions about individual pathology, researchers have become less optimistic about the consequences of family disruption for children. For the past six years, my colleagues and I at the University of Wisconsin—Madison have been examining the intergenerational conse-quences of family disruption, focusing specifically on the long-term costs of single parenthood for children. Our analyses are based on data from three longitudinal surveys, the Panel Study of Income Dynamics (PSID), the National Longitudinal Survey Youth Cohort (NLSY), and the High School and Beyond Survey (HSB) as well as data from several cross-sectional surveys, including the 1980 Census public use tapes, the National Survey of Family Growth, and the National Survey of Families and Households. Taken together, this body of research points to a number of consistent findings about the effects of divorce on children.

First, children who live apart from one or both parents appear to be disadvantaged across a wide range of outcomes: They are more likely to drop out of high school than children who live with both parents (McLanahan 1985; Sandefur et al. 1989; Astone and McLanahan 1989a, 1989b); they are more likely to marry and have children while still in their teens (McLanahan and Bumpass 1988a); and they are more likely to form single-parent fami-lies themselves, either through marital disruption or nonmarital births (Mc-Lanahan 1988). All of these outcomes increase the risk for long-term poverty and economic dependence.

Second, we have found that family disruption is associated with lower educational attainment across a variety of racial and ethnic groups. However, the cumulative effects of single parenthood appear to be stronger (more negative) for whites than for other groups. Single-parent living arrangements decrease the risk of high school enrollment by 122% for whites, 32% for blacks, 43% for Hispanics, 55% for Native Americans, and 39% for Asians (McLanahan and Bumpass 1988b). These differences could occur either because the institutional supports for single mothers are stronger in minority communities or because stress is higher across all types of minority families. Either way, divorce is less important in determining the life chances of minority youth than of white youth.

Third, the demographic characteristics of nonintact families do not matter very much. Whereas children of widowed mothers are less likely to drop out of school than children of divorced, separated, or never-married mothers, they are similar to children from other types of nonintact families in other ways. For example, children living with widowed mothers are approximately 30% more likely than children living with separated mothers to be enrolled in high school at age 17 (McLanahan 1985). In contrast, children in widowed families are virtually indistinguishable from children in other single-parent living arrangements with respect to premarital births. In both cases, the children are about 120% more likely themselves to give birth out of wedlock than children in intact families (McLanahan and Bumpass 1988a). Nor does the sex of the child or custodial parent make much difference. Both boys and girls are more likely to drop out of school and start families early if they come from nonintact families, and daughters living with single fathers are just as likely to give birth out of wedlock as daughters living with single mothers (McLanahan, 1985; McLanahan and Bumpass 1988a). There is some evidence that the presence of a grandmother in mother-only families reduces the risk of a daughter's premarital birth (McLanahan and Sandefur 1990).

Fourth, among whites, remarriage does *not* reduce the disadvantages associated with family breakup, even though stepfamilies have more income than single-parent families. In fact, when income is taken into account, children living with stepparents appear to be even more disadvantaged than children living with single parents. For example, white children in single-parent families are 62% more likely to drop out of high school than those in intact families, whereas white children in stepfamilies are about 97% more likely to drop out (McLanahan et al. 1988). Whether stepparents have other economic commitments outside the household or whether they are unwilling to share income with their stepchildren is not clear at this point. However, the evidence that remarriage may not be a solution to the problem of single parenthood is consistent across several studies.

Finally, family disruptions in adolescence seem to have the same consequences as disruptions in early childhood, though perhaps for different reasons (McLanahan and Bumpass 1988a). Early disruptions increase the risk of long-term exposure to single parenthood, whereas later disruptions reduce parental authority during adolescence, which is a time in which children require much parental guidance and control.

DIVORCE AND DISADVANTAGE:
CAUSE OR EFFECT?

The studies described above show a positive correlation between family stability and children's long-term socioeconomic attainment. They do not, however, establish that the relationship is causal. One might argue that the lower attainment of children from divorced families is due entirely to conditions predating the parents' divorce. If this were true, children from divorced families would be expected to be worse off than children in two-parent families, even if the divorced parents had remained together. In fact, they might have been worse off. This argument, which is called the *selection hypothesis,* assumes that predivorce conditions resemble those of the family described above, in which the father provides neither emotional nor financial support to the mother and the household is chaotic. If all family disruptions were of this type, we would still be concerned about the welfare of the children in such families, but not about the parents' decision to divorce.

If we assume that at least some marital disruptions resemble the case in which both parents love their children but not each other, what evidence do we have that divorce itself reduces children's well-being? In such a family, wouldn't both parents continue to love and support the child after a divorce, and wouldn't the child benefit from less conflict and more parental satisfaction? Apparently, children do not always think so. In their recent book, Wallerstein and Blakeslee (1989) report that children in conflict-ridden families were angry and disappointed to learn that their parents were getting a divorce. Even after 10 years, many of the offspring in their sample still resented their parents' decision and felt they had lost something very precious because of the divorce.[8]

Apart from children's perceptions, there are theoretical as well as empirical reasons for believing that divorce itself has negative consequences for children. Perhaps the most important change after a divorce is the decline in parents' economic investment in children. In part, this is due to a loss of economies of scale: Parents' income must support two households instead of one. In part, it is due to changes in the costs and benefits of children. Parents who live apart from their children are less likely to experience the psychological benefits of parenthood than parents who live with their offspring, and the costs of supporting their children go up, because the nonresident parent loses control over expenditures (Weiss and Willis 1985).

Divorce also alters the quantity and quality of the time parents spend with their children. Time with the nonresidential parent declines because of increases in transportation costs and the costs associated with interacting with the residential parent, and time with the residential parent declines because single mothers must work more hours to compensate for the loss of income. The quality of parent-child relations is affected by the fact that parents are under a considerable amount of stress during the first year after separation and also by the fact that parental conflict over child support and visitation may continue for many years. In families where fathers continue to contribute substantial amounts of money to their children, the father is likely to resent the fact that the cost of the child is high. In families where fathers pay little child support, the mother is likely to resent the fact that she must bear the cost of the child alone. In the latter case, direct parent conflict may be low, but the mother's attitude toward the father may be hostile, which itself has negative consequences for the child. Stress and parental conflict undermine parental authority and interfere with the child's internalization of parental role models and values. Socialization theory (see Hetherington et al.

1978; Hetherington and Arasteh 1988; Wallerstein and Blakeslee 1989) suggests that such disruptions have negative consequences for children's cognitive and emotional development.

Finally, divorce affects the quality of children's community resources and their claim on these resources. Divorce increases the likelihood that a child will live in a disadvantaged community, where jobs are scarce and schools are poor. The benefits of completing high school and delaying parenthood are lower in such communities and, therefore, adolescents are less likely to stay in school and more likely to become teen parents. Even among children living in middle-class neighborhoods, divorce may interrupt community ties and promote membership in deviant subgroups. Residential mobility is much higher among recently divorced families than among two-parent families, which means that a substantial proportion of children from newly divorced families must adjust to new schools and make new friends. When parents are under considerable stress, teenagers turn to peers for support, which can have either a positive or negative effect, depending on the culture of the group.

My colleagues and I have been testing many of these ideas, and the evidence is far from conclusive. The most consistent finding is that income is an important factor in explaining differences between children in one- and two-parent families. Differences in family income account for between 25% and 50% of the difference in high school graduation (McLanahan 1985) and for about 15% to 25% of the difference in early family formation (McLanahan 1988).

Aside from income, we have been able to shed *some* light on which parenting practices and which community characteristics are important for children's attainment. We know, for example, that single parents and stepparents are less likely to monitor their children's schoolwork and social activities and have somewhat lower educational expectations than parents in intact families (McLanahan et al. 1988; Astone and McLanahan 1989a). We also know that children from nonintact families are more likely to live in disadvantaged neighborhoods, to attend poor-quality schools, and to associate with deviant subgroups than children living with both parents (Astone and McLanahan 1989b; Sandefur et al. 1989). Finally, it is clear that family disruption is associated with relocation and that children living with stepparents experience the greatest number of moves (Astone and McLanahan 1989b). Unfortunately, we have not been able to demonstrate that these differences account for very much of the contrast in school achievement and family formation behavior among children in one- and two-parent families.

Last, we have made some progress toward testing the selection hypothesis. We have determined that inherited ability does not account for the difference in the educational attainment of children from intact and nonintact families

(Astone and McLanahan 1989a, 1989b). We have shown that *changes* in family structure (going from a two-parent household to a one-parent household) lead to *changes* in parental practices, neighborhood conditions, and children's school behavior (Astone and McLanahan 1989a; Sandefur et al. 1989). And, finally, we have shown that family structure effects persist after the use of statistical techniques to control for unobserved heterogeneity (Manski et al. 1990). While we are fairly confident that divorce itself has some negative consequences for children, we do not have a good estimate of the magnitude of that effect.

RESOLVING COMPETING INTERESTS

In the concluding section of this chapter, I want to return to the issue of women's and children's competing interests in divorce and say a few things about what might be done to resolve the conflict. Let me begin by explaining why I chose to focus this chapter on the trade-off between women's and children's interests as opposed to simply talking about the effects of divorce on children, which is the subject of my empirical research. The reason for choosing the former was to highlight what is often a hidden tension between those who view divorce from a woman's perspective and those who view it from a child's perspective. Many people, and women in particular, are uncomfortable with the notion that women's and children's interests may conflict. This is not surprising, given that our society views women (and women view themselves) as the primary caretakers of children. Men may be criticized for neglecting their parental obligations, but a mother who places her own interest above that of her child is the subject of great scorn. Consequently, liberal and feminist discussions of single parenthood often take one or two directions: Analysts either argue that single parenthood is *harmful* for both women and children—for example, that mothers and children are victims of male irresponsibility (Ehrenrich 1983) or poverty (Wilson 1987)—or they argue that single parenthood is *beneficial* for both women and children—for example, that women and children are better off living independently from men (Delphy 1984). While all of these descriptions are true in some cases, I suspect that many couples break up because one or both of the parties find their relationship lacking in personal fulfillment, and I suspect that, in a majority of these families, the father has something valuable to offer his children.

The research on the intergenerational consequences of family disruption contains important information for women who are in a position to choose whether or not to end their marital relationships. Surely mothers who are in this position will want to know that divorce has costs for children, if only so that they can take this information into account in deciding whether or not to end an unsatisfactory union. Ultimately, these women may find that the gains of living independently outweigh the costs for themselves and their children, but this is quite different from operating on the assumption that family disruption has *no* negative consequences for children or that women's and children's interests are *always* the same.

What are the policy implications of this research? Should the government outlaw divorce for couples with children? Should it make divorce more difficult by changing the tax code? To answer these questions, the costs and benefits of such an action must be evaluated from society's as well as the individual's point of view. With respect to costs, outlawing divorce would impose major restrictions on individual freedom and expose women and children who live in abusive situations to considerable harm. Thus the social costs are clearly high. With respect to benefits, the answer is less clear. Until the selectivity issue is resolved, we cannot be sure how much of the negative impact of family disruption is due to divorce per se. Moreover, the magnitude of the effect of divorce on society as a whole is not always large. Outlawing divorce would raise the national high school graduation rate from about 86% to 88%, assuming no selectivity into divorce. It would reduce the risk of a premarital birth among young black women from about 45% to 39%.[9]

While outlawing divorce is probably not justifiable, less draconian measures may be in order. Reducing economic insecurity in mother-only families, for example, would go a long way toward reducing some of the negative consequences of family disruption for children. At this time, there are at least two major strategies for increasing the income of single mothers. One set of policies is designed to increase family income by increasing the earning capacity of single mothers. These policies, which include employment and training programs for welfare mothers, child care subsidies, and pay equity proposals, are aimed at increasing a single mother's ability to support herself and her children on her own. A second set of policies is aimed at increasing the role of fathers in supporting their nonresident children. Child support reform includes proposals for (a) increasing the proportion of children with awards, (b) increasing the level and collection of awards, and (c) instituting a minimum child support benefit for children with a living nonresident parent.[10]

These strategies have somewhat different implications for mothers and children. Policies aimed at increasing women's earnings are consistent with the notion that one parent is sufficient for raising a child so long as that parent has an adequate income. As such, they benefit women, whereas they may have costs for children insofar as they reduce the amount of time mothers spend with their children, and they may increase the prevalence of mother-only families.[11] Child support reform, on the other hand, limits parents' freedom and redistributes the cost of children from mothers to fathers. A guaranteed minimum child support benefit shifts some of the cost from individual families to the public, as is true of child care subsidies. Child support reform is clearly in children's interest in that it strengthens their claim on the nonresident parent's time and resources. In doing so, it redistributes the economic costs of children from mothers to fathers, which increases the cost of divorce for men. At the same time, it redistributes domestic power from mothers to fathers, which increases the cost of divorce for women. Because of the latter, some families may view child support reform as undesirable (McLanahan and Booth 1989). One of the few advantages that divorced mothers currently have is the more or less exclusive control over child-rearing decisions. However, if nonresident fathers are held accountable for child support, mothers must be prepared to relinquish some of their parental power. While this may be difficult at first, in the long run, I suspect it will be good for children in terms of both economic advantages and greater father involvement.[12] At a minimum, the symbolic value of knowing that one's father has maintained an economic commitment is important to the child.[13]

Strengthening the link between fathers and children may also be good for women. The fact that so many women today feel torn between motherhood and their quest for economic independence is evidence that the conflict *between* mothers and children is also a conflict *within* women themselves. Whereas, in times past, economic production and domestic production were complementary activities, today, the time and energy a mother invests in the labor market is usually time and energy *not* invested in children. Most women recognize this fact and experience a major dilemma over how to be good mothers without jeopardizing their future economic security. If women invest all of their time in caring for children, they increase the risk (for themselves and their children) of being poor at some future date. If they invest heavily in market work, their children receive less parental attention.

The only way to ensure that children do not suffer a loss of parental investment in the future is to encourage fathers to become more involved in domestic production. Not only does increasing fathers' obligations reduce psychological uncertainty, it ultimately increases mothers' earning capacity. Child support increases the benefits of working outside the home for low-income mothers, because it is taxed at a much lower rate than welfare benefits. It also permits middle-income mothers to be more discriminating in their employment decisions, which should enhance long-term earning capacity. In sum, child support and employment/training programs are complementary policies that strengthen family ties while promoting women's economic independence. Both are necessary for resolving the conflict between women's and children's interests.

NOTES

1. The gender wage gap, which remained constant at about .60 between 1950 and 1980 has been declining since 1980 for younger cohorts of women (Gunderson 1989; Blau and Beller 1988).

2. This is not to say that women's economic independence is the only cause of family reorganization. Changes in family structure may also reflect shifts in social values and institutions as well as fluctuations in job opportunities for male workers. Some argue that the liberalization of attitudes about divorce and single parenthood has made it easier for couples to dissolve unhappy marriages or relationships. Others argue that changes in the characteristics of a desirable spouse have increased uncertainty and undermined marriage (Oppenheimer 1988). Still others claim that increases in welfare benefits for poor single mothers accompanied by declines in jobs for low-skilled male workers have made it more difficult for young couples to establish and maintain families. While each of these arguments has merit, I believe they are less important than women's economic independence in accounting for the long-term trend in family structure (see Cherlin 1981 and Garfinkel and McLanahan 1986 for further discussion of these arguments).

3. For a discussion of the trends in families headed by single mothers, see Garfinkel and McLanahan (1986). The proportion of families headed by single mothers did not change very much between 1900 and 1960. Increasing divorce rates were offset by decreasing widowhood, which meant that the "flow into" mother-only families remained relatively constant. Moreover, remarriage rates were high, which meant that the proportion of single mothers remained low.

4. From this point on, I will refer to marital disruption and divorced-separated mothers as opposed to never-married mothers. Much of what is said about divorce and families headed by divorced women, however, also applies to informal unions that lead to parenthood. Although this may seem inappropriate to some persons, I believe that the similarities between the statuses of divorced mothers and never-married mothers are greater than the differences. With respect to children's well-being, their effects are quite similar.

5. Feminists have long debated the issue of divorce and its consequences for women. For a description of the historical debate, see Phillips (1988, chap. 12). For examples of the modern debate, see Weitzman (1985) and Delphy (1984).

6. At the bottom of the income distribution, the absolute gains from marriage have also declined due to the loss of jobs for low-skilled male workers. For this group, therefore, the increase in nonmarriage is less likely to indicate an increase in overall well-being.

7. The seeming disparity between women's subjective reports of postdivorce economic well-being may arise from several factors. Divorced women may minimize the economic costs of divorce to justify their decision to live independently. Alternatively, these women may be accurately describing their situation. Whereas their total family income (adjusted for family size) may have been greater prior to divorce, control over that income may have been much weaker. In this case, the women may indeed be better off economically. (I am grateful to Timothy Smeeding for pointing out this last possibility.)

8. Because Wallerstein does not have a control group in her sample, she does not compare her respondents with adolescents in two-parent families. Therefore, it is possible that many of the problems reported by the young adults in her sample are common to all young people, regardless of the parents' marital status. What is clear from the Wallerstein study is that children who have been through a divorce attribute many of their personal problems to the fact that their parents divorced.

9. The estimate for high school completion is based on McLanahan (1985); the estimate for premarital birth is based on McLanahan and Bumpass (1988a). Both sets of estimates assume

that all of the negative impact of family disruption is due to the disruption itself as opposed to preexisting characteristics of the parents.

10. See Garfinkel and McLanahan (1986) for a more detailed discussion of child support reform.

11. There is considerable debate over the extent to which the quantity of time with the mother is important for children's well-being (Desai et al. 1989; Belsky 1988; Phillips et al. 1987; Phillips 1987). The recent evidence suggests that the strongest negative effects associated with mother's employment are for middle-class boys (Desai et al. 1989). Note that this finding is consistent with our own evidence that the effects of divorce are more negative for middle-class, white boys and girls than for other groups.

12. The question of whether contact with the nonresident father has benefits for children is also unresolved at this time. While a number of small studies indicate that the postdivorce father-child relationship is very important for children's well-being (Hess and Camara 1979; Wallerstein and Kelly 1979), other researchers have found no significant effects of father contact (Furstenberg et al. 1986).

13. Studies show that fathers who pay child support are more likely to spend time with their children and to participate in making decisions about their children's lives (Seltzer and Bianchi 1988; Seltzer et al. 1989; Seltzer 1989; Furstenberg et al. 1986). For more information on the potential impact of child support reform on parent-child relationships, see Garfinkel and McLanahan (1986).

REFERENCES

Astone, Nan M. and Sara S. McLanahan. 1989a. *Family Structure and School Completion: The Role of Parental Practices.* Institute for Research on Poverty, Discussion Paper 905-89. Madison: University of Wisconsin.

———. 1989b. "The Effect of Neighborhoods on School Completion." Madison: University of Wisconsin, (mimeo). Institute for Research on Poverty.

Belsky, Jay. 1988. "The 'Effect' of Infant Day Care Reconsidered." *Early Childhood Research Quarterly* 3:235-72.

Bergmann, Barbara. 1986. *The Economic Emergence of Women.* New York: Basic Books.

Bianchi, Suzanne and Daphne Spain. 1986. *American Women in Transition.* New York: Russell Sage.

Blau, Francine and Andrea Beller. 1988. "Trends in Earnings Differentials by Gender, 1971-1987." *Industrial and Labor Relations Review* 42:513-29.

Bumpass, Larry and Sara McLanahan. 1989. "Unmarried Motherhood: Recent Trends, Composition, and Black-White Differences." *Demography* 26:279-86.

Cherlin, Andrew. 1981. *Marriage, Divorce, and Remarriage.* Cambridge, MA: Harvard University Press.

Delphy, Christine. 1984. *Close to Home: A Materialist Analysis of Women's Oppression.* Amherst: University of Massachusetts Press.

Desai, Sonalde, Lindsey Chase-Lansdale, and Robert Michael. 1989. "Mother or Market? Effects of Maternal Employment on the Intellectual Ability of 4-Year Old Children." *Demography* 26:545-62.

Duncan, Greg and Saul Hoffman. 1985a. "A Reconsideration of the Economic Consequences of Divorce." *Demography* 22:485-97.

———. 1985b. "Economic Consequences of Marital Instability." Pp. 427-50 in *Horizontal Equity, Uncertainty, and Economic Well-Being,* edited by M. David and T. Smeeding. Chicago: University of Chicago Press.

———. 1988. "What Are the Economic Consequences of Divorce?" *Demography* 25:641-45.

Ehrenreich, Barbara. 1983. *The Hearts of Men.* New York: Anchor.

Fuchs, Victor. 1988. *Women's Quest for Equality.* Cambridge, MA: Harvard University Press.

Furstenberg, Frank, Philip Morgan, and Paul Allison. 1986. "Paternal Participation and Children's Well-Being After Marital Disruption." *American Sociological Review* 52:695-701.

Garfinkel, Irwin and Sara S. McLanahan. 1986. *Single Mothers and Their Children: A New American Dilemma.* Washington, DC: Urban Institute.

Gunderson, Morley. 1989. "Male-Female Wage Differentials and Policy Responses." *Journal of Economic Literature* 27:46-72.

Guttentag, Marcia, Susan Salassin, and Deborah Belle. 1980. *The Mental Health of Women.* New York: Academic Press.

Herzog, E. and C. Sudia. 1972. "Children in Fatherless Families." Pp. 141-232 in *Review of Child Development Research.* Vol. 3, edited by B. Caldwell and H. Ricciuti. Chicago: University of Chicago Press.

Hess, Robert and Kathleen Camara. 1979. "Post-Divorce Family Relationships as Mediating Factors in the Consequence of Divorce." *Journal of Social Issues* 35:79-96.

Hetherington, E. M. and J. D. Arasteh. 1988. *Impact of Divorce, Single Parenting, and Stepparenting on Children.* Hillsdale, NJ: Lawrence Earlbaum.

Hetherington, E. M., M. Cox, and R. Cox. 1978. "The Aftermath of Divorce." Pp. 149-76 in *Mother-Child Relations,* edited by J. H. Stevens, Jr., and M. Matthews. Washington, DC: National Academy Press.

Manski, Charles, Sara McLanahan, Daniel Powers, and Gary Sandefur. 1990. "Alternative Methods for Estimating the Effects of Family Structure During Childhood on Educational Outcomes and Family Formation." Paper presented to the annual meeting of the Population Association of America.

McLanahan, Sara. 1985. "Family Structure and the Reproduction of Poverty." *American Journal of Sociology* 90:873-901.

———. 1988. "Family Structure and Dependency: Early Transitions to Female Household Headship." *Demography* 25:1-16.

McLanahan, Sara, Nan Astone, and Nadine Marks. 1990. "The Role of Mother-Only Families in Reproducing Poverty." In *Children and Poverty,* edited by A. Huston. New York: Cambridge University Press.

McLanahan, Sara and Karen Booth. 1989. "Mother-Only Families: Problems, Prospects, and Politics." *Journal of Marriage and the Family* 51:557-80.

McLanahan, Sara and Larry Bumpass. 1988a. "Intergenerational Consequences of Family Disruption." *American Journal of Sociology* 93:130-52.

———. 1988b. "A Note on the Effect of Family Structure on School Enrollment." Pp. 195-203 in *Poverty and Social Policy: The Minority Experience,* edited by G. Sandefur and M. Tienda. New York: Plenum.

McLanahan, Sara S. and Irwin Garfinkel. 1989. "Single Mothers, the Under-Class, and Social Policy." *Annals of the American Academy of Political and Social Science* 501:92-104.

McLanahan, Sara and Gary Sandefur. 1990. Manuscript. University of Wisconsin, Madison, Institute for Research on Poverty.

Oppenheimer, Valerie. 1988. "A Theory of Marriage Timing." *American Journal of Sociology* 94:563-92.

Phillips, Deborah. 1987. *Quality in Child Care: What Does the Research Tell Us?* Washington, DC: National Association for the Education of Young Children.

Phillips, Deborah, K. McCartney, and Sandra Scarr. 1987. "Child Care Quality and Children's Social Development." *Developmental Psychology* 23:537-43.

Phillips, Roderick. 1988. *Putting Asunder: A History of Divorce in Western Society.* New York: Cambridge University Press.

Sandefur, Gary, Sara McLanahan, and Roger Wojtkiewicz. 1989. *Race and Ethnicity, Family Structure, and High School Graduation.* Discussion Paper 893-89. Madison: University of Wisconsin, Institute for Research on Poverty.

Seltzer, Judith. 1989. "Relationships Between Fathers and Children Who Live Apart." Paper presented at the annual meeting of the American Association for the Advancement of Science.

Seltzer, Judith and Suzanne Bianchi. 1988. "Children's Contact with Absent Parents." *Journal of Marriage and the Family* 50:663-77.

Seltzer, Judith, Nora Cate Schaeffer, and Hong-wen Charng. 1989. "Family Ties After Divorce: The Relationship Between Visiting and Paying Child Support." *Journal of Marriage and the Family* 51.

Sweet, James, Larry Bumpass, and Vaughn Call. 1988. *The Design and Content of the National Survey of Families and Households.* NSFH Working Paper 1. Madison: University of Wisconsin, Center for Demography and Ecology.

Thomson, Elizabeth and Sara McLanahan. 1989. "Family Structure and Parental Practice." Paper presented at the annual meeting of the American Sociological Association.

Wallerstein, Judith and Sandra Blakeslee. 1989. *Second Chances: Men, Women, and Children a Decade After Divorce.* New York: Ticknor and Fields.

Wallerstein, Judith and Joan B. Kelly. 1979. *Surviving the Breakup: How Children and Parents Cope with Divorce.* New York: Basic Books.

Weiss, Robert S. 1979. *Going It Alone.* New York: Basic Books.

Weitzman, Lenore. 1985. *The Divorce Revolution.* New York: Free Press.

Wilson, William Julius. 1987. *The Truly Disadvantaged: The Inner City, the Underclass, and Public Policy.* Chicago: University of Chicago Press.

14

Mountains or Molehills:
Just What's So Bad About
Aging Societies Anyway?

Timothy M. Smeeding

Those who are terribly worried about the demographic impact of an aging (baby boom) society on the economic status of today's and tomorrow's children have missed a golden opportunity. Public policy toward smoking has moved (and continues to move) in exactly the wrong direction over the past 20 years. The providing of free cigarettes in middle and high schools in the early 1970s would have increased the number of addicted lifetime smokers. This would almost surely have resulted in enough low-cost (quick, albeit painful) deaths from lung cancer to persons in their sixties by 2020 to have eradicated the retirement income problem among the baby boom generation.

Economists have long known that the fiscal health of public old age pension systems varies inversely with the incidence of smoking and the subsequent rate of death from lung cancer (Leu 1979). In other words, the more we smoke, the more we have workers who are healthy enough to be productive. In fact, according to the Tobacco Institute, they are more productive due to the beneficial impact of smoking on stress. Hence smokers are the perfect subjects for public insurance programs: They contribute payroll taxes through their working years and die quickly and relatively cheaply just as they reach retirement age, obviating their claims to social

AUTHOR'S NOTE: *I would like to thank Richard Easterlin (1988) for the mountains versus molehills metaphor, Rich Burkhauser and Tom Espenshade for comments, and Kelly Johnson and Crystal Ball for research assistance, but I accept full blame for errors of theory, fact, and fancy.*

insurance benefits. Unfortunately, we did not follow this policy; we went in the opposite direction and drastically reduced the incidence of smoking. Hence economists are left to estimate the *increased* costs of smoking reductions on the U.S. social security system (Shoven et al. 1989) and society is left to suffer the ills of an aging society.

Having missed this opportunity, what are we now to do? Is the dire and dismal demography of an aging society really our destiny? To mention two recent books on the subject (Aaron et al. 1989; Boskin 1986), *Can America Afford to Grow Old?* or have we made *Too Many Promises?* To be sure, these questions have spawned several volumes and conferences, much handwringing, and even a Society for Generational Equity. I must confess that I have even taken some part in this handwringing myself (Palmer et al. 1988). But, as the title of this chapter indicates, the endless string of conferences, papers, and volumes on this topic has led me to conclude that we are more likely to be arguing about molehills than mountains. That is, I believe that the "bad" economic and demographic consequences of aging societies will not really be so bad after all. My conclusions are based largely on economists' tools—behavioral response to expected changes in supply and demand—and hence may not appeal to many readers who believe in other tools—straight line extrapolation, stereotyping, or total political inflexibility, for instance. I will also argue, however, that there is one large black cloud on the horizon that could make an aging society terribly uncomfortable. That problem, the severe underinvestment that we are making in a large fraction of today's children, could, if allowed to continue, create a society in which none of us will want to live, regardless of our age.

Though an economist by training, my remarks will attempt to deal with the assigned topic, consequences of aging societies for individuals, in the context of the macro-micro sociology thematic focus of these sociology meetings. In other words, I intend to focus on the contrast between aggregate trends in aging and individual behaviors within these aggregates.

FACTS VERSUS PROBLEMS

Why should we worry about aging societies? It cannot be because we individually fear growing old; nothing yet known to human kind, including Ponce de Leon and plastic surgery, will stop individual aging. Our worry cannot be because older persons do not like to interact with one another. If this were a problem, 18% of Florida's population would not be elderly. There would be much less emphasis among the aged on living together (retirement communities), vacationing together (golden age cruises), or joining groups that are mainly segregated by age, from the American Association of Retired

Persons on down the list. The negative consequences must instead be that we are afraid of the impact of demographic trends, a baby boom followed by a baby bust, on our future economic well-being as older members of an aging society. Should we be worried? What can we learn from where we have recently been, and where we appear to be headed over the next decade, before turning to stargazing into the twenty-first century?

THE ELDERLY: TODAY AND TOMORROW

The economic status of today's elderly at least equals that of the non-elderly (Smeeding 1989; Hurd 1989). To be old is no longer to be poor in America. Forty years ago (1950), 59% of the elderly fell below the U.S. poverty line. Today (1988) that figure is 12% (Smolensky et al. 1988), and 6% if you count noncash income other than health care (Smeeding 1989). Though some degree of insecurity among the lower-income classes remains (Smeeding and Holden 1989), today's elderly are by and large more healthy and wealthy than any generation that has preceded them. What about tomorrow's elderly?

Recent evidence from the 1950 to 1980 Censuses (Smolensky et al. 1988) and from wealth surveys taken between 1962 and 1984 (Wolff 1985; Avery et al. 1984) indicate that the next generation of elderly—that is, those born between 1925 and 1935, who will reach age 65 between 1990 and 2000—will be even better off than today's elders. This age group (aged 25-35 in 1960) has had the good fortune to be in their prime working years during the earnings growth of the halcyon 1960s, to find the value of their homes soaring during the inflation of the 1970s, and to have large liquid assets during the period of high real interest rates and the stock market boom of the 1980s. Indeed, individuals born in the 1930s have been dubbed the "good times" generation by demographer Carl Harter. A recent Federal Reserve Board study (Avery et al. 1984) indicates that the mean net worth of those 55-64 in 1983 (many of whom are good timers) was 84% above the national mean net worth. Similar earlier surveys for 1962 and 1969 indicated that the 55 to 64-year-olds in those years (whose survivors are among today's elderly) had net worth holdings that ranged from 39% to 56% above the average. This emerging generation of elders is also more likely to have a greater fraction of long-term two-earner families, hence they will have a larger share of persons in households with private pensions and also larger entitlements to social security benefits than any preceding generation. Based on these indicators, and even discounting a continued stock market boom into the next decade, tomorrow's elderly will on average be better off than today's.

Table 14.1 Nursing Home Discharges in 1985: Proportion of Discharges that were Medicaid at Admission, Medicaid Spend Down, and Nonmedicaid

Length of Stay	Medicaid at Admission	Medicaid Spend Down	Nonmedicaid	Total %	Weighted Cases
< 3 months	23.8	2.5	73.7	100	473,338
3-6 months	35.8	8.5	55.7	100	194,539
7-12 months	46.1	10.8	43.1	100	119,627
1-2 years	48.0	9.6	42.3	100	100,703
2+ years	49.6	13.5	36.9	100	174,912
All stays	35.0	7.0	58.0	100	1,063,119

SOURCE: 1985 National Nursing Home Survey as reported in Liu et al. (1989).

One concrete indication of the meaning of these income and wealth figures is found in the 1985 National Nursing Home Survey as reported by Liu, Doty, and Manton (1989), shown in Tables 14.1 and 14.2. Contrary to the popular opinion that most elderly who enter a nursing home quickly spend down their assets and incomes until they end up on medicaid, almost 60% of those who were discharged (dead or alive) from a nursing home in 1985 did not need to rely on medicaid at all. Five out of six nursing home patients who were medicaid coverees when discharged were already on medicaid when they were admitted, having spent down their incomes and assets in prior hospitalization (or nursing home) episodes.

Of course, we should be concerned about elderly people who are forced to give up their entire financial security (income, assets, even homes) and fall back on welfare (medicaid) due to nursing home costs. With this in mind, the recently otherwise repealed 1988 Catastrophic Health Care Act kept provisions to protect the assets and homes of spouses whose partners end up in nursing homes. This measure, which protects at least $12,000 in liquid assets, the home, and $1,000 per month of income for a spouse whose partner is institutionalized, should reduce the specter of "nursing home poverty" even further. Suppose we say that, because of the catastrophic health care bill and rising incomes and assets, 67% of all nursing home discharges in 1999 will not need to rely on Medicaid (versus 58% in Tables 14.1 and 14.2). Given a 43% chance at age 65 that an elderly person will enter a nursing home even for one day (Kemper and Murtaugh 1989) and a one-third chance that such persons will leave under medicaid finance, the chances of "nursing home poverty" are less than 15%. Even ignoring the growing market for private long-term care insurance and related mechanisms for self-insurance, a one in seven chance of nursing home poverty does not really seem so

Table 14.2 Nursing Home Discharges in 1985: Proportion of Discharges for Each Medicaid Payment Group

Length of Stay	Medicaid at Admission	Medicaid Spend Down	Nonmedicaid	All Stays
< 3 months	30.3	15.9	56.6	44.5
3-6 months	18.7	22.1	17.6	18.3
7-12 months	14.8	17.3	8.4	11.3
1-2 years	13.0	13.0	6.9	9.5
2+ years	23.3	31.6	10.5	16.4
Total	100.0	100.0	100.0	100.0
Weighted cases	372,815	74,435	615,869	1,063,119

SOURCE: 1985 National Nursing Home Survey as reported in Liu et al. (1989).

difficult to bear. This is particularly true when one recognizes that many of the real beneficiaries of the elderly's ability to pay their own bills are their children, who would otherwise have had to pay these bills!

So, if the elderly aren't really doing all that badly currently, and if the near future looks even brighter, why should we be so worried about the distant future? Let's review the arguments.

THE FAR FUTURE: BEYOND 2030

Economists, and I fear demographers, are not very good at forecasting the far distant future, such as 2030 and beyond. The literature on the economic impact of an aging society tends to focus on either the near term, say 2000 or just beyond, or the truly long term, say, 2030 and beyond, up to even 2050 in some Office of Economic Cooperation and Development (1988) publications. The usual disclaimer, such as "prediction is a dirty job, but someone has to do it" (Lazear 1988, p. 2) doesn't buy much peace of mind or faith in such predictions. I put demographers and sociologists all into the same basket here. You may recall that demographers were the ones who told us in the 1960s and 1970s that, when the baby boom left their teens and reached working age in the 1980s, crime in America would fall precipitously!

Though my lack of respect for forecasting should be fairly clear at this juncture, combating the forecasters on the topic of an aging society and its economic consequences for individuals does require that we also gaze into the murky crystal ball. And so we shall.

The economic costs of aging societies in the thirtieth year of the twenty-first century will depend heavily on three related factors:

(1) demography (dependency ratios),

(2) future patterns of retirement and retirement income and wealth, and

(3) the long-run rate of economic growth (including the effects of labor force aging on productivity).

Other factors such as trends in health care costs among the elderly, both acute and long term, and immigration patterns are issues that should not be ignored, but they are less crucial and even murkier than the three cited above.

Demography. There is no doubt that the ratio of the population 65 and over relative to the working-age population (16-64) will rise by 2020. But the overall dependency ratio, those not in the labor force (under age 16 and over 64) to those of labor force age (16-64), will be lower in 2020 than it was in 1960 (Easterlin 1988).

Granted, the current *public sector* cost of elderly persons is more than twice that of younger generations. But average total (public plus private) expenditures per dependent are roughly the same (Wander 1978 as cited in Easterlin 1988). The question, then, is whether or not we have the political wherewithal to reallocate resources from young to old if we really need to do so—the total economic cost is about the same. We shall return to this topic below.

Retirement. The median age of retirement for men is 62 years of age today, as compared with age 70 in 1950 (Burkhauser and Quinn 1990). At age 62, today's retiree has a life expectancy of 18.9 years (National Center for Health Statistics 1986), thus spending a longer expected time in retirement than in childhood. By 1984, life expectancy for a 72-year-old (12.5 years) was the same as that of a 65-year-old in 1940, just after the Old Age Social Insurance (OASI) system was created (Fuchs 1984). We are, as a society, spending a lot of time being retired! This trend toward early retirement, if continued on into the mid-twenty-first century, coupled with continuing increasing longevity at older ages, could create a substantial fiscal burden, by the middle of the next century, on public old age pensions as currently structured.

Fortunately this trend toward early retirement is unlikely to continue. In fact, there is a good reason to expect that it will reverse itself over the next 40 years. The major influence on early retirement in the 1980s has not been the age of eligibility for Old Age and Survivors Insurance (OASI or social security) benefits but the incentives, of the defined benefit variety (see notes to Table 14.3), built into employment-related pension plans (Clark 1988; Kotlikoff and Wise 1987). In fact, between 1999 and 2027, the age of eligibility for full OASI benefits will be increased gradually from 65 to 67 with corresponding increases in reduced benefits for those retiring at age 62.

Moreover, the benefit from deferring acceptance *after* age 65 will increase from 3% to 8% per year between 1990 and 2008 (Clark 1988). Hence the OASI system will encourage later—not earlier—retirement. What about private pensions? They are sure to increase in both scope (number of workers, particularly women, who are covered) and depth (level of benefit) over the next few decades, but will they continue to have actuarial patterns that encourage early retirement? The answer is likely to be no, for several reasons.

Unless there is an unexpected rapid and drastic increase in either immigration or fertility over the next 20 years, labor force growth will slow and actually decline after 2015 (Lazear 1988). In fact, the economy is likely to generate new jobs much faster than the labor force will grow over the next several decades (Briggs 1987; Bloom and Bennett 1989). If so, workers will be scarce, wages will be high, and the cost of retirement will also be high both for employers who must pay defined benefit private pensions and for the employees who must quit work to take them. Employers who responded to the baby boom labor market glut of 1970-85 by inducing older workers to retire early are just as likely to reverse these incentives as labor markets become tight.

Moreover, to the extent that employees (and employers) continue the trend toward defined contribution benefit versus defined benefit pension plans, employers will continue to have reduced influence on retirement patterns in any case. Over the 10-year period of 1975 to 1984, the proportion of pension plans that are of the defined contribution type grew quite rapidly, from 26% to 44% (Table 14.3). If this growth continues, employees will increasingly have greater control over how long they want to work and at what job.

"Retirement" from a lifetime or career job, with pension, need not also mean total work stoppage. Increasingly, younger retirees are working at part-time or other full-time jobs after they have "retired" from their lifetime jobs (Quinn et al. 1989). Hence pension acceptance does not necessarily mean total retirement from work, especially among younger retirees.

Additional factors such as health and mobility of older workers (likely to continue to rise), the labor force and job status of wives (typically younger and increasingly likely to be in career jobs), and changes in the workplace to accommodate slower labor force withdrawal will all work to encourage reversing the trend toward early retirement and to encourage work beyond retirement during the next century. Public policies to tax larger fractions of OASI under the personal income tax could also work to slow early retirement by reducing the net benefits of OASI receipt.

Thus tomorrow's retirees are increasingly likely to be economically independent, with increased assets and incomes from nonpublic sources, and to be facing strong incentives to work until they can truly afford to retire.

Table 14.3 Pensions Trend, Number of Participants (in millions)

Type of Plan	Year 1975	1976	1977	1978	1979	1980	1981	1982	1983	1984
Defined benefit[a]	33.0	33.2	35.0	36.1	36.8	37.9	28.9	38.6	40.1	40.9
Defined contribution[b]	11.5	13.4	15.2	16.2	18.2	19.9	21.7	24.6	30.0	32.0
Total	44.5	46.6	50.2	52.3	55.0	57.8	50.6	63.2	70.1	72.9
Defined benefit (percentage)	74	71	70	69	67	66	57	61	57	56

SOURCE: Ippolito and Kolodrubetz (1986).
a. "Defined benefit plans" are governed by formulas that typically rely on number of years of service, age, and wages to determine pension eligibility and payout. Employers are able to use special windows or other incentives to change the actuarial value of the pensions and, therefore, to increase early retirement or to encourage continued years of employment.
b. "Defined contribution plans" are those whereby a specific sum is set aside by the employer and/or employee in each period of employment. The decision on when to take the accumulated amounts of funds is at the discretion of the employee. Beyond a specified retirement age, the value of the pension is "actuarially fair" (that is, the benefit of postponing retirement for one year is an actuarially fair increase in benefits over the expected remaining lifetime of the employee).

Moreover to the extent that employer-subsidized retiree health insurance and employer-subsidized private long-term insurance grows, they will also be able to protect themselves against the risks of expensive acute or chronic health care needs.

Economic growth. Palmer et al. (1988, pp. 208-9) write that Americans of tomorrow in all age groups will almost certainly have a much higher level of material well-being than Americans in similar age groups have today. He claims that, since World War II, per capita real GNP increased at an average annual rate of nearly 2%, leading to more than a doubling of the overall standard of living. Even if this rate of growth were to slow to 1.5% annually (about the rate assumed in the intermediate projection of the social security actuaries), per capita real GNP would double once again by the time the baby boom generation was fully retired. If the reader can accept, as I do, that such a rich society as this can afford a large retired population, the important question to ask is this: What are the major threats to this continued growth?

The labor force of the next decade will clearly become an older one. Between 1990 and 2020, the proportion of the labor force aged 55-69 will increase from 12% to 18% among men and from 9% to 17% among women (Lazear 1988). The ratio of workers aged 20-34 to those aged 35-64, which was about .60 in 1960, increased to .85 in 1980 but will fall below .50 by 2020 (Easterlin 1988). Should we be worried about this trend? Easterlin (1988) argues that there is no evidence that older workers are less productive than are younger workers. Age, experience, and, perhaps most of all,

216   PERSPECTIVES ON SOCIAL ISSUES

education (human capital) are the traditional factors that contribute positively to economic growth. The *older* workers of the early twenty-first century are likely to have more of each of these attributes than are the older workers of today.

In addition to human capital, physical capital is a key ingredient in economic growth. While U.S. economists continue to worry about personal savings rates, our major concern is the U.S. federal government deficit. If the government can stop sopping up personal savings, more will be available for private capital accumulation. Alternatively, we will continue to depend on the less satisfying but clearly valuable influx of foreign financial capital (Japanese, European, or from wherever) to meet our financial needs.

What, then, of the burden of social security payroll taxes on future generations? Palmer (1988) indicates that, between 1985 and 2030, the percentage of GNP devoted to medicare and OASI will have to increase from 6.4% to 11.0%, an increase of 3.6 percentage points. This may entail increases in payroll taxes from the current 15.0% to 23.0% or 24.0% by 2030. If real incomes double, while expenses for children decline, we surely can afford such levels of taxation. Moreover, if we act soon to change the future rules of OASI, as we changed the rules of OASI in 1983; or, if the recently adopted physician payment reforms under medicare are effective in reducing the growth of health care costs, we could experience an even smaller expected increase in public pension costs.

In summary, the elderly individuals of the twenty-first century are likely to be even healthier and wealthier than are today's senior citizens. They will be more self-reliant, be less dependent on public pensions, and have a greater number of choices concerning work, leisure, and location. The increased social security cost of supporting these elders should be modest, even under current projections. Will these elders be happier and more secure as well? That, I think, depends on public policy between now and 2030.

PUBLIC POLICY

What will it take to ensure a generally happy and secure as well as a healthy and wealthy old age for the baby boomers? Prediction is, as I have stressed, a highly inexact science. If one had tried to imagine where the elderly would be in 1987 based on 1950 information, one would have had to make the guesses shown in Table 14.4. It is just as unlikely that anyone knows where we will be in 2030. But if we are to move closer to the rosy scenario that I have laid out above, rather than the gloom and doom of the generational warfare predictors, some modest policy steps need be taken

Table 14.4 Guesses on Status of the Elderly in 1987 Based on 1950
Information

Item	1950	1987	2030
Percentage poor	59	12	?
Median age of retirement	70	62	?
Life expectancy at age 65	13.3	16.8	?

within the next decade. And there is some evidence that we are willing to make these changes.

First, government must act to protect the employment-based pension rights of today's workers. Europeans are just coming to realize that employment-related pensions provide an attractive alternative to fully publicly financed retirement. We already have these and should continue to maintain the advantage we have in this arena. In the realm of retirement income security, then, increased enforcement of pension guarantees via the Pension Benefit Guarantee Corporation (PBGC) and related agencies are needed to ensure the fiscal integrity of employment-related pensions. The current savings and loan crisis is evidence enough of the fiscal consequences of public guarantees backed by poor regulatory control. As the growing number of dual-earner families become secure, dual-private-pension families, the specter of impoverished widowhood will become less frequent among very old women, without great public expense. For those who wish to do more to supplement their pension plans, wise public policy might trade a higher than $9,500 limit on tax-free pension set-asides for supplemental retirement accounts for tighter provisions against early withdrawal of funds from these and other tax-deferred pension vehicles. If we promote putting money aside and making it secure, personal savings and private pensions will become a solid pillar of retirement upon which the baby boom generation can depend.

Second, if public resources for the elderly are to become scarce next century, they should be targeted on those most in need. Only 10% of the top third of the elderly ranked by income rely on OASI for more than half of that income (Smeeding and Holden 1989). If we were to restructure OASI benefits so as to increase the share going to low-income very elderly women (those 75 and over), particularly widows and survivors, while reducing the amounts of OASI received by upper-income elderly (mainly younger elderly couples), we could increase the security that the system provides and reduce aggregate outlays at the same time.

The extended medicaid coverage and increased measures to reduce spousal impoverishment due to nursing home costs that were retained in the otherwise defunct 1988 catastrophic medical care bill provide another good example for the type of modest public policy changes needed in the near future: low overall budgetary outlays providing well-targeted aid to the disadvantaged elderly.

The funds to pay for these benefits are also within our grasp. For instance, additional taxation of the OASI income of well-to-do retirees could be used to purchase higher widow benefits. Although across-the-board OASI cost-of-living adjustment (COLA) reductions would hurt the lower-middle-income elderly, modest decreases in the COLA for higher-income families might be used to finance acute care medicaid buy-ins for lower-income elderly units between 100% and 200% of poverty.

There remains, however, one large black cloud on the future happiness and economic security of tomorrow's elderly, and it has nothing to do with private or public pensions or medical care costs. The sustainable rates of economic growth and productivity necessary to provide resources for the future elderly and nonelderly depend heavily on the future productivity (physical and educational development) of today's children. For those with a good education, the future is bright indeed. The economic rate of return to a college education today is greater than in the 1960s; college graduates face a bright economic future. But, for high school dropouts and disadvantaged youth, the situation is likely to be quite different. Wise economic investments in health, education, and related areas for disadvantaged children can have substantial positive payoffs, but only if such investments are made at an early age. The poverty status of today's children is truly alarming. The United States had a higher rate of child poverty at the turn of the decade than that which existed in eight other major industrialized countries (Smeeding and Torrey 1988). According to a recent paper (Dooley 1989), the poverty rate of Canadian children, using U.S. income cutoffs, in 1986 was less than 9% as compared with 20% in the United States.

Thus, if we are going to change the social security system in the near future, we should perhaps add a C (for children) to the letters of Old Age Survivors Disability and Health Insurance (Sugarman 1988). A .5% payroll tax on both employers and employees would yield $20 billion next year. Earmarking these funds for the health, education, and other basic needs of disadvantaged children are the type of outlays that will pay large dividends next decade. We may be able to get by without these expenditures, but I fear that, unless we have the foresight to invest now in the human capital development of tomorrow's work force, the security, happiness, and economic status of tomorrow's elderly, no matter how much is set aside today, will be poor indeed.

REFERENCES

Aaron, Henry, Barry Bosworth, and Gary Burtless. 1989. *Can America Afford to Grow Old?* Washington, DC: Brookings Institute.

Avery, Robert, Greg Elliehausen, Glen Canner, and Thomas Gustafson. 1984. "Survey of Consumer Finances, 1983." *The Federal Reserve Bulletin* 70:679-92.

Bloom, David and Steven Bennett. 1989. "Future Shock." *New Republic* 19:18-21.

Boskin, Michael. 1986. *Too Many Promises: The Uncertain Future of Social Security.* Homewood, IL: Dow Jones-Irwin.

Briggs, Vernon. 1987. "The Growth and Composition of the U.S. Labor Force." *Science* 238:176-80.

Burkhauser, Richard and Joe Quinn. 1990. "American Patterns of Work and Retirement." Pp. 91-113 in *Redefining the Process of Retirement from an International Perspective,* edited by W. Schmahl. Berlin: Springer-Verlag.

Clark, Robert. 1988. "The Future of Work and Retirement." *Research on Aging* 10:169-93.

Dooley, Martin. 1989. "Demography of Child Poverty in Canada: 1973-1986." Paper presented to the Population Association of America.

Easterlin, Richard. 1988. "Population and the European Economy: Making Mountains Out of Molehills?" Paper presented to the symposium on Population Change and European Society.

Fuchs, Victor. 1984. "Though Much Is Taken: Reflections on Aging, Health, and Medical Care." *Health and Society* 62:143-65.

Hurd, Michael. 1989. "The Economic Status of the Elderly." *Science* 224:659-64.

Ippolito, Richard and Walter Kolodrubetz. 1986. *Handbook of Pension Statistics, 1985.* Washington, DC: U.S. Department of Labor.

Kemper, Peter and Christine Murtaugh. 1989. "Long Term Care Financing Reform: Implications of New Evidence on Lifetime Nursing Home Use." Paper presented to the meeting of the Gerontological Society of America.

Kotlikoff, Lawrence and David Wise. 1987. "Employer Retirement and a Firm's Pension Plan." Working Paper 2323. Cambridge, MA: National Bureau of Economic Research.

Lazear, Edward. 1988. "Adjusting to an Aging Labor Force." Working Paper 2802. Cambridge, MA: National Bureau of Economic Research.

Leu, Robert. 1979. "The Effect of Smoking and Lung Cancer on Public Retirement Systems." *Social Science and Medicine* 21:108-21.

Liu, Ken, Pamela Doty, and Kenneth Manton. 1989. "Medicaid Spenddown in Nursing Homes and the Community." Washington, DC: Urban Institute. (mimeo)

National Center for Health Statistics. 1986. *Vital Statistics of the United States, 1984.* Vol. 2, section 6. Washington, DC: U.S. Department of Health and Human Services.

Office of Economic Cooperation and Development. 1988. *Aging Populations: The Social Policy Implications.* Paris: OECD.

Palmer, John. 1988. "Financing Health Care and Retirement for the Aged." In *Challenge to Leadership,* edited by I. Sawhill. Washington, DC: Urban Institute Press.

Palmer, John, Timothy Smeeding, and Barbara Torrey, eds. 1988. *The Vulnerable.* Washington, DC: Urban Institute.

Quinn, Joe, Richard Burkhauser, and D. Myers. 1989. *Work and Retirement in America.* Kalamazoo, MI: Upjohn Institute.

Shoven, John, Joseph Sundberg, and John Bunker. 1989. "The Social Security Cost of Smoking." Pp. 231-53 in *The Economics of Aging,* edited by P. Wise. Chicago: University of Chicago Press.

Smeeding, Timothy. 1989. "The Economic Status of the Elderly." Pp. 362-81 in *Handbook of Aging and the Social Sciences,* edited by R. Binstock and L. George. San Diego: Academic Press.

Smeeding, Timothy and Karen Holden. 1989. "Economic Insecurity Among the Elderly: How Much Is Not Enough?" Nashville, TN: Vanderbilt University. (mimeo)

Smeeding, Timothy and Barbara Torrey. 1988. "Poor Children in Rich Countries." *Science* 242:873-77.

Smolensky, Eugene, Sheldon Danziger, and Peter Gottschalk. 1988. "The Declining Significance of Age in the U.S.: Trends in Well-Being of Children and the Elderly Since 1939." Pp. 29-53 in *The Vulnerable,* edited by J. Palmer, T. Smeeding, and B. Torrey. Washington, DC: Urban Institute.

Sugarman, Jules. 1988. "The Children's Trust." Seattle: Washington State Department of Social and Health Services. (mimeo)

Wander, Herbert. 1978. "Short, Medium, and Long Term Implications of a Stationary or Declining Population on Education, Labor Force, Housing Needs, Social Security, and Economic Development." Liège, Belgium: University of Liège.

Wolff, Edward. 1985. "Estimates of Household Wealth Inequality in the United States, 1962-1983." Paper presented to the 19th General Conference of the International Association for Research in Income and Wealth.

Part IV
Demographic Perspectives

15

Multilevel Analysis in the Study of Social Institutions and Demographic Change

Karen Oppenheim Mason

This chapter grows out of a long-standing dialogue in demography about the determinants of fertility change, a dialogue most recently carried on in a paper by Herbert Smith (1989). The dialogue concerns the role of social institutions versus the individual decision maker in promoting demographic change. After more than a decade of domination by micro-economic models of fertility, focused on individual decision making, the field of fertility studies has turned to a sociological model focusing on social institutions as the ultimate determinant of fertility change. This chapter offers a partial course correction to the sociological viewpoint. Although social institutions are likely to have major importance for fertility change, there is, I will argue, a need to concern ourselves with individual decision makers as well, in particular with their role in changing social institutions. I also discuss some potential methodological implications of this argument. For convenience of organization—and because it is the clearest and most recent statement of the sociological view of fertility determinants—I organize my discussion around Smith's paper. My intent is to deal with a general set of theoretical and methodological issues, however, rather than to critique Smith's paper.

Before turning to Smith's argument, a brief review of what is meant by *social institution* is in order.[1] In normal sociological usage, an *institution* refers to a set of enduring, enforced social norms (widely agreed upon rules for behavior) that deal with basic problems of social life, such as the recruitment and socialization of new members of the society (the family institution) or the production, distribution, and consumption of goods (the economic institution). Thus Eisenstadt (1968, p. 409) asserts that institutions are characterized by their focus on the perennial, basic problems of any society, by their organized regulation of behavior, and by the use of norms and sanctions in this process of regulation. In this chapter, I will emphasize the social norms that, when enforced over generations, constitute the driving force of social institutions. This is not to deny that there are other factors that pattern the behaviors involved in a social institution. The coercive force of the modern nation-state is often important as is the power wielded by other social actors. In most sociological discussions of institutions, however, it is their normative quality—and the fact that a substantial portion of the relevant population internalizes, abides by, and enforces these norms—that is definitive. Thus the family institution of a society does not simply comprise the most common social arrangement for recruiting and socializing new members of the society or the arrangement that the law of the state prescribes. It comprises the social norms that define the ideal or expected arrangement, whose acceptance and informal enforcement by the population helps to guarantee that this arrangement is indeed common. Thus, although a social institution is not the same as a social norm, in the discussion that follows, I will focus on the social norms whose internalization and enforcement define social institutions.

Let us now turn to Herbert Smith's argument, which in many respects exemplifies recent thinking about the institutional determinants of fertility. In his paper, Smith argues that the most promising theories of fertility determination are essentially macro social in character. These theories argue that individuals are constrained by a set of social institutions that establish incentives for them to behave in particular ways with regard to reproduction. It is these ways of behaving that, when aggregated, produce a given demographic regime. The methodological implications of this viewpoint are, according to Smith, twofold. First, because institutions vary across sociocultural groups, rather than across individuals (or so Smith argues), adequate empirical tests of the institutional theories must incorporate the appropriate macro level, that is, they must compare sociocultural groups differing in institutional characteristics. Second, however, Smith also argues that empirical studies must incorporate data on individuals. Simply comparing the institutional and demographic traits of social aggregates to see whether these traits are empirically associated in the manner theory predicts is inadequate.

What I want to add to this argument is a point that goes to the heart of sociocultural systems, namely, the relationship between individual choice and social institutions. Smith's commentary implicitly accepts a theoretical tradition in which social institutions are assumed to have a life of their own and to impinge upon but not result from individual choice or action. Because individuals are assumed to be constrained *by* institutions, but not to influence them, the most sensible analytical model is one in which the behavior of individuals located in different institutional contexts is compared. Although this is a common assumption in sociological theory, it is ultimately a dissatisfying one. What I would like to suggest, for the sake of argument at least, is that (a) individuals frequently have varying understandings of and views toward the social institutions of a given society or group and that (b) individuals can and frequently do shape social institutions through the choices they make. Institutional contexts cannot, therefore, be regarded as simply constraining or impinging upon individuals. Thus, while it may be analytically convenient to assume this is the case, if we are to understand demographic change, we ultimately need to discard this assumption.

It is instructive to review why it is that Smith feels empirical research cannot afford to ignore individuals, given that his reasoning suggests his underlying assumption that social institutions are exogenous to individual reproductive choice. One point he makes is that fertility varies across individuals, not just across sociocultural aggregates; hence, the study of fertility needs to be conducted at the individual level, although incorporating a comparison across culturally distinct groups. Although it clearly is true that fertility varies across individuals, I would argue that this is often no less the case for how individuals perceive and hence are influenced by social institutions. Once one recognizes that there is nonuniformity in people's perceptions of norms, in their experience with or anticipation of the enforcement of norms, and in their own choices about how to behave in those situations where certain norms might apply, it becomes difficult to assume that institutions are invariant across individuals. This not only suggests that it may be theoretically relevant to make individuals the unit of comparison—rather than the social aggregates to which they belong—but also suggests one way in which individual behavior can help to reshape social institutions. If a set of individuals begins to perceive social norms in new ways—that is, views their prescriptive content differently than has traditionally been the case, develops a new sense of the probability of enforcement or the costs of sanctioning, or changes their perception of the social situations to which the norms apply—then their behavior vis-à-vis the norms or the associated sanctions may alter sufficiently to shift the nature of the social institutions of which these norms are a part. This is at least a possibility to which students of demographic change needs to be sensitive.

Smith's other theoretically based argument about the need to incorporate the micro level into studies of demographic change is that the modernization that normally accompanies fertility decline involves an elevated importance of the interests of the individual relative to those of the group (Smith 1989, p. 175). Fertility rates fall, in other words, because the traditional sociocultural props for high fertility are undermined and because new institutional conditions combine with the increase in individualism to create incentives to which individuals respond by restricting their fertility within marriage. An understanding of how institutional change influences demographic change thus requires attention to the manner in which institutions impinge upon individual consciousness and influence individual decision making.

This argument again assumes that institutions affect individual choice (at least when individuals have any choices to make) but are themselves unaffected by such choice. Indeed, in some versions of this argument (not made by Smith but by others), both institutions and individual responses to them are virtually fixed in stone under premodern conditions. "Traditional" peoples abide without question by the "props" for traditional ways of life. It is only with "modernization" that they become rational calculators of self-interest who respond to but are not automatically controlled by social institutions.

Do we really have evidence that social institutions are a product of individual choice? In these brief comments, I am unable to go into this question very deeply but will try to make a case for the idea that they are. Before doing so, it is important to note that I am not claiming that social institutions necessarily result from atomistic decisions by individuals or that they necessarily arise in a random fashion. Neither am I arguing that institutions are without force in influencing people's behavior. With regard to social atomism, it is obvious that collective action is often critical for the form social institutions take. Even where it is not, large numbers of individuals may make predictable choices about social norms in response to material changes or other "environmental" shifts. For example, in parts of South Asia, poor families have redefined *purdah* from a system in which women are secluded within the household to one in which it is permissible for them to leave the home to earn much-needed money so long as they wear a headscarf while doing so (Shireen Jejeebhoy personal communication 1989, based on fieldwork done in 1989 in Tamil Nadu, India). It also seems obvious that, although the relationship of individuals to social institutions may vary within groups, institutions, nonetheless, influence how individuals behave much of the time. If they did not, it would not make sense to talk about institutions in the first place. With these qualifications in mind, however, I am prepared to make two arguments for the endogeneity of social institutions.

The first is the logical necessity of assuming something along these lines if we are to explain why social institutions change. Whether done consciously or not, somebody changes social institutions; the institutions do not literally spring from the ground. To be sure, one can argue that it is only a small segment of the population that makes the decisions shaping social institutions, for example, the people who wield the greatest power. But it makes just as much sense to argue that *many* people play a role in shaping these institutions, although the powerful more strongly than the weak. The mass character of individual decision making in the formation of social institutions seems especially plausible for behaviors such as sexual relations within marriage that are conducted in the privacy of a dyadic relationship and that are consequently more difficult to control through sanctions than are behaviors that are visible to larger groups. Thus a social norm within the family institution prescribing the deliberate control of fertility within marriage may arise precisely because scores of couples find reasons to begin to practice such deliberate control, with the result that older norms proscribing such behavior—or at least not prescribing it—are undermined and eventually replaced by a new normative order concerning the reproductive behavior of married couples.

The other argument for the idea that individual choice influences social institutions is the empirical evidence that individual perceptions of social norms vary considerably, perhaps more in "modern" societies than in "traditional" ones but certainly in the latter as well. This is important because, with the exception of social norms that have been formalized as state-enforced laws, the ultimate resting place of the norms that together constitute an institution is inside the heads of the individual members of a group. Varying perceptions of norms, of their applicability to particular situations, or of the severity or probability of sanctioning, therefore, means that the manner in which individuals experience a social institution varies. And where the experience of institutions varies, I am arguing, individual choices about the institution may vary as well, something that in turn raises the possibility of institutional change arising through individual choice.

Examples of interindividual variation in the perception of social norms abound. One particularly relevant to fertility is variation in responses to the ideal family size questions included in dozens of fertility surveys in developing countries during the past three decades (Mason 1983). Although there are clear differences across populations in the average number of children named by respondents as ideal in every population there is also considerable internal variation in such responses—too much to be readily explained by the internal sociocultural (i.e., institutional) heterogeneity of populations (Mason 1983). It would thus appear that not all individuals perceive norms for childbearing identically or respond to what they perceive these norms to be in the same manner.

The next question I want to discuss is whether there is anything wrong with assuming that social institutions are exogenous "givens" and reproductive decisions endogenous "responses;" in particular, whether we are likely to undermine our ultimate understanding of demographic change by making this assumption. As I have already suggested, the most obvious problem with this assumption is the issue of how it is that social institutions change. This is important because the demographic transition itself involves institutional, not just demographic, change. The shift from high to low fertility involves the establishment of new norms about sex and reproduction within marriage (or, in some settings, outside of it), just as the shift from high to low mortality involves, among other things, change in the ways that parents rear their children. If we assume that social institutions are simply "out there," imping-ing upon and constraining individuals but basically unaffected by individual decisions, then it is very hard to explain how, historically, change in familial institutions and hence the demographic transition occurred.

What are the methodological implications of this argument? One of Smith's (1989) major points is that institutional theories of fertility deter-mination require a particular type of multilevel empirical analysis, one in which a comparison among cultural groups as well as among individual women is made. Appropriate studies of fertility change must, according to Smith, compare women from different institutional contexts but must also incorporate individual-level information as well. The specific model he suggests (1989, p. 181) as appropriate for the study of institutional theories of fertility change has the form,

$$F_{ik} = a_0 + b_k + g_k I_{ik} = e_{ik} \qquad [1]$$

where i refers to individuals and k to communities; F_{ik} is an individual-level measure of fertility or one of its proximate determinants (e.g., contraceptive use); a_0 is a constant, for example, some minimal level of fertility or the average level across all communities; b_k represents the effect of the kth context and is constant across individuals (or households) within that com-munity; g_k is the coefficient—also constant for all individuals within the kth community—measuring the effect of the individual-level variables I_{ik} on F; and e_{ik} is an error term representing individual variation in F not captured elsewhere in the model. This model is argued by Smith to be preferable, in principle, to one that is wholly concerned with interindividual variation (i.e., a model in which the b_k terms are set equal to zero) as well as preferable to one wholly concerned with aggregate-level variation (one in which the g_k terms are set equal to zero).

What implications, if any, does viewing social institutions as influenced by individual decision making have for this model? It is possible, I think, to argue that, in many cases, it has few implications. If one is dealing with a short time frame, one involving months or years, not decades or centuries, then one can argue that treating institutions as unchanging does not seriously misrepresent reality.[2] Because it presumably takes years or decades, rather than weeks or months, for institutional norms to change, treating these norms *as if* they were exogenous to individual reproductive choices may be adequate where the analysis is focused on the relative short run. If one is dealing with a lengthy time frame, however—that is, a time frame during which it is reasonable to expect institutional change to occur—then my argument in this chapter suggests the need for a structural equation model with two, jointly endogenous variables: fertility change *and* institutional change. This would be especially important when analyzing historical situations in which institutional or demographic change was rapid. It is thus important for analysts to be self-conscious about whether the assumption of the exogeneity of social institutions is in fact tenable for the particular type of analysis and sociohistorical setting with which they are dealing. When analyses deal with long-term demographic change in settings where social institutions are changing rapidly, this assumption may prove inadequate.

I would also like to suggest that, in short-term studies of demographic change, purely individual-level analyses may offer insights into the institutional determinants of such change. This can occur if there is significant interindividual or interhousehold variation in perceptions of the social institutions that are thought to influence demographic regimes. The force of a social institution for reproductive decision making presumably operates through individual perceptions. Hence when individuals within a particular sociocultural group *think* they are operating under different incentives, asking whether they in turn make different reproductive choices can suggest to what extent these incentives indeed contribute to demographic change. To be sure, to be successful in testing institutional theories of demographic change, an individual-level analysis focusing on a single sociocultural group must employ sensitive and valid measures of institutional norms *as individuals perceive them*. Unfortunately, such measurement is often difficult and rarely occurs in the average national fertility survey (e.g., Caldwell 1985). It, nonetheless, is important to recognize that the types of studies that Smith (1989) and others perhaps rightfully criticize as being irrelevant to institutional theories of demographic change can *in principle* contribute to our understanding of these theories. This is at least one of several suggestions I offer in the hopes of contributing to the continuing dialogue about theory and research on demographic change.

In sum, then, I am arguing that institutional and demographic change both involve a shift in the choices that individuals make over historical time, choices that are potentially predictable and that consequently can be modeled quantitatively. Because institutional change is often as much a matter of individual behavior as is demographic change, assuming that social institutions are exogenous to individual reproductive behaviors is no longer satisfying from a theoretical perspective, at least when the time frame employed is a lengthy one. In a time frame of years rather than decades, or decades rather than centuries, assuming that social institutions are exogenous to individual choices may be "good enough." When the focus is on the longer term, however, then models that incorporate aggregate measures of institutions as exogenous predictors of individual fertility or mortality are likely to be misspecified. The recognition that individual perceptions of institutional norms often vary also suggests that comparisons among individuals within a single sociocultural setting may be sufficient to test institutional theories of demographic change, although only if it is possible to measure individual perceptions of institutional norms in a sensitive and valid manner. Thus the recognition that social institutions change through individual action not only has theoretical implications for studies of demographic change but has methodological ones as well.

NOTES

1. It is striking that most demographers who have written on the topic, including students of institutions such as Geoffrey McNicoll (1980), rarely discuss what they mean by this term. For example, in the penultimate page of his 1980 paper, McNicoll mentions that "institutions have been depicted in this paper as more or less stable social or economic arrangements," but this is after 30 pages of discussion!

2. I am indebted to Barbara Entwisle for pointing this out to me.

REFERENCES

Caldwell, John C. 1985. "Strengths and Limitations of the Survey Approach for Measuring and Understanding Fertility Change: Alternative Possibilities." Pp. 45-63 in *Reproductive Change in Developing Countries: Insights from the World Fertility Survey,* edited by J. Cleland and J. Hobcraft. Oxford: Oxford University Press.

Eisenstadt, Shmuel N. 1968. "Social Institutions: I. The Concept." Pp. 409-21 in *The International Encyclopedia of the Social Sciences.* Vol. 14, edited by D. L. Sills. New York: Macmillan & Free Press.

Mason, Karen Oppenheim. 1983. "Norms Relating to the Desire for Children." Pp. 388-428 in *Determinants of Fertility in Developing Countries.* Vol. 1, *Supply and Demand for Children,* edited by R. A. Bulatao and R. D. Lee et al. New York: Academic Press.

McNicoll, Geoffrey. 1980. "Institutional Determinants of Fertility Change." Working Paper No. 59. New York: Population Council, Center for Policy Studies.

Smith, Herbert L. 1989. "Integrating Theory and Research on the Institutional Determinants of Fertility." *Demography* 26:171-84.

16

Problems in Quantitative Comparative Analysis: Ugly Ducklings Are to Swans as Ugly Scatter Plots Are to . . . ?

William M. Mason

For the past several years, I have struggled with theoretical and data analytic articulation of micro-macro linkages for human fertility "careers" on, first, a stupendous scale that involves the use of the World Fertility Survey, where *micro* has referred to the ultimate reproductive units of society (couples) and *macro* has referred to less developed "countries" ranging in size and nature from small, peninsular, or otherwise contained states to rather large populations with large land masses.

Second, I have attempted multilevel formulations and analyses on a much less grand scale. Working with data for Malaysia, I have tried to tease out relationships in which cumulative fertility and contraceptive use are the dependent variables of interest, couples are the micro units, and villages are treated as contexts. Using more formidable technical machinery, I have attempted much the same thing for Taiwan.

Third, I am in the process of attempting a multilevel formulation and analysis of fertility using the *ethnic group membership* of Jews in Israel as the contexts or sources of macro variability.

Now, in all of my research, I have struggled to get meaningful results based on careful, a priori theoretical articulation. However, I have only had a little bit of success. In particular, the macro effects are typically small; my scatter plots are typically "ugly," either in the sense that you have to be desperate to envision any kind of line describing a pattern or in the sense that the plot is actually too perfect, and in some way the main action has been missed. Why the confession? Not because I enjoy public self-flagellation, but because I think there are some object lessons that, if shared, could lead to progress.

With no pun intended, let me place these micro-macro divigations in a particular context. Sociology, and that includes social demography, is in a period of intense self-scrutiny. From within the profession, the war between quantitative and nonquantitative factions has never been more intense. Further, quantitative social science has never before received the intense criticism that it is now experiencing from the field of statistics.

The writings of two well-known figures in the fields of sociology and statistics illustrate my point well. In sociology, we have Charles Tilly's (1984) well-aimed attack on quantitative comparative analysis in his *Big Structure, Large Processes, Huge Comparisons*. From statistics, we have a decade of serious, grounded criticism of quantitative social science research by David Freedman (Freedman 1981, 1985, 1987; Freedman, Rothenberg, and Sutch 1983; Freedman and Peters 1984a, 1984b; Daggett and Freedman 1985; Freedman and Navidi 1986; Freedman and Zeisel 1988). Tilly and Freedman have much to say that is of value. I am led to consider it because my scatter plots are still ugly ducklings, and the metamorphosis is not foreordained.

Recently, the quantitative, multilevel perspective has undergone rejuvenation with the development of estimation procedures for stochastic parameter models in the unbalanced case. This has given new hope to those like myself who seek to build on the rich qualitative constructions provided by the likes of, for example, Jack Caldwell (1982), Barrington Moore (1966), or Theda Skocpol (1979). In essence, a multilevel perspective enables analysts to operationalize the notion that *relationships* estimated using units of analysis at one level can be treated as functions of characteristics measured at another level. Moreover, outside of comparative analysis—in fields as diverse as the study of education within societies and biological clinical trials and growth studies done on laboratory animals as well as humans— multilevel analysis has come to enjoy great cachet as a major analytic framework not just an estimation procedure. The technology is popular. It facilitates research on conceptualizations that, elementary though they may be, are a quantum leap beyond what was previously envisioned or possible. Nevertheless, the big question is whether the hope engendered by the multilevel perspective is justified in the realm of sociological comparative analysis.

In this chapter, I want to address the critical stances of sociologists like Tilly and statisticians like Freedman as they apply to quantitative, comparative, multilevel analysis. Neither of them has tried this, though neither would have trouble making the stretch. Nevertheless, it may amuse you that a statistician soulmate to Freedman—David Ragosa (1987)—has praised a version of multilevel modeling in contrast to structural equations modeling. So the exercise has value—though, like other forms of exercise, the benefit may be exclusively the doer's, not the observer's.

MAJOR POINTS

I spend the rest of the chapter reaching the following conclusions.

(1) Multilevel analysis brings with it much conceptual baggage in the form of assumptions that need to be checked. But so important is the checking that it takes on a life of its own. Journal editors and the groups that support the journals, and book publishers as well, should encourage this assumption checking, just as they encourage the building up of detail in qualitative forms of discourse. Right now, this is not sufficiently allowed, because the push is always to get to the end of the story: "Does X affect Y, controlling Z—as you said it would in the preceding pages of theoretical development?" We need that theoretical development, but we should not be so quick either to build on it or to reject it. More *public* effort should be expended on assumption checking.

(2) Multilevel models provide no inherent protection from the major criticisms by statisticians concerning the use of observational instead of experimental data. It is possible to carry out a series of experiments and to model variability in the results across experimental contexts (Fienberg, Singer and Tanur 1985). This kind of design might involve randomized assignment at the contextual level, depending on circumstances. If it does not, then the design is a hybrid of observational and experimental procedures. Multilevel analysis cannot overcome design deficiences.

Thus, we can not fend off the inevitable point, well known to us: In the vast majority of circumstances, we are not going to be able to do experiments in comparative analysis. What then? We do statistical analysis aimed at capturing the effects of covariates based on actual configurations of phenomena, not laboratory isolation of bivariate covariability. I do not see the fatal flaw in this strategy. After all, our critics from sociology and from statistics tell us that we should be doing case studies and careful observation—writing it all down for some future date when we finally have enough "right" facts. No kidding, this is what they are saying to us. In no way does this get us closer to the experimental ideal, which in any case is imperfect, as Smith (1990) among others has pointed out. All of those careful case studies and all of that close observation still must attempt to deal with covariability and the lack of the experimenter's ability to manipulate in order to observe cause and effect. So my bottom line here is that quantitative analysis offers us a framework in which to sift arguments. The framework is worthwhile because, using it, arguments can actually be rejected, even if they can never be accepted unconditionally. I join, therefore, a line of predecessors that includes Zelditch (1971) and Somers (1971), who defended quantitative comparative analysis before the recent interest in micro-macro interactions.

These are the two main conclusions, but there are also some subsidiary conclusions, as follows.

(3) Major criticisms coming from antiquantitative sociologists have a degree of verisimilitude. They have taken on a life of their own in the war of "hard" against "soft." This is unfortunate, because some of the criticisms are flawed and have answers, or at least reasonable partial answers. One example is the so-called Galton's Problem. The modern label for this is "spatial autocorrelation," a problem that can be tackled with statistical tools but requires—for those who espouse nonquantitative methods as well as for those whose taste runs to quantitative work—the development of a substantive theory to account for the lack of independence across space. Thus just because spatial autocorrelation exists, it does not follow that quantitative research is necessarily invalid or impossible to practice informatively. Nor does it suffice to say that it exists because of diffusion processes. How does or did the diffusion take place? Of what relevance is the diffusion to the particular dependent variable under consideration? How do you know?

(4) Quantification forces us to make explicit lots of assumptions and concept usages that otherwise slip by without examination. The point here is that rigor and "quality" are in the eyes of the beholder, and "beholders" divide into groups. In a passage extolling the virtues of a particular work of historical sociology, Tilly (1984, p. 79) remarks on the " 'supple' adaptation of Bolshevik programs to workers' own articulated objectives." What is *suppleness*? How do we know it when we see it?

(5) The next point is related to the first one: The things that statisticians would have us do, such as looking at scatter plots of residuals and examining conditional distributions, are inherently good, and we should do more of them. However, *stopping* there—as Freedman and perhaps others would have us do—is not acceptable to me, because the process encourages endless speculation on the one hand or mindless empiricism on the other.

(6) Moreover, stopping the humming of the computers in favor of "going back to the basics" and "really getting the facts right" won't result in progress, or a greater rate of progress, either. The reason is that we are already struggling with what we think is fundamental, and, of course, we already want to get the facts right. Waiting for the facts to build up is futile. Even when they are "right," our *choice* of which facts are interesting changes with time and circumstances.

(7) Finally, if the Hegelian dialectic of thesis, antithesis, and synthesis is really at work in this sphere of discourse—and that, I claim, is an empirically testable proposition—then there is a gain in muting the "hard-soft" battle. At least some of the time, we need people with diverse tastes attempting to work together on the same subject matter and toward the same end. If we don't have more of this, then the goal of sound generalization is unlikely to be attained. To bring this about may require a revolution in the political economy of sociology departments.

THE MULTILEVEL MODEL AND WHAT IT DEMANDS IN PRACTICE

Now I want to turn to a simple version of the multilevel model and ask what needs to be accomplished from the perspective of state-of-the-art practice.

The multilevel model is given in its simplest, commonest form by Equations 1 through 5. In these expressions, $i = 1, \ldots, n_j$ denotes micro observations in the jth context, and $j = 1, \ldots, J$ denotes contexts.

$$Y_{ij} = \beta_{0j} + \beta_{1j} X_{1ij} + \varepsilon_{ij} \qquad [1]$$

$$\varepsilon_{ij} \sim N(0, \sigma_j^2) \qquad [2]$$

$$\begin{aligned} \beta_{0j} &= \eta_{00} + \eta_{01} G_{1j} + \alpha_{0j} \\ \beta_{1j} &= \eta_{10} + \eta_{11} G_{1j} + \alpha_{1j} \end{aligned} \qquad [3]$$

$$\begin{pmatrix} \alpha_{0j} \\ \alpha_{1j} \end{pmatrix} \sim N\left(\begin{pmatrix} 0 \\ 0 \end{pmatrix}, \begin{pmatrix} \gamma_{00} & \gamma_{01} \\ \gamma_{10} & \gamma_{11} \end{pmatrix} \right) \qquad [4]$$

$$\mathrm{Cov}\,(\varepsilon_{ij}, \alpha_{kj}) = 0, \qquad \text{all } i, j, k\ (k = 0, 1) \qquad [5]$$

This two-level stochastic parameter model is described in detail by Mason et al. (1983). Though it has not been absorbed into the mainstream of sociological research practice, it is well on its way. What can we say about it?

Comment 1. First, the specification is cross-sectional. It is open to the criticism that we are attempting to infer dynamic relationships from disparate units measured more or less at a single point in time. This is an old, old criticism offered nicely by Tilly (1984), among recent sociological commentators, as well as by statisticians. There are a couple of backs-to-the-wall replies: One is that, when you can't do an experiment, working with covariates is better than nothing. At this point, the debate needs to be joined: In what ways is the cross-sectional analysis better than nothing? There are answers, but we don't hear them often enough or applied with sufficient concreteness. One kind of answer defends the usefulness of cross-sectional analysis in its own right. Even if coefficients are biased relative to the "true" time-series model (if such a thing exists), it is informative to have *an* explanation of between-context differences that has the virtue of being falsifiable.

Another reply is that the cross-sectional approach is "thumb-in-the-dike," awaiting rescue by time-series analysis. Here, we are embarrassed by the cross-sectional approach and point to a brighter future when there will be sufficient data and insight to estimate the "right" time-series model. Well, maybe, but one time-series analysis begets another, as anybody knows who has ever tried to do it. With regard to the cross-sectional nature of the specification, then, the multilevel model labors under the same criticism as a single-level model.

Comment 2. The micro specification is incomplete. To some, this is a fundamental criticism. Expand the number of regressors, and it's still incomplete. What do we do about this? First, let's rule out intervening variables, on the grounds that experimental designs have just as much trouble as nonexperimental designs in dealing with them. This leaves us with contemporaneous and exogenous omitted regressors. The omission of correlated regressors will bias the coefficients of the included variables. There is no satisfactory answer to this challenge *even* for those working with experimental designs, let alone those working with nonexperimental designs or those not subjecting their thoughts to the rigors of such formulations. From the perspective of analysts working with cross-sectional or time-series data, it is not unreasonable to try to take account of those factors that are thought to be most important. As for the experimentalist, even if you get one of the "causes" right in an experiment, it is surely not the only one, and it does not operate in isolation in the real-world setting (possibly interactive), so the progress that results from a good experiment is far from overwhelming. Here, I do not see that the multilevel model is especially at risk. If anything, it enhances our ability to cast a broader theoretical net.

Comment 3. My third observation involves choice of functional form for the distribution of the errors: Social science theory is rarely so detailed as to specify the nature of the error distribution, much less "normality" as distinguished from other, similar distributions. Here, the multilevel model is on the same footing as virtually all other models in the social sciences. We just don't concentrate our theoretical energies on the most basic of the stochastic assumptions of the statistical models we employ. We need to try harder to do so or else work harder to restrict our attention to those instances where the choice of distribution is not important (for example, because sample size is very large), or demonstrate, empirically, that it just doesn't matter very much if we assume, for example, normality when some other related form is correct.

Now, when we do specify the assumed distributional form of the disturbance, the assumption needs to be checked. So too do the assumption of constant error variance and the assumption of conditional independence. The use of widely dispersed respondents in a sample survey may suffice to satisfy this last assumption. The use of clustered samples, as often occurs for practical reasons in data collection in small, rural villages in less developed countries, suggests the need to question the assumption. There are reasonable technical fixes to these problems, so that we don't need to feel undone by encountering them.

Comment 4. Although this simple model (Equations 1 through 5) assumes constancy across contexts in the functional form of the distribution of the disturbances, there can, in fact, be variability. This is certainly a genuine problem in multilevel analysis, but it is not usually thought to occur in single-level conceptualizations. The errors might follow one functional form in one context and some other form in another context. For example, if fertility is Poisson-distributed in contexts in which families do not control their fertility, it is non-Poisson in contexts in which fertility control is present. What does that imply for statistical model formulation and for estimation? This is a hard question and I don't know the answer. At the very least, it would appear that, if we assume a single functional form for the error distribution, when several apply across contexts, then the meaning of "parameter estimates" is unclear, and our parameter estimates, and conventional estimates of the *variability* in the parameter estimates, lose desirable characteristics associated with commonly employed estimation principles such as maximum likelihood.

Comment 5. The model also assumes independence of the micro errors *between* contexts. For comparative analysis, this is usually a reasonable assumption. For example, if the micro units of observation are individuals, then there is no reasonable way to match up people across countries. So that, even if relevant omitted micro variables are the same for a pair of countries, we still can't argue that a micro force in one country affects a micro outcome in another country.

Now let us turn to the macro equations.

Comment 6. The model assumes dependence of micro coefficients on other macro variables. Of course it does; this is a way of stating the innovation of the multilevel model. The assumption of this kind of asymmetry plays no role if we purge the macro equations of their error terms. In that case, the multilevel model reduces to the ordinary regression model, except that the specification includes regressors that are constant within contexts. So the crucial point here is that there is dependence of micro coefficients on other macro variables, with stochastic error. *The assumption of causal asymmetry needs to be justified substantively, by well-articulated theoretical development. If such theoretical development is absent, then the specification is arbitrary.* Note that the micro coefficients are not allowed, in this specification, to affect other macro variables. Such a possibility could be allowed in a design that allows for changes over time. Also, macro variables that are not included in an expanded version of Equation 3 could be endogenous with respect to the micro coefficients.

Comment 7. That the macro specification allows for macro disturbances is itself disturbing as well as conceptually appealing. The appeal is that we find it congenial to think of our "prediction equation" as allowing for imperfection. It is counterfactual to specify a model in which we are forced to assume that we know the exact regressor list. Nevertheless, from a classical statistical perspective, we need to define the population from which our contexts are a *random* sample. Does it make sense? How much trouble do we take to justify it? Analysts must work on this. Equivalently, from a Bayesian perspective, we assume that the disturbances are *exchangeable.* For each context, there is an n-tuple of macro disturbances. Suppose we move these n-tuples around, so that they are no longer necessarily matched with their own contexts. If we are totally indifferent to this mixing up, then the disturbances are exchangeable. This is a revealing way of stating the randomness assumption in the classical inferential framework, because it treats the disturbances of all of the macro equations *simultaneously,* not equation by equation. To satisfy ourselves that the macro disturbances are exchangeable (a) we have to be convinced that our macro specification is full and complete, and (b) we need to explore the computed residuals to determine whether there is omitted structure. For example, suppose we are conducting a comparative analysis in which countries are the macro units of analysis and *world region as such never appears.* We might be well advised to check the residuals to see if their averages vary across regions.

Comment 8. The model assumes normality of the macro disturbances: This is the same problem observed at the micro level, except that it is raised one level higher. We can examine residual plots to check for normality, and because we are likely to know something about the contextual units, we can consider whether departures from normality are substantively telling or apparent flukes.

Comment 9. The model assumes constancy of variance for each defined macro error term. We assume this to make the whole edifice tractable. We can check this assumption in the same way that it is checked in single-level models when there is only one observation per value of the regressor. That is, we can't expect to have replicate values of residuals for fixed values of G.

Comment 10. The model assumes independence of micro and macro error terms. I have stated this as Equation 5, which is correct given the normality of the micro and macro errors. Is the independence assumption innocuous? First of all, let's ask how *lack* of independence could come about.

At the micro level, suppose there exists some variable W that should be an included regressor but is in fact excluded. Suppose further that the *contextual* means of W covary with the Y means. These are plausible conditions under which the assumption of independence of errors across levels will be violated. When this happens, (a) one or more of the coefficients in the macro intercept equation will be biased; (b) all of the micro coefficients, to the extent that the micro regressors are correlated with W, will be biased, context by context; (c) there will now be at least one additional covariance component to estimate, and this is very hard; and (d) in general, there is likely to be loss of efficiency, and the computed standard errors of the estimated coefficients are likely to be incorrect.

One response to this potential problem is to admit that we can't guard against all omitted micro variables. However, for key variables, sometimes an aggregated proxy will be available. For example, the World Fertility Survey lacks consistent and detailed micro information on abortion for each country. For a substantial number of countries, though, it may be possible to obtain aggregated, country-level information on abortion. If countries are the unit of analysis, then inclusion of such aggregate information in the relevant macro equation will reduce bias as well as allow us to come closer to the assumption of independence of micro and macro errors. This is likely to be especially pertinent to the macro equation for the intercept.

Comment 11. There is another big assumption, which is that, across contexts, the macro errors are independent. This is the assumption of no spatial autocorrelation. Is it valid? In some instances it may be, in others it may not. You can't rely on a relative lack of geographic proximity of the contexts, because there are other bases of similarity (e.g., the contexts may be ex-colonies, so that dispersed countries have similarities that could exist only because of their common link to a former colonial power). Here, good prior knowledge, as well as theory, are needed. In principle, it is possible to extend the estimation framework to take account of such knowledge. For example, Benefo (1990) has carried out a fascinating analysis of reproductive regimes among some 34 West African tribes using World Fertility Survey data from four closely situated countries. Because of the proximity of these ethnic groups, it is reasonable to ask whether his macro specification satisfies the assumption of no spatial autocorrelation. A random coefficient regression (RCR) model estimated for these data might not. Why? Because these ethnic groups have countries in common. Because each macro equation of the RCR model reduces to an intercept and an error term, there is no macro structure to account for the within-country similarity of ethnic groups. Thus the assumption checking requires us to examine the residuals from any such multilevel method to see if they differ, on average, by country. In sum, the assumption checking can be done. It is a feasible task, though one not yet accomplished, to extend the computational formulas consistent with Equations 1 through 5 to allow for some forms of autocorrelation. We need to engage in assumption checking, however, to justify the statistical work entailed by specification of models that allow for spatial autocorrelation.

PROBLEMS, PROBLEMS

I have encountered three additional problems, each of them important, in the conduct of qualitative comparative analysis. The first concerns the question of varying meaning across contexts. The question of meaning can be addressed by supposing that in some way the variables we have in our equations are not quite the variables we want. At least, I think that is one reasonable way to conceptualize the claim that a variable means one thing in one context and another thing in a different context.

Why is this important? Because it is inadequate for critics to argue that, because the "meaning" of something varies over contexts, comparative analysis is impossible. Yet that is the most frequently voiced criticism of comparative analysis. The *meaning* of this criticism needs to be articulated within a given analytic context.

For example, Equation 6 says that our X variable is a combination of two variables—one of them what we thought we were measuring (X^*), and the other one (λ) something else. Furthermore, Equation 6 says that this other variable actually varies over individuals. It also says that the impact of this other variable can be different across contexts.

$$X_{1ij} = (\omega_{1j} X^*_{1ij} + (1 - \omega_{1j}) \lambda_{1ij})$$ [6]

Equation 7, in contrast, says that our measured X variable is off by a constant, with the constant differing across contexts. This is another way of thinking about the "comparability" issue.

$$X_{1ij} = a_j X^*_{1ij}$$ [7]

Equation 8 provides yet another way of conceptualizing constant errors within a context and also allows for variable errors across contexts.

$$X_{1ij} = (\omega_{1j} X^*_{1ij} + (1 - \omega_{1j}) a_j)$$ [8]

Equations 9, 10, and 11 provide parallel characterizations of errors, but for the dependent variable.

$$Y_{ij} = (\varphi_j Y^*_{ij} + (1 - \varphi_j) \xi_{ij})$$ [9]

$$Y_{ij} = z_j Y^*_{ij}$$ [10]

$$Y_{ij} = (\varphi_j Y^*_{ij} + (1 - \varphi_j) z_j)$$ [11]

Some general conclusions about the "varying meaning" problem, as construed above, are possible. Let us consider errors in the dependent variable first. Within a context, as long as these errors are random, there are no particular estimation problems—at least in the ordinary Gaussian regression case. The reason is that random errors in Y are absorbed into the stochastic disturbance of the equation, with no damage to parameter estimation.

What about nonrandom errors in Y? These cause us real problems within a *single* context. Working with multiple contexts amplifies the problems. Is there a technical correction? The answer here is that the analyst needs to work very hard to try to pin down the source of the nonrandom errors and find improved measures. Note, however, that there is no *particular* reason to think that any nonrandom errors are *meaning* errors.

What about errors in X? Here there is bad news. The reason is that *any* errors in the measurement of X leads to biased and inconsistent estimates of the *effects* of X on Y. Does this problem mean that we should give up? Not necessarily.

The reason we should not give up is that measurement errors in X do not *necessarily* eliminate the possibility of carrying out comparative analysis. Why not? The answer is contained in the macro equations, which have stochastic error terms. Where do they "come from"? Of course, one source of error is the counsel of realism: Not even a genius could create a model that would predict the true micro coefficients perfectly. The processes we try to model are not deterministic. But let us set this point aside and concentrate on the issue at hand. Another source of macro errors is errors of measurement (i.e., bias) in the micro coefficients themselves. These errors can vary from context to context. Indeed, all of the "meaning"-generated errors listed by Equations 6, 7, and 8 can be thought of as producing errors in the micro coefficients. Now, the magnitude and distribution of these errors may be such that they totally swamp any systematic variability in the coefficients across contexts—hence my "ugly scatter plots." But this is an empirical question in any research setting. If the analyst finds that the theoretically driven specification of the macro equation yields *nothing*, that is an indication either to dig deeper into the problem or to junk the theory. On the other hand, if estimation of the macro equation yields results consistent with the a priori reasoning, in what sense has variation in meaning across contexts rendered impossible the comparative analysis? I claim that, under this circumstance, quantitative comparative analysis has not been demonstrated impossible; quite the contrary. To me, this is a major, yet elementary conclusion.

The remaining problems, of the total of three mentioned in this section, can be dealt with succinctly, because satisfactory solutions are elusive. The problems are superficially identical but have distinct epistemological bases. They are as follows:

- The functional form can vary across contexts. Thus, in one context, a power term may be appropriate; in another, it may not. Or a variable may be *defined* conceptually in one context but not in another. For example, polygyny is common in sub-Saharan Africa, but not in Asia. This can prove intractable.

- Even if a variable, that is, a dimension on which there is in principle variability, is *defined* in a given context, it may not actually vary over micro units in that context. In this instance, the variable disappears, and we are left with a data-driven difference in functional form across contexts.

I don't have solutions, but it is clear that there is no universal tool. Our kit needs a variety of tools, including multilevel analysis. Of one thing I am convinced: If you take seriously all of the assumption checking I describe here, your micro-macro formulation and analysis will benefit. I wish I could practice what I preach.

REFERENCES

Benefo, Kofi. 1990. "The Determinants of Family Size Preferences and Traditional Child-Spacing Practices in West Africa." Ph.D. dissertation, Department of Sociology, University of Michigan, Ann Arbor.

Caldwell, John. 1982. *Theory of Fertility Decline*. New York: Academic Press.

Fienberg, Stephen E., Burton Singer, and Judith M. Tanur. 1985. "Large-Scale Social Experimentation in the United States." Pp. 287-326 in *A Celebration of Statistics*, edited by A. C. Atkinson and S. E. Fienberg. New York: Springer-Verlag.

Freedman, David. 1981. "Some Pitfalls in Large Econometric Models: A Case Study." *Journal of Business* 54:479-500.

———. 1985. "Statistics and the Scientific Method." Pp. 345-90 in *Cohort Analysis in Social Research: Beyond the Identification Problem*, edited by W. Mason and S. Fienberg. New York: Springer.

———. 1987. "As Others See Us: A Case Study in Path Analysis." *Journal of Educational Statistics* 12:101-223 (with discussion).

Freedman, D. A. and W. C. Navidi. 1986. "Regression Models for Adjusting the 1980 Census." *Statistical Science* 1:3-39 (with discussion).

Freedman, David A. and Stephen C. Peters. 1984a. "Bootstrapping an Econometric Model: Some Empirical Results." *Journal of Business & Economic Statistics* 2:150-158.

———. 1984b. "Bootstrapping a Regression Equation: Some Empirical Results." *Journal of the American Statistical Association* 79:97-106.

Freedman, David A., Robert Pisani, and Roger Purves. 1978. *Statistics*. New York: Norton.

Freedman, David, Thomas Rothenberg, and Richard Sutch. 1983. "On Energy Policy Models." *Journal of Business & Economic Statistics* 1:24-36 (with discussion).

Freedman, D. A. and H. Zeisel. 1988. "From Mouse-to-Man: The Quantitative Assessment of Cancer Risks." *Statistical Science* 3:3-56 (with discussion).

Mason, W. M., G. Y. Wong, and B. Entwisle. 1983. "Contextual Analysis Through the Multilevel Linear Model." Pp. 72-103 in *Sociological Methodology 1983-1984*, edited by S. Leinhardt. San Francisco: Jossey-Bass.

Moore, Barrington, Jr. 1966. *Social Origins of Dictatorship and Democracy*. Boston: Beacon.

Skocpol, Theda. 1979. *State and Social Revolutions: A Comparative Analysis of France, Russia, and China*. Cambridge: Cambridge University Press.

Smith, Herbert L. 1990. "Specification Problems in Experimental and Nonexperimental Social Research." *Sociological Methodology* 20:59-91.

Somers, Robert H. 1971. "Applications of an Expanded Survey Research Model to Comparative Institutional Studies." Pp. 357-420 in *Comparative Methods in Sociology*, edited by I. Vallier. Berkeley: University of California Press.

Tilly, Charles. 1984. *Big Structures, Large Processes, Huge Comparisons*. New York: Russell Sage.

Zelditch, Morris. 1971. "Intelligible Comparisons." Pp. 267-307 in *Comparative Methods in Sociology*, edited by I. Vallier. Berkeley: University of California Press.

17

Poor People and Poor Places:
Deciphering Neighborhood Effects
on Poverty Outcomes

Marta Tienda

The growth of urban ghettos characterized by chronic poverty and joblessness, pervasive welfare dependence, broken families, widespread teenage
parenthood, and other indicators of social malaise (i.e., high rates of criminal
activity) has rekindled academic and policy interest in the behavior of poor
people. However, the discourse of the 1980s has called attention to several
issues that, if no less salient during the 1960s, currently are framed somewhat
differently. Prominent among these is an interest in the persistence and
resilience of poverty as well as in its spatial configuration.[1] Concern with
the racial dimensions of poverty—notably, the appreciably higher risks
experienced by minorities—is a theme common to both periods, except that
Latinos figured more prominently in the discussions of 1980s.

Contemporary anxiety over the spatial dimensions of poverty has been a
response to evidence that poverty has become more concentrated over time,
that the behavioral correlates of concentrated poverty deviate from those of
the general population, and that concentrated poverty appears to be largely
a minority phenomenon. These circumstances lead to the testable proposition
that the spatial configuration of poverty is *directly* responsible for the growth
of a (largely minority) urban underclass (Wilson 1987).[2] The numerous and

AUTHOR'S NOTE: *This research was supported by a grant from the Office of the Assistant
Secretary for Planning and Evaluation of the Department of Health and Human Services to the
Institute for Research on Poverty of the University of Wisconsin. V. Joseph Hotz, Ross Stolzenberg, and William J. Wilson provided useful comments on an early draft. William Mason provided
the deadline that brought my ideas to print.*

compelling claims made in its support notwithstanding, this proposition remains to be validated empirically.

Recent academic and policy debates about persisting and concentrated poverty have been productive, if partly asynchronous, because they have reenergized endeavors to determine whether and in what ways social environments shape the behavior of poor people. Contemporary debate on the origins of the urban underclass has spawned research designed to formulate, test, and refine arguments about the mechanisms producing ghetto poverty and provides a new arena for ascertaining the existence of context effects on behavioral outcomes.[3] Two master research themes concern us here. One focuses on the evolution and deterioration of neighborhoods, while a second centers on whether and how proximate social environments, namely, ghetto poverty neighborhoods, shape the lives of their residents. Both of these research themes are vital for the current discourse on the causes, consequences, and cures for ghetto poverty. Moreover, they hold some promise of clarifying a highly contested and poorly understood aspect of persisting poverty, namely, whether it is transmitted through a fundamental altering of norms and "tastes" for nonnormative behavior (e.g., welfare dependence, chronic joblessness, or nonmarital fertility) or whether it is structurally produced and maintained and merely reflects intergenerational continuity of social and economic disadvantages.

Although research on both themes will help explain why and how the urban underclass emerged, progress toward this broader goal should be expedited by integrating the analytical implications of both research themes. This chapter discusses the nature of evidence required to establish the existence of neighborhood effects on poverty outcomes, such as chronic welfare dependence or prolonged joblessness, in light of information about the process of neighborhood change. The major theoretical issues addressed are the *social processes* through which neighborhood effects operate, while the key methodological issue bearing on the assessment and interpretation of social context effects on individual behavior is the role of *selection processes* in producing concentrated poverty areas. I argue that researchers must arrive at some resolve on these matters before making definitive claims about the forces producing an urban underclass or before confirming the existence of neighborhood effects on the behavior of ghetto populations.

Of course, sociological interest in structural influences can be traced to early theorists, particularly the writings of Durkheim and Simmel. That intellectual debate over the existence of context effects has waned at times reflects the limited success of analysts in establishing their existence rather than fundamental differences of opinion on theoretical grounds. It remains to be seen whether future empirical undertakings will succeed in establishing neighborhood effects on poverty outcomes, given the formidable methodological and conceptual problems I identify.

Accordingly, as a critical analyst, I identify gaps in theorizing about transmission progress and selection mechanisms and suggest testable hypotheses that advance existing studies. I review the existing interpretations of social context effects as a way of framing the subsequent discussion, which considers, respectively, the forces producing neighborhood change and the importance of adequately modeling selection and exposure processes in assessments of whether and how neighborhoods shape behavioral outcomes. I conclude with a brief discussion of theoretical issues that can enlighten and advance the current state of research on neighborhood effects but also alert readers to the difficulty of establishing pure "context" effects using conventional correlational designs.

SOCIAL CONTEXT AND BEHAVIOR: A SELECTIVE SKETCH

How social context influences individual behavior is an old theme in social science research. Numerous empirical studies claim to show systematic regularities in behavior according to social contexts (for a recent review, see Jencks and Mayer 1989). Examples can be found in the social psychological literature (Berger et al. 1980), in the demographic literature (see Freedman 1974; Casterline 1982), and especially in the literature on educational outcomes (Bryk and Raudenbush 1988; Burstein 1980). Because schools are organized as hierarchical social settings, examples of multilevel research designs abound in the voluminous literature on educational outcomes. A relatively new interest in the arena of social context effects is in neighborhoods. The idea that units as diffuse as neighborhoods influence individual behavior beyond what one would expect (or predict) based on characteristics of individual actors is entirely consistent with the sociological precept that social structure constrains behavior in semipredictable ways. Less well understood is *how* neighborhood effects are transmitted, whether such effects are of short-term duration, and whether they persist in contexts other than those where they emerged.

Jencks and Mayer's (1989) insightful review on the social consequences of growing up in a poor neighborhood acknowledges that it is not obvious whether neighborhoods actually influence behavioral outcomes, even when suggestive evidence supports such an interpretation. I concur, but for somewhat different reasons. Determining whether there are neighborhood effects on individual behavior poses formidable methodological difficulties but equally important conceptual challenges. The conceptual issues are thornier than the methodological ones because of major statistical innovations for dealing with multilevel social processes, as evident in the development of hierarchical linear modeling techniques (Bryk and Raudenbush 1989; Mason et al. 1983). Conceptual development of multilevel processes has not kept pace. Rather, the inclusion of indicators representing social contexts has proceeded as if "contexts" were independent variables whose influence on behavior is additive and exogenous or, at worst, control variables whose influence must be statistically removed. Such formulations estimate place effects without adequate attention to the sorting processes that produced highly differentiated contexts in the first place.

Another problem plaguing neighborhood analyses centers on the appropriate *definition* of a neighborhood. In sociological and economic conceptions, neighborhoods

> have in common the meaning of physically bounded areas characterized by some degree of relative homogeneity and/or social cohesion . . . [T]he economic literature on neighborhoods [includes] the concept of "neighborhood external-ity" . . . [to acknowledge] the economic reality that the behavior of an individual and a neighbor are not independent. (White 1987, pp. 3-5)

Cohesion arises from shared facilities and institutions (e.g., parks, schools, churches, and neighborhood organizations) and also partly from shared preferences and norms. Size and cohesion are important criteria for demarcating neighborhood boundaries. Not only is it easier to predict the behavior of persons residing in small and cohesive as compared with large and disengaged neighborhoods, but it also is easier to enforce sanctions, to generate cooperative strategies, and to control free-rider problems (Mueller 1976).[4]

As a theoretical construct, a neighborhood embraces both social and spatial dimensions, yet empirical measurement focuses primarily, if not exclusively, on the spatial to the neglect of the social foundations. A related issue is the matter of neighborhood boundaries. For convenience, and largely dictated by administrative reporting practices, researchers use either census tracts or zip code areas as proxies for neighborhoods. Essentially this represents "statistical neighborhoods," which may or may not correspond to neighborhoods defined in social terms. Social dimensions of neighborhoods are crucial because they derive from interaction patterns, which are the ultimate mechanisms through which neighborhood effects can be transmitted. In other words, spatial proximity may be a necessary condition for producing neighborhood effects, but interaction patterns are sufficient. Physical contiguity per se might activate "demonstration effects," for example, but these will depend on the social ecology of the neighborhood and on whether individuals come into contact with one another. It is puzzling, then, that attempts to establish the existence of neighborhood effects on behavior largely are based on global or contextual ecological characteristics of places, to the relative neglect of social interaction within spatial domains.[5]

Conceptually, what is at issue are boundaries of social areas as defined by interaction patterns, rather than administrative boundaries, and how these exchanges vary depending on the object of interest. In some instances, the physical boundaries of neighborhoods may be obvious, as in the case of neighborhood schools (Jencks and Mayer 1989) or other types of service delivery areas. However, for behavioral outcomes such as joblessness, non-marital fertility, or welfare dependence, it is difficult to envision a situation where physical contiguity coincides with, or takes precedence over, interaction patterns.

That physical contiguity does not guarantee the existence of social cohesion is easy to appreciate in a highly segregated context where income segregation cross-cuts administrative boundaries or the micro units of census geography. Chicago provides a good example because several census tracts are so highly differentiated in their income structure (e.g., Kenwood) that neighborhood characterizations based on measures of central tendency would portray the prevalence of neither wealthy nor poor families. This example underscores the importance of considering not only measures of central tendency to characterize neighborhoods but also measures of dispersion to portray the extent of homogeneity or heterogeneity. At a minimum, one can determine the reasonableness of equating geopolitical or statistical boundaries with social neighborhoods.

The matter of how physical contiguity promotes social cohesion is so critical for theorizing about neighborhoods and "neighborhood effects" on behavior that it warrants further consideration (see also Sampson 1988). Consider a large public housing project consisting of several high-rise buildings. In this "bounded space," it is conceivable that interaction among neighbors, if it occurs at all, is restricted to the residents of a given building or members of a given floor. But if there is sufficient distrust among neighbors, interaction patterns may be confined entirely to persons residing outside the project. Under these circumstances, a so-called neighborhood characteristic, such as percentage on welfare or percentage jobless, would reveal very little about the social processes that produced the structural attributes of a place. Stated differently, if income status is a condition for being selected into a housing project, then the average level of joblessness and welfare use is likely to be higher in projects by virtue of the rules governing access to subsidized housing. Thus what a mechanical analysis might substantively attribute to "neighborhood effects" on individuals' propensity to use welfare would reflect nothing about social interaction (e.g., imitating behavior or restructured preferences) but fundamentally capture a selection process governed by eligibility rules for residence in low-income housing projects. From a theoretical standpoint, what is of interest are the social relations that define neighborhoods; from a modeling standpoint, both the selection processes governing residential choices and the interaction patterns within designated social ecologies are of interest.

A third issue clouding the interpretation of neighborhood effects derives from theoretical notions of how neighborhood effects operate. Again, the thoughtful review by Jencks and Mayer (1989; see also Mayer and Jencks 1989) provides a good point of departure. These authors identified several processes through which "neighborhood effects" operate, including (a) *contagion* mechanisms, which result from imitating behavior and peer pressure and are conditioned by the differential susceptibility of individuals to conform; (b) *socialization,* which entails the internalization of social norms and learning the boundaries of acceptable behavior, even as these change; (c) *institutionalization,* which produces behavioral regularities through structured and semistructured organizations and actors, including employers, schools, enforcement agencies, and other social institutions; and (d) *social comparison* processes governed by levels of relative deprivation and status organizing processes (see, for example, Berger et al. 1980).

Jencks and Mayer claim that it is nearly impossible to distinguish empirically among these alternative mechanisms that produce "neighborhood effects" on individual behavior. Perhaps this is accurate for the current state of affairs, but it need not be so. The reasons are both conceptual and methodological. Conceptually, what is lacking are efforts to determine *which* transmission mechanisms are more germane for specific behavioral outcomes. Indicator selection should be guided accordingly. Methodologically, what is lacking are valid empirical measures of diverse transmission mechanisms. This is a far cry from multilevel modeling, which simply combines person and place characteristics without regard to the potential endogeneity of the neighborhood characteristics, the extent of heterogeneity in neighborhoods, or direct measures of interaction patterns.

Contagion processes appear to be the most general mechanisms producing neighborhood effects on behavioral outcomes, but they require interaction perforce. To illustrate with example, for peer pressure to activate gang behavior, prospective members must come into contact with "certified" gang members and not merely be aware that gangs exist. Similarly, conceptualizing the widespread use of welfare behavior as a contagion process necessitates interaction at some level so that behavior can be copied. Of course, if social workers are the culprits promoting the widespread use of welfare, interaction with other welfare users would not be required to trigger a welfare epidemic. In this instance, neighborhood effects would be irrelevant, yet they might appear because of the institutional processes that sort welfare users into public housing. Models that posit contagion processes as key mechanisms producing neighborhood effects should represent these using *direct* measures of interaction, such as measures of social networks, rather than average measures derived from behavioral outcomes that presumably are produced by residential patterns. Doing so borders on tautology, yet, unfortunately, it appears to accord with current practices.

Furthermore, the appeal of one or another transmission mechanism depends on the subject of interest. To study many aspects of youth behavior, such as sexual activity, gang behavior, or school performance, all four transmission mechanisms proposed by Jencks and Mayer (1989) might be viable. This suggests that the development of models that distinguish among alternative transmission mechanisms would be fruitful. However, for adults, it is difficult to envision under what conditions socialization processes might be posited as the primary mechanisms transmitting neighborhood effects on nonnormative behaviors, such as chronic joblessness, economic dependence, or criminal activity. Contagion processes involving mimicking the behavior of others are reasonable, as are institutional processes that may disconnect some individuals from the job market, allow others to remain on public assistance, or indirectly promote criminal activity through lax law enforcement. To the extent that socialization processes produce "neighborhood effects" on adult behaviors, they may capture either prior family experiences or a *re*socialization process that results directly from sustained exposure to nonnormative social arrangements. The latter case involving the restructuring of norms in accordance with actual life circumstances might be regarded as a true "neighborhood effect." Although such instances of restructured norms have not been examined, this idea is implicit in many discussions about the emergence of an underclass. It must be made explicit.

Wilson's (1987) thesis about social isolation is critical in this regard. However, acknowledging the existence of socially isolated neighborhoods still begs the question as to how the neighborhoods came to be socially isolated and whether residents' behavior would be different under alternative social environments. The obvious test for neighborhood effects operating through resocialization of adults would require, as Jencks and Mayer (1989) noted, physically changing the neighborhood environment of adults and observing changes in behavior after such a move—a highly unlikely and unethical social experiment. Nonetheless, this does not excuse the need to design studies that adequately establish the existence of neighborhood effects and that convincingly adjudicate among alternative mechanisms that conceivably produce them.

Finally, while there is no clear agreement about the mechanisms that produce neighborhood effects on specific behavioral outcomes, the dominant view appears to be that they exist. Neighborhood effects generally are conceptualized as contextual effects derived from the collective aggregation of individual attributes rather than global characteristics of places that do not have an individual analogue.[6] A consideration of the importance of global ecological characteristics of poor places raises an alternative hypothesis, namely, that neighborhood effects derive from the resource stock of a place, which includes the extant formal and informal institutional structures that, in turn, provide the basis for neighborhood cohesion or disintegration. In terms of how interneighborhood inequities emerge and unfold, and how place characteristics ramify on individual behavior, the resource stock of a neighborhood might be conceived as a proximate determinant of interaction patterns and an ultimate cause of specified behavioral syndromes.

To use the example of youth criminal activity, the incidence of juvenile delinquency might result because of the proliferation of gangs. But gang activity is highly correlated with the presence or absence of organized activities that can engage youth in constructive behavior. In addition to potential endogeneity problems, use of a contextual measure, such as percentage of youth ever arrested, to ascertain the existence of neighborhood effects on the propensity of youth to engage in criminal activity could merely reflect the absence of suitable alternatives for channeling behavior. In this instance, the ultimate cause of juvenile criminal activity would be a resource stock deficiency; the proximate cause would be the prevalence of gang activity; and the mechanisms through which neighborhood effects on individual behavior were transmitted might be contagion processes (see Crane 1988), maladaptive socialization, or a misguided social comparison process reinforced by the widespread deviance. Alternatively, institutionalization as a social mechanism producing neighborhood effects on juvenile delinquency rates ultimately might reflect the absence of a resource base for adequate law enforcement.

My point is that neighborhood effects generated through contextual measures of places themselves probably have ultimate causes rooted in resource stocks. If so, then conceptual frameworks and empirical models used to depict neighborhood or context effects should reflect this. That policy implications vary depending on how a resource stock is conceptualized within a neighborhood context makes this a hypothesis worthy of empirical scrutiny. If resource stock problems are the *root causes* of social dislocation observed in ghetto neighborhoods, then solutions focused on neighborhood revitalization might be more productive than those aimed at rehabilitation of individuals. If, however, the nonnormative behavior of poor people residing in extremely poor neighborhoods largely results from selective sorting processes, then neighborhood revitalization strategies almost certainly will meet with limited success unless accompanied by programs to rehabilitate individuals.

These points bring into focus two issues that should aid in future attempts to conceptualize and decipher neighborhood effects on behavioral outcomes. The first is the *evolution of neighborhoods* themselves. As my example of juvenile delinquent activity illustrates, it matters a great deal whether the spatial concentration of delinquent juveniles results from the declining resource base of neighborhoods, from the nonrandom migration processes involving delinquent youth, or from contagion processes operating on differentially susceptible individuals.[7] Hence, an important step in deciphering neighborhood effects of any sort would appear to be establishing the source and sequence of neighborhood change. This topic is considered briefly in the next section. The second issue involves the interface between neighborhood status and social behavior. The notion of exposure, which is a fundamental precept in demography, can be applied fruitfully to the analysis of neighborhood effects on behavioral outcomes to avoid exaggerating place effects based on incidence measures, as discussed in the last section.

THE PROCESS OF NEIGHBORHOOD CHANGE: SELECTION OR TRANSMUTATION?

The importance of studying the process of neighborhood change prior to assessing neighborhood effects on individual outcomes revolves around the role of nonrandom selection in producing poverty ghettos. It matters a great deal *how* residential turnover contributes to the emergence of spatially and socially isolated neighborhoods. For example, neighborhoods characterized by a high concentration of low-income and poor families can arise because of the out-migration of the more affluent, the influx of low-income families as the housing stock ages, or some combination of both (Bond and Coulson 1989). Assuming a constant poverty rate, both processes would produce a spatial reshuffling of families by poverty status. What combination of forces actually occurs, and what mechanisms precipitate or avert neighborhood decline, should have direct bearing on whether a neighborhood becomes a low-income working-class area or a ghetto poverty area characterized by the social pathologies identified with the urban underclass.[8] Selective out-migration is a dominant hypothesis summoned to explain the emergence of concentrated poverty areas, but the empirical evidence supporting this claim is sparse, albeit apparently consistent (Jencks 1988).

It is not obvious that neighborhood decline, once begun, must culminate in poverty ghettos. This premise is important for conceptualizing how neighborhood effects influence individual behavior and, alternatively, how the aggregation of individual behaviors produce alternative trajectories of neighborhood change. The comparative analysis of urban poverty areas by

Bane and Jargowsky (1988) has documented appreciable diversity in the course of ghetto poverty between 1970 and 1980. Based on the concrete experiences of individual cities, the extensive variation in the proportion of poor families residing in high-poverty areas defies simple generalization about the constellation of factors that eventuate in neighborhood decline. That some cities witnessed a spatial concentration of poverty during the 1970s while others did not challenges researchers to identify the root causes of neighborhood deterioration. Put differently, poverty level at time 1 may be an important predictor of ghetto poverty at time 2, but the correlation is far from perfect, and we seem not to know why.

Models of neighborhood evolution posit a general sequence, or set of stages, through which most neighborhoods pass. The stages of neighborhood evolution generally consist of initial urbanization, transition, downgrading, thinning, and, finally, renewal (White 1987; Schwirian 1983). This evolutionary sequence need not be perfectly replicated in all places, but the general pattern seems to describe the progression of most large urban areas. An alternative paradigm for stages of neighborhood change is that of Downs (see White), who focuses on the "health" of the neighborhoods. His five stages are (a) healthy and viable; (b) incipiently declining; (c) clearly declining; (d) declining with acceleration; and (e) abandoned, unhealthy, and nonviable. Reversibility in the process of decline prior to reaching the final stage of Downs's scheme is important for our interest in the circumstances structuring alternative paths of neighborhood change. From the standpoint of understanding whether neighborhoods become "physically and spatially isolated," in Wilson's (1987) terminology, or whether they experience renewal, what needs to be ascertained are the *minimum and necessary conditions* that can reverse the process of decline or, alternatively, criteria for establishing at what point neighborhoods cease to be socially viable.

Neighborhood succession has been investigated mainly in terms of residential segregation and, to a much lesser extent, in terms of socioeconomic composition, especially income distribution.[9] The succession model is useful for theorizing about the dynamics of neighborhood change, notably turnover, replacement (especially differential rates of replacement by socioeconomic characteristics), displacement, and depopulation. Of particular interest for generating hypotheses about the way neighborhood environments influence individual behavior are the *thresholds* or *tipping points* that determine whether individuals remain in or depart from a neighborhood (Taub et al. 1984). Taken collectively, these decisions are part and parcel of the dynamics of neighborhood change and could bring into focus the minimum and necessary conditions for low-income neighborhoods to become ghetto neighborhoods.

The public choice literature in economics also is instructive on this point because it provides a framework for thinking about the mechanisms by which consumer-voters register their preferences for public goods and amenities. Tiebout (1956) defined *public goods* as collective consumption goods enjoyed in common in the sense that each individual's consumption of such a good does not subtract from any other individual's consumption of that good. Two points are relevant for our interest in the process of neighborhood change. First, even though public goods are shared, and costs cannot be charged back to individuals based on actual consumption, ability to pay *does* influence the distribution of public goods. This is clearly evident in the uneven quality of schools and other social amenities (e.g., parks, clubs) available across neighborhoods. Second, a given residential configuration itself reflects a level of demand for public goods of a given quality. This is so because individuals "vote with their feet," and thus residential mobility is a mechanism for registering demand. That mobility also represents a *cost* of registering demand for public amenities partly explains the nonrandom sorting patterns that result. These reflect differential ability to pay as much as sheer preferences or more so.

The Tiebout (1956) public choice model provides important insights into the dynamics of neighborhood change insofar as it sets forth the economic foundations of the selection mechanisms producing interneighborhood inequalities. However, its underlying assumptions are rigid and especially unrealistic for low-income groups. The idea that consumers "vote with their feet" is a sensible proposition, but it is not reasonable to assume that consumer-voters are fully mobile, that they have full knowledge of revenue and expenditures for public goods, and that they have many options in selecting where to reside (or relocate), as the Tiebout model stipulates. That race and class severely constrain the residential options of poor and minority families reduces the appeal of Tiebout's framework for explaining residential choices among the poor but less for middle- and high-income groups. However, Tiebout's framework calls attention to the importance of deciphering the selection processes that set in motion turnover and succession processes in neighborhoods.

This discussion indicates that researchers interested in neighborhood effects on the behavior of the poor can benefit from a solid understanding of paths of neighborhood change if for no reason other than to avoid confusing causes and consequences. But there are other reasons as well. A clearer understanding of how selection mechanisms operate may improve the ability of researchers to *predict* the course of neighborhood change. It would be especially helpful if researchers could determine *which* neighborhoods experiencing declining economic bases or aging housing stocks are destined to become "deadly neighborhoods" (Jencks 1988) and *which* are likely to remain viable working-class neighborhoods, albeit with lower resource stocks. Analytically, this requires moving from uni- or bidimensional to multidimensional conceptions of neighborhood trajectories. Candidates for the development of multidimensional tipping or threshold models of neighborhood change analogous to those used to study racial segregation include (a) changes in the housing stock, (b) changes in business activities, (c) and changes in the institutional environment, with particular emphasis on institutions that have the potential to promote social cohesion, such as schools, churches, neighborhood clubs, and the like (Sampson 1988).[10]

There is little reason to focus on the extremes. Affluent neighborhoods have low rates of high school noncompletion, male joblessness, welfare dependence, mother-only families, and criminal activity; high-poverty ghetto neighborhoods have high rates of these behaviors. However, between these extremes, there exists a wide range of experiences and circumstances that provide analytical leverage to determine why the dynamics of neighborhood change result in the formation of dangerous neighborhoods in some instances and not in others. It is critically important to distinguish among alternative trajectories in the design of public policies.

To summarize, the importance of studying neighborhood change in its own right is that it determines our success in assessing neighborhood effects on individual outcomes. It is essential to understand mechanisms producing alternative neighborhood trajectories to avoid confounding selection effects with neighborhood effects in the study of spatially concentrated deviant behaviors that have come to be associated with the underclass. The problem is not simply a matter of controlling for background characteristics of individuals, as Jencks and Mayer (1989) seem to imply, for the indiscriminate application of controls in the face of selection can produce highly distorted results (Lieberson 1985). Once the selection processes are adequately understood, then it makes sense to proceed in deciphering the "social consequences of growing up in poor neighborhoods." This is the subject of the next section.

NEIGHBORHOOD EFFECTS ON THE BEHAVIOR OF POOR PEOPLE

I have already discussed the mechanisms through which neighborhood effects can be transmitted and elaborated the importance of the sorting processes that homogenize residence patterns. Although the modeling of transmission and selection mechanisms poses formidable challenges by themselves, I will raise two additional issues that dare researchers to detect pure neighborhood effects. One concerns the matter of *exposure* to particular environments, and the second concerns the issue of *feedback* effects between individuals and their social environments. An adequate grasp of exposure and feedback effects is essential to sort individual from context effects. For the underclass debate in particular, it is necessary to establish whether the spatial concentration of poor people alters the normative environment in which individuals interact and, through a feedback link, modifies behavior from what it would be under circumstances of dispersed poverty. Absent this information, it will be impossible to verify Wilson's (1987) hypothesis about the existence of "concentration effects."

Wilson's notion of concentration effects revolves around whether and how living in ghetto poverty areas shapes the lives of the poor beyond what one would expect on the basis of their social and demographic characteristics. In lay terms, the question is whether, for example, a mother is more apt to receive welfare benefits if she resides in a neighborhood where this practice is the norm when compared with another (statistically identical) mother who resides in an environment where welfare dependence is the exception. There is some tautology in this line of reasoning because, by definition, a greater share of mothers actually are welfare dependent in the poor neighborhoods compared with rich neighborhoods, but this problem is not inherent to the thought experiment that undergirds the question.

Leaving aside the potential endogeneity, selection, and aggregation biases that complicate this example, it is not obvious whether a neighborhood effect should emerge once the circumstances that determine the risk of welfare receipt (i.e., single parent status with few or no job skills) are modeled, *unless*—and this is critical—the spatial concentration of welfare mothers actually encourages or prolongs welfare use among those who might otherwise be disinclined to do so.[11] We do not know whether this occurs, but it is plausible if the spatial concentration of welfare users produced an environment where its use was legitimated (at least in the eyes of its users) or, at a minimum, if spatial concentration reduced the social stigma associated with welfare dependence. Both possibilities are reasonable, but it is not obvious how one would establish the increased legitimacy or decreased stigma associated with different levels of welfare use without encountering serious selection problems or conducting unethical social experiments.[12]

It bears repeating that physical proximity per se is not a mechanism of transmission but a circumstance that structures transmission mechanisms. Demonstration effects, however, might be activated through residential propinquity, particularly if a case can be made for relative deprivation or social comparison as transmission mechanisms. This would not appear relevant for the welfare example developed in this section except insofar as welfare users were perceived as better off by mothers working at minimum wage jobs that did not subsidize health care or food costs. In this instance, the social comparison or relative deprivation models would be implied as mechanisms activating the "concentration" effects, but the actual transmission mechanism might best be conceived as "demonstration effects."

It should come as no surprise to find a positive correlation between residence in ghetto poverty neighborhoods and a mother's propensity to receive welfare at a given time. But a cross-sectional correlation will not be particularly informative, even if the background factors specifying the "risks" of welfare usage are adequately modeled (or partialed out) unless time spent in a ghetto environment also is modeled. We do not know whether simple *exposure* to environments where many women are on welfare alters the susceptibility of a given individual to utilize welfare or whether susceptibility increases only with *sustained exposure* to such environments. Thus, in addition to monitoring the influence of personal characteristics that dispose individuals to engage in a particular behavior, it is necessary also to model directly *exposure* to the nonnormative social environments that allegedly influence individual behavior.

Social background characteristics are important indicators of life experiences, but the controversy about the intergenerational transmission of dependence, for example, cannot be solved without concrete information about individuals' exposure to environments where welfare dependence is pervasive as compared with environments where welfare use is episodic and typically rare. Conventional practices, which usually involve introducing current individual characteristics into models predicting past behavior, are obviously inappropriate. However, the extent of distortion in the measured context effects depends on whether individuals remained in similar social environments throughout the period that a particular behavior (say, welfare use) was measured.

Temporality is more problematic in the measurement of neighborhood effects on behavior than in the measurement of school effects on achievement. For the latter, temporality seldom poses measurement problems because the context effects hypothesized to operate usually correspond to the spatial arrangements and to the period when achievement occurs. This is not so for neighborhood effects, partly because neighborhoods are diffuse constructs, partly because of residential mobility (which may covary with the outcome of interest and hence produce selection biases), partly because the outcomes of interest (i.e., out-of-wedlock childbearing, welfare dependence, gang activity, chronic joblessness) often occur episodically over long periods of time, and partly because, as argued in the previous section, the neighborhood contexts themselves change, such that even stable residents are not exposed to "constant" neighborhood environments. These circumstances increase the need to think of neighborhoods as fluid rather than fixed social constructs.

The second issue bearing on the empirical assessment of neighborhood effects concerns the extent to which nonrandom sorting produces the observed correlations between social context and behavior. Because the selection issue was addressed at length in the previous section, an abbreviated discussion should suffice to make my basic point. If systematic selection processes are the primary mechanism bringing together individuals with similar socioeconomic characteristics and behavioral dispositions within spatially bounded areas, then selection processes will be confused with neighborhood effects unless one can show that concentration itself accentuates the manifestation and ramifications of particular behaviors. At a minimum, until the *feedback mechanisms* between individual behavior and the social context are adequately modeled, the notion of "concentration effects" remains, at best, an intriguing hypothesis to be tested or, at worst, a statistical artifact of selection and aggregation bias. It is difficult to envision a test of Wilson's notion of "isolation effects" or "concentration effects" without a clearer understanding of the feedback mechanisms between individual actors and the environment they shape through their concrete actions.

CONCLUSION

Evidence that residence in high-poverty areas is associated with a higher incidence of nonnormative behaviors that have come to be identified with the syndrome of persisting and resilient poverty provides a challenging opportunity to disentangle the social forces ultimately responsible for the growth of the urban underclass. At this point, it is difficult to be optimistic about the prospects for detecting substantively and statistically significant neighborhood effects on behavioral syndromes associated with concentrated poverty. This was not my view when I began this exercise, but I see the source of the problem as resting on two issues that can, in my judgment, be resolved by investigators who choose to do so. I state these in the form of two tentative conclusions:

(1) Before encouraging further statistical modeling to capture neighborhood effects, more conceptual groundwork is needed to specify adequately the exposure, selection, and feedback effects that define how neighborhoods shape the behavior of the poor, and

(2) Given the nature of available data, it is virtually impossible to determine with any degree of confidence the existence of neighborhood effects on poverty behaviors.

In brief, neighborhood context should be treated as a time-varying rather than a time-invariant covariate in the analysis of individual behavior. At a minimum, researchers should take great precautions in assessing neighborhood effects when there are temporal disjunctures between the dependent variable of interest and the length of exposure to alternative social environments. Once the thorny issue of "exposure" is adequately handled, and when feedback effects between context and behavior are modeled, then we may assert with confidence that social context *does* (or does not) influence individual behavior beyond what one would expect based on individual characteristics alone.

I see further promise for determining whether and how neighborhood contexts shape individual behavior pending the conceptual advances discussed above. To do so, I believe, requires that we define neighborhoods, first, in *social* terms and, secondarily, in *spatial* terms. This is a tall order, and there is no single prescription for doing so, but the "appropriate" definition of neighborhoods surely must depend on the object of interest. The idea of defining neighborhoods according to the outcomes of interest is not original (see Schwirian 1983), but the failure of prior scholars to address it is troubling. This state of affairs reflects both data constraints and, perhaps, the unwillingness of analysts to strive for conceptual clarity in specifying neighborhood effects. Most of my arguments can be accommodated by expanding the concept of neighborhood to include a family of definitions that can be tailored to specific outcomes of interest.[13]

Concrete illustration is in order. *Geographic neighborhoods,* limited by major streets, highways, parks, rivers, and schools, or *demographic neighborhoods,* defined by discontinuities in the population characteristics of places, might be appropriate for studying residential segregation, but they are not suited to detecting the effects of concentrated poverty on individual behavior. For this, *social neighborhoods,* defined by the boundaries of social networks and the density of interaction patterns, are necessary. In rare instances, geographic neighborhoods will coincide with social neighborhoods, but this should not be a deterrent to pursuing empirical work to establish neighborhood effects on individual behavior. Unless a researcher is particularly interested in establishing the coincidence or crystallization of multiple dimensions of neighborhood structure, the task at hand is simplified by focusing on patterns of interaction and methods suited to portraying the nature and frequency of interaction.

The appeal of defining neighborhoods in social terms is all the more compelling because it will mesh with the conceptual work of specifying what transmission mechanisms are particularly suited to specific types of behaviors. In comparison with the task of conceptualizing neighborhoods in social terms and theorizing about particular transmission mechanisms, empirical estimation will be relatively straightforward. This is because the nature of the data required to establish neighborhood effects will be clearly in view and because computational techniques have proceeded ahead of conceptual development.

Coleman's (1987) notion of "social capital" provides a compelling way to think about how to represent the social cohesion that defines neighborhoods (White 1987, p. 3), but there are other forms of "capital" that are equally germane, such as financial and cultural capital (see Browning and Rodriguez 1985). By *social capital*, Coleman refers to the norms, networks, and relationships among actors that bear on individual behavior. The appeal of this concept is heightened by virtue of the fact that it exists within families, neighborhoods, and communities and because it provide a basis for placing *cohesion* at the forefront of a social definition of neighborhoods. The notions of social, cultural, and financial capital, while abstract concepts, provide a frame of reference for thinking critically about how individuals are linked to a social context and about the social forces that foster cohesion or isolation.

In conclusion, my skepticism about the prospects of deciphering neighborhood effects is based largely on past empirical modeling effects, given the nature of data currently available and given the inadequate handling of exposure, selection, simultaneity, and endogeneity in prior empirical work. On the theoretical side of the matter, I am more optimistic because I envision considerable opportunity for expanding upon the ideas set forth by Wilson (1987), Coleman (1987), and Jencks and Mayer (1989). Once this challenge is met, the necessary advances in empirical modeling will follow, I am confident.

NOTES

1. Focus on the spatial aspects of poverty during the 1960s highlighted differentials between rural and urban areas and between central cities and their suburbs. While the problems of the inner-city ghetto were clearly acknowledged, no theoretical propositions about spatial and social isolation were forthcoming.

2. Although there is no clear consensus about how to define the urban underclass, there appears to be some consensus that the underclass includes men who are chronically jobless and women who chronically depend on welfare to survive (Ruggles and Marton 1986). Major disagreement about the definition of the underclass centers on whether the dysfunctional behavior (e.g., criminal activity, drug addiction, and alcoholism) that is pervasive in high-poverty neighborhoods is a defining feature, or a consequence of, persisting poverty and chronic joblessness (see Wilson 1987; Ruggles and Marton 1986) and at what levels of poverty concentration the deviant behavioral syndrome becomes ineluctable.

3. I use various phrases to describe concentrated urban poverty associated with the urban underclass, including *ghetto poverty, concentrated poverty,* and *persistent poverty.* Editorial rather than substantive reasons underlie this decision.

4. Social cohesion as a defining feature of neighborhood boundaries is a rather stringent requirement and is problematic from an operational standpoint. However, underclass neighborhoods have been characterized as having experienced a process of disintegration—the obverse of cohesion.

5. The schooling literature may be an exception to this criticism because social interaction often is bounded by classrooms and instructional programs. My interest in the underclass debate focuses on neighborhoods as social and spatial arenas for interaction, not schools.

6. An obvious exception to this generalization emerges from the schooling literature, which is replete with examples about how characteristics of schools and classrooms influence achievement, above and beyond measures of social heterogeneity based on class composition. My interest in neighborhoods rather than schools makes this a moot issue.

7. Of course, one must establish what determines different levels of susceptibility, but this consideration is beyond the scope of the current discussion. This issue is discussed briefly in Crane (1988).

8. Bond and Coulson distinguish between a "filtering model" and an "externality model." The former views income segregation as resulting from selective sorting propelled by an aging (and presumably deteriorating) housing stock, while the latter emphasizes the role of neighborhood income levels or racial composition per se in precipitating turnover.

9. For a noteworthy recent exception, see Massey and Eggers (1989). Other exceptions are studies that focus on the renewal (or gentrification) of neighborhoods, which place great emphasis on class composition along with racial composition.

10. An obvious question is why these institutions promote social cohesion. I have selected these examples because they represent opportunities for engagement of neighborhood residents in the pursuit of collective and common goals. Of course, the mere presence of a school, church, or club does not ensure that residents will be involved, but, in principal, the possibility for participation is greater than in the absence of these institutions in the neighborhood.

11. I use the welfare behavior example for convenience, but other behaviors associated with ghetto poverty, such as chronic joblessness or nonmarital fertility, can be substituted without altering the basic point.

12. One possibility is measuring attitudes toward welfare use among individuals, but this is not a satisfactory solution because individuals who have ever received welfare (either as a child or an adult) may have different views (either positive or negative) as a result of having received a grant. In essence, measures of attitudes could not be regarded as totally exogenous to the outcome of interest.

13. I am grateful to Ross M. Stolzenberg for this constructive suggestion based on his critical reading of my earlier manuscript.

REFERENCES

Bane, Mary Jo and Paul Jargowsky. 1988. "Urban Poverty Areas: Basic Questions Concerning Prevalence, Growth, and Dynamics." Policy Discussion Paper Series. Cambridge, MA: Harvard University, Center for Health and Human Resources.

Berger, Joseph, Susan Rosenholtz, and Morris Zelditch, Jr. 1980. "Status Organizing Processes." Technical Report 77. Stanford, CA: Stanford University.

Bond, Eric and Edward Coulson. 1989. "A Hedonic Approach to Residential Succession." Unpublished manuscript, Pennsylvania State University.

Browning, Harley and Nestor Rodriguez. 1985. "The Migration of Mexican Indocumentados as a Settlement Process: Implications for Work." Pp. 277-98 in *Hispanics in the U.S. Economy*, edited by G. Borjas and M. Tienda. Orlando, FL: Academic Press.

Bryk, Anthony and Stephen Raudenbush. 1988. "Toward a More Appropriate Conceptualization of Research on School Effects: A Three-Level Hierarchical Linear Model." *American Journal of Education* 97:65-108.

———. 1989. "Methodology for Cross-Level Organizational Research." *Research in the Sociology of Organizations* 7:233-73.

Burstein, L. 1980. "The Analysis of Multi-Level Data in Educational Research and Evaluation." *Review of Research in Education* 8:158-233.

Casterline, J. B. 1982. "Community Effects on Fertility Intentions." WFS/Tech. 1952. London: World Fertility Survey.

Coleman, James. 1987. "Families and Schools." *Educational Researcher* 16:32-38.

Crane, Jonathan. 1988. "An Epidemic Model of Social Problems in Ghettoes." Unpublished paper, Harvard University.

Freedman, R. 1974. "Community-Level Data in Fertility Surveys." Occasional Paper 8. London: World Fertility Survey.

Jencks, Christopher. 1988. "Deadly Neighborhoods." *The New Republic,* June 13, pp. 23-32.

Jencks, Christopher and Susan Mayer. 1989. "The Social Consequences of Growing Up in a Poor Neighborhood: A Review." Unpublished paper, Northwestern University, Center for Urban Affairs and Policy Research.

Lieberson, Stanley. 1985. *Making It Count.* Berkeley: University of California Press.

Mason, William, George Wong, and Barbara Entwisle. 1983. "Contextual Analysis Through the Multilevel Linear Model." Pp. 71-103 in *Sociological Methodology 1983-1984,* edited by S. Leinhardt. San Francisco: Jossey-Bass.

Massey, Douglas and Mitchell Eggers. 1989. "The Ecology of Inequality: Minorities and the Concentration of Poverty 1970-1980." *American Journal of Sociology* 95:1153-88.

Mayer, Susan and Christopher Jencks. 1989. "Growing Up in Poor Neighborhoods: How Much Does It Matter?" *Science* 243:1441-45.

Mueller, Dennis. 1976. "Public Choice: A Survey." *Journal of Economic Literature* 2:395-433.

Ruggles, Patricia and William Marton. 1986. "Measuring the Size and Characteristics of the Underclass: How Much Do We Know?" Unpublished paper, Urban Institute.

Sampson, Robert. 1988. "Local Friendship Ties and Community Attachment in Mass Society: A Multilevel Systemic Model." *American Sociological Review* 53:766-79.

Schwirian, Kent. 1983. "Models of Neighborhood Change." *Annual Review of Sociology* 9: 83-102.

Taub, Richard, Garth Taylor, and Jan Dunham. 1984. *Paths of Neighborhood Change.* Chicago: University of Chicago Press.

Tiebout, Charles. 1956. "A Pure Theory of Local Expenditures." *Journal of Political Economy* 64:416-24.

White, Michael. 1987. *American Neighborhoods and Residential Differentiation.* New York: Russell Sage.

Wilson, William Julius. 1987. *The Truly Disadvantaged: The Inner City, The Underclass, and Public Policy.* Chicago: University of Chicago Press.

18

Markets, States, Nations, and Bedrooms in Western Europe, 1870-1960

Susan Cotts Watkins

Between 1870 and 1960, demographic diversity in Western Europe declined markedly. Countries became more similar to one another in their levels of marital fertility and marriage. More striking was the decrease in demographic diversity within countries. That is, in 1870, provinces (departments, cantons, counties) within the same country had quite different levels of marital fertility and marriage, whereas, in 1960, one province was much like another: National boundaries had come to enclose distinct demographic regimes. A trio of macro-level processes—the integration of national markets, the proliferation of state functions, and nation-building—paralleled these changes (Watkins 1991).

In the end, however, accounting for aggregate demographic change with macro-level economic, political, and social change seems unsatisfactory. Our intuition is that there is something particularly "individual" about childbearing and marriage: To feel satisfied that we have sketched out a plausible account for greater demographic homogeneity, we would want a way of linking changes in markets, states, and nations to individuals in their bedrooms and courting parlors. The rational actor framework that is usually used to model demographic change seems a priori unpromising as a way to think about declines in demographic diversity. The individuals in these models are too isolated, too concerned with their own interests—particularly, in most versions, their economic interests—as they approach their "fertility-relevant bedtimes." While such models have been useful in organizing explanations for demographic behavior, in the end, they accord poorly with observations that more than the individual is involved at these bedtimes.

Not only is there a spouse but also a veritable Greek chorus of relatives and friends. Although it is possible to think of these others as elements of the individual's utility function, it seems useful at this stage to think more explicitly about the nature of the interaction of the individual with relevant others.

In this chapter, I propose that we can come closer to understanding the way that markets, states, and nations intruded into the private lives of individuals if we consider the effects of these structural changes on the interactions of individuals with each other. I characterize this interactional level largely in terms of women's gossip, which I have come to think is a useful way of summarizing some of the influences of others on individuals.

Gossip has often been scorned as idle and malicious talk, particularly associated with women. Gossip is certainly a form of social control: Some behaviors are condemned, others praised. But, at its best, gossip provides narrative, explanation, and judgment: In the stories of others, the talker narrates a sequence of events that imply an explanation, and talker and listeners alike speculate on the meaning of the events, reach a common point of view, and reassure themselves of what they share (Spacks 1988).

I focus on women for two reasons. First, it is appropriate because the demographic indexes I use to describe the reductions in demographic diversity are based on the fertility and marriage of women. Second, births and marriages are often well recorded, but what preceded them is not. Thus I have had to imagine the interactions, and it was easier to imagine women than men talking about childbirth and marriage. I do not, however, want to exclude the possibility that these were topics of men's conversations. In addition, I assume that men and women may talk about these things with each other.

I will begin by briefly describing the demographic changes. I will not present the supporting evidence, because this would require lengthy discussion of the measures used, the quality of the data, and so on and would leave little time to discuss the macro-micro linkages that are the theme of the meetings on which this book is based. I will then summarize the important determinants of demographic behavior around 1870, before the onset of the decline in marital fertility, and sketch out a role for the local community in accounting for demographic variation. I will subsequently summarize the major relevant changes in market integration, state expansion, and nation-building and how they may have contributed to the creation of a national demographic community by extending the range of social interaction from local to national. Let me emphasize at the outset that, while the demographic changes themselves have been well documented elsewhere (Watkins 1991), the story that I am proposing to make sense of these changes is far more speculative—and, because of its emphasis on the sort of past interactions that cannot be observed, is likely to remain so. It does, however, suggest directions for research in contemporary countries.

DEMOGRAPHIC NATIONALISM

There were major changes in marital fertility and marriage between 1870 and 1960. Before 1870, women married late (at age 23 or older), and substantial proportions remained unmarried (10% or more; Hajnal 1965, 1982). Marital fertility was high; more significantly, at the national level and outside France, there is no persuasive evidence that married women deliberately and successfully controlled their fertility. Instead, most women began childbearing at marriage and continued until menopause or widowhood.

In 1960, in contrast, fertility was low (marital fertility in the median province in 1960 was about 50% of the 1870 level), and fertility control was nearly ubiquitous. This change in behavior was rapid and pervasive. Before 1870, only in France and a handful of provinces elsewhere was there deliberate control of fertility within marriage; by 1930, the fertility transition had begun almost everywhere. Information on social groups is much less comprehensive, but virtually all participated in the fertility decline, typically with rather small differences in timing. The pace and pervasiveness of the fertility decline suggests that some mechanism of diffusion was involved (Watkins 1987); this points to the importance of social interaction. The decline in marital fertility was loosely accompanied by an increase in the proportion married, which has been much less well studied (Watkins 1981).

Although fertility decline and the rise in proportions married are important, they are not the changes of interest here. Here the concern is not with level but with variation. The changes in demographic diversity can be best summarized by imagining a demographic map of Western Europe in 1870 and another one in 1960. If we were to color the provinces on the 1870 map according to their levels of marital fertility and marriage, we would see that national boundaries would be faint on that map. There was so much diversity within countries that it mattered little whether a province was in one country or another.

Between 1870 and 1900, demographic diversity within countries increased temporarily, as some provinces adopted the new demographic behavior earlier than others. Diversity subsequently, however, decreased. An equivalent demographic map for 1960 would show national boundaries to be deeply etched. Country location accounted statistically for some of the provincial-level variation in demographic behavior in 1870, but far more in 1960. Differences among countries diminished as well, but the reduction of diversity *within* countries was greater than the reduction of diversity *among* countries. In addition, a country-by-country examination of change showed that, in most countries, differences among provinces had diminished, sometimes by as much as 50%. This reduction in diversity occurred not only for marital fertility (where levels fell) but for marriage (where levels rose) and are rather robust (that is, they are evident using a variety of measures that take level and location on the scale into account). Data for social groups are much less comprehensive, but surveys for several European countries in the mid-1970s show that absolute differences in fertility by social groups were rather small, rarely more than .50 of a child (see Jones 1982).

Market integration, state expansion, and nation-building can plausibly be related to the greater demographic uniformity in 1960 than in 1870 in two ways. The first account is located primarily at the level of the individual and would argue that market integration and state expansion made the circumstances in which individuals lived more similar across the provinces within any country. Thus, following a standard neoclassical or rational actor model, the costs and benefits of childbearing, or the determinants of the timing of marriage, would be more similar across provinces, and, as a consequence, individual behavior (and, in the aggregate, provincial behavior) would be expected to be more similar. This account cannot be ruled out, not the least because the available data are aggregate, not individual. It fits some of what is known about changes in markets and states: for example, Jeffrey Williamson's (1965) findings that provincial differences in income and prices first increased and then decreased. It does not fit other findings. For example, in France, departmental demographic diversity was associated with income differences in 1870, but, in 1960 (when there was much less variation across departments both in marriage and marital fertility and in income), the association between income and demographic behavior had almost disappeared (Watkins 1991).

An alternative account, and one that I will explore below, is that the demographic behavior of individuals is influenced by those with whom they live and talk, that is, by members of their community. In 1870, the relevant community seems to have been largely local. By 1960, the relevant community was largely national. Recently, there have been attempts to include "community-level" variables in demographic analyses (see, for example, H. Smith 1989; Entwisle and Mason 1985; Casterline 1981). Although these attempts are salutary, too often the "community-level" variables are simply aggregates of individuals: for example, the proportion with an elementary education. The communities I have in mind here are somewhat closer to anthropologists' folk communities—people who talk to each other, where communication is the essence of community (although the local communities of Western Europe in the nineteenth century were not as closed or as homogeneous as archetypal folk communities).

The emphasis on interaction, and particularly conversation, raises the issue of language, because a common language is necessary for conversations. In 1870, most countries had subgroups that did not speak the national language (or languages). The countries that were relatively demographically diverse were those that were most linguistically diverse (e.g., Belgium, France, Germany, and Switzerland) while the countries that were more homogeneous demographically were also relatively homogeneous linguistically (England, Scotland, Ireland). Between 1870 and 1960, linguistic diversity declined, except in countries where a second (or third) language was an official language.

Thus, in language as well as in demographic behavior, local communities were increasingly integrated into larger national communities. While this argument is largely based on parallel macro-level changes, an intensive case study of France suggests a more direct relation. As noted before, in France, departmental diversity diminished between 1870 and 1960 in per capita income as well as in marriage and marital fertility. Linguistic diversity also decreased: In 1870, about a quarter of the population of France spoke languages other than French (Breton, Basque, and so on; Weber 1976; Levasseur 1889), while, by 1960, virtually all spoke French. In 1960, however, the linguistic history of a department was a better predictor of its marital fertility and nuptiality than was its per capita departmental income (Watkins 1991).

LOCAL COMMUNITIES
AND NATIONAL COMMUNITIES

Let us begin by considering the determinants of demographic behavior before the onset of the fertility transition. In the absence of deliberate attempts to space births or to stop childbearing once a desired number of children has been reached, differences in marital fertility can be accounted for fairly well by differences in breast-feeding. Studies in developing countries show that, among women who do not use contraception, much of the variation in marital fertility can be attributed to lactation (Casterline et al. 1984; Bongaarts and Menken 1983). Although direct evidence of breast-feeding is not available for the past, the conclusion that breast-feeding accounts for much of the variation in marital fertility is compatible with evidence from English parish registers and German village genealogies in the eighteenth and nineteenth centuries (Wilson 1986; Knodel 1988).

Patterns of breast-feeding varied widely. In some areas of southern Germany, women did not breast-feed, giving their children pap instead. In other areas, between 85% and 100% of the women nursed their children (Kintner

1985; see also Knodel and van de Walle 1967 and Knodel 1988). In southern Bavaria, exceptions to the practice of never breast-feeding "were subject to sever social sanctions, including ridicule from neighbors and threats from husbands," suggesting the mobilization of village opinion (Kintner 1985, p. 168). Customs of extended breast-feeding or never breast-feeding seem to have been long standing. The German villages where breast-feeding was most common among women married at the end of the eighteenth century were also those where it was most common among women married a century later (Knodel 1988, p. 324). In southern Bavaria, fifteenth-century scripts of the Christmas plays of farmers in Oberbayern show Mary cooking the Christ child a meal of pap rather than breast-feeding (Kintner 1985, p. 168).

Whatever the reasons for variation in breast-feeding across communities, the communities themselves seem relatively homogeneous in this respect. Variations in infant mortality provide indirect evidence. In German villages in the eighteenth and nineteenth centuries, village customs of breast-feeding accounted well for village differences in infant mortality. There was little difference in infant mortality among occupational groups within a village. Knodel (1988, p. 447) concludes: "The fact that all social strata within a village appeared to have shared a more or less common risk of child loss emphasizes the probable role of local or regional infant-feeding customs, common to all classes, as a key determinant of infant mortality" and thus of marital fertility.

What about marriage? The distinctive Western European marriage pattern—relatively late female age at marriage and a relatively high proportion of spinsters—is associated with nuclear family households, a tolerance for unmarried women (Watkins 1984), and a close correspondence of the spouses' ages (Laslett 1972; Gaskin 1978). These were apparently quite long standing (Hajnal 1965, 1982). Within this broad Western European pattern, however, there were regional patterns (R. Smith 1981) as well as sharp local differences.

What was local about marriage? Most young people married those that they had met, which meant that the marriage market would be circumscribed by their movements. For the upper classes, the relevant community extended beyond the village and the province: In England, the marriage market for the nobility was national (Stone and Stone 1984). For ordinary people, the marriage market was far more local. In France in 1865, 52% of couples marrying in rural communes in Ardèche were from the same commune; in the department of Loir-et-Cher, in only 13% of marriages between 1870 and 1877 did one of the spouses come from outside the department (Sutter 1958). And three-quarters of brides and grooms in the Bavarian village of Hetzenhausen in the first half of the nineteenth century came from settlements within a radius of one mile from the village (Lee 1981, p. 102).

Because the ability to set up a new household at marriage depended on economic resources, presumably these were important in the timing of marriage. Markets were largely local or regional, so that incomes and prices differed from one part of a country to another. This would lead to considerable variation across communities in the age of marriage. Markets also brought together people from a number of villages or, in the case of regional markets, from a number of provinces. As William Skinner (1964, 1985) has argued for China, there is probably a relation between markets and marriage: News of nubile young women could be exchanged along with grain, then introductions made, and friendships formed. Additional local variation probably came from substantial flexibility in the interpretation of the rule linking marriage to economic circumstances; what satisfied the prerequisites for a new household seems more likely to have been defined by the community than by the individuals themselves. Only rarely is there evidence of community control of marriage at its most extreme form, as in some areas in nineteenth-century Germany, where marriage was forbidden if the couple were judged not to have sufficient resources to support their new household and thus would be a burden to the community (Knodel 1967).

This brief discussion of the determinants of demographic behavior in late nineteenth-century Western Europe points to the role of the community, and particularly the local community, in influencing demographic behavior. This is not to say that individual decisions and individual circumstances were not relevant. But it seems likely that relatives, friends, and neighbors had a say.

New mothers would have learned how to feed their children from their mothers and their neighbors, through observation and conversation. Historical records yield glimpses of the circumstances of these conversations. On market day, the women of the French village of Auffay walked together (without men) to the market. We can imagine them chatting as they walked (Gullickson 1986, p. 84). Martine Segalen (1983, pp. 138-39), in her account of French peasant life in the nineteenth and twentieth centuries, cites a work on Brittany:

> The wash-house is one of the principal places of gossip in the region. Women of all ages meet there, and soaping and beating their linen often seems only a secondary activity, so enthusiastically do they exchange scandal and tell each other of the loves, marriages, births, and other major events of the district.

The picture of Breton women washing and gossiping together does not seem to me to be peculiar to Brittany or to France, and it is at least plausible that the way to feed a new infant was among the topics women discussed and that the stories of scandal they exchanged would have included stories of women who did not do it right.

More direct evidence comes from the accounts of *Spinnstuben*, gatherings for work and sociability that were common across Western Europe. Sometimes mixed sex and sometimes single sex, they were "one of the places around which the sexual culture of youth concentrated" (Medick 1984, p. 323). Here the women talked about everyday problems, and "the censuring and settling of village conflicts were in the forefront" (Medick 1984, p. 334). A contemporary observer (from a publication of 1799) wrote that women "talked intimately of one's babies, of a cousin, of a neighbor, of flax, spinning; of geese, ducks, chickens, and eggs" (p. 334). Men, in their own *Spinnstuben*, would also gossip, but apparently about somewhat different topics: agriculture and everyday life.

Even in the nineteenth century, however, personal networks linked communities. Marriage and migration were important in creating such links. Spouses were often from different villages; marriage would have created a path among villages, as the outmarrying spouse returned to visit friends or relatives. Migrants maintained links with their community of origin (Garden 1970; Poussou 1983; McBride 1976; Moch 1983). The heterogeneity of provincial demographic behavior in the nineteenth century, however, suggests that the paths that connected communities became more attenuated as distance increased.

MARKETS, STATES, AND NATIONS

Between 1870 and 1960, the scale of these interactions expanded. The expansion of markets from local to national extended personal networks. Long-distance migration increased considerably; presumably as a consequence, there was also an increase in the proportion of marriages in which one spouse was born in another province (e.g., Courgeau 1970, p. 85; Sutter 1958; Sutter and Tabah 1955). As in the earlier period, links with the local community were often maintained by those who left. Writing about contemporary France, Laurence Wylie notes that virtually everyone in the village of Chanzeaux has relatives, close friends, neighbors, and landlords who are emigrants, and it is through them that the village gains "intimate and personal contact with the 'New France', which in many other respects has bypassed the small villages" (Wylie 1966, p. 183).

More speculatively, the distribution of goods across the nation would have meant that people in one part of the country could eat the same foods and wear the same clothes as those in another. Consider, for example, the Bon Marché, the large French department store. It disseminated advertisements and pictures that showed people in the provinces what a proper bourgeois family (i.e., the Parisian upper-middle class) looked like. To advertise its winter season in 1894, 1,500,000 catalogues were mailed out, of which half (740,000) went to the provinces (Miller 1981, pp. 61-62). The Bon Marché and other department stores "made the culture of consumption a national one"; through them, Paris and the countryside became more alike (Miller 1981, p. 165). The result would have been that, when one encountered someone from another province within the same country, he or she would appear, at least outwardly, to be more like oneself than would have been the case in the nineteenth century. This would have, I think, facilitated inter-action: It is reasonable to assume that people are more likely to feel that they have something in common with those who dress the same, to gossip with them, and to take their interpretations seriously.

Market integration was both national and international in the period before 1870. International integration continued to increase, aided considerably by reductions in transportation costs, but seems to have been at least partially compensated for if not overbalanced by state-driven moves toward national economic autarky (Pollard 1981). In the late nineteenth century and on into the twentieth, national economies were defined by tariff walls, the removal of internal customs barriers, and national subsidies. Somewhat paradox-ically, pan-European events played a role defining national economies. During the Depression, international flows of labor and capital were severely restricted (Kenwood and Lougheed 1983, p. 249). Both world wars vastly enhanced the powers of the nation-states over their own economies. There would almost certainly have been more national market integration without war, but there was more yet as a result of the wartime mobilization of the civilian economy.

State functions expanded enormously, increasing what Braudel (1984, p. 51) has called its " 'diabolical' power of penetration." In the nineteenth century, the state became more extensive and more intrusive than it had been earlier. Governments rarely implemented policies explicitly intended to affect either fertility or marriage (policies of Fascist Italy and Germany are obvious exceptions as are the pronatalist policies of France). The most direct link between state expansion and demographic behavior is through the expansion of social rights. If children were valuable as a source of social security, then the implementation of welfare programs would have decreased their value in this respect. The last quarter of the nineteenth century and the first quarter of the twentieth saw the "collectivization of providence": Social welfare became collective, compulsory, and nationwide (de Swaan 1988). In France, for example, public assistance had been supported almost entirely from local funds, but during the Third Republic (1870-1940), these responsibilities were increasingly interpreted as national obligations (Weiss 1983). Just as market integration would have made the circumstances in which provincial populations lived more similar by evening out income and prices, national welfare programs would have made the costs and benefits of children more similar across provinces within the same country. But these and other national programs would also have encouraged a sense of identification with others in the same state.

State development was similar in the countries of Western Europe during the last century (Grew 1984), and welfare programs eventually became rather similar in all. But it is likely that these programs were perceived by citizens as social rights that belonged to them as citizens of a *particular* country. During the Depression, expanded welfare schemes must have further increased people's perceptions that their survival depended on national policies, thus enhancing the consciousness of interdependence within the national community and enlarging the distance to communities on the other side of the border (Pollard 1981, p. 74).

While state formation began well before the nineteenth century, mass identification with a nation almost certainly grew during that century (Tilly 1975; Hobsbawm 1987, p. 146; A. D. Smith 1986). Nation-building includes the insistence by the state that everyone should be able to communicate in the official language (or languages) and the invention of national traditions (Agulhon 1981; Hobsbawm and Ranger 1983). War heightened intergroup solidarity (Simmel 1955). The creation by the state of the home front as an integral part of the war effort brought Western governments closer to their people (R. Smith 1981; Winter 1986). In time of peace, the enemies of the nation were international (e.g., the Catholic church and socialism) and regional (e.g., regional patriots; Hobsbawm 1987; Grew 1984).

Most important in nation-building, I think, was education. It is not only the higher levels of education that are relevant but also that students attended either state schools or schools subject to a considerable degree of regulation by the state. Schools deliberately inculcated civic loyalty (Katznelson and Weir 1985) and insisted on a minimum common curriculum (e.g., national history). They provided a common set of myths and symbols as well as a degree of common knowledge upon which strangers could draw, thus facilitating interaction. Particularly significant was the insistence that students be taught in the national language. The implication of a common language for expanded interactions is suggested by an account of a small village in France around the turn of the century: "One knew—dimly as yet—that wherever French was spoken, a peasant born and bred in Mazières-en-Gâtine could fit in and live his life" (Thabault 1971, p. 165).

Market integration, state expansion, and nation-building are obviously intertwined, separable only for analytic purposes. And they are not an exhaustive list of influences associated with the growth of a national community. Sports, for example, also tied people together. In the United Kingdom, "the topic of the days' matches would provide common ground for conversation between virtually any two male workers in England or Scotland" (Hobsbawm 1983, pp. 288-89). Increased literacy made provincial boundaries increasingly porous. Newspapers (and later radio) brought in models from outside the local community that could serve as topics of gossip as well as permitting metaphorical long-distance conversations via advice columns in which issues such as child care were discussed. The role of newspapers in the creation of a national community has been elucidated by Benedict Anderson (1983), who emphasizes the interactions of capitalism, printing, and the growth of standard vernacular languages in the formation of "imagined communities." One of his central images is that of a newspaper: a one-day best seller, out-of-date tomorrow, read in privacy.

> Yet each communicant is well aware that the ceremony he performs is being replicated simultaneously by thousands (or millions) of others of whose existence he is confident, yet of whose identity he has not the slightest notion. . . . What more vivid figure for the secular, historically-cloaked, imagined community can be envisioned?

The influence of newspapers stops at the frontiers of the language in which they are written; in most countries, this increasingly coincided with the nation-state. Thus Tarde concluded that, even though nations have increasingly intermingled, imitated each other, assimilated, and morally united, the demarcation among them appeared increasingly irreconcilable (Tarde [1898] 1969, p. 306). Newspapers made the exchanges of ideas between people speaking the same language even more rapid than the exchange of merchandise and ideas among distant people. Therefore, "even though the *absolute* difference between nations diminished, their relative and conscious differences grew" (Tarde [1898] 1969, p. 306).

CONCLUSIONS

This chapter began with a brief description of the formation of national demographic regimes in Western Europe. I argued that what we know about the determinants of demographic behavior in the past suggests an important role for the community. When we compare this past with the modern era, we see that, despite a rhetoric (on surveys, for example) that assumes a model of individual decision making, the greater similarity of demographic behavior across provinces (and probably across social groups as well) suggests that the community currently influences demographic behavior as well. What has shifted, I argued, is the locus of that community: from largely local to largely national. The increasing importance of national communities is also shown in the decline in linguistic diversity—the move from local languages to a national language (or languages, in some cases). To try to account for the decreased demographic diversity within the countries of Western Europe, I pointed to parallel macro-level changes: the integration of national markets, the expansion of state functions, and nation-building. As an explanation, this is obviously unsatisfactory, in part because the argument is made simply by noting plausible parallel changes. But it is also unsatisfactory because simply describing parallel changes in macro-level phenomena omits the linkages between markets and states, on the one hand, and bedrooms, on the other. I have thus tried to sketch out what I think these links looked like on the ground and, to do so, have emphasized the level of interaction, and in particular conversational interaction among women, what I have called the best kind of women's gossip.

This kind of gossip provides what Giddens (1979) has called "interpretive schemes" that permit the evaluation of new behavior. It has been argued that people cannot verbalize the social rules guiding their behavior; what gossip does, I think, is to provide an arena in which social rules can be given a highly contextual and situational formulation. The demographic changes between 1870 and 1960 suggest that what was acceptable and what unacceptable, or desirable and undesirable, changed a great deal between 1870 and 1960. It was, I think, through gossip that people tentatively tried out the possibility of change by talking of other people and assessing the reaction of their friends.

Both the gossipers and the stories they tell are important. In particular, I think that women are far more likely to talk about sex and marriage with others who are considered to be "like us" such that their opinions are relevant. In addition, the stories told—about an imprudent marriage, for example, or a woman who had too few or too many children—would be seen as more relevant for one's own behavior if they concerned people "like us" rather than exotic people. One consequence of market integration, state formation, and nation-building is that increasingly people were more likely to have actual conversations with those in other parts of the country as well as to have metaphorical conversations via advice columns in the press. Moreover, those with whom they talked could be seen as "like us," members of the same community by virtue of their common language, common education, common dress, and so on.

There are at least two problems with the preceding analysis. The first is the issue of evidence. Because the demographic data are aggregate, and because women's gossip is particularly evanescent, the story that I am telling is unsatisfactory for those who want to see empirical tests of these models. Gossip is not only difficult to record but, by its nature, is closed to the outside observer. But we can study some of the prerequisites for conversations, such as language, and attempt to measure the degree and amount of interaction of women with others outside the local community by looking at visits, travels, relations with kin outside the community, and so on. Such an approach would not supplant the individual-level analyses that have dominated in the past two decades (Coleman 1986). It would, however, attempt to integrate micro and macro levels of analysis by focusing on the effect of change in macro-level structures on interaction.

The second problem is to reverse direction, to understand how the purposive actions of individuals combine to produce a social outcome—how individual choice becomes collective choice (Coleman 1986; Collins 1988). The issue is to understand the potentially strong interdependence between one person's behavior and another's. Coleman asks how the returns of education to an individual change depending on the education of others. But one could easily substitute fertility or marriage: How is the fertility of a couple influenced by the fertility of others?

While I cannot answer this question, I can propose two lines of thinking. Both involve a sort of tipping process, such that, as more and more people changed their behavior, those who did not were increasingly pressured to follow suit. The first is that, as fertility fell, those who retained the old patterns became—and came to see themselves—as more unusual, required to justify to their friends why they continued childbearing. We have some indication of this process in an account of a Sicilian village. There, the gentry began to practice fertility control before World War I, the artisans in the interwar period, and the laborers (the *bracciante*) only after World War II. The laborers speak of their blindness in not controlling their fertility earlier. They reproduced, they said, "with their eyes closed." The *bracciante* themselves look on the few families with many children with disgust, describing them as primitive, as animals (Schneider and Schneider 1984).

The second line of speculation would pay more attention to shifting constraints as those who produce for the market, and bureaucrats who produce the many forms that we fill in, think of their clientele in terms of averages. It is an argument similar to that of John Meyer, who says that, while modern society extols individualism ideologically, it insists on "standardized individuals" (Meyer 1986). I can illustrate with a homely and personal anecdote. One evening recently I went to McDonald's with a friend who has three children (the youngest of which were twins). It turns out that, in McDonald's, the tables seat a couple or a family of four: they are not designed for families that exceed the average. Similarly, causal observations suggest that government bureaucrats are highly "menu driven." They expect to be dealing with typical individuals or typical families, not those who are different. I would suggest that it is not only that larger families are more expensive but that those who manufacture goods and produce forms think in terms of averages; by doing so, they subtly communicate to those who might not want to be average that it would be easier for them if they were.

The result is that, while we live in societies that rhetorically value individual diversity, and ones in which improvements in contraceptive technology and a relaxation in views about the relation of sex, marriage, and childbirth have made possible much more diversity than in the nineteenth century, we have witnessed what I expect was an unintended consequence of these changes, a greater demographic uniformity. The integration of market, the expansion of states, and nation-building are macro-level changes that expanded the scope of interaction and thus, I think, influenced the marriage and childbearing of some: as these became an increasingly large proportion of the population, it seems likely that more and more segments of the population participated, further reducing demographic diversity. We can expect within-country diversity to increase during times of change, such as with the move toward cohabitation and higher divorce in Western European countries after 1960, but I predict that the same chain upward, from micro to macro, will produce greater uniformity within countries in these behaviors as well, and sooner rather than later.

REFERENCES

Agulhon, Maurice. 1981. *Marianne into Battle.* Cambridge: Cambridge University Press.

Anderson, Benedict. 1983. *Imagined Communities.* London: Verso.

Bongaarts, John and Jane Menken. 1983. "The Supply of Children: A Critical Essay." Pp. 263-307 in *Determinants of Fertility in Developing Countries,* edited by R. Bulatao and R. Lee. New York: Academic Press.

Braudel, Fernand. 1984. *The Perspective of the World.* London: Collins.

Casterline, John B. 1981. *Community Effects on Fertility Intentions: The Effect of Aggregate Levels of Contraceptive Use on Individual Intentions to Use.* London: World Fertility Survey.

Casterline, John, Susheela B. Singh, and John Cleland et al. 1984. "The Proximate Determinants of Fertility." In *WFS Comparative Studies.* Voorburg, Netherlands: International Statistical Institute.

Coleman, James S. 1986. "Social Theory, Social Research, and a Theory of Action." *American Journal of Sociology* 91:1309-35.

Collins, Randall. 1988. "The Micro Contribution to Macro Sociology." *Sociological Theory* 6:242-52.

Courgeau, Daniel. 1970. *Les Champs Migratoires en France.* Cahier no. 58. Paris: Institut National des Études Demographiques.

de Swaan, Abram. 1988. *In Care of the State: Health Care, Education and Welfare in Europe and the USA in the Modern Era.* Cambridge: Polity.

Entwisle, Barbara and William M. Mason. 1985. "Multilevel Effects of Socioeconomic Development and Family Planning Programs on Children Ever Born." *American Journal of Sociology* 91:616-49.

Garden, Maurice. 1970. *Lyon et les Lyonnais au XVIIIe siècle*. Paris: Société d'Édition Les Belles-Lettres.

Gaskin, Katherine. 1978. "Age at First Marriage in Europe Before 1850: A Summary of Family Reconstitution Data." *Journal of Family History* 3:23-26.

Giddens, Anthony. 1979. *Central Problems in Social Theory: Action, Structure and Contradiction in Social Analysis*. Berkeley: University of California Press.

Grew, Raymond. 1984. "The Nineteenth Century European State." In *State-Making and Social Movements*, edited by C. Bright and S. Harding. Ann Arbor: University of Michigan Press.

Gullickson, Gay L. 1986. *Spinners and Weavers of Auffay: Rural Industry and the Sexual Division of Labor in a French Village, 1750-1850*. Cambridge: Cambridge University Press.

Hajnal, John. 1965. "European Marriage Patterns in Perspective." Pp. 101-43 in *Population in History*, edited by D. V. Glass and D.E.C. Eversley. London: Edward Arnold.

————. 1982. "Two Kinds of Pre-industrial Household Formation Systems." *Population and Development Review* 3:449-94.

Hobsbawm, Eric. 1983. "Mass-Producing Traditions: Europe 1870-1914." *The Invention of Tradition*, edited by E. Hobsbawm and T. Ranger. Cambridge: Cambridge University Press.

————. 1987. *The Age of Empire, 1875-1914*. New York: Pantheon.

Hobsbawm, Eric J. and Terence Ranger, eds. 1983. *The Invention of Tradition*. New York: Cambridge University Press.

Jones, Elise F. 1982. "Socio-Economic Differentials in Achieved Fertility." *Comparative Studies: ECE Analyses of WFS Surveys in Europe and USA*. Geneva: U.N. Economic Commission for Europe, Population Activities Unit.

Katznelson, Ira and Margaret Weir. 1985. *Schooling for All: Class, Race, and the Decline of the Democratic Ideal*. New York: Basic Books.

Kenwood, A. G. and A. L. Lougheed. 1983. *The Growth of the International Economy*. London: George Allen & Unwin.

Kintner, Hallie. 1985. "Trends and Regional Differences in Breastfeeding in Germany from 1871 to 1937." *Journal of Family History* 10:163-82.

Knodel, John. 1967. "Law, Marriage, and Illegitimacy in 19th Century Germany." *Population Studies* 20:279-94.

————. 1988. *Demographic Behavior in the Past*. Cambridge: Cambridge University Press.

Knodel, John and Etienne van de Walle. 1967. "Breast Feeding, Fertility and Infant Mortality: An Analysis of Some Early German Data." *Population Studies* 21:109-31.

Laslett, Peter. 1972. "Introduction: The History of the Family." *Household and Family in Past Time*, edited by P. Laslett and R. Wall. Cambridge: Cambridge University Press.

Lee, Robert. 1981. "Family and 'Modernisation': The Peasant Family and Social Change in Nineteenth Century Bavaria." Pp. 84-119 in *The German Family*, edited by R. J. Evans and W. R. Lee. London: Croom Helm.

Levasseur, E. 1889. *La population française*. Vol. 1. Paris: Arthur Rousseau.

McBride, Theresa M. 1976. *The Domestic Revolution: The Modernisation of Household Service in England and France 1820-1920*. London: Croom Helm.

Medick, Hans. 1984. "Village Spinning Bees: Sexual Culture and Free Time Among Rural Youth in Early Modern Germany." Pp. 317-39 in *Interest and Emotion: Essays on the Study of Family and Kinship*, edited by H. Medick and D. W. Sabean. Cambridge: Cambridge University Press.

Meyer, John W. 1986. "Myths of Socialization and Personality." Pp. 208-21 in *Reconstructing Individualism: Autonomy, Individuality, and the Self in Western Thought*, edited by T. Heller et al. Stanford, CA: Stanford University Press.

Miller, Michael B. 1981. *The Bon Marché: Bourgeois Culture and the Department Store, 1869-1920.* Princeton, NJ: Princeton University Press.

Moch, Leslie. 1983. *Paths to the City.* Beverly Hills, CA: Sage.

Pollard, Sidney. 1981. *The Integration of the European Economy Since 1845.* London: George Allen & Unwin.

Poussou, Jean-Pierre. 1983. *Bordeaux et le sud-ouest au XVIIIe Siècle: Croissance Économique et Attraction Urbaine.* Paris: Editions de L'École des Hautes Etudes en Sciences Sociales.

Schneider, Jane and Peter Schneider. 1984. "Demographic Transitions in a Sicilian Rural Town." *Journal of Family History* 9:245-72.

Segalen, Martine. 1983. *Love and Power in the Peasant Family,* translated by Sarah Matthews. Oxford: Basil Blackwell.

Simmel, Georg. 1955. *Conflict and the Web of Group Affiliations.* New York: Free Press.

Skinner, G. William. 1964. "Marketing and Social Structure in Rural China." *Journal of Asian Studies* 24:3-43.

———. 1985. "Rural Marketing in China: Revival and Reappraisal." Pp. 7-47 in *Markets and Marketing,* edited by S. Plattner. Lanham, MD: University Press of America.

Smith, Anthony D. 1986. *The Ethnic Origins of Nations.* Oxford: Basil Blackwell.

Smith, Herbert. 1989. "Integrating Theory and Research on the Institutional Determinants of Fertility." *Demogracy* 26:171-84.

Smith, Richard. 1981. "The People of Tuscany and Their Families." *Journal of Family History* 6:107-28.

Spacks, Patricia Meyer. 1986. *Gossip.* Chicago: University of Chicago Press.

Stone, Lawrence and Jeanne Stone. 1984. *An Open Elite? England 1540-1880.* Oxford: Clarendon.

Sutter, Jean. 1958. "Évolution de la Distance Séparant le Domicile des Futurs Époux (Loir-et-Cher 1870-1954; Finistère 1911-1953)." *Population* 13:227-58.

Sutter, Jean and Leon Tabah. 1955. "L'évolution des Isolats de deux Départements Français: Loir-et-Cher, Finistère." *Population* 10:645-74.

Tarde, Gabriel. [1898] 1969. *On Communication and Social Structure.* Chicago: University of Chicago Press.

Thabault, Roger. 1971. *Education and Change in a Village Community: Mazières-en-Gâtine 1848-1914.* New York: Schocken.

Tilly, Charles. 1975. "Reflections on the History of European State-Making." Pp. 3-83 in *The Formation of National States in Western Europe,* edited by C. Tilly. Princeton, NJ: Princeton University Press.

Watkins, Susan Cotts. 1981. "Regional Patterns of Nuptiality in Europe, 1870-1960." *Population Studies* 35:199-215.

———. 1984. "Spinsters." *Journal of Family History* 4:310-325.

———. 1987. "The Fertility Transition: Europe and the Third World Compared." *Sociological Forum* 2:645-73.

———. 1991. *From Provinces into Nations: Demographic Integration in Western Europe, 1870-1960.* Princeton, NJ: Princeton University Press.

Weber, Eugen. 1976. *Peasants into Frenchmen: The Modernization of Rural France, 1870-1914.* Stanford, CA: Stanford University Press.

Weiss, John. 1983. "Origins of the French Welfare State: Poor Relief in the Third Republic, 1871-1914." *French Historical Studies* 13:47-78.

Williamson, Jeffrey G. 1965. "Regional Inequality and the Process of National Development: A Description of the Patterns." *Economic Development and Cultural Change* 13:3-84.

Wilson, Chris. 1986. "The Proximate Determinants of Marital Fertility in England, 1600-1790."
    In Lloyd Bonfield, Richard Smith, and Keith Wrightson, eds., The World We Have Gained,
    pp. 203-30. New York: Basil Blackwell.
Winter, Jay. 1986. *The Great War and the British People.* Cambridge, MA: Harvard University
    Press.
Wylie, Laurence. 1966. *Chanzeaux: A Village in Anjou.* Cambridge, MA: Harvard University
    Press.

19

Micro-Macro Theoretical Linkages in Social Demography: A Commentary

Barbara Entwisle

Susan Watkins begins with the fact that, between 1870 and 1960, differences in marriage and marital fertility between provinces of Western Europe decreased sharply. The reduction in diversity within countries was greater than that between countries, increasing the significance of national boundaries over time. To account for these changes, Watkins points to the integration of national markets, the expansion of state functions, and nation-building and links these processes to changes in conversational interaction, especially among women. Her speculative chapter proceeds along promising lines, especially in its emphasis on communication among women. All too often in fertility research, women are treated as sexless and genderless respondents, representing households rather than themselves. I agree with Watkins that women are likely to gossip about childbirth and marriage, although men may discuss these topics from time to time as well.

However, Watkins's arguments have two weaknesses. First, the link between macro-level change and micro-level interaction—specifically "the best kind of women's gossip"—is more clear for market integration and nation-building than for state expansion. The arguments about state expansion should be developed. The second point concerns the relationship between the expanded networks and sense of community that accompanied macro-level change and gossip—who gossiped with whom about what. I do not agree with Watkins that an increase in the number of people viewed as "like us" necessarily leads to corresponding increase in the number of people with whom gossip is exchanged.

For Watkins, the link between macro-level change and micro-level processes involves network expansion and a widened and more inclusive sense of community. That the expansion of markets extended personal networks strikes me as a reasonable proposition, and, for the moment, let us accept the argument that, as a result, models from the outside were more likely to be brought in and that others would more likely be experienced as "like us" and, therefore, the topic of and participants in gossip. Her arguments regarding nation-building, with its insistence on one or more official languages, also seem reasonable. This has obvious implications for the expansion of personal networks: Interpersonal links require a common language. Another consequence of nation-building was the conscious promotion of a national identity, especially through education, and with it an enlargement of the pool of people "like us." But what of state expansion? The arguments relating state expansion to personal networks and the content of interpersonal communication are not as clear. Watkins refers to the effect of national welfare programs such as social security on the sense of identification with others in the state. Nothing is said about networks per se or the role of gossip. This part of the argument needs to be elaborated.

The second point concerns the implications of network expansion and a widened sense of community for gossip. Watkins believes that we gossip with and about people "like us." An increase in the number of people "like us" due to market integration, nation-building, and growth of the state leads to an increase in the number of people with whom we gossip. Really? This description does not ring true. Gossip is intimate conversation—in terms of not only the topics discussed but the people with whom we typically gossip. Why should an increase in the number of people "like us" necessarily lead to an increase in the number of intimates, that is, people with whom we gossip?

To use the language of network theorists, it seems to me that gossip characterizes communication among those with strong ties. The expansion of networks that accompanied market integration, state expansion, and nation-building and the increase in the numbers of people "like us" that resulted from these processes would tend to increase the number of persons linked by weak ties. The description of micro-level processes confuses different kinds of interpersonal links. What is needed is an account that explores the implications of expanded networks based on weak ties for the content and import of gossip exchanged with intimates. For example, it is my impression that new information—such as that concerning a job opportunity or the address of an abortion clinic when abortion is illegal—is more likely to flow across weak than strong ties. The expansion of personal networks resulting from market integration, extension of the state, and nation-building could thus have increased access to new information and provided conduits for the inflow of new models. Then these new models could have been discussed, judged, and interpreted among intimates. To me, explicit recognition of weak versus strong ties and the incorporation of both into the arguments would provide a more satisfying account of the macro-micro linkage.

What I like about Karen Mason's chapter is the attention given to social change. Mason observes that multilevel modeling in social demography (and also other fields of sociology) is peculiarly static. To borrow her language, the social institutions that shape reproductive behavior are "out there" and the direction of effect is top down, reminiscent of the trickle-down theories of the Reagan era. Given this kind of model, how can we account for change? Do not individuals help to shape the world around them?

The theoretical contribution of Karen Mason's chapter is to note that an adequate account of demographic change must include processes that are bottom up as well as those that are top down. Individuals *do* help to shape the world around them and as such participate in as well as respond to processes of social change. How this works for the social institutions most closely related to fertility behavior is left unexplored, however. This part of the argument needs to be developed.

Arguments about the likely endogeneity of social institutions in the explanation of fertility behavior and change lead Karen Mason to criticize a body of empirical work that treats these institutions as exogenous. In her view, statistical models that incorporate macro as well as micro variables as determinants of individual reproductive behavior are misspecified. Moreover, although not stated explicitly in the chapter, the misspecification involved is very serious, leading to biased and inconsistent estimates of the effects of fertility determinants.

Is endogeneity a threat? Absolutely. But Karen Mason has overstated its enormity. All statistical models require simplifying assumptions. The question is this: Under what circumstances is it reasonable to treat social institutions *as if* they are "out there"? In answering this question, the time horizon is critical. In the cross-section, or over short periods of time, assuming that pervasive social institutions are "out there" strikes me as reasonable. Over longer periods of time, this assumption is less tenable. (The size of the macro unit is also important; endogeneity poses more of a problem at lower than higher levels of aggregation.) The multilevel models with which I am familiar—specifically those addressing fertility behavior and decline—incorporate relatively short periods of time (from a macro perspective). I hesitate to call them misspecified because of the assumed exogeneity of macro determinants.

But suppose we did expand the time horizon. Would we end up with "a messy set of simultaneous equations in which the aggregate as well as individual variables on the right-hand side in some equations appear on the left-hand side in others"? Not necessarily. Individuals affect social institutions *over time,* not in a moment of time. Consequently, if the goal were to incorporate social institutions as endogenous variables, I would do so within the context of a multilevel panel model in which social institutions at time 2 are the result of individual behavior, reproductive and otherwise, at time 1. Such a model is doable, although certainly not easy.

The rejection of multilevel statistical models as not feasible or analytically tractable leads Karen Mason to call for macro-historical studies of institutional and demographic change. I agree that such studies can usefully address theory that is essentially multilevel in thrust, but they are not immune from the problems of simultaneity that lead Karen Mason to criticize multilevel statistical modeling in the first place. Indeed, macro-historical studies are subject to many of the same threats to validity as studies based on the multilevel statistical approach. Also, just as macro-historical research can shed light on cross-level relationships, studies that focus on micro-level phenomena can provide useful insights if placed within the right theoretical context. Of course, no one type of study will answer all of the questions about the micro-macro linkage in social demography. Ultimately, what is needed is a full range of research approaches.

Bill Mason's chapter makes a strong pitch for checking assumptions in analysis, qualitative as well as quantitative, and illustrates how this might be done for one approach to multilevel statistical analysis. Of particular interest is a two-level stochastic parameter model in which micro coefficients depend on macro variables. His review of the assumptions underlying this model is detailed and thorough. The discussion of assumptions about error terms, including the issue of varying meaning across context, is especially helpful. Two points should be added. The first concerns change and how it might be incorporated into the multilevel model, and the second addresses fit with various theories of macro-micro linkage.

In his description of the multilevel model, Bill Mason comments on its cross-sectional character and the assumed dependence of micro coefficients on macro variables. As I noted earlier, the two go hand in hand: Given the cross-sectional nature of the model, it makes sense to view macro variables as constraints on micro processes. How might the multilevel statistical model be extended to encompass change over time? Bill Mason suggests in passing that one could allow micro coefficients to affect macro variables. Relaxing the assumption that micro coefficients depend on macro variables, and not the reverse, is an important step toward a multilevel model that can account for social change. Let me illustrate the substantive rationale for such a specification with an example coming from the study of fertility decline in developing countries.

Although analysts do not agree on the importance of family planning programs in explaining fertility decline in developing countries, no list of potential fertility determinants would be complete without some mention of these programs. But the assessment of family planning programs is complicated by the fact that, frequently, fertility decline is already under way when such programs are introduced, and their impact on subsequent change is often misstated. How might the implications of prior changes in fertility behavior be taken into account?

One possibility is that the beginnings of fertility decline might be revealed by differential fertility behavior within a population. After all, a response to conditions leading to fertility decline is unlikely to be simultaneous and across the board. If this reasoning is correct, then a micro coefficient capturing differential fertility behavior may help to predict a macro variable such as family planning program effort at a subsequent time point. This potential effect represents one way in which the behavior of individuals might influence their social context and as such responds (at least in part) to Karen Mason's criticism of multilevel statistical models. That said, it is also important to recognize that this extension of the model will not answer all questions about social change.

The multilevel specification under discussion accords well with theories that are concerned in some fashion with opportunity structure. It does less well with theories concerned with interpersonal interaction and the transmission of new ideas. This is my second point. The model allows for cultural constraints and variability in these constraints in the cross-section but does not capture the dynamic aspects of these theories as they play out over time. Imagine trying to capture what Susan Watkins has labeled "the best kind of gossip" and the expansion of personal networks in terms of this model. We would not want widely dispersed respondents in a sample survey. Rather, a highly clustered sample would be ideal, so that we could imagine our respondents talking with one another and incorporate their conversations into the structure of the model. A different approach to data collection would be required as well as new modeling strategies that would incorporate the operation of personal networks into the framework that Bill Mason has described.

Marta Tienda addresses a range of problems that arise in the attempt to study neighborhood effects, especially in the context of social change. Her instructive review begins by stressing the need to define neighborhoods sociologically, according to patterns of social interaction, instead of relying on convenient statistical areas such as census tracts or zip code areas. Indeed, drawing boundaries is primary regardless of the size of the sociospatial units one wishes to study, although the difficulties are more pronounced at lower than higher levels of aggregation. Given the general importance of the boundary problems, and given the attention that Tienda devotes to them, it is appropriate to elaborate this part of her chapter, drawing on work that I have done recently in connection with design and planning for a national study of adolescent sexual and contraceptive behavior to be conducted in the United States.

Put simply, the goal in operationalizing the concept of neighborhood is to map locally based social interaction onto a spatial grid. A major advantage of doing so is the ability to tie in to the rich array of data collected for spatial units in the study of neighborhoods. One might take at least two approaches. The first borrows from social geography the concept of an activity space—that is, where individuals go to carry out their daily routines. Presumably, the paths followed on an everyday basis involve patterned encounters with others and thus delineate meaningful sociospatial units. This approach struck me as promising, so I adapted it for possible use in the adolescent study I mentioned, even conducting a pretest. It failed, unequivocally. Adolescents, even those with drivers' licenses and access to cars, could not trace their daily travel patterns on a map. They could not even locate their homes! I relate this experience because it is as important to learn about failures as well as successes.

An alternative approach builds directly on friendship patterns. Knowing the home addresses of, say, five or ten friends provides a basis for moving from a set of social interactions to spatial units whose characteristics can be measured and assessed. Questions to obtain the relevant information can be included in sample surveys, although the coding of friends named and their addresses is not a trivial matter. For instance, plans for the adolescent study call for a complete canvas of schools selected for the sample. Respondents will be asked to name up to five friends of each sex and will then identify these friends from a roster of all students in the school. They will also report their own home address. With data available for an entire school, the home addresses of school friends can be derived. The detailed geographic identifiers and mapping routines recently developed for use in the 1990 census make it possible to create a variety of spatial units from this information and to generate characteristics of these units. (It would certainly be desirable to study more than a handful of neighborhoods.) I hope this approach will prove to be more successful than the first one I tried.

The other problems Tienda addresses involve social change directly and its causes and implications at a local level. For example, selection processes are a concern. What may appear to be an effect of neighborhood characteristics may in fact be the result of persons selectively moving into and out of certain neighborhoods. Not only does the tendency to "vote with one's feet" make it difficult to determine to which contexts respondents were exposed, and for how long, but the macro changes induced by migration guarantee that contexts will change even for respondents who do not move. There is a further problem that should be added to the list: Contextual boundaries are not fixed, especially at a very local level such as a neighborhood. Not only do the characteristics of neighborhoods change, and not only may their effects vary over time, what constitutes the neighborhood may also change. This has obvious consequences for the analysis of neighborhood effects.

The chapter ends on a gloomy note. Tienda is not optimistic about the prospects for detecting substantively and statistically significant neighborhood effects. This bleak assessment is based on the methodological and statistical concerns identified, namely, the inadequate handling of exposure, selection, simultaneity, and endogeneity in modeling and estimating these effects. Without in any way denying the importance of these concerns, I would like to suggest that theoretical weaknesses pose an even more fundamental threat. The area that needs work most urgently involves theories about micro-macro linkages, especially the development of theories about change, and even more especially theories about change at the micro level affecting the macro level, whether the latter is conceived in institutional terms as Karen Mason does or in sociospatial terms as the other authors have done.

Index

Abbott, A., 84, 86
Abortion issue, 113, 114
Accounting profession, feminization of, 175, 184
Action scripts, organizational roles and, 86
Action theories, social structure and, 33
Affirmative action, 177, 179, 187
Africa:
  fertility rates in, 143
  food crisis and, 131-133
Aging:
  economic status and, 210-212
  public sector cost of, 213
Aging societies, 208-218
  beyond 203, 212-216
  demography and, 213
  economic growth and, 215-216
  facts about, 209-210
  public policy and, 216-218
Agrarian (plow-based) farming systems, 109, 130
Agriculture, U.S. labor force in, 144
Alexander, J., 11, 12, 78
Alexander, K. L., 161, 162, 165
American Sociological Association, 6
Anheier, H. K., 89, 92, 93
Anthropology:
  exchange and, 35, 36
  gender stratification and, 15, 109
Antidrug crusade, 115
Astone, N. M., 197, 200, 201
Attitude studies, 87
Authority, role relations and, 83

Babies, artificial feeding of, 17, 142
Baboon social organization, 17
Baby boom, 15, 19, 147, 208, 214
Baking profession, feminization of, 177, 185
Bank management, feminization of, 177, 179

Barley, S., 83, 89
Baron, J. N., 175, 185
Bartending profession, feminization of, 176, 178, 183, 184
Becker, G., 63, 64, 180
Behavior:
  archetypal patterns of, 65
  institutional regulation of, 224
  neighborhood effects on, 246-247, 249
  prediction of, 48, 84
  roles and, 81-82, 84
  social context and, 246
  See also Individual behavior
Behaviorism, 11
Beijing Spring, 55
Berger, J., 12, 104, 105, 246, 249
Berger, P., 65
Bielby, W. T., 175, 185
Bird, C., 170, 179
Black civil rights movement, 118
Black power movement, 13, 31
Blacks:
  antidrug crusade and, 115
  out-migration of, 102
Blakeslee, S., 199, 200
Blalock, H., 92, 93
Blau, P., 12, 29, 30, 31, 35, 39, 46, 77, 78, 84, 90
Blumberg, R. L., 8, 15, 17, 109, 118, 121-137, 142, 143, 148
Book editor profession, feminization of, 177, 179, 182, 183, 184
Boserup, E., 15, 129, 143
Bourdieu, P., 52, 86, 157
Bravery, social movements and, 51, 53
Breast-feeding:
  fertility and, 267-268
  infant mortality and, 268
  substitutes for, 142
Broadcast reporting, women's progress in, 178, 179
Bumpass, L., 197, 198

ABV-1640